BOOKS BY JACK DENTON SCOTT

Pug Invades the Fifth Column (co-author)
Too Lively To Live (co-author)
The Weimaraner
All Outdoors
Your Dog's Health Book
Forests of the Night
How To Write and Sell
The Duluth Mongoose

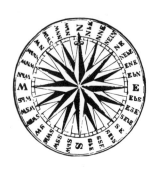

For to admire an' for to see,
For to be'old this world so wide—
                              —Kipling

Passport

to Adventure

by Jack Denton Scott

with photographs by Maria Luisa Scott

Random House • **New York**

145838

Library of Congress catalog card number: 66-12163

Manufactured in the United States of America

A portion of the first chapter appeared in *Playboy* magazine.

For Maria Luisa,
who shares my tent
and climbs my mountains

ACKNOWLEDGMENTS AND AUTHOR'S NOTE

We wish to express gratitude to the Scandinavian Airlines System that took us to the far places—and brought us back; also to SAS personnel, who went far beyond the call of duty to help us on our way. Our thanks also go to Som Nath Chib, Director General, Department of Tourism, Government of India, and the department's New York directors, S. D. Khanna and Leela Sivamani Nadhan; to Professor Walter Minarz and Rudolph F. Mattesich of the Austrian State Tourist Department; to Peter Prag and Malfrid Bernhard of the Norwegian National Travel Office; to Jaime Segarra of the Spanish Tourist Office, and Marcelino Arias Artola, director of the Hostal de los Reyes Católicos. Further appreciation should be offered Lefteris Ant. Katsanis, Mytilene, Greece; and Jeanne Steinmetz of the National Travel Association of Denmark, and Salvador C. Pena of the Philippine Tourist and Travel Association.

My wife and I are greatly indebted to Bernard and Inez Hoffman for advice, and to their Hoffman Laboratories for producing photographs from negatives that had been exposed to tropic swelter and arctic cold. Our thanks must also be included for the thoughtfulness of Ted Kesting, editor of *Sports Afield,* where several of the sporting experiences that follow appeared in different form.

If this proves indeed to be a book, then much of the credit goes to my editors at Random House: senior editor Harry E. Maule, a Merlin who makes words behave; and Leah Gadlow, who brought order from confusion and sense from nonsense.

Very special thanks go to the patient Tony Wimpfheimer who, between trips, fed necessary encouragement along with superb *cappelletti al burro* and *vitello tonnato* at New York's San Marino.

From 1959 to 1963 we traveled more than five hundred thousand miles, using seven types of aircraft, besides elephants, pirogue, rickshaw, jeep, Land Rover, burro, Chinese junk, aluminum Rolls-Royce, arctic ketch, coastal steamer, cruiser, *bankero* canoe, Greek caïque, feet, and, occasionally, hands and knees.

The journeys described in this book were not made consecutively, but rather at intervals over a period of four years.

J.D.S.

CONTENTS

ILLUSTRATIONS

PASSPORT
TO ADVENTURE

CHAPTER ONE

INDIA

He wore a rose-pink turban, white trousers, an open brocade jacket showing bare brown chest, and he came in softly without a word. Placing the tea tray on the low bedside teak stand, he bowed gracefully to the knees and withdrew, backing out, his bare feet whispering.

It was a classic bedroom scene from a Cecil B. De Mille Oriental epic in full color. My bed was huge, splashed with gilt, canopied in silk, its four posts of rosewood crawling with realistically carved cobras; huge draperies of gold silk were drawn over the window; the floor was white marble; the rug near the bed was the velvety soft pelt of a leopard, the head mounted in a snarl.

A sip of fragrant, scalding Darjeeling tea brought the whole thing back to near-reality: that mad dash through the most colorful and confused city in the world, Calcutta; then New Delhi overnight, the drive to Bharatpur and the palace, Moti Mahal, or White Pearl, of my friend, the Maharaja of Bharatpur.

He had come to meet us at his summer palace at Deeg, a once magnificent place with fountains and great flower gardens, but now, since India's independence, rapidly becoming a crumbling wreck. The Maharaja drove us back to Moti Mahal in his aluminum Rolls-Royce. Servants were waiting in the great circular drive before the entrance to the white palace. Strung over their arms were leis of fragrant flowers, mostly sweet peas. The Prince of Bharatpur personally draped them around our necks as welcome garlands. We had met his teen-age daughters, Parvat and Renuka, had cold drinks on the great emerald lawn, and after dinner we sat on cushions and listened to the palace orchestra playing their *sitars, tablas* and *tamburas.* Their bright turbans of red, pink, white and orange made them look like a bed of Oriental poppies nodding in a breeze as they swayed to the beat of the high, weird, strangely haunting music.

We had sat up most of the night talking about the duck hunt the following day. The location was one of the most famous in the world where kings, princes, shahs, rajas, viceroys, generals, ambassadors and political greats from everywhere had gathered to try to outshoot each other. No one, however, outshot the Prince of Bharatpur.

At this moment of early morning, in other bedrooms of this lovely columned pile, the four duck hunters who had come to India with me were going through the same routine—tea by turban in canopied bed.

We had flown from New York two days ago, with brief stops in Copenhagen, Abadan and Calcutta. The trip still seemed wrapped in a dream web. Jet transportation does that: it carries you away from the familiar and the accustomed so fast that mental and physical adjustments take hours, sometimes days, before you are prepared to look upon the new scenes with a normal and unconfused eye.

This whole situation had much of the confusing in it. It had started in Carlton House, on Madison Avenue in New York City, exactly a month ago. I was there with four friends, C, H, W and Y, and we were talking about a subject that occupies many in Manhattan—boredom with the routine of a big city. Suddenly a wild thought struck me.

"Let's go to India duck-hunting!" I said.

Silence. It was obvious that all four of my drinking companions thought I had quaffed a dozen before arriving at Carlton House, or that I was desperately in need of a psychiatrist.

I quickly explained. While writing an adventure column for the New York Herald Tribune Syndicate, I had been to India and shot ducks with the Maharaja of Bharatpur. I found him a fascinating and friendly man who liked Americans. He had developed this liking for us during World War II when he came in contact with our soldiers. We struck it off and he tendered me a permanent invitation to bring some friends and come back and shoot ducks.

The silence was finally broken by C. "Well, what are we waiting for?"

He went on. "This is a once-in-a-lifetime offer! I'll give up vacation time for the next five years to shoot ducks with your maharaja and sleep in his palace!"

"And I," said W, "will sell everything but my wife to make a trip like that!"

Suddenly, with the cathexis of this remark, these were men of courage who decided in few words to do what they had always dreamed of. This was a welcome breakout from their cocoon of complacency, of dully doing the same thing day after day: work, home, cocktail parties, maybe the beach for week ends, sometimes a sail around Manhattan on a friend's boat, perhaps a fast trip to Florida, the Bahamas, Bermuda or even Europe—the planned year, the predetermined, almost predigested vacation.

Over the face of Y, a bald man of five feet with a gentle but puckish face, came the bold look of an adventurer. His faded blue eyes gleamed, the air conditioning stirred the fringes of his side hair, and suddenly, magically, he looked exciting, almost romantic.

Something of the sort happened to each of us. In describing it afterward, H, a six-foot-six realist, said, "It was like reaching out and taking hold of a dream that had always just eluded me. And I decided then and there that I'd go to India, no matter what happened. I'd been dreaming about it ever since I looked at pictures of the Taj Mahal when I was twelve years old."

Similar expressions came from the others. I understood that I wasn't the favorite conversation piece in their homes but I had stirred up adventure and proved an important social point: there is life in conformed man yet.

Carlton House president Gaston Lauryssen gave us bon voyage three weeks later with his rarest burgundy and prime tenderloin embedded with *pâté de foie gras*. A few members of the press were present, who refused to believe the whole thing. In less than a week, after three more planning sessions which included things like shipping cases of shotgun shells ahead and clearing the whole project with the Maharaja of Bharatpur and Som Nath Chib, director of the India Government Tourist Office, we walked up the ramp into an SAS DC-8 at Idlewild and, within minutes, the dream was cloudborne.

The four men sat silently in what seemed to be a state of shock, probably with visions of white-faced, silent wives behind. This was not a group of wealthy dilettantes off on a lark. H, tall and blondly handsome, with an infectious sense of enthusiasm, was under forty and director of communications of a large chemical complex. With his ruddy complexion, his fierce, blue-gray eyes and his thrust, he was the only one of the four who looked like an adventurer. C and Y were short, cheerful men who looked life in the face and laughed at it. C had a wholesale meat business in Manhattan; Y worked for a public relations firm. C, an aggressive bantam, had tried almost everything; Y was also a bantam type who wanted to try the world on for size but hadn't had the opportunity. W, dark-haired, a meticulous dresser, had a slight German accent, wore horn-rimmed glasses that gave him a sedate, owlish look. He was a working motion-picture cameraman, a "cinematographer" as he frequently pointed out. He was quiet with an encouraging air of competence.

I was just restless. I had seen moonlight on the Ganges, sun on the Alps; waded a foaming stream in Spain, watched the rain sweep over a Scottish moor. Now I was sick of cities and routine. I wanted to put the commonplace out of my life, step out of the python coils of civilization that squeeze from us every thought except survival and security. Adventure was the answer, and I was willing to show the way "to sail beyond the sunset" as Richard Halliburton, who had the same sort of urge years ago, put it. To make my point I even quoted a stable citizen, Supreme Court Justice William Douglas: "The richness of life is found in adventure. It develops self-reliance and independence—then life teems with excitement."

Now, through the miracle of this century's magic carpet, the jet, here we were in India, at the White Pearl Palace. Through the open window I could smell the dewy wet of predawn and hear the cough of arriving cars, the click of closing doors, the low murmur of voices. They were gathering for the duck shoot. I should get dressed. It was a difficult bed to leave; it held you like an embrace. The teapot on the teak stand was still sending fragrant tendrils of steam into the room. The leopard snarled as I stepped over his head. The dream was clearing into reality.

Since I expected to spend some time abroad gathering material to keep my typewriter in motion, my wife, Mary Lou, had come with me. She was waiting outside her bedroom as I closed my door.

"The others are outside," she said. "I doubt if they slept a wink last night. They looked like sleepwalkers as they passed. I don't think our group is going to establish any shooting record."

Shooting had been a ruse. We all knew it. I confess that this going to India to shoot ducks was really a psychological gambit to put us in motion. It had a ring to it, an impossible quality that made it all the more appealing to the imagination.

Can you imagine a serious discussion of five men making a trip slightly less than the distance around the world to spend a few hours to see the Taj Mahal by moonlight or view the burning ghats on the Ganges? No one would be tempted. Moreover, it was a situation that wives and friends could laugh off. We had read about these sights. But the lure of a hunt with one of the princes of India, of staying with him at his palace, had a pull that put it into the realm of the must-do. And don't let the shotguns and the shooting disturb. It is a scientifically established fact that it takes the average hunter twenty-five shots to bag a single duck. These are fast-flying, wary birds who know how to take care of themselves.

So the shotgun becomes the object that we verbally wave as the reason for coming to this far place. Even if we don't fire it. Besides, there are millions of ducks, and the few that we down, if we are lucky, will end in a curry to feed many people. It will be a curry created by the Maharaja of Bharatpur himself. I know that Y has never even held a shotgun in his hands. I wonder if his wife knows?

But there he was, standing beside the Maharaja's jeep station wagon, leaning on his shotgun with all of the aplomb of a man who has stood in many a dawn like this waiting to hear the whistle of wild wings.

The others looked equally nonchalant, or perhaps they were dazed. The dawn was coming now in a butter-spread across the bottom edge of sky, and the Maharaja was bustling about getting things in motion.

"Let us go!" he said in his high voice. "We must be in the butts before full light. Let us go!"

He is a short, dark man with a mustache, sleek dark hair with slight touches of gray, warm brown eyes, and an erect, proud carriage as befits the twentieth prince in an unbroken line. Now he herded everyone into his three Rolls-Royces and jeep wagon and we rolled toward the duck water.

The Colonel His Highness Maharaja Sir Brajindra Sawai Brijendia Singhji Bahadur Jang doesn't do anything the ordinary way: the jeep we were in had a custom body that would hold a dozen passengers. Now it held the six of us and our guns. The Maharaja drove, leading the way. Behind us in the three Rollses and several other cars were a German baron, all the male teachers from the nearby college, and some American 4-H Club members who were visiting their counterparts in India, brought to help fill the shooting butts by Brigendra Singh, the Maharaja's brother-in-law. Gardner Bump, an expert from the U. S. Fish and Wildlife Service, gathering live specimens of India's game birds, had taken a day off to join the shoot.

The Maharaja talked while he drove as fast as the jeep would go, taking his eyes from the road to look back at us, a habit that had us jumpy before we left the palace grounds.

"We keep the birds in the air and on the move by gunfire," he said. "To do this we should have most of the ninety-two butts filled. It is a large piece of water to cover." His English was as elegant as his tailored shooting jacket and his ten-thousand-dollar matched Purdey shotguns.

We had received blueprints of the seven thousand-acre Keola Dev Ghana Sanctuary showing the position of the shooting butts, plus an engraved invitation embossed in gold at the top with the House of Bharatpur's coat of arms, an upright lion and an elephant. On the back of each blueprint was a list of the important duck shoots since 1902. The impressive roll started with the Viceroy, Lord Curzon, and ran through such names as Lord Kitchener, the Crown Prince of Germany, the Prince of Wales, dozens of maharajas, much more English royalty, some U. S. Senators, a sprinkling of shahs and kings, and a score of famous soldiers. Opposite each name was the number of ducks that had fallen to their guns. The whole thing was enough to give anyone an inferiority complex. To compound the feeling further, the Maharaja turned to me and said, "You are going to shoot in the Shah of Iran's butt. You'll have to do well to keep up with him!" H drew the King of Nepal; C, Lord Mountbatten; Y and W, two maharajas.

We passed through the graceful marble arch of the Prince of Wales Gate, and within minutes saw the polished metal gleam of water. Also, within minutes, I saw and identified a black drongo, a pied bushchat, a redstart, a Brahminy myna, two yellow-headed wagtails, a purple sunbird, a crow-pheasant, an osprey, a hoopoe, a Siberian and sarus crane, and a dozen white and three black ibis. This was a birdwatcher's paradise.

The Maharaja told us that it had been declared a nonmigratory bird sanctuary and that it was attracting bird-lovers from all over the world.

"It is the largest in Asia," he said. "Hardly a day passes that a brace of ornithologists doesn't appear and ask our permission to study birdlife."

Then he added, laughing, "I hope *our* kind of birdlife will be in evidence. If we had as many sporting birds as we do spoonbills, cormorants, shags, darters, terns and storks, this would be the best ducking water in the world."

I think it is.

Twenty minutes later we were in the butts, which actually weren't erected to hide the gunner, but were merely bamboo uprights to mark the position. I sat on a shooting seat, a turbaned boy in loincloth, body gleaming with oil, on either side.

His Highness would signal the shoot to start by firing two shots. They came quickly. And with the sound came the birds.

This was an expert's duck shoot. The birds were high and moving

The secretary of the Maharaja of Bharatpur (in black beret) selected retrievers for the royal duck hunt.

fast. They came first in bursts of a dozen, then in twos and threes. It took me most of a box of shells to get the hang of it. The two Indian retrievers sat morosely watching the unscathed wildfowl wheel over us.

When I started connecting, the birds going down in a wide, spiraling arc, the boys hit the water as fast as a Labrador, splashing out to get the fallen, shouting to each other as they made the retrieve.

By noon it was over. I had gone through a half-dozen boxes of shells; my shoulder was burning, sore to the touch. My duck take wasn't large enough to cause any exuberance, but the two Indians seemed happy and kept nodding and smiling at me.

I have been on many duck shoots but never have I seen so many birds in the air, birds that kept coming even after we walked back to meet the rest of the party. And the variety was amazing to a man who was accustomed to mallards and bluebills. Wigeon, pintails, tufted pochard, nukta, green- and blue-winged teal, and two new species of geese, the graylag and the barheaded.

The Maharaja counted my take. "The Shah outshot you," he said. "But then he had three guns and a bearer for each gun."

H and C had done well; Y, who confessed that he had secretly

taken skeet lessons before we left, discovered that ducks were
different from clay targets, and W found they "flew too high and too
fast."

The Maharaja announced that we would shoot again tomorrow. "I
expect to have other guests in for my duck curry," he said. "I implore
you gentlemen, get a good night's rest and shoot for my curry pot
tomorrow."

A group of tattered-turbaned Indians, evidently villagers, lined up
to watch us as the ducks were gathered and the cars loaded. They
stood staring in a single line, looking like hill brigands about to loot a
town.

Dinner that night was at the huge family table in the formal dining
room under four great crystal chandeliers. There was a servant behind each chair in white trousers, long black side-slitted tunic and a
white turban with a tail that trailed down the back. The Maharaja
had two chefs, Eastern and Western. All of us caught the spirit and
chose Eastern food. A mistake. It was served on large, sectioned
silver plates without flatware, which was messy for clumsy Westerners. We ate with our hands, scooping up the rice and rich chicken in
heavy cream with round, crisp wheatcakes, the *chapatties*. This was
washed down with endless bottles of *liebfraumilch*. Ripe, sweet mangoes were dessert, with tiny, crisp, powdered cakes.

Service was superb, with a man at your elbow instantly when you
had finished a portion. After the food, silver bowls of warm water
floating rose petals were brought. You washed your hands and were
handed a towel, also warm.

The young princesses sat demurely, answering questions flung by
their father, making tabletalk pleasantries with their guests. The conversation mostly involved the dodging ducks, the 4-H effort in India,
Nehru's tirelessness, the prince's prowess with a gun (he had bagged
four times as many ducks as anyone else) and the miracle of the jet.

Our jet had propelled us so fast from New York to this Far East
White Pearl Palace that unreality sat with us at dinner. To coin a new
word, it was jet-real—as if you were sitting back looking at yourself
through someone else's eyes, or watching the scene on a cinema
screen. It was difficult to believe that this was actually happening to
me and four friends who had discussed it half-jokingly just a few days
ago.

But it was real all right. "Let's adjourn to my game room for
brandy and coffee," the Maharaja said. The floor of the game room
was carpeted in tiger pelts skillfully sewn together. There must have

been fifty tigers in the rug. There was no orchestra tonight. The Maharaja talked.

He spoke of his sorrow at the government letting his Deeg palace fall into ruin, of his interest in tourism, in attracting more people to his country. Then he got into shooting and sport. You didn't need fifty tigers on the floor to prove that he was a past master.

H and Y kept asking questions about leopards and tigers until the Maharaja finally laughed and threw up his hands. "I didn't want to alarm you by telling you this. But there is a leopard, or panther, as we call them, roaming the palace grounds. I suggest that H and Y go sit in a tree and try to bag it."

Silence.

Then they both agreed. But you could see that this hadn't been part of their dream of India. This was somewhat different from the duck shoot and the desire to see the Taj Mahal.

They were gone three hours. All of that time was spent in a tree, each of them holding one of the Maharaja's rifles.

They returned, Y trembling with excitement. "We saw it!" he said. "H flashed the light just in time when we heard this creepy sound. But we didn't shoot. Why?" He turned to H.

H, who knew guns and hunting, said, "The leopard was moving too fast. We would have missed, or we might have just wounded it. Then there would be the devil to pay."

"*Hell* to pay, you mean!" said the Maharaja grimly. "Nothing more dangerous than a wounded panther! Thank you for not firing upon a running cat."

Again brandy. Then the canopied beds.

The climax of the next day was the Maharaja's curry. That evening we began drinking chilled champagne before the other guests arrived, while the Maharaja had his staff set up the cooking operation. He supervised the filling of dozens of silver bowls with tiny red chilies, cardamon, coriander, black pepper, honey, onion, and other mysterious ingredients. In the center of the room was an Indian charcoal brazier. The coals were burning now, and the guests began arriving in parties of six and eight. The Maharaja, after seeing that everyone had a drink in his hand, sat on a cushion beside the brazier, and a servant brought in a huge American pressure cooker.

"Marvelous gadget," he said to me, "gets these ducks tender in no time."

Then came a platoon of servants in pastel turbans. One had four ducks on a platter, the next a silver bowl of spices. Twenty approached the Maharaja on his cushion. He placed ducks in the cooker, sprinkled in spices, airily waving each servant on when he had what he wanted.

The heady Eastern aroma of freshly crushed spices permeated the room soon after the lid was fastened. In a half-hour the curry was finished, and passed on silver plates with rice and glasses of *liebfraumilch* (the Maharaja's favorite)—duck so tender, so sweet, so rich in the prince's secret seasoning that every man there wished aloud that he had been a better shot so the plates could be refilled.

The orchestra played tonight: again the swaying of Oriental poppies; again the high, strange music that I will never forget.

Duck-shooting would never be the same again.

After the Taj Mahal and some sightseeing in Agra and Delhi, C, H, W and Y would go home, but I intended to do some more wandering in India and the East. After telling me of the places I should see (it would take at least a year to see India, and even then you would miss much of it), the Maharaja called to his brother-in-law, Brigendra Singh. "Tell Jack about India Shikar and Tours. He's an adventurous fellow who wants more than temples and burning ghats."

It seems that the *shikar* (a big game hunt organization) was owned by three friends, rajas, tiger hunters, who used elephants and worked out of a fascinating area in the foothills of the Himalayas.

"You don't have to shoot a tiger if you don't want," Brigendra said, "but it is an exciting part of our world. I can alert them if you'd like to go out for a few days. I know that they are always booked up, but I'm sure they can fit you in between assignments."

Before we left to see the Taj by moonlight that night, Brigendra called Delhi and talked with one of the brothers. "They have an open week," he said, "and would be delighted to have you as guests. I'll meet you in Delhi and introduce you to Giri, their Delhi-based partner. Then you can take it from there."

Good-byes to the Maharaja and his family took over an hour—we were all so grateful, the stay had been so pleasant, he so generous, that it was difficult for any of us to find exactly the right words of appreciation.

H probably said it better than anyone. "Your Highness," he said, "you have made ordinary life livable for me again. When the walls of New York begin closing in, all I'll have to do is turn on the memory of your hospitality."

It was still light when we left the palace, but before we had traveled five miles we were stopped by two boys with a toothless old bear and a rhesus monkey. One boy wrestled with the bear; the other put his monkey through a few tricks. The monkey collected some annas from us while the boy with the bear did a little rhumbalike dance for us before we drove on.

It was dusk when we arrived at Agra where a representative of the department of tourism was waiting for us. A skinny man in a tropical suit, with a dark heavy moon face and polished black eyes, he was friendly and helpful. We waited for the moon as we drank Lion beer which the tourist man cooled with ice cubes.

When the moon came up, gilding the lawn before the hotel, he said, "We should go now to see the most impressive sight in India, maybe the world."

He wasn't exaggerating. "Towers of fables immortal, fashioned from mortal dreams," Walt Whitman sang of India. I don't know whether he ever saw the Taj Mahal, but *dream* is the word. As we drove to the Taj I had thought the moon was particularly beautiful this night, clear, full, floating free of clouds, but now it was dwarfed as the marble dome of the Taj Mahal rose, bathed in moonlight. Silently we walked past the great red sandstone gate with its dozen cupolas—everywhere were silent people caught in the spell of the place—and entered the garden. At the end, surrounded on three sides by lush evergreens stood the Taj. Cypresses flanked each side of the water, canaled in marble, that ran to the entrance; the reflection of the dream-white tomb lay on the water. This is where Richard Halliburton swam or splashed—it was too shallow to swim—and obligingly got himself arrested. What a silly thing for him to do, I thought now, as I saw the splendor of the scene. It was adventure enough just to stand and appreciate this masterpiece.

This "lover's tear on the cheek of immortality" fills those who stand and stare with emotion that grips all but the guides who move around muttering, "*I* am the official government guide. *I* know all the history. All the facts. Do not leave this great place without knowing . . ." But fortunately our tourist department man sent them away. "Bloody bores!" he said. "As if anyone had to do any more than *look* at the Taj!"

We stood a few feet inside the gate doing just that—looking. H whispered, "I never would have believed it!" C looked as though he had been poleaxed; Y's lips were moving as if he were saying a silent prayer; W fumbled with his camera case for a moment, then decided to record it with his eyes, not the mechanical lens, and stood staring.

The Taj Mahal—"This result of the fusion of two cultures . . . has brought us the supreme architectural achievement of man."

Mary Lou's eyes shone, and the tourist official kept nodding his head at our appreciation. "Yes, yes," he whispered. "This result of the fusion of two cultures, two architectures, two ways of thinking and feeling, has brought us the supreme architectural achievement of man."

Now the central dome of the Taj rose before us in purest white marble, seemingly floating in the night, its proportions geometrically perfect. All of the walls were filled with intricate floral carvings and inlay.

Inside the main domed chamber of the Taj Mahal, behind a tall marble eight-sided screen, were the sepulchers of Shah Jehan and Muntaz Mahal, his second wife. This most beautiful building on earth was created by the Shah as her monument.

An old man with a beard and long dirty robes came out of the shadows as we entered, saying, "I am the guardian of the sepulchers." He chattered on, his words completely ignored by all of us as we stood admiring the magnificent inlay on the chaste white marble of the graves. Directly beneath them the bodies are entombed. Ceiling and floor were also laid with white marble.

Now the guardian's voice began to pierce our consciousness. "The walls have many precious stones embedded in them—sapphires, jasper, emeralds, onyx. Many of the emeralds have disappeared."

As we left, he held out a wrinkled old hand. "Five rupees please for my services."

We were all still silent as we walked back through the red gate and got into the car. Our tourist friend took over.

"Shah Jehan and Muntaz Mahal were married eighteen years. She went everywhere with him. Even on his battles of conquest. Their love was proverbial. She was not only strikingly beautiful but had a fine mind, and it is said that he consulted her on everything, even military matters. She died giving birth to their fourteenth child, a daughter."

The car purred through the night. Looking back we could see the main dome rising like a second moon.

Our education continued. "The Shah was inconsolable. To construct her mausoleum he sent everywhere for architects, masons, sculptors, calligraphists. Persia, Arabia, Turkey sent their finest craftsmen. But one of our own people, artist Isa Afandi, submitted the model that won the emperor's approval. It took twenty thousand men twenty-two years to build this ode to love."

At Agra we left our American hunting companions and fortunately got a ride to Delhi the next morning with the department of tourism official. He kindly gave up the back seat of his car and sat with the driver, turning his dark moon face toward us for the entire ride, delivering a patter of philosophy that gave a clue to Indian mentality.

"Oh," he said brightly as we left Agra, "I almost forgot. I have a gift for the lady." He produced a small soapstone replica of the Hindu elephant god, Ganesh. Reaching back, he tenderly placed it in Mary Lou's hand.

"I am a follower of Ganesh," he said. "He is one of our most interesting gods."

He went on to say that most of the Hindu religion is based on Shiva worship, the oldest living faith, which was practiced in the Indus Valley over five thousand years ago. The God Shiva seems to flit mainly around graveyards and is the number one ghost in India. Brahma's granddaughter, Sati, married Shiva. One day, to honor her departed god-husband, she leaped into sacrificial flames and was burned to death, thus beginning a Hindu practice that even plagues Nehru's India, with widows sometimes committing suicide by

jumping into the flames and becoming respected Sati saints. Shiva has
another wife, Kali, the Goddess of Destruction, who is inordinately
pleased when she is offered a human sacrifice. Those who worship
her are considered a left-hand caste, not on the same level with the
Shiva people, who are the right-hand caste.

"There is still another wife of Shiva," our tourist man said. "She is
Parvati. Her son was Ganesh. One day, angered because Ganesh followed him through the forest, Shiva cut off his son's head. To console
his horrified wife, the god commanded his servants to walk into the
forest and return with the head of the first living creature they saw."
Here our man halted solemnly. "They saw an elephant and returned
with its head. Shiva placed it upon Ganesh. Thus was our elephant
god born. Dramatic, is it not?

"You know, good people," he went on, "with what they are doing
in modern medical science, transplanting hearts, giving the blind the
living eyes of others, transplanting kidneys, it is entirely possible that
this could have happened to Ganesh. Isn't it? You know also, I suppose, that the Hindus were practicing advanced surgery when the rest
of the world was having trouble descending from trees?" He hesitated. "I hope you do not think I am being boastful, but by the year
500 the doctors of India had identified and classified seven hundred
drug herbs."

I wondered what Nehru and his intellectuals would have said to
this nice man, who obviously believed every word he was uttering.
The Indian people have more of a struggle ahead than most of us
realize. Of their 461 million (one-seventh of the human race), 300
million are Hindus, embracing Shiva and the "entirely possible" Ganesh.

As we left our pleasant philosopher at the Ashoka Hotel, thanking
him for the ride and the statue of his god, we remained thoughtful
travelers. And to the thoughtful traveler, Delhi is a sobering city. In
its great red sandstone government buildings and in the half-mile
columned rotunda of its Parliament, the stuff of slavery or of freedom
is currently being compounded. Delhi, the city that has embodied
many forms and moods, has reached her most important moment in
history. A social revolution is being launched from this ancient place,
caught up in the complicated mesh of modern problems.

In this free but grotesquely shrunken society of India, a bitter
battle is being fought for a world of free men. If this experimental
revolution succeeds, all of us who believe that we live in the un-
shackled world of democracy can breathe a sigh of relief. But if the

sea-strong terror from China or Russia engulfs this struggling subcontinent, then communism will control Asia. If this awakening giant who speaks haltingly of freedom should topple, the world may stumble and fall with it.

At the desk in the hotel was a message that changed this serious stream of thought and brought us back to the reality of our mission in travel: adventure. We were to meet Rajkumar Giriraj Singh, Delhi-based owner of India Shikar and Tours, the next day. We would leave for his jungle camp immediately.

As we left the *shikar* offices with Rajkumar Giriraj Singh into the confusion of ASAF Ali Road (bullocks blocking traffic, car horns blaring, trying to push through the milling crowd of head-shaven Hindus, bearded Sikhs, short, fierce-looking Gurkhas, gaily turbaned Punjabis, Madrasis and dozens of Indians I couldn't identify, beggar women pushing diseased babies at you, a half-naked fortuneteller blatting in your ear, "A rupee, sir, will tell what lies ahead!"), one of those incredible things happened that would trouble a fiction writer.

Stepping briskly from a tailor shop was a dapper man with a mustache, snapping blue eyes and the relaxed manner of a baron. Beside him was a pert, attractive woman. They were our neighbors, the Alastair MacLeods from Roxbury, Connecticut, some ten thousand miles from home.

It was beside their hearth many months ago that Mary Lou and I sat and talked tiger. Now we chatted in that sophisticated manner of jet travelers trying to be nonchalant about running into one another on the streets of New Delhi. Of course all of us were secretly shaken with surprise. The MacLeods proved my contention that romance and adventure are not items to be vicariously pulled from a TV tube.

Those months ago when we met in Connecticut, Mrs. MacLeod had phoned me after reading a book I had written on India's jungles and asked if we would come for cocktails and talk. Every winter they traveled and she explained that they had been almost everywhere, even India. They took turns choosing places to go. This was her winter to plan, and she had an unusual idea that she wanted to talk about.

"I'd like to go hunt tigers," she said. "Alastair is willing. He thinks it would be fun."

Taken aback, I explained as diplomatically as I could that tiger-hunting was a serious business requiring experience, physical fitness, a calm shooting eye, and several other qualities that I didn't think they might have, inasmuch as they were not youngsters. Both were sparkling, live people; neither had any sign of advancing age or infirmity, and Mrs. MacLeod positively shone in her energy and exuberance.

"But we really don't want to shoot a tiger," she explained. "Only—"

Her Scotch husband cut in brusquely, "We just want to observe. See how the thing is done. Taste the jungle life. Go through the routine. Sounds exciting."

She laughed. "Neither of us has ever had even an air rifle in our hands. I'm scared to death of guns."

"But Bernice is not afraid to take a chance on most anything," her husband said. "This tiger thing is her idea. Rather yours. Your bloody book started all this."

The rest of that Connecticut cocktail hour was spent answering questions: names of *shikar* organizations, what kind of clothing they should take, how they should travel, where they should stay in India, what was the best type of tiger-hunting, the ideal terrain, did anyone hunt them from elephants? It was skillful questioning. Enough so that there was no doubt of their sincerity. Several weeks later we left on a trip and I never did get the opportunity to talk to the MacLeods again about their tiger plans.

And now here they were. They had just been measured for shooting clothing and were going out with the same *shikar* organization that we were. They would be about fifty miles from our camp.

We didn't see them again until long after this meeting in India— then just briefly in Roxbury—but the *shikar* people told us that they were excellent clients, that they took the cold, the sitting in trees, the camp food, the winds from the Himalayan foothills, the entire jungle experience without turning a hair.

"Amazing people!" said the *shikari,* the professional hunter who had been with them. "They sat high in a tree during some of the coldest hours we have had in this territory. And never complained."

What they actually had done was go through the entire tiger-hunting program, the baiting, the sitting up, even to the classic moment when the great cat came out of the jungle and approached their tree.

"The most thrilling thing I have ever done!" Mrs. MacLeod said.

"Quite!" said her husband.

Any reader who thinks it takes a great white hunter with courage, youth, stamina and nerves of steel to go on a tiger *shikar* in India, should think of the MacLeods.

. . .

Minutes after that meeting with our Connecticut neighbors we
were in Giriraj Singh's jeep station wagon heading north out of New
Delhi, moving through traffic resembling a temple mural: near-naked,
ash-smeared holy men; slim, elegant women in brilliant red, green
and purple saris; Hindus in white Gandhi hats and tight, narrow
pants, with turbans of all colors and shapes. Herds of buffaloes were
ambling along the road ahead; people were squatting on the roadside
beside cooking fires. We passed a man with a cobra and a scrawny
little mongoose setting up his sideshow, the snake thrusting its head
out of the basket, the mongoose in his cage, running, running.

Now we drove beside the laden camels and mules of the hill people
who had come in to barter, beside pedal-rickshaws and old, dusty
taxis, most of them with two bearded Sikhs in the front seat, many
with bewildered-looking Westerners peering from streaked back windows. Near the flaming walls of the Red Fort, a man in dirty white
turban and dhoti, standard Indian loincloth, was pushing long sticks
of sugar cane through a hand press. The oily juice was being received
by a dirty brass pot into which he dipped glasses, quickly topping
each with chopped ice. He would sell a glass, then dry it with a
corner of his dhoti as it returned empty. The day was getting warm
now and people were lining up before his sugar press.

The huge onion dome of Shah Jehan's Great Mosque loomed
ahead, and suddenly we found ourselves beside the ring of stone steps
leading to the building. The broad stone ledges were crowded with
nearly naked beggars, many lifting their hands for alms as we drove
by. Leading away from the mosque were lopsided little buildings that
looked as though they had been flung together by madmen, the tot-
tery shacks of the thieves' market where everything from a toilet seat
to a tiger's-claw brooch had been stolen and was offered for sale.

Giri, as he insisted we call him, was dark, had a mustache, thinning hair and much natural charm, with a genius for quickly putting
people at ease. In fact, he was the front man for India Shikar and
Tours, the organization that he and his brother Shem Sher Jung
owned. He met clients at the plane, wined them at his country club,
dined them at the best restaurants in Delhi, and squired them around
the shops, all the time filling them in on the *shikar* that lay ahead.

Both he and his brother, once great landholders though not of
royal blood, were still called rajas by the many people who used to
live on their land. Now, in a free, independent India, with rajas and

maharajas swept out of power, the land that Giri and his brother once owned belonged to the government but they were permitted to hunt on it—properly licensed, of course. They knew the region and its animals well.

Giri explained why he was taking us to the *shikar* camp by jeep. "It has rained more than usual this month," he said. "The road to the camp will be soft. We will need the jeep. But I'm afraid that even with it we will have rough going."

After running out of gas once and waiting at several railroad crossings while freight trains crawled by, we finally lost civilization. In one bleak, terrible area that looked like a desert, we crossed the noble Ganges at a point where it was barely a trickle, but even here Hindus were filling bottles with water from the sacred river.

Commenting on the vastness of India, a noted reporter once said that writers became so confused with its richness and variety that they often captured only bewildered glimpses of the land and its people. I hoped not to let that happen.

We were on our way to see how tigers are hunted from elephant back, to hunt partridge from trained elephants, and take a look at the unusual people from Nepal who make the basic ingredient for betel chewing.

We drove slowly through the medieval village of Kotdwara, a place of ancient stone buildings, open markets and a road full of wet ruts with buffaloes and wagons mired in mud, donkeys loaded until you didn't see how they could walk, even if they weren't buried to their knees, and a howling bedlam of drivers trying to get them out of the mud onto the solid road shoulders. Here man as beast of burden was doing better. These were mountain people, their backs loaded with animal skins, cages of screaming rhesus monkeys, huge gourds of milk, baskets of fruit, wicker containers of curds—all here from the hills to barter in the open markets.

"As the vulture flies," Giri said, "this village is less than one hundred miles from Tibet. We are now about forty miles from camp by forest roads."

With the jeep in four-wheel drive, its horn blatting constantly like an animal in pain, we managed to get past Kotdwara and to the entrance of the road that would take us into the jungle.

A forest guard stood there in a handsome gold-and-red peaked turban, khaki shirt and shorts, with an obvious air of authority. He held up a large black hand, palm out, halting us.

The second language in India is English and practically everyone in authority speaks it. Hindi and Hindustani are supposed to be used more often, but we found that English in several accents, Welsh, Scotch, Oxford, is the first language, really the status or prestige tongue. The guard had a broad Welsh accent and was adamant.

"Very sorry, sirs," he said, "but you cannot travel this forest road. We have had seven inches of rain in three hours. Rain has washed it out in places and in others it is so soft that you cannot travel."

Giri showed him our *shikar* papers and hunting licenses, and introduced Mary Lou and me, saying, "Our camp is already set up forty miles from here. We have made the trip many times in this jeep."

The guard bowed his head at the introductions. "You see, sir," he said, "I have my instructions due to the fact that if people become mired in the road, then it is necessary for us to go in and bring them out. As you know, this is a bloody bother."

But he finally waved us on. The roads were indeed terrible. But Giri, through knowledge of the road, driving skill and use of all the gears the jeep had, almost got us there—almost. This was the first time I had seen the doughty jeep defeated. One stretch of the jungle road stood deep in water. Trees were thick on either side, so we couldn't go around. Giri decided to run through the water. We got out, walked close to the trees and waited on the other side.

The jeep, roaring mightily, got to the center, sank to the top of its wheels, and stalled. Walking through muck up to his knees, Giri came to the roadside and said, "Camp isn't too far. Why don't you wait and I'll go for help."

As we waited, a peacock watched us from a clump of thick young bamboo, his presence betrayed by his royal blue head and the sun striking light from his eyes. We sat quietly but the bird never stirred a feather. A mongoose came from the grass fifty yards away, raised his weasel head at us, then flowed like water back into the undergrowth. Life was all around us, you could hear it rustle, hear its stealthy whisper.

As the subtle sounds continued, I thought, Here you are deep in jungle. Your guide is gone; your guns are in wraps in the jeep. Around you could be anything: cobras, leopards, tigers. But the situation seemed so unreal, so much like something out of a book, that I looked at the reality of the jeep in the mud, the brass disk of sun, my wife sitting calmly beside me, and knew nothing would happen. It didn't. But as Giri finally came up the road on an elephant, I realized that many things could have happened in that wild place as we sat and waited.

It has been said that there is nothing more dependable than a jeep, and I have agreed. But there is—a trained elephant. This one, using a chain harness, yanked that jeep out of the mud like a waiter taking a cork from a wine bottle. We were in camp in a half-hour.

Camp was something that you must dream about if you think of adventure in the far places. Beyond stood the Shavlik Range wreathed in blue mist, the foothills of the Himalayas. Three hundred yards from the tent compound ran the Sonanadi, the "River of Gold," making a sound like someone tuning a guitar. In a grove of trees before camp, four elephants stood fanning their ears while mahouts baked bread for them on flat stones over open fires. Behind the cooking tent an old man in dhoti and white turban was scraping a large, circular brass pan, the sun making it gleam like a huge coin.

This was Mota Sal, "The Place of the Fat Sal Trees." These trees, known to Indians as "the poor man's teak," have huge, hand-sized leaves and look like a combination of oak and maple. They circled the camp. Some of the camp helpers had spread belongings in the open beneath them; others had erected little tents. When the mist burned off and the sun became bright, the sal leaves cast shadows that lay like temple frescoes. In the leaf-shadow the elephants became strange spotted beasts out of a dim past.

Our tents were fifty yards apart, encircled by a head-high wall of canvas, making a compound. There were two tents for the *shikar* people, one for us and a dining tent. Just outside the compound were the cook and laundry tents.

The tents were a large double-fly type of exceptionally heavy canvas made by Khyaliram and Sons in Delhi, and the most luxurious I have ever camped in. Ours, lushly floored with Oriental rugs, had a little sitting room, a large bedroom, a small storage or closet area, and a separate bathroom with a washstand, a toilet, and a three-by-two galvanized tub, a "hip bath." With this came a boy in his teens, of the untouchable caste, who took care of the tent.

The first morning when we came out of the canvas he was squatting in the little anteroom sweeping the floor with a bunch of reeds. He was more efficient than any electric sweeper or plumbing system yet devised. As for the tentbearer, Inait Tulla, I have yet to see any modern mechanical gadget that can so pleasantly bring a cup of steaming tea to you of a cold morning, smiling shyly as it is placed on the bedside stand.

The untouchable boy couldn't combine jobs, although he was perfectly capable of making the beds and bringing the tea. But as an untouchable, the cups he touched, the clothing he handled would have been destroyed by the Indians of other castes.

The Indian caste system is something the Western mind has trouble grasping. It is in a strange way something like our trade unions. There is a caste for everything—sweeping, gardening, driving, waiting on table, guarding, even a terrible caste that lives by stealing and selling children. I was told in Delhi that although free India is doing its best to abolish the system, many castes are fighting it in fear of losing their employment, which is handed down from father to son for generations. But the untouchables, 50 million of them, are born into such a sad way of life that it automatically keeps them out of all the temples, forces everyone to avoid coming close to them, and reduces them to getting their drinking water from gutters and ditches. And yet there is nothing different about them; there is no physical feature that sets them apart. Our tent boy was a handsome, happy lad who smiled as he did the work that no one else would stoop to do.

The hot tea brought by Inait Tulla this morning was necessary; it brought life back to two frozen bodies. It was so cold when we awoke that Mary Lou's face cream was frozen solid. We could hear the four elephants trumpeting gently, a peaceful, somehow reassuring sound, and a crow cawed coarsely as he swooped low over the tent. The heavy morning dew was dropping like rain on the canvas as the camp stirred into life.

January in the jungles of India, especially here in the northern mountains, was much colder and damper than we had been led to believe—less than twenty degrees. This morning the mists came like smoke from the nearest mountain—a spiny ridge called Hathi than Ka Danda, "Ridge of the Elephants of Old"—and from the river that flowed by, sending up steam as if it were afire.

We had gone to bed shortly after arrival that first night; this morning we would meet the full *shikar* crew at breakfast. They were waiting in the anteroom of the dining tent before a potbellied stove. Giri made the introductions: Shem Sher Jung, the senior partner of India Shikar and Tours, a man of noble bearing, short-cut gray hair over a well-shaped Roman head; his son Devendra Singh, slim, dark, a bit arrogant; H. C. A. Singh, called Daju, or brother, slightly on the effeminate side with sparse hair that he brushed up from the back in an impossible attempt to disguise the fact that he was fast becoming bald. He was married to the sister of the Queen of Nepal, had brought his special valet along, and was to delay many a *shikar* day with the making of his toilet, his valet helping him with the hopeless and endless hair brushing. He was immaculately clad in crisp khakis and tweed jacket and wore a dark red ascot. He turned out to be cheery and an excellent shooting companion.

A slim little old man, wearing a woolen pullover stocking cap that covered everything but the face, much like the gear skiers wear, came in and stood at attention.

He wore an old blue suit jacket at least one size too large—obviously somebody's hand-me-down—narrow, slightly flaring jodhpur-type breeches, and his oak-brown feet were bare. His thin, gentle, sensitive face was dominated by darting brown eyes and a huge white mustache.

"This is Jait Ram," Giri said. "Our tracker. We can't move without him. He knows more about tigers than their mothers."

Jait Ram removed his head cover and bowed a head of thick gray hair.

"I don't think we will hunt cats today," Shem Sher said, "but put out the baits. We will go for them tomorrow."

I knew from our 1958 experience that this meant tying out young buffaloes in a likely place, leaving them there all night for the tiger to kill. A rather cruel, but I am told necessary, way to mark that the great cat was in a specific area.

"We don't want to shoot a tiger," I said. At that Jait Ram waited.

"Oh?" said Shem Sher.

"No, the bird-shooting is what we are eager for. But we would like to see how you hunt tiger. See a tiger in his natural element. Actually go through everything but the killing, if that is possible. I hope you don't have to tie out buffaloes to do this."

"No," Shem Sher said, "we can run scratch beats. Drive our elephants through places where our trackers find sign that a tiger has been, without trying to shoot him." He then told Jait Ram not to tie out the baits, but to spend time looking for fresh tracks.

Jait slowly pulled on his cap, straightened, bowed once, then turned and made a dignified exit. He left an air of confidence behind.

"I'm leaving for Delhi after breakfast," Giri said, "but as you can see, I leave you in good hands. I told them you wanted to shoot partridge from elephant back. Maybe that can be done today?"

Shem Sher nodded. "Certainly. The camp also can use the fresh meat."

"Good show!" Daju said. "Sporting thing to wing away at the birds from the big beasties."

Devendra, wiping his mustache with a long forefinger, said nothing.

Breakfast in the dining tent with its long table covered with white linen and silver was unexpectedly good. It was served this morning by the cook, an old Moslem with a long white beard and a black skull-cap, who shuffled in with oatmeal, liver and scrambled eggs.

After breakfast Shem Sher, a man who had obviously studied ornithology and botany, launched into a description of the bird that we were to hunt. He later proved able to identify a bird or a tree from any distance, and his facts were so neatly arranged and came out so precisely that you knew that anything he said was true. He had spent much of his time in the jungles, not for the hunting but because he liked nature. I've found that many of the men who have linked themselves to the quiet places are great talkers—when they get a captive audience.

"*Kala teetar* is the bird's Hindi name," he said. "*Francolinus francolinus* is about half the size of the ordinary village hen—"

"Come, come, Shem Sher," Daju said. "It's the black partridge we're going after—"

"That's what I'm saying," Shem Sher said impatiently. "Perhaps you have no desire to learn more of anything but hair lotions and vitamins, but I'm certain that these are people who would like to know more of the feathered creature they will be hunting."

We nodded that we would. What else could we do?

He went on in his high, schoolteacherish voice, detailing the bird as accurately and completely as a naturalist.

Devendra, the dashing son, was impatient and embarrassed as his father described the partridge. He kept taking off his big green bush hat and flapping it in the air, while he scrubbed his booted feet on the ground, making a sound like an animal digging for survival. His father ignored him.

"They feed in early morning and about dusk. They are one of the fastest of all game birds on their feet, and seldom take to the air unless driven or suddenly come upon—"

And that was all; that was the end of the dissertation. His son had gone and stirred up the elephant drivers, the mahouts, and they were awaiting us with Champa Kali, Anarkli Kali, Chattra Kali, and one just called "Daju's elephant," donated by him to the *shikar* organization. This one raised her trunk and made a noise like a waterfall. "Noisy beast," grumbled Shem Sher, "just like her master." Daju laughed.

And then the mahouts had their *ankuses* out (small, hooked goads), and the elephants were kneeling for us to mount. Devendra,

Shem Sher and Daju went up their backs, using the beasts' tails as hand holds, but Mary Lou and I used the small ladder and grabbed the metal piece on the saddle. Guns and shells were handed up and we lumbered off. It was surely the most unusual bird-shooting setup I had ever encountered.

The mist was as thin as cigarette smoke now as we moved about three miles an hour, just a little slower than a man-walk. Amazingly, it was a smooth ride; we swayed a bit, as if standing on shipboard, but there was no jerky movement and the big animals required little direction.

I wondered about firing a shotgun so close to the elephant's head (I was just back of the mahout, not three feet from the big beast's flapping ear) and asked Daju, my shooting partner, the question.

He laughed. "Don't worry," he said. "In the old days we used to fire five hundred express rifles from their backs, standing in a *houdah*, equipment we don't use any more. No, these ladies are trained hunting beasties. Don't give it a thought."

So the scene was set: the mist had lifted and we walked into spear-headed tiger grass over twelve feet high. The wind moved it ahead of us like waves on a golden sea.

The elephants walked softly on their huge pads. Ahead of us sounded the incessant trill of the weaver bird, monotonously shrill. Then to our right we saw a fluttering in a sal tree, and Daju said, "Green pigeons. Let's go closer. You can try your luck. Give you an idea of how the elephants stand to gunfire before we get into partridge territory—"

The big animal obediently moved close to the trees; the pigeons coöperated, flashing green fire as they hurled themselves into the air. I swung the Browning 20 superposed easily, and fired twice. The handsome brace of pigeons kept on going, ignoring the strange creatures on the large animal. Not a feather fluttered. But the experiment was a success. The elephant stood like stone, steady to shot and, as it proved, to wing. I've seen many a supposedly well-trained field trial pointer who was more fidgety under fire.

Mary Lou, on her elephant fifty yards away, waved her gun in derision, and the mahout had his elephant flip her trunk. We kept moving forward, the three elephants abreast, until we reached the center of the huge grassy *maidan,* or meadow, the giant grass still moving like sea waves in the wind. Then Shem Sher halted and shouted. "We have chased the birds on the groun⌐ ⌐head of us. We will now move forty yards apart and get ready to shoot. They will have to fly over a stretch of road, so I think that we will get birds into the air shortly—"

He knew his *kala teetar*. In five minutes there was a burst of feathers a dozen feet ahead of my mount: two partridge. They flew like grouse, only faster. I got one, Daju took the other. Then the mahout marched his elephant over and the marvelous animal picked up both birds with her facile trunk and handed them back to her master.

The others took four more partridges as we moved forward in this regal fashion. Never have I seen a neater, faster job of retrieving than these elephants accomplished. If I hadn't been aboard on this maneuver I never would have believed it.

Now we could hear the birds: they were agitated and their chik-cheek-cheek-keraykek calls were far-reaching.

Accustomed to the swaying motion now, I waited briefly when the elephant halted, to get proper range and let the animal's breathing subside. Mostly the birds flew singly or in pairs, but as we reached the edge of the grass and neared a narrow dirt road, there was a terrible flurry and at least two dozen burst out. I nearly fell off the elephant. It is unnerving enough to see and hear that many partridge hit the air, but to get an elephant-back view of them is a startling experience.

When we reached the road we slid off our mounts and gathered for a talk. We had taken eighteen birds from the three elephants and each man had missed a half-dozen shots. There may be more interesting bird-shooting somewhere. If there is I'd like to know more about it.

We decided to go back to camp by way of the road, the two other animals preceding us and sending up feathery spirals of dust with their huge feet. One mile from camp, Daju bagged a bold red jungle cock that decided to try flying over our elephant, and I took a brace of green pigeons that made the mistake of thinking elephants don't use shotguns.

Jait Ram, the tracker, was waiting for us when we got back. Eagerly he reached up for the birds.

"My belly cries!" he said in Hindi. "What would hungry tiger hunters do without our great elephants?"

The answer to that was nothing. Hunting wouldn't be possible in this terrain where elephant and tiger grass often grew to a height of twenty feet. I had thought of what might happen if one fell from an elephant while bird-shooting and got lost in that ocean of grass. Anything could be concealed in its golden depth—tigers, leopards, wild boars—a host of animals.

When I mentioned it to Shem Sher he laughed. "All wild animals are more afraid of us than we are of them." Then he frowned. "With the exception of the abnormal ones, of course. The injured, the terribly old, and those that have an unnatural appetite created by the laziness and stupidity of people."

He went on to say that in these hills religion had actually created many man-eating tigers. When people died they were supposed to be cremated. But usually this wasn't done. An arm, a leg or a forehead would be seared, signifying that the dead one had been consumed by fire, and the corpse would be rolled over the mountain to be "buried" by wild beasts—hyenas, jackals, vultures—and sometimes by tigers.

As a result many a tiger hereabouts had picked up a taste for human flesh, and some, when corpses weren't available, went out and made them.

"You know of Jim Corbett, of course," Shem Sher said. "He was very popular in your country."

Jim Corbett had specialized in hunting man-eaters and had written a best-selling book, *The Man-Eaters of Kumaon*. I knew his work and respected his prowess as a hunter and a writer.

When I told Shem Sher that, he nodded. "I knew him well," he said. "His mother was an Indian. The Kumaon Hills he wrote about are a day's walk from this camp. Also, not many miles from here is the Corbett National Park that has been set aside as a memorial to him, where you can sit and watch wild animals. It is a protected area and full of all kinds of wild life."

"Did Corbett actually hunt tigers on foot in this region? With all this grass? It doesn't seem possible that he could do it and live to write about it."

Shem Sher smiled. "The grass isn't always this tall, and it wasn't precisely here that he hunted. Usually it was nearer villages in cultivated areas. But he has hunted here. He was a brave man."

Back in the dining tent over "boily brown" partridge and rice (the freshly bagged birds are boiled in water until tender, then sautéed in ghee, or buffalo butter, until brown), Shem Sher—with many a verbal and unappreciated assist from Daju—told us about those wonderful beasts, the hunting elephants. They dominated the camp as they stood regally in the grove of sal trees eating the leaves and the bread the elephant boys brought them, seemingly aware of the fact that they were the masters of the situation, that without them there wouldn't be a camp, for there wouldn't be any tiger-hunting or bird-shooting.

The Indians do not believe in training elephants through fear. The first step is to assign a mahout who will live with the elephant, perhaps for the rest of his life. They are at least twenty-five years old before they begin their training as hunting elephants. The temperamental streak is gone at that age; the animal is quiet and will take to specialized training more easily. Shem Sher's animals were all females; the tuskers are too temperamental to make reliable hunters. During breeding season the males often go mad, attacking other elephants and people.

Daju broke in to say that the captive elephant is placed in a stall between two others, who are already well-trained or at least well-advanced, where it is left alone with sufficient food and water. In this manner the wild one can see that she is safe, that nothing alarming is going to happen. Once the captive starts eating normally and quiets down, training begins.

The trainer stands in front of the animal with two assistants on tame elephants on either side controlling the captive. Four other men then run their hands gently over the wild one's hide uttering soothing and endearing words. Often the elephant doesn't take to this and starts whipping her trunk. The trainer then shows and uses his *hawkus* or *ankus,* the pointed metal rod with the curved hook on the side. The elephant will take some punishment with the goad, then fold up her trunk in protection and quiet down, enduring the hands of the men attempting to gentle her.

After submitting to this, she is led to a stream, and her mahout, again using the goad, will induce her to lie down in the water where she is bathed, has her belly rubbed and water splashed on her. This delights her and after a while she looks forward to the bath as a reward if she has been a good girl all day. Then comes the ordeal of getting her accustomed to the riding saddle, *khatola* or *char-jarma,* which is a huge pad with an oblong frame lashed on it. Long rides with several people aboard finish this phase. Then follow the hunting lessons.

Shem Sher Jung said that these usually take four years. First, the elephant is ridden into the field where a pack of barking dogs is driven out of the brush toward her. When she becomes toughened to this hellish racket—and this can take a long time—they ride her into the jungle, throwing lighted firecrackers ahead of her and snapping a huge bullwhip over her head. For riders, Shem Sher uses men with slingshots, who search out trees loaded with noisy parakeets. The birds are slinged into screaming mass-flight from the trees, making a racket that would raise the dead.

When the tyro hunting elephant has learned to take all this in stride, she is brought out with a pair of experienced animals, saddled with a *houdah,* the big boxlike riding contraption, and the gunner stands and shoots at whatever game may be flushed. After this point is reached the weaknesses are worked on until she is as steady to shot as a polished field trial pointer.

The burden of training falls upon the mahout, who begins his trade as a fodder cutter for the skilled elephant men. He is usually the son of a mahout, the profession in India passing from the father. The finished mahout makes about forty rupees (a rupee is twenty-one cents) a month plus food, board and tips. The latter can be substantial. Mahouts seem happy people.

Every morning the delightful aroma of elephant bread baking permeated our camp. This is a mixture of wheat, salt and water, emerging from the coals as a huge brown loaf, which is fed to the hunting elephants daily. One animal consumes ten pounds, plus all the *ficus* leaves he can eat. The *ficus* is a variety of fig, and a favorite of the big beast. The remainder of the hunting elephant's diet is varied with millet, milo, green corn stalks, young bamboo, kans grass (related to sugar cane) and tiger grass. They prefer young trees with a milk sap, and the mahouts offer it to them as a reward after an especially good or hard day.

The "riders of the great" have a special language for communicating with their charges, a tongue few understand.

But Shem Sher Jung knows many of the words and he translated a few: *Dhut* means stop; *mall,* go; *bhit,* sit; *tul,* a special canter lifting the left leg. *Jhuk* means drop one shoulder and lean sideways; *mall agah,* go forward. *Dub* commands an elephant to knock down a tree; *tali,* to step on the tree once it is down. A hunting elephant can understand thirty words and several phrases.

The pleasantest memory of the elephants I have is the day Mary Lou and I rode Champa Kali to the camp of the strange people from Nepal. After breakfast we waited for our mahout to finish smoking his long water pipe. He was a slim, swarthy man wearing an old British Army coat and a black skullcap that looked as if it had once been velvet. He had flashing brown eyes, a small mustache, a gentle voice, and smiled often. He was training his ten-year-old nephew to become a mahout. The boy would be assigned an elephant in ten years. Now it was his task to feed and bathe Champa Kali, help saddle her, and bring her whenever the mahout summoned.

The sun lay hard and bright as yellow paint on the tents this morning; the mist had vanished by nine o'clock and the *shikar* men in the area before the camp were just finishing up their flat wheatcakes, *chapatties,* and tea as we walked over to look at Champa Kali. The elephant boy stood beside his charge smoking a *bidi,* a brown hand-rolled cigarette that smelled like burning garbage. Champa Kali was bored and had her trunk in her mouth, one front foot cocked over the other.

Daju, his hair gleaming from his valet's morning brushing, said: "They get bored standing around. They like action. This morning we are going to ride the girls to a *catechu* camp where the Nepal people help us with our vice. Betel chewing, y'know. A beastly habit that is turning all the teeth in India black. Disgusting!"

Daju wasn't one to wait while a mahout smoked his way through a three-foot water pipe. *"Aajao!"* he said in Hindi. "Come!"

With that the camp sprang into action, the elephant boys and mahouts saddled their mounts, the boys up on the beasts' backs tugging, the mahouts shoving up the large saddles.

In fifteen minutes we were on the road, a winding track with the River of Gold on one side still smoking in mist, and the great stands of amber elephant grass on the other. Beyond the mahouts occasionally mumbling at the elephants, the only sounds were the slight shuffling of the big beasts plodding along, the sigh of the river, and the screams of parakeets as they flew from the tops of sal and tun trees—a banner of red, green and yellow flowing over our heads.

Shem Sher led on Daju's big elephant, Daju and Devendra were next, and we brought up the rear. A couple of miles up the road, the elephant traffic stopped, Shem Sher slid down the back of his animal, using the tail as a hand hold, and bent over some marks in the road.

"Tiger!" he said loudly. "A big male crossed here early this morning!"

Then he got back on his mount, going up the back again, pulling himself hand over hand up the elephant's tail.

We left the river road now. Off to our right were peaks powdered with snow—the Himalayas humping against the sky.

The camp of the betel people was marked by long streamers that rose in the sky like a giant puffing of cigar smoke. Shem Sher waited for us. "These are the Chais," he said. "They are from Nepal and don't care much for guests. I believe they think visitors come to spy and learn how to chop the *catechu.* Often they don't even speak Hindi. So I don't think we should stay overlong. But we wanted you to see this *catechu* camp. Few ever get the opportunity."

The camp was beside a small stream, the buildings consisted of poles covered with grass, and along the far sides were open-faced sheds, constructed the same way. There were several men, all in short dhotis and crude turbans, actually just a cloth twisted around the head; women wore soiled saris and cloths over their heads; children of all ages were everywhere dressed in long shirts and nothing else. They were light brown, handsome people, all with serious expressions —even the children—and they completely ignored us after Shem Sher spoke to a man who was standing in the center of the crude compound dipping a fiery red liquid out of clay pots.

Before the open shed two men in dirty dhotis were chopping a peeled log, perhaps a foot in diameter, that was braced by two long poles and wedged over a block of wood. In superbly skillful motions they were chopping in unison—first one, then the other—and chips the size and thickness of potato chips, nearly all exactly the same, were flying with unerring precision into the shed.

"One-tenth of the human race chew *pan* or betel," Shem Sher said. "And only these people from Nepal know how to chip the *catechu* and prepare it in the pots. This kiln or *bhatti* is run by just one family. There are others in the jungle, all just like this. As *catechu* paste is the base for all good *pan,* these Chais are much in demand. They refuse to teach anyone else their trade. They will work a couple of months, sell eighty pounds of *catechu* to a contractor for 325 rupees, then return to Nepal."

We were to see people chewing betel all over the East—a habit more prevalent than smoking in the West—and the end result is black teeth.

Catechu paste comes from one of two acacia trees native to India, *A. Catechu* and *A. Sumam.* Forest plots are marked according to a twelve-year plan, and contractors bid on them at public auction. The product is called "minor forest produce," even though it brings millions to the forest department and makes millionaires out of many contractors.

The chips are placed in boiling water in pots, twenty-one on each kiln, seven on two sides, seven on the top. When the juice thickens, it is poured, with a handmade wooden ladle, into the top pots. The boiling goes on for days, with the *catechu* juice being dipped from one pot to the other to keep the color consistent. Then it is strained into carrying pots, taken to storage sheds and placed in huge clay tubs where it solidifies. Eventually it is placed in pits.

Remaining in the pits for one month, it is then cut in ten by twelve-inch slabs and dried. When it begins turning black from the sun, it is cut into pieces the size of a small cake of soap. The contractor arrives, pays by the pound at a price agreed upon, and the Chais dismantle their crude camp and walk back to Nepal.

Called *pan* because the mixture is rolled in a leaf from the betel vine of that name, the product contains more than *catechu* paste. Mixed into the leaf with the *catechu*, which gives color and flavor, is shell lime to brighten the color; dried, sliced areca nut to exercise the teeth; cardamon to make it aromatic; and often aniseed and cloves for additional flavor. The finished article is wrapped in the *pan* leaf

In a catechu *camp of the Chais of Nepal, the national betel-chewing habit began with wood chips in smoking pots.*

and vigorously chewed into a cud. I tasted it and found it astringent, with a sweetish taste.

There were few Indians I met who didn't chew *pan*. Some claim that the combination in *pan* contains a drug. Most Indians deny this, but the educated admit that black *catechu* is often prescribed for diarrhea, dysentery and intestinal hemorrhage.

So perhaps in the countries where these afflictions are so common, *pan*-chewing isn't a vice but a sensible habit. None of the rajas of India Shikar and Tours chewed it, but of the forty others making up the *shikar* camp, at least thirty-five had the black teeth of the betel chewer.

Our mahout must have picked up some fresh *catechu* from the Chai camp. He spouted blood-red liquid like a wounded whale all the way back to camp. But apart from the hazard of that fine red spray, it was a pleasant, even romantic ride. We rolled on Champa Kali's back watching the Pariah kites sailing in a cloudless sky—even more agile and graceful than vultures or gulls—admired the high ermine collar of the Himalayas, and listened to the River of Gold singing in the sun.

Back at camp we had some strong Assam tea and delicious little partridge sandwiches. There we decided on the two-hour run to the Jim Corbett National Park.

It was a huge area dedicated to the man who saved so many lives in his courageous campaign against man-eating tigers and leopards. Bounded on the north and west by the Ramganga River, on the east by the Kosti River and on the south by the Shavlik Range, 125 square miles of wild, beautiful country had been set aside as a game sanctuary. There are several excellent guest houses where you can spend the night; meals are served and a jeep can be hired to drive you around the one hundred miles of roads. Going in we saw a herd of chital grazing peacefully fifty yards from the road, two crocodiles on the banks of the Ramganga, and a dozen wild boar rooting in a field not a mile from the guest house.

Watchtowers are spotted in strategic places. Mary Lou and I climbed one and saw five wild elephants come out of a grove of sal trees. The wild-life warden told us that one hundred tigers are in the park; over two hundred elephants, fifty thousand deer of several species, sloth bear, langur monkeys, jackals, hyenas, leopards, peacocks and sambur. Even pythons inhabit the sanctuary.

We stood in the watchtower for two hours hoping to catch sight of a tiger, the lord of the jungle.

"Don't worry," said Devendra, who had driven us, "you will see tigers before you leave camp. There are more of the big cats in our area than any place in the world. Tomorrow we plan to put on a scratch beat with the elephants."

When we got back to camp the elephant boys were bathing their charges in the river. The four giants were lying on their sides like dowagers on a masseuse's rubbing table, while the small boys splashed water on them, and the mahouts directed operations. Champa Kali was having her stomach rubbed with a river rock and grunting in delight.

Jait Ram, in the tent compound, conferred with Shem Sher and Daju. "We will go for tiger in the morning," Shem Sher said. "Jait Ram has tracked a big male to the Nimbu Sot beat. He believes that the tiger has eaten and is lying up there. If so, we stand a good chance of seeing him in the morning."

"We will go by elephant," Daju said. "So we must get started early. We will have to move through the mist."

Dinner was early. We had junglefowl curry so hot that it should have kept us warm all night. But it didn't. The cold winds came off the Himalayas, and the wet mist settled down from the Sonanadi. Mary Lou and I tried to sleep in a sardine wedge, but the cold was a knife that kept pricking us awake.

The nickering of the elephants was a welcome sound, signaling that the camp was awake and it was time to get up.

Inait Tulla came shivering in with the soul-saving Assam tea, strong enough to carry us out of the canvas to watch the mists swirl and the morning dew run off the tents. Shem Sher was in front of Daju's tent shouting in Hindi.

The red and black rooster, which was kept behind the cook's tent, flapped up on the strip of canvas wall that encircled the tent area, and stood wobbling as he tried to pull the sun up with a crow as shrill as a siren. He didn't make it. If the sun was there, it was masked in mountain mist. Breakfast was fast but good: sausage, potatoes and an omelette, served by two barefoot bearers who rushed around to keep both themselves and the food hot.

We must have made a strange scene moving single file from camp that morning. I thought we looked like something out of an old wall tapestry of an Indian prince's hunting party: the elephants muttering in their trunks, the mahouts wrapped to the tops of their turbans, Daju and Shem Sher in heavy shooting coats and pith helmets, Devendra in his swooping green bush hat, Jait Ram and five others

At a jungle camp in the foothills of the Himalayas, hunting elephants were being bathed in the Sonanadi, the "River of Gold."

We moved through tall elephant grass at the start of the search for a tiger on the Nimbu Sot beat.

walking ahead, leading the way through morning mist that streamed over the Ridge of the Elephants of Old.

Mary Lou and I hadn't been told about a traveling trick of the elephant. On our way to the *machan,* or tree platform, where we would watch for the tiger, we left the road. Moving through rough country, the big animal picked her way carefully, stepping over fallen trees, avoiding holes in the ground, going around gullies, without any direction or prodding from the mahout. At one place we came to a hill. This time the mahout had to say a few sharp words and slap the elephant's head. These extremely intelligent beasts don't like toiling up a hill any more than a person does. But Champa Kali did it, grunting a bit. When she started down the other side, suddenly she sat down and did it the easy way, sliding all the way to the bottom, with us hanging on to the sides of the saddle, nearly falling over backward.

The mahout looked back at us, laughing and spraying red *pan* juice, as Champa Kali righted herself. Trumpeting softly, the elephant went through a grove of trees in her rolling-ship gait, atoning for her surprise slide by breaking the low-hanging branches that might slap back into our faces.

The place where Jait Ram had found tiger sign was called Nimbu Sot for good reason. Nimbu meant lime tree and Sot was a stream. The area where we stopped was a young forest of lime trees with a little stream singing through it. On all sides were dense foliage, creepers and thick bamboo. Shem Sher and Daju had come with us, and the other two elephants had circled, waiting to start through the heavy growth toward us. Jait Ram and the men he brought with him would walk beside the elephants, shouting and whacking trees to drive out the tiger. Devendra, armed with a 500 express rifle, rode an elephant as a precaution, should the tiger be a crafty one and break back toward the advancing party.

Our elephants now moved up to the *machans.* Standing upright on the saddle, all we had to do was step off onto the tree platform, sit down and wait. The mahouts took the elephants off and stood hidden in the lime trees. Daju sat with me, armed in case of an emergency; Shem Sher in the *machan* with Mary Lou for the same reason.

One of the rules of a sit-up is silence; another, complete lack of motion, no wiggling, no scratching, no slapping at flies. A tiger has remarkably keen eyes and ears. On one hunt a cat turned and retreated when he saw a hunter in a *machan* adjust a camera setting. Another time when a man lifted a rifle bolt, the tiny click alerted the tiger, who jumped fourteen feet and killed the two hunters in the tree.

Mary Lou and I had done this tree-sitting three years before, but I had forgotten the patience it requires. We had never seen elephants beat out tigers, which promised excitement. There we were, sitting on a platform in a seventeen-foot sal tree, waiting for the largest cat in the world to emerge from the tangle, very conscious of the fact that tigers can jump eighteen feet vertically. This rated as a new spectator sport that dwarfed all others. Our vision was obscured by a thick tangle of young bamboo, lantana vines that looked as if they had been spun by a giant spider, tun, sal, teak, lime, and dozens of other trees I couldn't identify.

Now, in the distance, we heard the sound of voices. The beat had begun. It would take an hour for the elephants and men to reach us, during which time our thoughts ran the scale from the height of expectancy of seeing the tiger, to the low of fear of the many things that could happen. Branches cracked like pistol shots under the huge feet of the elephants, men shouted, axes splatted against tree trunks, elephants trumpeted—all accompanied by the crashing and tearing of bushes.

I confess that the sound effects of this drama were unnerving and that the cymbals of fear rang constantly as the elephants crashed through the jungle toward us. I felt Daju straighten. Turning my head, I saw his hands turning white on the rifle. From that dense screen before us, like a cued actor in a play, burst an agitated wild boar, bristles up, his six-inch white tusks gleaming. He disappeared like something in a conjuror's act.

Then, as if the boar had gone before to set the stage, out stepped a tiger. Immense, orange-gold, his stripes as black as velvet, his black and white ears twitching. One hundred times the size of my hearth-side Siamese, he stood there for a moment that seemed forever. His liquid green eyes, shining like jade in the sun, roved the area before him.

Even with the elephants crashing and the men screaming behind him, he stood, master of the moment, in full control, and one could almost feel the enormous strength of the cat. His forelegs were nearly as thick as a man's body, his head the size of the seat on which we trembled.

Our bodies needed no adjuration from the mind to sit still; fear froze us there. A tiger standing in his own terrain seems three times the size of the one pacing a cage in a zoo, and his beauty is a thing to behold; glossy-gold, majestic, unafraid. He is a lord of the jungle.

Turning his head slowly, he surveyed the space he would have to cross. Now he looked up and saw us. Neither of us moved. We sat hypnotized, held in his spell. With a flick of his tail, he crossed before us, vanishing in a streak of gold flame into the underbrush on the other side. Then I remembered that I held a camera in my hand. But such was the fascination of the moment that I had forgotten to snap the shutter. It was a good thing I hadn't.

The elephants came out of the jungle, crashing through the same spot from which the tiger had stepped so gracefully. Tree dew gleamed on their slaty-gray hides. The mahouts and Devendra were also soaking wet, both from this and from the moisture of the grass that reached above the elephants' backs. Jait Ram, his magnificent mustache reduced to a scraggle, his five wet and shivering men behind him, stepped along beside the lead elephant. The Nimbu Sot beat was over.

The next morning, Giri arrived with his jeep to take us back to Delhi. The road had hardened, making departure less dramatic than arrival. We had little trouble getting through the ancient village of Kotdwara this morning. Just the usual waiting while cattle got out of our way.

Giri laughed. " 'Brake inspectors' we call them. Poor brakes and you end up with a lapful of holy cow."

On a long, rough, unpaved stretch, women in billowy black garments were repairing the road. Some lifted their heads as we passed, and jewels flashed in their noses. Using wicker baskets, they would dig soil from one part of the road, creating little holes as they filled the larger ones.

Giri was thoughtful. "To look at this," he said, "you'd never believe that in 400 A.D. India was using algebra. Something has happened to our clock of civilization. Somehow, some place, it got stuck—"

Going through many of the villages, we noticed the holy cattle—holy because they and the highest, Brahmin caste were born on the same day. They were followed by women or children carrying shovels and wicker baskets to collect the freshly manufactured manure which they would form into flat cakes and dry for fuel—100 million tons a year.

We also saw cows with bleating calves being milked at the doorsteps of huts by men who obviously owned them and sold milk. Until then I thought these 140 million animals that had free run of the streets in the villages and cities belonged to everyone, that they were a living religious symbol.

Mainly they were a wretched-looking lot—dusty, thin, hip bones shoving up against the skin. This cow culture, this worship of cattle, is another of the many problems delaying the progress of India. Turn a couple of hundred thousand half-starved cattle into the streets of New York, Chicago or Los Angeles, and make it against the law to molest, drive away, or rout them from the city, and you have a small idea of what confronts India.

Giri thought it insoluble. "We have our beliefs," he said; "some seem impossible, others make good sense. But how can everyone be expected to think alike in a country that has thousands of subcastes, all with their own rules of life? The British listed three thousand, but there are many more they knew nothing about. There are two thousand divisions of the Brahmin, or priest, caste alone. For example, there are different rules for different sects of Brahmins. One who eats in a house seven days after a person has died there, will never intermarry with Brahmins who wait eleven days. This goes right on down the line in differences of eating, farming, walking, doing almost anything."

He laughed. "Many of us also live by our astrological almanacs, often published by various state governments. Did you know, for example, that it is extreme good fortune in Lucknow if a bat falls from the ceiling into your lap? But not if it falls on your neck." He shook his head. "I would caution against trying to understand us too quickly. It would take years to try to make Western sense out of our civilization." Then he said proudly, "After all, it took us thousands of years to create probably the oldest civilization on earth. So it is reasonable for us to take a few more years to straighten out some ancient tangles. But we're catching up fast."

Before he left us at our hotel in Delhi, he said, grinning, "I can promise that it won't take so long to build an affection for our food. Would you join me for dinner at Moti Mahal? It is a restaurant in the old quarter that I think will give you a good impression of us."

I have heard the complaint that dining in India leaves much to be desired and have wondered if those who pass through cities like Delhi, Bombay, Calcutta and Madras too quickly have even tried the native dishes. I agree regarding the so-called international cuisine, which isn't international at all but one of the few disagreeable heritages left by the English, who were never inspired when it came to food. Without deviation, the English meal begins with a weak soup, followed by fish, then a joint of some kind, usually mutton or chicken. A watery pudding or custard always brings the meal to a sticky end. The trouble with this routine is that the food is barely warm and unappetizing. Bland, underseasoned, overcooked, it is the trademark of the British throughout the world, from Ceylon to Bermuda.

But anyone who complains about Indian food served in the good restaurants must be missing his taste buds. Giri introduced us to a classic dish, chicken *tandoori,* in Moti Mahal that night—a famous place that can rest on its food laurels amid the noise and squalor of the open markets and the overpopulated old quarter. *Tandoori,* a secret mixture of nine spices, is placed on cut-up chicken, which is then marinated in lemon and yogurt, speared on skewers and cooked over coals in a huge black pot buried in the ground. Served with *biyyani,* a spiced rice topped with thinly sliced hard-boiled eggs, it is usually preceded by another Moti Mahal specialty, *seekh kababs,* sausage-shaped minced lamb that also comes on skewers. Everything is eaten by hand with the aid of crusty hot *chapatties,* the round wheatcakes that are the national dish.

Chester Bowles, on his first time around as our ambassador to India, is supposed to have helped make Moti Mahal famous, holding dinner parties and business luncheons there. But *tandoori,* in my opinion, is its own best ambassador, at Moti Mahal or other places where it is available.

Restaurants in Delhi and other major cities are many and varied: Khyber, Volga, Embassy, Gaylord's and the Golden Dragon. The Imperial, Ashoka and Claridge Hotels in Delhi serve everything from a steak to *pulao,* which is delicious rice with raisins, cloves, onion and cardamon. India may lead the world in its varied rice dishes—all excellent, everything from soup to dessert. Chicken also appears in many forms in most Indian restaurants: kebabs, cutlets and *murg masala,* which combines it with garlic, ginger, tomatoes, red chilies, almonds and heavy cream. The Indian curries are nothing like ours. We use a gentle curry powder; the Indians use about a dozen fresh ingredients, the principal being red chili peppers, which are blended by hand. Very hot. Curried chicken, beef, lamb, mutton and kid are usually accompanied by chutneys which run from coconut, *chana dal* (yellow pea and chili), tomato, date and mango, to the tart and overpowering garlic chutney.

A favorite of mine is *mughul,* a robust mutton curry with garlic, green ginger, chilies, cloves, cardamons, cinnamon, coriander and roast coconut. The key here is *dahi,* the tart Indian yogurt which is beaten into the whole business and served over the browned meat.

Another favorite, chicken in curd, requires cut-up chicken to be placed in a pot with spices and milk curd, and mixed well. The top is sealed with dough and the chicken baked, coming to your table in its golden crust. Indians also fry spinach leaves and parsley and serve them crusty and hot as an appetizer. Excellent. Broiled steaks, chops and superb fish (*beckti* and pomfret especially) are served everywhere.

Unless you take the subcontinent in a straight in-and-out tourist run, sampling only the vapid aforementioned "international cuisine," India offers many new adventures for the palate.

There weren't many in the DC-3 departing New Delhi on this bright Sunday morning bound for the naughty temples at Khajuraho. A plane leaves for the temples every Sunday from Delhi, returning that evening. The trip is inexpensive; the whole thing including lunch is under fifty dollars and worth seeing. Three Frenchmen and two French women had rushed into the plane to get front seats. The women were dressed in flowery silken things and exuded perfumed femininity as only French females can, and the men were middle-aged, well-dressed in light sports jackets, flannels and bright ties. Each of the five, carrying a pair of binoculars, chattered like caged parakeets as the plane took off. There were also several turbaned Indians; one in a dhoti and a tweed jacket, the others in Western dress, also with binoculars.

I wondered about the binoculars, then remembered what I had heard about Khajuraho when it was discussed over tea in the Ashoka Hotel by three obviously well-traveled Americans, two older men and a college type. I was sitting four feet from them in a rattan chair drinking Lopchu tea.

"Boy, that Khajuraho temple trip was something!" said one of the older men. "The ways of love are infinite indeed. I never knew the Indians were so accomplished."

"Those secret rooms showing the art of love at Pompeii are boy scout compared to Khajuraho!" the college boy said.

The tourist department said it differently. Indians, even if they aren't employed by the tourist department, incline toward the ornate and flowery in speech—especially if it concerns temples. Our man was young and enthusiastic, and he gave it to me in full poetic presentation.

"Only 350 miles from Delhi," he explained, "lie the magnificent temples reputed to be among the most original works of Hindu architecture. Besides the beauty of outline, these temples have surface decorations that are marvelous. In the artistic arabesques of the lovely sculptures on the outer walls, you see celestial beauties, amorous couples, gods and goddesses, serpents and leogriffs.

"Once a large city, Khajuraho has now dwindled to a village of two thousand lying on the edge of Ninora Tal Lake. Its ruins spread over an area of over eight miles.

"Khajuraho reached its glory under the Chandella Dynasty from 950 A.D. to 1050 A.D. At this period were built those temples. Out of a group of eighty-five, twenty still remain."

He stopped, not to catch his breath, but to make this a dramatic moment. Then he went on, as if quoting holy words from the Gita. "During the great Hindu renaissance, Khajuraho became the center of a new imagery—sometimes grotesque, sometimes sublime—a synthesis of an art vital and alive. Temples of different faiths were built side by side, quite different from those in the rest of India, almost all of them in buff-colored sandstone, each on a solid, high masonry terrace.

"Other parts of the temples have a unique flowing architectural pattern. The roofs of the assembly halls are all dome-shaped and rise one above another, culminating in the graceful rise of the final spire, the *shikhara*. This crowns the central chamber where the idol lies enshrined. The gradual rise in height to the dizzy top symbolizes the mountain abode of the God Shiva."

After all this talk we took off. In two hours we came down, erratically circling Panna Airfield, almost like a moth at a flame. It was not really an airfield but a huge meadow that had been smoothed, the grass mowed and the lumps flattened, so that a plane could land without losing a wheel or a passenger's gold inlays. The pilot brought our craft in with the assurance of a crow landing in a cornfield, but he had difficulty avoiding a crowd that ran toward us as he slowed the plane, propellers chopping to a stop. The pilot padlocked the door and the crowd came closer.

Women in soiled purple saris and heavy silver anklets, tribesmen with painted faces, naked children, all staring, all unabashed as they came within two feet, ringed us. The women lifted their heads, laughing at the funny foreigners; the men scowled, the slashes of paint on their faces quivering; the children danced around howling.

There is this about India: you are never more than three feet from the unusual, even in your comfortable hotel in the great cities. Open a door anywhere and you will see people and sights to make you pause in awe. It is perhaps the last country in the world where the traveler can go and not be disappointed in what he finds. The West has not overwhelmed this subcontinent with its civilization, its clothing, its sights and sounds. India remains, with its saris, its dhotis, its naked and its painted, its many sects that wear their hair uncut, dangle silver from arms and legs, and shave heads to the top, leaving the remaining hair to be tied behind.

Now at Panna, villagers followed us to the bus that waited to take us the thirty-six miles to Khajuraho. They surrounded it, staring, breaking rank only when the bus driver came through them in a bull charge, nearly knocking down three laughing women, their saris opening like the wings of a butterfly.

As we jogged through the countryside, passing mango groves and cornfields that were turning brown under the relentless sun, the French party industriously changed into white sneakers that they had brought along in little canvas bags. Then they sat, chatting in their beautiful language, each one shining the binoculars that dangled from his neck. They were arming for the ogle.

It was 10:30 when we arrived at one of the main temples, the Eastern Group near the village of Khajuraho, a sorry place of dusty, sun-shattered buildings and apathetic people. The glamour and the glory of the past enshrined in the nearby temples was just a memory in stone to these modern Indians. Poverty was currently enshrining them in its grim sculpture. Dirty, naked children haloed with flies played in the unpaved streets; women in dusty, torn saris sat in the shade of trees; men sat by the side of the road in dejected attitudes of social surrender, occasionally raising a hand for alms.

There were six important temples in this group we were visiting: three Hindu, three Jain, with an enormous stone sculpture of Hanuman, the Monkey God of the Hindus, dominating. The French party ignored all except the sculpture of people in various poses. They walked about like strange insects, binoculars glued to their eyes, saying over and over, *"Formidable! Formidable!"* when they saw a particularly erotic scene. Stone carvings of women doing everything man at his most lustful has ever imagined were everywhere.

An old Punjabi in jacket and dhoti and a varicolored turban stood entranced, as still as the figures in stone he was watching, binoculars focused steadily upon a group of four women and a willing man. The women were big-busted and lustful, bending in many postures, some smiling, some sullen. Everywhere these women were burned in passion, clothed in nothing but silken ropes around the waist that dangled in tassels.

I never saw so many navels in my life. If you think bikinis at a beach are lascivious, you are in for a new adventure at Khajuraho, the temples of sensual sensation. It is a tribute to the superb art of those ancients that their stone sculpture is so alive and realistic. You have the feeling of intruding. I heard a woman near me say, "It's so

Khajuraho—"We sat quietly, held in the grip of art so powerful that it reached across the centuries to make us live again in an ancient time . . ."

real, it's embarrassing," thus wrapping up the sensitivity and genius of those sculptors of 922 A.D. If artists create to be appreciated, this group of nameless artists have achieved that goal at Khajuraho.

But even though men and women are graphically pictured doing what comes naturally—and unnaturally—this wonder of an age is still religious. And in India it is treated as such, with reverence and respect. Unlike the Italians who inhabit the ruins of Pompeii like vultures at a corpse, hawking pornographic pictures and pamphlets illustrating the erotic pleasures of old Pompeii just before its destruction, there were no sex salesmen here at the temples of Khajuraho.

And after you have been here awhile, that aspect of sculptured sex begins to tone down and you appreciate and admire the art for what it is: animals, birds, court scenes, dancing, trees in bloom, musicians, a happy people from the dim past at work and play, all mirrored vividly.

But the French didn't see much of this. They stood carefully using binoculars, whispering, taking notes. Perhaps these Gallic specialists had more than met their match here with the old sects of the East.

After seeing the Eastern Group we got back into the bus and went to a Circuit House for lunch. It was a red brick building surrounded by mango trees where we ate in pension style at one long table covered with a white cloth. Quart bottles of cold Lion beer—excellent but on the sweetish side as all Indian beer is—cold chicken and cold sliced potatoes, and *beckti,* a moist white delicious fish. There was also pudding and sago wafers and nonstop conversation, the French gabbling excitedly between bites, the Indians talking in Hindi.

There were pools of shade under the mangoes where we waited for the bus driver to take us to the Western Group, which was supposed to be the best of the temples. Here was Chaunsat Yogini dating back to 900 A.D., the shrine of Kali, the Goddess of Destruction. It is of solid granite and named for the sixty-four female goblins that attend the Goddess, all of whom are here in their weird forms and faces. In another temple is Vishnu, the God of Preservation, with his original head and the ten others of his incarnations. There are six main temples here too, and much more of the erotica, the loving and the loved, the nude dancing girls, winged gods and goddesses, snakes and crocodiles and terrible, unidentifiable creatures that came from the minds of the artists. The last is the Southern Group of two temples. The sculpture here is not so inspired, but the overall effect is still impressive.

Finally, even the French took their eyes from their binoculars and began to appreciate that there is much more to Khajuraho than graphic lessons in the art of love. Few spoke in the bus ride to the plane, and conversation was sparse in the DC-3 returning to New Delhi. We sat quietly, held in the grip of art so powerful that it reached across the centuries to make us live again in an ancient time of grandeur and violence, of gaiety and abandon.

I certainly wasn't tired of sightseeing. It is impossible to get too much of India. True, there can be too many temples, too much emphasis on the various gods and too much symbolic carving and statuary, but with the diversity of people and scene, there is enough in this subcontinent to keep a traveler coming back for years. Yet somewhere I had read that the British had introduced an American fish, the rainbow trout, into some Indian mountain streams, and I was curious. Our Orvis rods were also panting in their cases, and I still clung to my belief, even here where nearly everything is extraordinary, that a fishing rod is often the magic wand waving you on to unusual experiences and adventure. And again it proved to be true. If I hadn't pursued this thought about the rainbow trout, Mary Lou and I would have missed an encounter with one of the most unusual tribes in the world.

The quest started off in such silly fashion that it almost stopped before it started. Since Brigendra Singh, that singularly intelligent fellow who had made possible the Shavlik Range experience with the hunting elephants, worked with the American Embassy in Delhi, I approached him. He was a sportsman and I thought he would probably know all about the rainbows. It rapidly developed into a comedy.

"Are there rainbows in India?" I said. "I've heard that some English sports—"

He smiled. "They need rain. There are some beautiful ones during monsoon, but I don't think I've ever seen one during this dry season—"

He had me there. This was new information about one of my favorite subjects. "You mean they need rain to survive in India?"

"Of course, my dear chap, they need rain. Let me remind you that a rainbow is a bow or arc of prismatic colors appearing in the heavens opposite the sun, due to the refraction and the reflection of the sun's rays in drops of rain."

I laughed. "My rainbow, *Salmo gairdnerii,* is a native to coastal waters and streams from Lower California to Alaska, but has been introduced elsewhere. It is also an arc of prismatic colors, especially when it leaves the water, wet and shimmering—" If he wanted to play, I'd play.

"I don't understand," Brigendra said, frowning slightly. "I didn't know that rainbows differed, *even* in America. Are you sure?"

Everything can be carried too far. When I told Brigendra what my rainbows were he laughed until the tears came.

"A fish! A fish! My dear fellow, *mahseer,* yes. This rainbow, no. I don't know. This is a splendid joke!"

But another clever fellow, Som Nath Chib, director of the department of Indian tourism, didn't think it was a joke. I got right to the subject this time. He knew all about the project. There is little about India he doesn't know.

"Well," he said, "I've been told that those tenacious Englishmen who did many good things and some bad things for my country, after years of trying successfully introduced your trout in two or three streams in the Nilgiri Hills in southern India, near a place called Ootacamund. It's many miles from here, but I will write ahead and make arrangements for you, if you must make the trip."

I must. Two things that Som Nath Chib said intrigued me. The rainbow were in streams straight up in a mountain elevation of more than seven thousand feet, and they were ready to be caught in February. Both circumstances seemed unusual for this fish.

Mr. Chib was right. It was a long way from New Delhi to Ootacamund, the tiny town high in the Nilgiri Hills, or "Blue Mountains." We flew to Coimbatore where we met R. Ramaswamy, a member of the Government Tourist Office, out of the Madras regional office. He was a tall, heavy-set, jolly man who out-haggled the local taxi king, getting us a beat-up bald-tired car—about a 1940, I think— and an old but alert-looking driver.

As we got in and started out of Coimbatore, raising dust that followed us as if it was tied to the car, I saw that the heap had one hundred thousand miles registered, and worried aloud. "How high are the Nilgiris?"

"Seven thousand feet above sea level," Ramaswamy said. "They're beautiful, with a blue light always on them. I've seen them from the air and they're an oval-shaped, undulating plateau, about thirty miles across."

"But will we see them?" I said.

He was puzzled. "What do you mean, sir?"

"Our car has two badly worn front tires and more than one hundred thousand miles. That's like riding a seventy-five-year-old horse with bad feet."

The driver said, "Sound car, sir. And don't be concerned about the tires. I am a most careful driver."

In India you have to be. Nothing—goats, Brahma steers, water buffalo, people, or bullock carts—gets out of your way. It is understood that you get out of theirs. Our driver was adept at this, but often the car wasn't coöperative. It stalled; it sputtered fitfully when we tried to pass a bullock cart, alarming the white-turbaned driver so that he put on extra speed. I could hear those worn tires pancaking. The trip up the mountains was a terror. Trucks hurtled; the road narrowed as we climbed; unprotected drop-offs threatened every foot of the way.

Think what you may about British colonialism, but anyone driving that twisting snake of a road into the clouds of the Nilgiris would have to admit that they accomplished a masterpiece of engineering to lay any road at all up the rocky side of these steep, blue-misted, wild mountains.

Ootacamund, nestled in a curve between folds of the hills, was an amazing replica of a completely unspoiled English village, with retired British army officers walking about in tweeds, smoking pipes and walking black Labradors on leashes. There were English women in sweaters and skirts, carrying shopping baskets; schoolchildren in blue uniforms and caps. The flash of scarlet saris, the slanted dark eyes and Oriental faces of the Indian women brought us back to India. We were taken out of reality again by tall, bearded men in black-and-red-striped white Roman togas proudly stalking the streets. These were the Todas, most unusual of the many tribes of India.

As our car shivered to a stop beside a small office building, tires smoking, Ramaswamy said, "I will go see about the fishing."

This is what a little curiosity about trout fishing does. It delivers strange tribal men, fantastic villages, magnificent mountains, a remarkably dangerous roller-coaster ride, and sometimes, if you are very lucky, perhaps even some fish.

E. R. C. Davidar, a slim, handsome young man, thought we would get rainbow trout. A lawyer, he was a member of the Nilgiris Game Association and not only would offer us a complimentary angling license but also tell us where to fish and furnish us with a guide.

As we drove to the comfortable Savoy Hotel to stow our bags and rig our gear, Davidar said, "The rainbows here are a story of British persistence."

Obviously on a favorite subject, he went on. "I believe they tried at least a dozen times before the experiment took; all serious, scientific attempts, too. Dr. Francis Day, an authority on Indian fresh-water fish, tried twice. He tried to import and breed trout in 1863, then again in 1866. He even got to the stage of actually planting fish. But he failed; so did all the others, until H. C. Wilson, another accomplished pisciculturist, went to work on the problem in 1906. This, as you probably know, was, and still is, a famous hill station where the English fled to escape the heat of places in the south, and I think nearly every English male is a fly fisherman. Anyway they spared no expense or scheme to establish trout here where it would be a heaven for flyrodmen. They spent a pretty penny on Wilson. But it paid. He came up with the idea of rainbows and bought ova and stock fish from New Zealand and Ceylon. These took. On September 11, 1911, Avalanche, Emeral Valley, Krurmund and Mekad waters were opened to the public."

Davidar suggested that he have a guide call for me at the Savoy Hotel early the next morning. It was cold when Konnamoto came wearing a slouch hat, looking like an English gardener who had stood in the sun too long. His English was slow but good. Ramaswamy had rooted himself out of bed and stood shivering beside the car.

"We will try the Avalanche, sir," the guide said. "It's only a half-hour from here and we should arrive at the right time. I must warn you, sir. These are most wild fish."

It was early enough and cold enough for frost. It lay on the fields and the rolling downs in silver sheets, and the mountains dark against the sky. We turned off the main road, entering a narrow, rutty, dirt lane, and bounced through acres of rhododendron the size of apple trees with the scented, flaming red flowers as large as your hand. They must have been at least a hundred years old.

Suddenly we rounded a curve and the Avalanche lay before us, mist spiraling from it. I knew I was in trouble as soon as I saw the stream: it was small, perhaps twenty-four feet wide, but the edge was bare, not a tree or a bush. This meant that if these trout were as wild as claimed, they could be easily spooked by the sight of us or even by shadows, if the sun ever got strong enough to etch a shadow.

"No cover," I said hopelessly to Konnamoto as we got out of the car.

He smiled appreciatively. "Right, sir," he said. "That is one reason the trout of Ooty are so shy—and so famous."

Konnamoto carefully examined my flies, selecting a Hardy Spirit, a Silver March and a Peter Ross. I tried them all, getting two rises on the Silver March. But it wasn't easy fishing. The lack of cover was an advantage in casting, of course, but without this we would be altogether too easily seen by the fish. The cast had to be longer, fuller, and you had to stand well back from the stream. This meant that the targeting was poor, for you couldn't see much of the water. And if you walked in, no matter how stealthily, the fish would vanish in silver streaks.

When the sun got warm enough to melt the silver-frost and take some cold out of the water, I waded in my sneakers and made upstream casts, letting the fly drift back into the pools. I tried my few tricks or techniques for more than two hours and didn't raise a fish. Then Konnamoto took command. Taking from his pocket some flies that he identified as a Green Wool Glory, a Cock and Bundle, a Butcher and an Alder, he used my rod. His smooth, practiced cast made the rod look like an extension of his right arm.

But master that he was, he didn't move a fish. He came wading back. "We'll have to fish only rough water, sir, where the fish can't see us."

He had the Alder on. I took the rod, and we walked for a mile until we came to a stretch where the stream moved swiftly and brokenly over rocks. I took two in five casts—scrappy fellows, flinging themselves into the air in the prismatic arc I had described to Brigendra Singh.

Konnamoto and I walked for ten miles, leaving Ramaswamy dozing in the sun near the car, and took a total of twenty fish. I gently released all but a half-dozen that we had for breakfast the next morning, appreciating, as we ate the crusty, juicy fish, the English gentlemen who had tried so hard to bring them here to the tall Nilgiris.

While I had been out getting breakfast, Mary Lou reconnoitered. The Todas had intrigued her to the point that she passed up the bout of trout-fishing—the first time it had happened. Ramaswamy, in his effective way, had introduced her to the local tourist representative, who had in turn taken her around to a Toda *mund,* or village.

"Tomorrow," she said, so excited she nearly ate a trout head, "the Toda elders sit in judgment on a man who has broken their laws. They will hold the council right in the village center!"

They were there all right, squatting in a semicircle in the village center. Wearing white togalike garments crossed with single bands of red and black, these handsome copper men with curling black hair and full beards managed to give the gathering an air of dignity despite the people stopping to stare.

After a while the gapers passed on, and the Todas continued their trial, muttering, some of the older men raising their hands in anger. Ramaswamy managed to find out what it was all about. It seemed that one of the younger Todas had escorted a tourist to a temple and permitted him to take photographs. This was a crime.

"They are against anyone other than a Toda seeing any of their rituals or sacred objects," he said. "But I think we are in luck. Our fishing friend Mr. Davidar has managed to arrange a meeting with a leader. Lawyer Davidar's wife is a doctor and has attended several of the more important Toda clan leaders. So we have a bit of influence working on our side."

Davidar had gone with a law firm in Ootacamund shortly after he got his degree, and being an intelligent young man, had learned much about the Todas. Just before he introduced us to the clan leader, he gave us some background.

"They are the most unusual of the Indian tribes," he said. "Keeping their heritage almost completely unchanged, they live today as they must have when they came here many, many years ago. Ethnologists know little about them and where they originated. Some think Babylon; others that they are the descendants of the legions of Alexander the Great. I met one expert who thinks he has proved that they are Jews who fled from Babylon. There seems little doubt that they came from the West, perhaps the Mediterranean."

On the way to the Toda *mund* to meet Pellican, the young leader who would tell us about his tribe, we were halted by a sight that froze time and stopped the clocks of civilization: a pretty Toda woman, also in the wrap-around togalike garment, her raven hair glistening and falling in strands down both sides of her face, was kneeling in the dusty road, placing the foot of a noble old Toda on her forehead.

"Their greeting," said Davidar. "No matter where they see the male Toda, they stop and place his foot on their forehead—a mark of respect for their males."

We met Pellican the clan leader that afternoon, a slim young man with sleek black hair cut the Western way, wearing a long white skirt and a brown three-button suit jacket. Like most of the Todas, he carried a staff and had an air of dignity about him. He had learned English in a missionary school, was the leader of the Narsh clan and head of the Toda Welfare Association, formed to try to woo the race out of its old ways.

"One of our leaders died a few weeks ago," he said. "He was

cremated, as is our custom, and we celebrated his death by killing all of his best buffalo. We still have his hair, which we will burn in another ceremony. But that date hasn't been set yet."

He went on to say that he was against the buffalo sacrifice ritual, that it was barbaric, a waste of valuable animals, and signified nothing worthwhile.

Davidar laughed. "It is good that you didn't come a couple of weeks earlier! The smell of dead buffalo was overpowering after that last funeral!" He looked at us. "Have you by any chance ever inhaled the perfume of dead buffalo lying in the sun for several days?"

Pellican didn't appreciate the levity. "As you know, Mr. Davidar, that is the Toda religion. When an important man dies, if he has been kind to his buffalo, they are slain so they can accompany him to the other world of the God On, who rules the Toda dead."

"I know," Davidar said. "I'm sorry. Knowing you were against this practice I thought—"

"Against, yes," Pellican said, "but not to the point of ridicule." He was thoughtful. "Besides, as you know, we are vegetarians. But we don't object to others taking the bodies of the dead buffalo. It is only their souls we want to follow the departed. Often after the funeral, the Badagas, those people who inhabit these hills in such numbers" (this with contempt) "come and get the dead animals."

"Besides," he said to Davidar, making that young lawyer blush in anger, "it seems a silly thing for a cattle-worshiping Hindu to criticize a people for their religious associations with buffalo. We don't go to the lengths you do. Our buffalo are sacred, true. Some of them. But they are well fed and cared for. They do not wander the streets like beggars."

If he had deliberately planned to discourage Davidar to the point of leaving, he was successful. "I have a client at the office," he said. "I'll see you later. As you can see, Pellican will take good care of you."

My first glimpse of a *mund,* or village, is etched in memory. Five Toda houses, on top of a green hill in liquid sunshine, looked like giant wine barrels half buried in the ground, and were surrounded by a low wall of stones. Five hundred yards from the houses was a cattle enclosure with twenty-five magnificent brown buffalo, great horns curving like cutlasses.

The dairy temple, or *poh,* several times the size of the dwellings, was set well back on a higher piece of ground overlooking the *mund.* Several women were sitting in front of one of the barrel huts, one having her hair done. A white substance was being vigorously rubbed into her sleek black head. "Ghee," said Pellican. "Buffalo butter. It is clarified by the priests. Pure white. It is also our main food." It also smelled. You could get the rancid scent even from where we stood. But it apparently did wonders for the hair of the pretty Toda women. Their heads shone bright as metal.

"We only number 650 now," Pellican said, "and we live all over these mountains in small family *munds* just like this. They don't differ by a blade of grass. If you see one you see them all."

Now a handsome Toda, with head that looked exactly like those sculptured ones of the gods I had seen in Athens, came and joined the family group. He nodded at Pellican.

I remarked what a fine-looking fellow he was. Pellican smiled. "Once we were the rulers of these Nilgiris. Even today the Badagas pay us *gudu* as a tribute, and the Indian Government is paying us a quitclaim for the land they have taken from us. But our men do nothing but tend the buffalo, sometimes sing and dance, and lately drink much toddy."

He went into some detail on toddy. "The Indians have a caste of toddy tappers," he said. "They climb a palm tree with a glass jar tied around their necks and carry a knife in their teeth. Near the top of the tree under the fronds the sap flows. They cut there and catch it. Sugar is added; it ferments and becomes a very alcoholic drink. It is forbidden in much of India today, since prohibition is the rule of the time. But we Todas aren't Indians, although they try to make us obey their laws. Sometimes I think my people drink too much toddy just to prove that they are an independent race."

Pellican told us that he was president of the fourteen clans through the virtues of his education and his aggression. As such, he was trying to get the Todas more money for their lands, hoping for educational privileges and better housing.

There are two divisions of Todas. The most important, the Tharthar Ahal, has nine clans; the other, the Tevili Div Ahal, has five. There is no intermarriage between divisions. If there is a death in a division, the other division does the celebrating at the first funeral. During that ceremony the buffalo of the departed are struck between the eyes with the blunt head of an ax and the deceased is cremated. The second funeral is held by the dead man's own division. His hair is wrapped in his toga, or *putkuli,* the beautiful robes that are embroidered by the women, and the corpse is burned. The ashes are then placed under a stone on a mountaintop. This ceremony also includes much drinking and dancing, for the Todas believe that the dead go to another world where they are happy. Pellican said that the fourteen clans gathered at their special cathedral temple on a mountain once a year in December.

He told us of a weird belief. "In the cathedral temple," he said, "is a huge black poisonous snake, a cobra. It is a strange snake, for it cannot be seen by good Todas but only by those who have committed a crime against our people, or have done something against our gods." This belief also serves as a protection, to keep the curious and the unbelievers out. No one knows whether the cobra is actually there or not.

He went on to tell of a Toda clan leader who permitted two Indians to photograph the holy stone in the cathedral temple. He needed money to rebuild his hut and was promised that he would get it if he brought out the stone.

"This man got his money," said Pellican, "but two days later he went to the main temple—probably to pray and ask forgiveness. The next day he was dead. We believe that he saw the snake. He did wrong against the gods and was punished." I couldn't help thinking that a snake of this sort might be a good thing in our Western world.

When we returned to the *mund* the next day, Pellican explained that the Todas believe that Tekirsi, a goddess, created the buffalo first, then the Todas. "The Todas for the buffalo, to care for them and protect them; and the buffalo for the Todas, to support us and give us food," he said. Their other chief god was On, who ruled the world of the dead.

He pointed to a large man in black robes who was milking an enormous buffalo, a calf beside her, while a handsome Toda with a staff looked on. "That is our priest, the Palol," he said. "He prays before he opens the buffalo pen, then takes the sacred buffalo to the temple and milks them. That is not a sacred animal he is milking. He does this for the owner because his skill and holiness enrich the milk."

Not only is the Palol celibate and not allowed near the Toda women, but he is the only one who can milk the sacred buffalo. These dairies in the *munds* are actually places of worship. As the priest churns the milk into ghee, or butter, and buttermilk, he chants a long prayer which Pellican quoted for us. It simply wishes all good things for the Todas. The milk can only be carried by the priest, in the bamboo milk pail that he himself makes. Sacred buffalo—the largest ones, specially bred—are called *ohrhaly*.

We were in luck today, Pellican told us. A Toda wedding had taken place at another *mund* and when the men came back to this *mund* they would probably be slightly toddy-took and would dance and sing and pray around their temple.

Within an hour they returned, laughing and singing. Then, each with a staff, they gathered before the temple, joining hands and dancing around the building, singing, "Rro, Rro, Rro, Rro, Rro." Suddenly the merriment stopped. The Todas stood as if in a trance. Then, almost as one, they bowed toward the temple and prayed.

"They are praying for the happiness of the bride and groom," Pellican said, "and that the children will be boys."

Mary Lou wondered aloud how the race could survive if the children were always male, as they prayed. Pellican smiled. "That is where they are wrong. I try to tell them. It is part of the program I am planning. Education. Modern thinking."

This led naturally into the question of polyandry, known to be practiced by the tribe. "This is the thing that is supposed to make our people so different, so terrible," he said. "But there is a tribe in Tibet that currently practices it. No one points at them. I agree that the idea is based on a bad action. Also I disagree with polyandry. I have one wife and three children."

Pellican went on to say that his grandfather told him that the real reason for the Todas practicing polyandry was to keep the family property intact. If each brother had his own wife, he would demand an equal share. But if the brothers all had one wife in common, there would be no necessity to divide the family wealth. The complication in the system arose when several men married one woman, yet there were many girls of marriageable age in the *munds*. This led to feuds, so the Todas began female infanticide.

"But that is legally banned today," Pellican said, "so we have almost as many Toda women as men."

But the Todas, a people who seem able to rise to the occasion when their habits are threatened, came up with another idea: polygyny. A Toda may have one wife, but he still has equal claim on his brothers' wives, and they on his. If a Toda wants to climb into bed with his brother's attractive wife, all he has to do is say so.

Pellican laughed. "I have no brothers, so I can lead a normal married life. I am doing my best to bring up the younger generation to do the same."

He suggested that we take a close look at the curious humpbacked huts. "No other people have them," he said. Measuring eight by six-

teen feet, they had a semicircular roof woven of rattan, grass and
bamboo, the two ends being gabled with heavy planks. The doorway
was less than three feet high. We had to crawl in.

Three women in their classic robes were sitting on an earthen floor,
one stirring something in a black pot that simmered over an open
dungcake fire, another combing ghee into a little girl's hair. There
were two rooms. One with bamboo mats on the floor was evidently
the bedroom. The room we were in was living and dining room and
kitchen. On wall ledges were brass and copper pots; some shining,
others fire-blackened. Large clay vessels sat beside pails of buffalo
milk. The fire smoked under the pot; steam and scent poured from it.
It smelled like refuse burning. The only ventilation came from the

Mary Lou Scott joined the Toda women beside their strange barrel huts.

little doorway; the room was close, almost fetid. It reminded me of an Eskimo igloo.

We stayed for lunch, eating on a grassy knoll in front of one of the huts with a dozen Todas. Lunch was rice with ghee and tiny red chili peppers and buttermilk. None of the Todas other than Pellican spoke English. Their language was a dialect, supposedly closely linked to two South Indian languages, Kannada and Tamil.

Pellican was trying to piece together Toda history but was having difficulty. "My father tells me he came from a certain *mund*. His father told him the same. As far as I have been able to discover, no Toda remembers any life beyond this in the Nilgiris. I have a theory that we came from Syria many years ago, perhaps a remnant people from an invading army."

After finishing his bowl of rice and butter, he got up, stretching slowly like a cat, and waved at a beautiful Toda woman standing on a hill a hundred yards away. "That's the wife of one of our clan leaders who is in jail in the next village. Too much toddy. The police say he was belligerent. I don't believe it. But I am going to have to walk to the village, post a bond and bring him back to his *mund*."

He shook hands with us, smiled, and said that he hoped that we would think kindly of his people and return. His long white skirt swishing around his ankles, the last hope of the Todas strode off.

Coming down from the Nilgiris, our old car sending up steam like a teapot, we were stopped by another like it—older than ours, if such a thing was possible—pulled across the road and blocking our passage. It was full of men, some in uniforms much like those railroad conductors wear on American trains. Dependable Ramaswamy got out of our car and lumbered toward them like a big bear, talking Hindi furiously as he went.

They were police and they wanted to search our car to see if we were smuggling alcohol. Prohibition was the senseless law of the land and we had been told that searches and comic-opera chases were commonplace. But we never left the car. Eventually Ramaswamy convinced them that he would vouch for our honesty and sobriety, inasmuch as we were honored guests of the India Government Tourist Office. We were respected charges of his, he told them, who never let a drop of the horrid stuff pass our lips.

Evidently actor Fredric March and his wife Florence Eldridge, who were traveling in India with their New Milford, Connecticut neighbors, a doctor and his wife, didn't have a Ramaswamy with them. On their way to visit Periyar Game Sanctuary in Kerala State, they were stopped, their taxi was searched, a small bottle of whiskey was found, and they were trundled off to the police station and severely questioned for several hours.

Apparently the police didn't realize who Fredric March was, but soon most of India did. The Marches had had tea with Prime Minister Nehru in Delhi a few days previously. Somehow word got to him. There was great embarrassment and the affair was headlined in all the newspapers.

We met the Marches in Madras, and again in Ceylon. The actor was relaxed about it, but his wife was still vociferously perturbed. A humorous sequel occurred in Ceylon. As they were driving to the temples at Kandy, their car was stopped by two policemen. They were asked if they were carrying any alcoholic spirits. Mr. March groaned words to the effect of oh, no, not this all over again, and said that he didn't have any alcohol in the car.

"No?" said the police official brightly. "Why not?" And according to the story, he pulled out a fifth of fine Scotch and presented it to the Marches.

Other than this annoying and often confusing situation, prompted by prohibition, I doubt that the traveler has little to complain of in India. We didn't. Using a combination of car and the sturdy planes available to us, we were able to catch glimpses of an India that visitors who stick to the tourist trail and cities don't get. Most of the welter of humanity, teeming like a colony from an overturned anthill (360 million), lives in the six hundred thousand villages that string across the subcontinent like beads in a necklace.

In nearly every mud-hut village there were Biblical scenes of women in scarlet robes at the well. As they dipped huge earthen jugs into the water, naked children watched, many haloed with flies. Great gaunt cattle sauntered over and nudged the imperturbable youngsters; skinny goats went braying through the dusty streets. The smell of burning manure, pungent as gunpowder, hung over most villages. In one, the entire side of the wall of a building was plastered with round cakes of dung drying in the sun. Poverty was often relieved by breath-taking beauty on the village edge, a Flame of the Forest tree bursting with color, the great red flowers hanging so large and brilliant that they looked like Japanese lanterns strung there for a celebration.

On the outskirts of many a rural settlement, men and women beat rice on the ground with bamboo rods; then, in the ancient way, picked up the hulls and flung them into the air, hoping that the slight breeze would carry the chaff away leaving the rice kernels to fall to the ground.

Scarcely a village was without the photographer's dream shot of a skinny man in a breechclout, his cigar-brown body gleaming in the fierce sun, as he stood halfway up a fifty-foot pole slenderer than his arm, while two oxen beneath plodded in a never-ending circle—an irrigation system old before the time of Christ.

Often we saw an old man and a boy standing in the road, surrounded by a ring of curious villagers, who watched them prod a mongoose and a cobra into a fight. The old man usually did the prodding and the boy tooted a small fat flute. The snake rose from his coil, hood extended, and the mongoose darted in, fast as flame. But the fight was never finished. The cobra was taken by his tail and flung back into his basket, the mongoose was yanked back on his cord, and the boy quickly passed a reed basket, hoping to get rupees from the spectators before the contest was resumed. Curiously, the old men and the boys always looked alike, the men with grizzled beards and huge hooked noses, the boys brown as coffee beans with smiles that were an impossible combination of the professional and the sincere.

We spent a morning on the beach at Madras, watching the stork-thin fishermen in their pointed duncelike caps and little else moving in the surf like minnows. They were shiny black men and boys who rode strange craft hollowed from slender logs less than two feet wide. They speared them skillfully through the water that broke in white explosions around them, and they waded up to their chins pulling nets in a circle. These were members of the Chempatavas caste, fishermen since the dawn of their recorded time. When not in the water, they lived like otters in reed huts on the shores of the Bay of Bengal.

At Hardwar, the holy city located almost at the source of the Ganges—seldom mentioned in the guide books, but to us more interesting than Benares that is always mentioned—we saw ten naked holy men with long, wild hair and gray ash-smeared faces and bodies walking along shore near the bathing ghats like ghosts or newly risen corpses. They had renounced all worldly things, even clothing, in their religious dedication. One of them was being buried in sand. He was quickly surrounded by a crowd that stood breathlessly watching to see if he would suffocate or survive.

There are eight million *sadhus* or holy men in India, many of them

"These were members of the Chempatavas caste, fishermen since the dawn of their recorded time."

The sadhu *with the three dung marks of Shiva, like scars on his forehead, used fierce monkeys to blackmail alms.*

mad, many of them frauds who deceive and prey on the public. I was told that there was a *sadhu* in Hardwar who lifts a fifty-pound weight with his penis; another who pulls his intestines from his mouth, washes them in the Ganges, then pushes them back where they belong.

I didn't find them, but I did talk to two stately old gray-bearded *sadhus* in saffron robes who spent an hour trying to convince me that I should give up this useless worldly existence, go back into the hills with them and learn how to meditate and live a worthwhile life in a cave.

At Rishikesh, where the sacred Ganges is a creek flowing from a mountain, we started to cross a swaying footbridge that spanned the river like a spider web. Blocking the entrance was a leper, parts of his nose and hands rotted away, the three dung marks of Shiva like scars on his forehead. His hand went out like the strike of a snake for alms. When we apparently didn't give him enough annas, he gave a strange bark and two rhesus monkeys scampered off a ledge above him and started tearing our clothing. When we dropped more annas in his hand he barked again, the monkeys went back to the ledge, and we were permitted to cross the bridge. An unpleasant memory even now.

But the sight of the sleek, dark, gaily saried women of Madras who rent their heads to carry tiffin was a pleasant one. Tiffin, or lunch, is placed in a nest of brass containers at the home of the customer; then the women run it gracefully to the client's office or place of business, the sun flaming the two-foot brass burden so the women look as though their heads are afire.

In the south it was interesting to watch men standing by the roadside tossing coffee and milk from containers in each hand in a yard-long stream of brown. They were as adept as professional jugglers, finally serving the coffee in brass cups with a graceful flourish.

Along many of the roads stone pedestals stand like monuments. These are places of rest where people relieve the weight of the burdens they carry on their backs and heads.

This is a country where you can wander in fascination for months. But we had an invitation to spend time in the central jungles and had to cut short this spectacular sightseeing. Our route to the jungles was by plane to Nagpur, then a drive to the wild area. We boarded a plane at Madras, deep in the south.

Planes from that city, Delhi, Calcutta and Bombay land at Nagpur, the geographic center, within five minutes of one another, to exchange mail and passengers for other destinations. The resultant confusion is appalling. It looks and sounds like a Hollywood-staged riot or mob scene, but even among Indians of all sizes, dressed in everything from dhotis to the formal high-necked *achkan* (the mark of the political servant or diplomat), we had little trouble locating Vidya Shukla, owner of Allwyn Cooper, Ltd., the country's leading *shikar* organization. He stood, lean and aloof, waving his hand at us as we deplaned. A handsome, light-skinned young man in his black *achkan* and white trousers, he loomed out of the bustle like a stork among barnyard chickens, tall, calm and unhurried.

He greeted us with the folded-hand, prayerlike gesture, the *namashthe,* which is the Hindu silent wish for good health and the mark of pleasure at seeing you.

And it was a decided pleasure to see him again. We had hunted with his organization in 1958—without bagging a tiger. Not through the lack of skill of his people, but just plain bad luck, on which nebulous asset all hunting depends. But he had been greatly disappointed and wanted us to return. Now he wrapped his arm around my shoulders, saying, "It's been a long time! It's great that you two are here again! Knowing you, we will get you into the jungle immediately."

Vidya Shukla is the son of the former Governor of India's Central Provinces, now part of Madhya Pradesh, and is a member of the House of Parliament. He created the *shikar* organization to keep himself busy, in contact with visitors to his country, and because he liked hunting and the jungle.

As we drove into Nagpur he went into detail on a new service his company was offering. "It's just for a week," he said. "We want to give visitors the chance to see what I consider the best part of India, her jungles and animals. Travelers who can't afford the time or money to take the monthly or half-month *shikar.*

"For $215 a person can stay in our *dak* bungalow for seven days with the full complement of servants, use our jeep and *shikari,* and have the opportunity to bag four kinds of deer, two antelope, the blue bull, the sambur, wild boar, sloth bear, about a dozen kinds of game birds, go fishing, hunt crocodile, get the whole taste of the jungle."

He went on to say that the hunting itself wasn't important. People could take advantage of this new program just to live in the jungle in luxury, drive its roads, photograph, or rest.

"Why didn't you let me know?" I said. "This appeals more than tiger-hunting."

He smiled grimly. "Oh no, Jack! Our reputation is at stake. We want the honor of your bagging the world's most important trophy with Allwyn Cooper."

He became solemn as we transferred equipment into his new black air-conditioned motor car, obviously the pride of that part of the country, with a crowd gathering to touch its shiny sides, cocking their heads to listen to the soft cat-purr of the motor.

"You will be at the jungle *dak* before nightfall. Don't be alarmed now at what I say. But I'm afraid our zeal to try to put you in the way of a tiger has backfired slightly. A monster awaits you."

He wouldn't say any more, assuring us that Rao Naidu, the chief *shikari,* whom we had hunted with before and were anxious to see again, would meet us. "He will explain," said our friend as he waved good-bye.

We arrived in air-conditioned comfort, courtesy of Detroit and Vidya Shukla, at the predetermined meeting place more than two hundred miles from Nagpur, in an area where the real jungle begins to form its green wall. Rao was there waiting for us in his jeep in an inkwell of shade thrown by a fat *mahwal* tree. He stepped from its shadow as Mary Lou and I got out of the car. We hugged like brothers long separated and he respectfully shook hands with Mary Lou, saying, "Welcome back to our jungles."

Rao Naidu is a Hindu, of the Kshatriya warrior caste, a man with a university education. As an intelligent individual, he has found his way in life, made his peace with it, decided what he really wanted to do with his short span and had the courage to do it. Loving the jungle since childhood, he decided that one day he would spend most of his time in its serenity, away from conformed man and the terrible bee-swarm of his cities.

As you read these words, Rao has made the break. He is his own man, head of his own *shikar* organization, which informed observers and hunters tell me is one of the best in the world. It would be. Rao is a neat, conscientious person who can bring order out of chaos, calmness from calamity. And, to the point, he can find the big cats when no one else can.

He walks with long-striding feline grace, talks softly almost in a purr, can climb a tree like a leopard, hear a twig snap at two hundred yards, tell from the track of a tiger its size, sex, when it ate last, how fast it was traveling. Rao is about five feet ten, with slightly receding hair the shade of a crow's wing in the sun. His complexion is the color of Italian coffee after it comes from the espresso machine and is heavily treated with milk—*cappuccino* they call it in Rome. He is slim, in excellent physical condition, can walk all day without breathing hard, and when he is your friend you are a lucky man.

We drove another three hours, probably one hundred miles, deeper in the jungle to a *dak* bungalow, a whitewashed sprawling building with a thick red-tile roof, on a rise five miles from the forest village of Mulni. The staff of cook, bearer, driver, tracker, skinner, room boy, each with an assistant, waited for us on the broad veranda.

After introductions Rao said, "As I promised, your tiger is here. I made sure by giving him a buffalo every two days to keep him. He is a big one. He finishes the bait easily in that length of time and is always ready for more."

"How many buffalo have you given him?" I asked in chilled fascination.

"Four. No, five. And one tonight makes six."

"Terrible!" said Mary Lou. "Isn't there another way?"

"Well, madam," Rao said, "I suppose so. But this is the sure way. I gave my promise that I would have your tiger here. I am keeping that promise. Mostly these buffalo are old and useless animals. So there is no great waste."

"Have you tried sitting up for him?" I asked. "Just to size him up?"

Rao smiled. "No. But the *machan* is ready. We will sit up tonight."

"Is there a dead bait?"

"No. He dragged it away and finished it."

"What do we do tonight then?"

"We tie a fresh bait."

"Alive?" my wife asked.

"Of course. It's the only way now, isn't it?"

Over hot Darjeeling tea laced with Dugson's honey we discussed that one, making it clear to Rao that we weren't at all happy with the thought of sitting in a tree watching the tiger kill a helpless animal. Rao said that it was the best method. The tiger was accustomed to getting fresh meat regularly. He had kept returning, apparently without suspicion. We could wait until he killed the animal, then follow to where he dragged it, then build another *machan* and hope that he would return. But he didn't advise it.

"Seeing that we have made this much of an investment in buffaloes," he said, "it is my suggestion that we sit up tonight. The buffalo is already tied at the place in the jungle. The *machan* is ready. If we disturb anything, or do wait until he makes his kill and then follow his drag, it is almost certain that he will be aware of us following him. He will hear the men making the new *machan*. He will know we are there. And he might not come back to finish his meal."

When you are with an expert on his own ground, it is considered intelligent to follow his instructions. That's exactly what we did.

We drove the jeep five miles into the jungle, then left it with the driver and walked another three miles until we came to a stream running through a sort of glade—an open spot in the jungle surrounded by giant creepers and other large, well-leafed trees. It was four o'clock and the sunlight was still falling through the leaves in blotches of gold on the ground, touching the tree trunks with color. Then we saw the bait, standing quietly and tied to a huge black *unjun* tree. The live buffalo.

Rao ignored it, walking directly across from it, perhaps forty yards, to a stately *kowa* tree that looks much like our oak. The *machan* was high up in the tree. A rope ladder dangled. Cautioning us not to speak, Rao went up the ladder like a langur; my wife followed almost as gracefully; I swayed up feeling like a bear shinnying a sapling. The *machan* was a good one. Thick branches with the twigs smoothly hacked off were plaited together with bamboo, forming a secure platform. A blanket was spread to soften it. As we sat, the clearing spread before us almost like a stage. Left center was the buffalo. Behind him the stream ran making its serene sounds.

We had been settled about ten minutes when we heard the sound, like an animal dragging something. We stiffened, each of us automatically searching his own piece of jungle. A porcupine came waddling out into the open, its long tail heavy with quills. This Asiatic type, nearly the size of a cocker spaniel and the world's largest, could bring death to a man, and is responsible for making many man-killers out of tigers and leopards. It fills their paws or mouths with fishhook barbs that fester and poison and prevent the cats from hunting normally. The porcupine took a long drink from the stream, eyed our buffalo, then waddled on.

We were in the tree at four-thirty and would probably have to wait most of the night before the cat came. Tigers, the sane, normal ones, are nocturnal. That means it would be late before this one came for his meal.

Nothing much happened now as we sat—except that discomfort grew as the night became darker. As the sun's radiation leaves the earth, melting away in the night, the cold comes. In the jungle it is a creeping cold that lays its chill deep in your bones and it is a physical impossibility not to shiver and shake, even with heavy pants and sweater. The picture of sultry India, land of sweat and humidity, is often a false one, especially high in a tree at night.

Now the moon had gone and the last heat had left the earth. The only warning as the tiger came in out of the darkness was a long, sighing gasp—the death sigh of the buffalo as it was choked, the most frightening sound I have ever heard.

Still we sat. Rao was to give the sign to shoot by pressing my knee, then shining his light on the tiger. We sat quietly for about five minutes. There was a splashing in the stream, then silence. Still no sign from Rao. Finally he flashed his light at the tree. There was nothing but a broken rope. The probing searchlight reached the stream. In the middle of its narrow bed was the buffalo.

In cold defiance the cat had killed the animal, dropped it in the stream, then vanished into the jungle. He was aware of us, probably had seen a movement, or had watched us arrive earlier. But it was still dark and we couldn't climb down until dawn. The tiger could be there waiting. Rao explained why he hadn't given the signal to shoot or flash the light. He was waiting for the tiger to start feasting on the kill, for the sounds of crunching bones. "Once he started eating," he said, "not even the light would frighten him. But if I flashed it earlier he would have run."

As dawn came we went down, rifles at the ready, and walked back to the jeep, wondering aloud why the tiger had killed and disappeared. Why hadn't he eaten? Why had he carried the buffalo only to the stream? Why hadn't he taken it deeper into the jungle?

Rao shook his head. "Strange. He is more clever than I gave him credit for. He knew we were here. Killing the buffalo and leaving it was contempt." This, then, was our monster, produced by a friend wanting to do us a favor.

Rao sent several men back to drag the buffalo out of the stream, cover it with branches and brush so the crows and vultures wouldn't get it, and retie it to the tree with double ropes so it couldn't be dragged off.

Now started a series of all-night vigils. We had the dead bait and we refused to sacrifice any more live animals, arguing that a meal was a meal, that the tiger would surely come back to this kill. Rao agreed, and we sat over the bait for three nights. The tiger didn't return. The fourth night we left before dawn. An impatient mistake. When we returned the next night the bait was gone; even the double rope was broken. It was necessary to wait until morning to try to follow the drag marks of the bait into the jungle. Even then we moved cautiously, rifles ready. Rao and the three trackers went first, then Mary Lou and I, then three more trackers—moving in single file. What we found was the head and a few bones. The tiger, hungry after waiting several nights, had polished off the animal in one sitting. Now what?

We still didn't want to go through the live-buffalo ordeal again, so Rao suggested that we rest for a couple of days and see what happened. The first night the tiger came out of his jungle and roared all night. He wanted his usual buffalo. The boys all came and huddled in the *dak* bungalow until dawn. Next day was Holi, a Hindu religious ceremony in which everyone hurled colored water into one another's faces and the lowliest had the privilege of painting the faces of the most respected. Everyone in camp had his face daubed in reds, blues and oranges. The men built a roaring bonfire and danced around it, screeching out songs. The skinner and the tracker, dressed like women, sang and danced with each other and the cook and the sweeper.

As we drove to Mulni to see the village celebrate the religious carnival, Rao explained Holi. As is usual with Indian beliefs, it was based on a story of horror and destruction.

Prahlad, India's child saint, was an ardent devotee of God even while still an infant. His father, the cruel King Hiranyakashipu was a God-defying tyrant who did not like his son's devotion and tried unsuccessfully to force him not to utter God's name. Prahlad's unbending determination and devotion enraged the king. Holika, the king's sister, enjoyed a boon of immunity from fire, so the king ordered her to take Prahlad and walk into a blazing fire.

The intention was that Prahlad would be consumed by fire and Holika would come out unharmed. When she did enter the fire with Prahlad, God intervened to save His devotee. Holika was burned to ashes, while Prahlad came out unharmed. According to this legend, the Holi bonfire is a reënactment of the burning of Holika, and the colorful revelry is the people's thanksgiving and joy for the triumph of Prahlad.

Curious little bullock-drawn wagons, humped with a screen of bamboo, were arriving as we drove in. These were the aboriginals, the jungle people, mostly Gonds, and they were poorly dressed, the men in crude, short dhotis, the women and children in dark, often torn saris. But everyone was happy: open stalls were everywhere; bare-chested jungle merchants squatted beside piles of brass and glass jewelry and **ornaments**; women joined hands and danced in the road to the beat of a drummer who shook his head madly; men were trying to shinny up a greased pole. Every face was splotched with color, and most of the men and children had vivid red, blue and orange splashes all over their clothing. Venders in turbans and little else hawked colored sweetmeats; roadside braziers cooked pieces of mutton; *chapatties* baked; goats and cattle bawled; babies rolled in the road dust; young men talked with shy girls—and they all stared at us as if we had just escaped from a zoo.

It had been a gay day but gaiety ended abruptly at dusk. The tiger

"Next day was Holi, a Hindu religious ceremony in which . . . the lowliest had the privilege of painting the faces of the most respected."

was hungry again and his roars circled the camp, growing closer as it got darker. I suppose some hunters would have charged out into that unknown darkness after the cat and settled the whole business then and there. But Rao's experience and my lack of courage teamed up and we sat and listened to the tiger talking—telling us how upset he was that we hadn't tied up a buffalo for him. Toward dawn we could hear him walking along the road in front of the *dak,* making as much noise as a bullock hauling a cart.

"Tigers just don't act that way," said Rao, shaking his head, just before we went to bed for an hour or so. Shortly after we awoke, a deputation awaited: four of the camp boys, the bearer, the assistant cook, driver and the room boy. They said that unless the great *shikari* and the brave sahib killed the tiger and stopped his walking around their tents threatening them all night long, they would leave—walk back to Nagpur.

Rao told them that Nagpur was three hundred miles off, that it would grow dark before they reached a place to stay for the night. He gently suggested that they come to the *dak* every night until we had settled with the tiger. They weren't happy but they agreed, at least for a while.

They were unhappier the next night. The tiger talked again and stalked along the road to the village. At dawn a group from Mulni told us that he had killed a calf in the middle of their village, carried it two miles and eaten it. What would he do tonight?

Rao rubbed his head in chagrin. "I'm afraid in my eagerness to see that you got your tiger this trip I created a problem. If we don't tie out a bait, apparently he will go and get his own buffalo. It could happen that if someone gets in his way we will have a tragedy on our hands. This is not a normal tiger. He's too bold. He comes too close to us. He walks like an elephant. I'm not sure what the plan should be—"

It turned out to be a daylight beat, with Rao assembling the able men of Mulni to walk through the last area where the tiger's tracks were seen. We loaded the jeep with trackers and started for the place. As usual Rao drove. We hadn't been driving a half-hour, getting to a point on the Kesla-Bori road where it crossed the Tawa River, when one of those unexpected jungle dramas unfolded. Sadly, terribly.

Rao stopped suddenly, pointing through teak trees that stood in a line, slim as fishing rods, with two enormous leaves sticking from the top of each tree like elephant ears.

At first I didn't see it, then Mary Lou gasped, and I saw the hor-

"It turned out to be a daylight beat, with Rao assembling the able men of Mulni to walk through the last area where tiger's tracks were seen."

ror. A dozen wild dogs, not much larger than fox terriers, red, with up-pointed ears and pointed muzzles, tongues out, stood by the stream. In it were two animals that they had chased to exhaustion and torture: a sambur doe (a huge, elklike animal) and her fawn. Evidently she had tried to fight the dogs off and was bleeding and gashed with great wounds; beside her, barely able to stand in the shallow river, was the fawn with its eyes eaten out. Quietly Rao and I reached for our rifles and got out of the jeep. We shot until the clips were empty and the barrels hot. But the wild red dogs were small targets and they were clever. We got three; the others vanished silently, the most feared killers in the jungle, able to take even a tiger in their relentless, never-tiring chase. Rao left two men to end the suffering of the sambur and we drove on to the beat area.

This turned out to be our day for unexpected drama. As we moved toward our tree *machan,* the sky darkened and the trackers walking ahead of me paused, glanced at the sky, then with troubled faces looked at Rao. He shook his head. "It looks like rain. I hope it doesn't. Strange things can happen in a jungle storm." Prophetic words.

I climbed into the *machan,* this time a rough one, and placed my foam rubber mat under me. An old man in a loincloth, looking older than my grandfather, monkey-agile, swung up beside me. He was a wrinkled, nut-brown fellow with a constant, toothless grin; he became helpless-looking when the rain came, and his smile vanished.

I have never seen rain fall this way; it was like having a fire hose turned on you full blast. The skies just opened and let it out. The old man touched my arm, pointing. Coming out of jungle tangle was a magnificent sambur stag with great antlers, noble even though he was soaking wet. Close behind was a wild boar.

They held their heads high. Suddenly they bolted, running as if all hell had broken loose. It had. Hail. A rain of stones the size of golf balls pelted. I waited for it to stop, as our hailstorms do, but this one didn't. We were being beaten and welted with the ice rocks from the sky. I took the foam pad, clutched the old tracker to me, and held it over our heads. It probably saved us from being seriously injured.

I worried about Mary Lou. Then, running through the hail, was Rao, followed by Mary Lou, both holding *machan* pads over their heads. They stood hunched up under my tree, trying to avoid the hail. Beaters were all around them, arms over their heads, some crouching under bushes. The storm ended after fifteen minutes. As I unclutched the old fellow, he leaped from the platform and slid down the tree like a fireman answering a four-alarm.

When I got down, the ground was covered with two inches of hail —the jungle floor a carpet of ice. We examined ourselves; bruises, some open and bleeding, were on our arms, but we had all protected our faces.

The sun came out as suddenly as it had disappeared, transforming the scene of terror into one of gleaming splendor. Mist rose in tendrils through the trees. The ground was a bed of brilliant diamonds. From behind trees and from under bushes, the villagers appeared, many of them bleeding.

As we stood there drenched to the skin, beaten with hail, shaking with cold despite the reappearance of the sun, Mary Lou began laughing—a little hysterically. I joined; then Rao. The villagers caught the humor, if humor it was, and began laughing. It would have made a mad scene if someone who had avoided the storm had suddenly come upon us. Bedraggled, beaten down, shivering, we started back toward the jeep, a tattered and defeated troop of tiger hunters.

The next night was quiet. We needed that. The boys did report seeing a big leopard in the road close to camp, but the tiger didn't talk that night—nor the next. And no kills were reported. But the big leopard was seen again, creeping up on two little white kids that we kept around the camp as mascots—or probably pot insurance. The little goats bleated so loudly that the cook came running, saw the leopard, and ran shouting to us.

"We better try to get the panther," Rao said. "These people are as frightened of them as they are of tigers, perhaps more so. The panther is more treacherous. I have no idea what happened to the tiger. He puzzles me. Perhaps he has found something dead that is keeping him happy for a while."

"Let's count our blessings," said Mary Lou.

"But we'll have to face up to it soon," I said. "We have to stay here until we get that tiger. I think he's confused. All that free, easy meat—"

"No doubt," said Rao stiffly. "But let's have a change of pace and see if we can get that leopard tonight. Here's the way we'll do it—"

He suggested that he take one of the kids, dig a hole in the ground, put the animal in it, and protect it by covering it with bamboo matting. The kid would bleat, luring the leopard. We would sit in a tree nearby and shoot the spotted cat as he crept toward the hole in the ground.

"Normally," Rao said, "we'd just tie the kid to a tree. Expose it. This way we usually get more noise from it, thus more attraction for the panther. But knowing you two, I suppose—"

"We like the idea of the pit better," said Mary Lou. "The kid will be safer."

We decided not to go too far from camp—less than a mile. The leopard had appeared in camp twice after the kids. He would not be far away. Rao didn't carry a rifle; Mary Lou took her Winchester .308 and I had the .338, a new caliber that hadn't been completely proven yet. Winchester had tested it, thought it was a great rifle, and I was going to see what it could do with India's big game. Its 250-grain bullet was supposed to have a muzzle energy of 4050 foot pounds. Winchester suggested that it was an excellent rifle for moose and bear. It should be plenty of gun for a leopard. Mary Lou was the better shot, and her .308, with a muzzle energy of 2730 foot pounds, would be right for the spotted cat.

So the hole was dug, the kid placed in it. He began bleating immediately. Rao selected a tree about fifty yards from the pit and perhaps twenty feet from the dirt road that ran into the village five miles away. It wasn't a tall tree and the *machan* was a makeshift thing.

Rao thought the leopard was eager for his young goat dinner and would show up within an hour. As darkness came swiftly, the kid stopped his bleating. As it grew darker, he would let out an occasional half-hearted bleat. But that was all. A leopard bait he was not. But maybe he had a brain. Down in that dark hole, silence might bring some kind of security.

After two hours, a noise. Something was creeping out of the jungle screen. It came in a creepy, wobbly gait—a striped hyena, a horrible creature that looked as if he had come right out of the graveyard. But Rao had secured the matting well. Finally the hyena gave up and continued his search for something easier and deader.

Then it came as all true drama does, completely without warning. The tiger returned. His roars began as before, starting low, then growing louder, fiercer, angrier. "Going away from us," I said. He sounded miles away. Mary Lou, keen of eye and ear, said, "I'm afraid not."

Rao said nothing. He sat there like a person caught up a tree, without a plan. Which is exactly what he was. For the first time, this exceptionally cautious hunter had ventured forth without his rifle, an effective .423 Mauser. But we were close to camp; we were out for leopard. Two guns were plenty.

Now the roars faded. Silence was all around us, a breathing, pulsating silence. Why didn't the tiger roar? Where was he now? We needed a noise.

We got it. The kid started bleating. He had been mute for nearly two hours. Now, of all times, he decided to cry for help. And his sharp, spaced little bleats sounded exactly as if that was what he was saying. Then he stopped.

Something was clumping along the road beneath us, heading for the village. Whatever it was, it didn't care about being heard. Then it started breathing heavily, and I felt Rao on one side, Mary Lou on the other, stiffen. Mary Lou took my arm in a hard, frightened grasp.

Suddenly Rao flashed his light. In the middle of the road stood an enormous tiger. He knew something was wrong, knew that he was caught in a strange light. He twisted his head. He turned and looked up at us. I shot carefully at the point where the spine joins the neck.

He roared, going down as if pushed by a huge hand. He went into a frenzy of motion in the road.

Rao gasped. "Shoot again!" Mary Lou, rigid beside me, put her .308 to her shoulder and shot twice. I placed one more shot below the shoulder in the twisting, roaring animal.

The tiger suddenly was still, spread-eagled in our light. The kid was bleating. Our driver was supposed to have been here ten minutes ago. Now the lights of the jeep came up the road. They fell upon the tiger. The horn began blaring.

Rao shouted that the men in the jeep should stay back until we made certain the animal was dead. He took Mary Lou's .308 and shot twice close to the body—no movement. Then he took a knife out of his pocket and threw it. It landed on the tiger's back. It didn't move. We climbed down.

As we stood there in the road looking at the great cat, Rao said calmly, "A good shot. If you had only wounded him, he would have been up after us in seconds. They can jump straight up eighteen feet, you know—"

"How high was our tree?" Mary Lou asked weakly.

"Fifteen feet," Rao said. "A little tree for a little cat. I wasn't counting on this surprise."

Why was our jeep late? Flat tire. If it had come roaring up on time, there is no telling what would have happened.

It took eight men to carry the great tiger on his last trip along the jungle road.

CHAPTER TWO

CEYLON

Some time ago a man named Alexander Graham Bell wrote words that have become my philosophy: "Don't keep forever on the public road, going only where others have gone. Leave the beaten path occasionally and dive into the woods. You will be certain to find something you have never seen before. Follow it up. One discovery will lead to another, and before you know it, you will have something worth thinking about."

I haven't made any big discoveries yet except for the pleasures of people and places, but I'm still trying. So when Som Nath Chib, chief of the government travel organization, talked with us the day before we decided to leave India, we followed his suggestion. One would have had to lack curiosity and spirit not to do so.

"It is believed that they are the world's happiest people," he said. "They live on an island that some call paradise. They play all day, seldom work, have plenty to eat and drink, live wherever they choose. It is also thought that they are the original gypsies. If I were you, I would try to find them. They are on the island of Ceylon."

Mr. Chib was a small, trim, relaxed man who always seemed to have the situation under control. When he got enthusiastic, he fizzed like Bromo in a glass. He was fizzing now.

"Fasss-cinating island," he went on. "And these people, the gypsies, are out of another world! Fasss-cinating! I'd suggest that you first move around southern India. Few tourists go there. You know their routine. Delhi, Agra, Benares, Jaipur, Bombay, and our visitors think they are old India hands."

So we had traveled the south where the "old India hands" are seldom found, and now we found ourselves airborne once more, flying from Madras to Ceylon. Mary Lou and I, as always, were amazed at the physical stamina of the tourists aboard. They were mostly Americans in their late sixties, some older, burbling now with the thought of the island. They probably had been up since 6:00

A.M., bustling around the shops and seeing the sights of Madras with the zest of teen-agers.

After twenty minutes aloft the aircraft captain's voice came over the sound system. "Flying time to Colombo airport in Ceylon is two hours, ladies and gentlemen. Weather en route is reported fine, but I regret to tell you that we are having some premature monsoons on the island and probably will be greeted with rain when we arrive."

The word *monsoon* created a stir among the older folks. Their tour director, his apostolic spade beard awiggle, scurried about putting them at ease. "*Light* monsoons. Not even monsoons, if you please," he kept saying. "Just a bit of rain."

Quite a bit. It was drumming so hard that you could hear the downpour above the sound of the aircraft's motors as we came in for a landing. The tarmac was polished ebony in the rainfall; rain sizzled and steamed as it hit the tin roofs of the airport buildings. A Sikh, tall and handsome in a white turban, and a slender brown man in a tan linen suit stood waiting for us under enormous umbrellas.

They came forward with their rain shields and the Sikh said, "Welcome to Ceylon, Mr. and Mrs. Scott! I am Mr. Sehti, Government of India Tourist Office for this island. And this is Stanley Learned of the Ceylon office. Mr. Chib has asked us to look out for you."

"I have a nice surprise for you," said Mr. Learned. There is a Singhalese wedding today. Perhaps you would like to see it?"

"We haven't an itinerary worked out yet," said Mr. Sehti, "but that is a small matter. We can arrange for you to see anything on the island."

"What about the gypsies?" I said.

They looked at each other blankly. "The gypsies?" said Mr. Learned.

"Yes, we understand they are interesting people and have a happy way of life."

"But tourists want to go to Kandy, to the temples, to the mountains," Mr. Learned said.

"We aren't tourists," I said. "Not exactly, that is. And, incidentally, we would be honored to go to that wedding. It is just that we are looking for out-of-ordinary things rather than tourist spots."

"Oh," they said in unison. Then Sehti took over. "Naturally," he said. "But these gypsies are not so easy to find—"

"No," said Mr. Learned. "They stay in an area less than a week, thinking that if they do not move on, all the food in that place goes rotten."

We got into an old car and drove through lush countryside. We passed through areas where the bougainvillaea was so colorful and profuse that the roadside seemed afire. It was interspersed by flame trees with giant red flowers. Pink, mauve and purple orchids were everywhere, and more different types of palm trees than I had ever seen. There were tall, graceful specimens; thick, squat types; the areca, the kitul, the royal, the cabbage and the great talipot palms. Then we were in Colombo, the capital; half modern West, half fascinating East. The streets were narrow and winding, full of open-stall shops. The broad, clean, tree-lined avenues were full of cool shadows. Color was everywhere—graceful, dark women in orange, red and purple sarongs; men in Western attire with English-type shorts, followed by one almost naked, his brown body gleaming as if oiled, his walk a stagger.

"He's slightly toddy-took," said Mr. Sehti. Stanley Learned said nothing. There was a slight, embarrassed silence, and I said, "A beautiful city. These streets are the equal of any."

Stanley brightened. "Colombo's expansion was created by Sir Patrick Abercrombie, the planner of Greater London, you know." He was about to fill us in on Ceylon as we made our way through the traffic, when we nearly collided with a figure on stilts, ten feet tall. It was a man dressed in women's clothes—a soiled white silk skirt and long red stockings. He carried a flaming red parasol.

"On his way to the railroad station or open market to get a few laughs and earn some money," said Sehti. He pointed at a line of cars moving slowly by, people leaning out, waving and shouting. "Another wedding," he said. "A good sign."

"Yes," said Stanley, "this is an auspicious day. A good day for travel, for betting, for love—and weddings."

He went on to explain that often there were days like this when, without any concerted planning, there were several weddings and it became "auspicious."

Stanley then ticked off Ceylon for us. "In case either of you fell asleep in geography class," he said, "Islamic legend has it that Adam came to Ceylon after he had been thrown out of the Garden of Eden. He had it better here. We don't have apples but our mangoes and pineapples are the best in the world. Actually we are only eighteen miles from India. You might say we are connected by sixty miles of sandbanks and reefs now called Adam's Bridge, touching Rameswaram at the southernmost tip of India. Singhalese is our language but many of us speak Tamil; quite a few know English. Sixty-five percent of us are Buddhists, twenty percent Hindus, nine percent Roman Catholics, six percent Moslems."

Putting all of Stanley's points together, we could describe Ceylon as an island separated from India on the northwest by the Gulf of Mannar and Palk Strait. It lies off the southern end of the sub-continent and extends 270 miles from north to south, 140 miles wide, with a total area of 25,332 square miles. Long a junction of Eastern trade routes, Ceylon has been called everything from "Land of the Lion People" to the "Emerald Isle," but is best known as the "Pearl of the Orient." Gem would be a better word, for the island is the home of the sapphire, especially the six-rayed star; the pigeon-blood ruby; the unusual alexandrite stone, green by day, red at night; and is the only place where that smoky, staring gem, the cat's eye, is found.

We were entering the suburbs of Mount Lavinia now. I could smell fragrant frangipani and see the flame of hibiscus beside the neat houses. On each side of the narrow road leading to our hotel were gem shops staffed by men whose long hair was coiled in knots at the nape of the neck. They stood in the doorways beckoning.

The Mount Lavinia Hotel was a sprawling, terraced, many-storied pile hulking beside the Indian Ocean, seven miles from Colombo. Managing Director Vogel, a Swiss, greeted us warmly, escorting us in the grand manner to our room. Mr. Sehti had returned to his office; Stanley Learned waited in the lobby to take us to the wedding.

We had a corner room, almost a suite, large, comfortable, with twin beds; an adjoining antiquated bathroom, with a huge claw-footed tub and no shower. The small balcony looked out on the ocean. We could see a thatched hut on the beach with catamaran fishing boats drawn up and breech-clouted fishermen coiling nets. Occasionally a huge rock, squatting like a giant turtle, broke the symmetry of the long spread of sugar-sand beach. A woman walked along it, the wind lifting her red sari, the blue tongue of sea washing white as it touched the shore. Forty slender palms bowed heads in an offshore breeze. It looked as though the tourist department had planned the colorful scene.

On the rail of the balcony sat a pair of crows, the gray-headed house crows we had known in India. They were a bold couple whose eyes glittered as they stared at us—a pair of creatures who would swoop in and give us a bad time at breakfast.

The rain had stopped and we could hear a soft drip from the eaves. There was a fresh salty-iodine sea smell coming through our open window. Far off above the Indian Ocean rain clouds still huddled in dark conference. We were ready in ten minutes, in a taxi and on our way to the wedding. The taxi was a polished ancient black Buick; the driver, a handsome man with curly black hair peppered with gray, Denzil Wirasinha. He was the most important person we were to meet on the island.

The ceremony had taken place by the time we arrived but the reception was going full blast at the Galle Face Hotel in Colombo, a monstrous place by the sea that reminded me of the great old heaps in Saratoga. More than five hundred guests were seated at long tables dressed in their best, mostly pastel print dresses and tropical suits, with a Chinesey-looking purple coat showing up at some of the tables, and now and then a startling blaze of color where one of the older women sat in a Singhalese sari, more colorful and somehow more feminine than those we had seen in India. The waiters, slim brown youths, swished about in long bright skirts, and there was a low rising hum of voices.

The bride was skinny and pretty, and shy as all brides are supposed to be but few are; in her long white gown she looked like an Audrey Hepburn who had stayed out in the sun too long. The groom, a distraught young fellow, said, "So nice meeting you," then went back into the daze of this complicated thing he had done with his life.

The twelve-foot trestle tables were littered with several kinds of fish, sliced cold fowl and meats, potato, rice and crawfish salads. Beside every place was a dainty piece of white-frosted wedding cake and a glass of white liquid that could have been a tepid kind of champagne—"The ginger ale of champagne," said Mary Lou, who doesn't like champagne anyway. Everyone was jovial, as they always are at wedding receptions, and food disappeared and reappeared with amazing rapidity, much of it being eaten gracefully with both hands.

I think Stanley Learned wanted to show us that the people on his island were not different from those in America—at least at a wedding. And the impression held until Mary Lou and I met the "broker," introduced just that way by Stanley. "Here is the man who made the wedding possible. The broker. Mr. and Mrs. Scott."

He said, "Glad you are here on this auspicious day."

He was a fat brown man in a spotted, untidy, once-white silk suit. He had a toothy smile but it failed. His eyes didn't enter into it; they were animal-like and watchful. This cold, calculating character stood staring at the happy goings-on at the reception much as a dealer watches cattle at an auction. The father of the bride paid dowry to the bridegroom and cash to the broker. This broker often worked both sides of the fence, collecting from both parties, Stanley explained, adding that it was a most valuable service.

He laughed. "This broker knows more about the young ladies on the island than their mothers."

As we left, Stanley said, "Your taxi driver, Denzil Wirasinha, comes from one of Ceylon's best families. He is an educated, interesting man. My thought is that he might prove useful—might even find the gypsies."

Denzil thought he could. After driving to the hotel, we walked to the beach, watched the Indian Ocean practicing to be a picture postcard, and talked. "Those gypsy chaps, sir," he said. "They are on the move all of the time. They have the run of the island. Our government lets them set up camp anywhere they wish, so it's hard to tell where they'll be. But we'll get to the chaps, sir. Meantime I'm wondering if you'd like to see a chap who walks on fire?"

"Why in heaven's name would anyone want to walk on fire?" Mary Lou said.

"Well, madam," Denzil said, "this chap is sort of a Hindu holy man, a swami. I'm told he does this to prove a point of mind over matter."

The next day we went to see the fire-walker, Swami Gauribala. He was a husky fellow dressed in flowing yellow robes, with long hair bushed on the sides, balding in front. He had a full beard, as gray and bristly as steel wool. A strand of heavy red beads hung across his bare chest. He was smoking a long black cigar and spoke excellent English. He was a German who had come to the East, was converted to Hinduism and had lived in Ceylon for twenty years.

We had driven quite a few miles to see him perform beside a Hindu temple where a fire pit had been dug and the area roped off. There were Hindus standing, sitting and squatting everywhere. The pit was over fifteen feet long, four feet wide, probably that deep, and it was filled with burning logs that were almost consumed. The coals would be ready and several men were fanning them by the time we had finished talking with the swami.

He claimed that he had walked barefoot across the flaming coals six times and had never had any ill effects. "I invited a Christian minister, the Reverend E. L. Robinson, to join me in a walk a few years ago at our most famous temple at Kataragama. He watched me go across the pit, then he tried it. Unfortunately, he spent the next two weeks in the hospital. But I felt fine and walked three miles to see a friend the night after I trod the pit."

Although he said they might help, the swami claimed that he followed no rituals like plastering his body with the holy yellow paste or bathing in sacred waters. He didn't use charms or fast. His technique was the rhythm of the walk; slow, even steps across the coals. He did like the white ash well fanned off so it didn't further insulate the red coals. "The feet should be well-soaked in cool water. The walk should be slow and steady, no skipping, jumping, hopping, sliding, dancing. Like walking a tightrope, balance and know-how are needed," he said.

Then he went a bit mystic explaining that the real secret was an inner conviction that material things didn't matter, that the mind without ego was the master of fire-walking. "You must get rid of the 'I' and attain an egoless state of mind," he said. Then he explained that those who get burned think, *I* would like to walk the fire unburned. *I* walked the fire pit. *I* am afraid that *I* might get burned. He thought the egoless state of mind could be attained with alcohol or drugs, indeed had seen people under the influence of one or the other walk the coals without harm. "Self-torture, self-surrender, love of God, use of some charms, the holy saffron paste, sometimes help achieve the egoless mind also," he said. "Yoga, a supreme stillness of speech, mind and body will also empty the mind, wipe out the ego."

It wasn't doubletalk, for we waited and saw him take ten long precise steps over coals burning as brightly as those in a barbecue pit, and no smoking flesh. His Hindu followers watched in silent awe as he walked the fire, then gave rousing cheers. Even Denzil was impressed and as we drove back to Mount Lavinia he said, "Can you believe a chap doing that, sir? Perfectly astounding!"

The Mount Lavinia Hotel with its Oxford Bar, its two-terrace cocktail lounges, three restaurants, all giving write-home views of the Indian Ocean, was a fine hotel because of Mr. Vogel, who paraded it like a soldier, his spectacled eyes missing nothing. His well-trained waiters, dressed in long, brightly colored skirts, moved quickly and efficiently, even with the cats in their way. For Mr. Vogel, fine hotel man that he was, had an outrageous love of cats. There must have been fifty in the place, all sizes, shapes and colors, some with a leg or a piece of tail missing where they had run into the whirling blades of a huge air-cooling fan before the trouble was discovered and the fan shielded.

Most guests took Mr. Vogel's cats in their stride, but an American film star and his wife had vocal fits when they found more than three under their table. I must admit it was a bit disconcerting to sit there trying to eat a shrimp curry while surrounded by ten lean cats staring at my fork in motion.

Denzil had a way with them. He came to the table, brushing them gently but firmly aside with his foot until they knew he meant business and found another table with less determined diners. He came in to dinner one evening, brushed off the cats, sat and had a cup of fragrant Ceylon mountain tea with us. "I haven't had much luck finding the gypsy chaps yet," he said, "but I have hopes." Then he said, "I am told that you like fishing and shooting and things like that, sir."

"We both do. Gives us something to focus on, takes us away from the tourist traps. Besides it's relaxing and fun."

"I agree," he said. "I think there is something in Ceylon that you will like. Teal-hunting."

I said that this was the most exciting of ducks.

"Shall we do it tomorrow?"

I thought it would be a good idea, wondering aloud where I could get some shells for the Browning shotgun I had lugged along. "And for my Winchester 21," Mary Lou said. "I like teal, too."

"That will not be necessary to hunt these chaps, sir," Denzil said. "I'll be around and pick you up about six o'clock in the morning. You just need your swimming trunks."

Denzil was having his little joke. "What do we do, outswim them?" I said, going along with the repartee.

He shook his head seriously. "In a way we are going to outthink these teal. I'll be waiting at six."

At breakfast the next morning we had the usual battle: seconds after the tray was brought, our two balcony crows were flapping around the room, diving to the floor when a crumb was dropped; one even sat on the back of my chair awaiting a handout. They made breakfast a mess, and no matter what we did they always came back. Mary Lou finally dreamed up a method of propping the balcony door shut with her dressing case. Apparently that door had never been tightly shut since the hotel had been built. Now the crows sat outside, long-billed faces against the window, glaring.

Denzil was waiting at the entrance with his usual encouraging smile, and we were off past the banks of gem shops whose hawkers even at this hour waved us in. He drove us through the huge market in Colombo, where fish of many colors, shapes and sizes were being arranged in open stalls that looked like an outdoor art exhibition getting under way. As we rode we looked for the gypsies; Denzil told us to watch for any small groups of colorful people with burros who might be moving along the many side roads.

Fifteen miles out, I shouted to stop. Coming down a side road were seven men dressed in dunce-type peaked hats, their clothing dusty but made up of every color in the spectrum; several had chains of bells around their ankles. They were carrying reed baskets and they waved them at us and said something in Tamil. Then after Denzil shook his head and waved them on, they went up the main road, several occasionally wiggling belled ankles into a mad tune.

"Not gypsies," said Denzil. "Betel sellers on their way to the city. Our bad habit here too, just as in India."

Another hour of driving through paddy-field country found us beside what looked like a lake, a body of water of perhaps twenty-five acres. In Ceylon these are called tanks, a term that needs some definition.

To irrigate this once populous but arid north central region, the ancient Singhalese kings constructed immense artificial lakes. Built without our modern equipment, the tanks of Ceylon are feats of engineering that inspired historian Sir Emerson Tennent to write, "The stupendous remains of reservoirs are the proudest monuments which remain of the former glories of Ceylon. No similar constructions performed by any race, whether ancient or modern, exceed in colossal magnitude the stupendous tanks of Ceylon . . ." This is not exactly accurate, for the tanks of Ceylon are far from being mere architectural relics of a glorious past. They still conserve water, mostly from the abundant rain that falls during the northeast monsoon period, and are used for irrigating ricefields and as water supply during drought months.

An earthen embankment is thrown across a hollow, or shallow valley, to trap rain water, which is gradually drawn off through cutstone sluices and along the *elas* or water channels to the fields below. Most of the tanks are small, but some—Kantalai (Giant's Tank) and Lakawewa—occupy three thousand acres. Denzil also told us that since most of the tanks are surrounded by scrub and forest, and have swamps and marshes at the shallow ends, they are attractive areas for all kinds of birdlife. "This one seems to interest the teal chaps," he said.

There were two men in loincloths waiting for us beside the tank as we got out of the car, their brown bodies gleaming with oil. They both carried pots larger than their heads, and they bobbed and smiled as we were introduced: De Alwis and Saravanamuttu.

There was an animated conference in Singhalese, and Denzil said, "They would like you to get your swimming trunks on. They're ready to get started. Teal have been here and have taken off, but are expected back. They think that the ducks went down on the other side of the far marsh."

The far side of the tank was swamp with lotus, water lilies and reed growth along the edge of the entire bank. The water looked dark and dangerous.

I went back to the car, got into shorts and came to the edge of the tank where they waited. De Alwis, evidently the tactician, handed me a brown pot, talked with Denzil for a moment and pointed at the tank. Floating about three hundred yards away were a half-dozen objects that hard staring finally identified as more brown pots.

Denzil said, "The technique, sir, is to wade into the water with the pot over your head and go and stand among those floating pots. Those pots have been there for many days and the teal are not afraid of them." Denzil now smiled sheepishly. "I have not seen this myself, sir, so I only tell you."

"You mean to tell me that Ceylon teal are so stupid that they will decoy to pots? Pots!"

"No, sir. The teal are supposed to come in and swim among the pots as is their habit. You quickly reach up, pull them under water and put them in this." He walked over to the two teal hunters and came back with a round rattan basket, roped so it fit around the waist. A neat trick if it worked. My knowledge of teal included memories not only of their swiftness in flight and their agility on water, but also their mental acuteness.

"It's not too late to give the whole thing up," said Mary Lou. "I wouldn't go into that mucky water if I could catch a diamond bracelet. Not only does Ceylon abound in snakes, but I wouldn't be surprised if you could pick up some dandy fungus in there. Let's just watch the experts."

"Look," I said. "Richard Halliburton swam the Hellespont, scaled the Acropolis walls at night, swam between Scylla and Charybdis. The least I can do is wade a little pond on this teal exercise."

"It is not a little pond," Mary Lou said. "It is twenty-five acres of centuries-old water that could contain anything, including the Loch Ness monster."

The teal yankers were fidgeting and indicated that I should put my head in the pot. I did, finding it surprisingly light, with openings for the eyes and nose. It was not uncomfortable. Denzil gave last-minute instructions as I waded into the tepid water.

"Use patience, sir, they tell me. Wait until the teal swim close, then reach out, pull them under the water by the feet, put the one you catch in the basket, then wait for another. Do not splash the water. Try to be quick and quiet. I'd suggest watching one of them first."

As I followed the hunters, the water quickly coming up to my neck, Mary Lou said in disgust, "This is teal zeal if I ever saw it! The fire-walking was probably safer!"

Moving slowly, watching my footwork so I didn't slip and fall, I followed the Singhalese to the floating pots, stood perhaps ten yards from them, near two pots, and waited. I could see small things wiggling through the water, and thirty yards to my left there was a long steady ripple that turned out to be a snake, a peculiar greenish one, head up, going shoreward.

The water was the color and temperature of tepid tea and I was sorry that I hadn't oiled myself heavily before I got into it, but no one had suggested it and I hadn't thought of it. Then a taggle of teal appeared low in the sky coming our way, and I forgot about oil, skin, snakes and fungus.

They were a pretty sight, these *mal-sera*—the cotton teal—with their swift no-nonsense wingbeat, their heads moving as they surveyed the situation before coming down on the water. Apparently all they saw were the pots. The water was cloudy enough to conceal our bodies, even from that high teal vantage point, and about three dozen came in, hitting the water smoothly with scarcely a ripple. I stood still, waiting for them to approach the pots.

This standing motionless up to one's neck in water—water that could have some strange things in it—takes some doing. A few fidgets and the teal would be out of here quickly.

I couldn't distinguish De Alwis from Saravanamuttu as they stood in their pots; matter of fact, I didn't know which pots had men in them, but the teal were near, and soon started disappearing, two at a time. I had counted fourteen; now there were six, and I hadn't detected a motion in the water. I could see that this was a brisk, skillful business. The teal didn't seem to notice the disappearance, and then three came right at me. I waited until one was within a foot, reached carefully under the water, grabbed a leg and pulled. He pulled back, let out a loud squawk and took off. So did the others.

De Alwis came over, took off his pot, put his finger to his lips for silence, then put the pot back on and gave me a lesson. His hand moved underwater like that movement of the snake I had seen, maybe even faster; then he clutched his fingers as if he had a teal, and pulled back gently, still underwater, to the basket on his hip. I nodded that I understood and he went back to his place.

I could see that this was really a matter of timing. There could be little lapse between the sudden grip on the bird's submerged legs and the yank underwater.

We waited for an hour for another flock, or for the same one to return. This time a dozen birds landed. The experts took only three before I had my chance with one swimming within ten inches. I made a grab and tried to pull the quacking teal under. But he was strong and he flapped and made a god-awful fluster. I hung on and finally got him into the rattan basket, lost my pot in the process and spooked the rest of the teal.

De Alwis and Saravanamuttu were generous about the whole matter, giving me a half-dozen teal for supper and asking me to join them again. Mary Lou's view of the proceedings was less enthusiastic, but there wasn't any light repartee when the Mount Lavinia's Swiss chef put the potted teal on our table the next night. They were stuffed with rice and so tender that they could almost be cut with a sharp glance.

A couple of days after the tank adventure I received a phone call from Stanley Learned, informing me that the best brains of the island's travel bureau had been working on an itinerary for us, that it was ready, in two parts, and that he would send it over. After dinner that night Mary Lou and I decided that Denzil Wirasinha would be our travel expert; the Ceylon bureau hadn't even vaguely caught our intentions.

The next day we made an all-out effort to find those elusive gypsies. I've always held that unusual people are more interesting than places, that in attempting to find them you nearly always come across much more than you would if you followed the old trails, stuck to the museums, the temples, the "sights to see."

In taking a side road along the ocean, that we ordinarily wouldn't have traveled unless we were searching for the gypsies, we saw a quartet of naked fishermen wading out to sea, paying out a net in a circle, two of them carrying rods and fishing as they laid the net. We passed a little market in a village that sold nothing but giant prawns the size of my hand, bought three for less than fifty cents, took them to the resthouse at Hikkaduwa and had them for lunch. The meat was so white, so sweet and succulent, that it compared favorably with the Maine lobster.

A few miles from our luncheon stop, fifteen men in colored sarongs, looking like a Broadway production of *The King and I,* were constructing a ten-foot dais by piling logs crisscross. "A funeral pyre," said Denzil. "The departed one will be placed on it this afternoon, the family and friends will gather, the fire will be lit, and the soul will depart."

We watched a funeral pyre go up beside the road while hunting for the mysterious Ceylon gypsies.

Passing through an out-of-the-way village so beautiful with flowers that it reminded me of Tennyson's line, "A little street half-garden and half-house," we ran into a procession making its brilliant way. There were nine Buddhist priests in bright orange robes, including two lads probably ten years old, also in robes, also with shaven heads glistening as if they had been oiled. They all carried bamboo fans and black umbrellas to shield their bald heads from the sun.

The boys were solemn and walked in a dignified fashion, heads high, steps measured, umbrellas held in their left hands, their right hands busy building up a breeze with the fans. They smiled but didn't turn their heads when Denzil spoke to them, and one answered in a shrill voice that came piping at us like the sound from a reed instrument. We watched them progressing in their stately, single-file line, a blaze of orange.

We had seen these bald, impressively robed Buddhist priests everywhere on the island, and Denzil had told us that the people consider it a privilege, actually part of their religion, to fill the bowl of any priest who asks. The Buddhist priests seem to be even more respected than the Catholic fathers in Rome or Madrid. We saw little flags flying atop many rooftops. On each flag was printed "Oh, thou jewel in the heart of the lotus flower," which is the most popular prayer to the Lord Buddha. The flags, we were told, were supposed to waft the prayer heavenward, thereby making the way easier for those who flew them. That single drop of water supposed to be found in the heart of the lotus is said to be the purest thing they can offer to Buddha.

We saw many people twirling prayer wheels by hand as they sat and walked. These were brass or wooden cylinders filled with thousands of prayers, or repetitive lines of "Oh, thou jewel in the heart of the lotus flower." Each spin of the wheel sent a prayer to Buddha.

Denzil broke in. "I should have thought of it before. The priests know everything."

"What?"

"That boy priest told me where some gypsies are," he said, smiling as we began to show excitement. "Those are clever little chaps." He ran fingers through his wiry hair, lit a cigarette, sighed and said, "Let's hope the gypsy chaps haven't moved since the priests saw them."

They hadn't. We drove fifteen miles and found them in a grove of coconut palms, their shoulder-high huts constructed of large, dried talipot palm leaves, in overlapping layers, giving the appearance of giant blond tortoises. Entrances were open, the palm leaves cleverly arranged to make the dwellings wind- and rainproof. A little gray donkey was hobbled near each hut, and there were a half-dozen small brown dogs that barked as we got out of the car.

Eight attractive women came out wearing two-piece varicolored cottons. The upper part separated, showing a rim of brown midriff; the skirts were long and flowing. Their dark slanted eyes flashed, then they smiled as Denzil explained our mission. We merely wanted to talk with them, perhaps spend a little time if they didn't mind. It seemed that the men were off on a hunt but would be back soon. The dogs stopped their frenzied barking but not before the camp was aroused and we could see little heads popping out of the huts looking us over. The children came tumbling out, brown, handsome, all smiles, most of them completely bare. A few wore cotton dresses. While we were sitting in the shade of the grove waiting for the men to return Denzil told us about the gypsies. He said that they fascinated everyone on the island.

I suppose if the truth were to be told, most of us are vagabonds at heart, at least in our dreams and inclinations. Having known some of the Romanies of Europe, I'll admit that I have envied their carefree life. Of course, the true gypsies there are fast dying out and being replaced by didicois (half-breeds) or mumpers, poor families who have taken to the road. In Europe the gypsies are considered a social anachronism and are hounded from their camping sites by civic-minded citizens. This strange race, which appeared in Europe from India in the fourteenth century, has spread in small bands throughout the civilized world, and has been persecuted for six centuries. In America their caravans and fortunetellers have been looked upon with joy by children and with suspicion by grownups.

In Ceylon it is different. The government gives them permission to enter nearly any area. Most landowners are happy to have them for a variety of reasons. It is believed that the shrill braying of their donkeys knocks the coconut beetle to the ground. The donkeys then eat the destructive insects. Also, the gypsies hunt things like lizards and rats that the other islanders won't touch. The lizards are eaten; the rats are fed to their captive cobras.

The Ceylon gypsies are also sleight-of-hand specialists with a trick that keeps many rural islanders in their debt. Often they will approach a farmer, or city slicker with a farm or country place, telling him they have seen a cobra on his land. For a fee they offer to take it away. This places the landowner in a quandary. The gypsies may be lying but also they might be telling the truth. The fee they ask is so small that he almost can't afford to refuse. So he tells them he will pay when they produce the cobra. They agree and start searching his land. He watches for a while; then growing tired of the elaborate, slow search, goes to his house. But he still watches as closely as he can. After about an hour the gypsies shout. One comes racing out with a wiggling cobra; the other approaches the owner for the fee, which he always gives with a mingling of reluctance and relief, uncertain whether the gypsies planted one of their own cobras there or actually did find a dangerous snake.

Gypsies raise nothing. They hunt, exhibit their snakes or monkeys in cities or get cash which they use to buy food, but mostly spend for illegal "pot" arrack, the rawest of white alcohol made from the flower of the coconut palm. There are two castes in Ceylon, the snake gypsies who we were with (Aihikuntikayo) and the monkey gypsies (Madhilio). The two never mingle, the snake gypsies holding the monkey clan in contempt, claiming that they eat rats and snakes.

Curried chicken is a favorite of the Aihikuntikayo. They actually go fishing for the birds—in someone else's chicken coop. Using long poles and lines with sharp hooks, they are adept at hooking the chickens in the throat, preventing them from squawking and alerting the owners. By the blunt but well-intended expedient of delivering a dozen bottles of cold beer every day, I became a sort of confidant, and one night I went on a chicken-fishing expedition with them. There were only three of them, two to watch, one to fish. They carried one pole over twelve feet long that reminded me of the old-time two-handed salmon rods. It was a bright night with the moon riding like an airfield searchlight. Mary Lou and Denzil were dead against my going.

" 'Jack Scott was arrested last night on the island of Ceylon as a chicken thief,' reported the Associated Press," Mary Lou said. "I refuse to go with you. If you want to be an idiot, be one by yourself."

"The authorities would be shocked," said Denzil.

Arguments faded after I put across the idea that all I wanted was to observe something remarkably different in fishing techniques. We walked three miles to a farm set back a quarter of a mile from the road. One gypsy went in to scout, returning in ten minutes. Apparently everything was all right, for we then proceeded, moving carefully, casting ten-foot shadows, soon coming to a small chicken house enclosed with a tall wire fence. Without a word one gypsy glided to the right about a hundred yards; the other to the left. The fisherman went to work, standing on a crate he had brought along. It took three casts to get his first bird, caught neatly in the throat. An underfed sort of white leghorn came flapping out. There were about three dozen hens in the enclosure; after the tenth cast and the third hooked chicken, the brood was beginning to get agitated. Without a sound the two gypsy sentries came, beckoned, and we left, the chickens held by the neck so they couldn't sound a warning.

I have seen good men with a flyrod on the rivers of New Brunswick, Newfoundland, Spain, Norway and Scotland, but my chicken-fishing gypsy could have given them all lessons in the art. His casts were long, skillful and deadly accurate—each cast a challenge that the average fisherman would not attempt. If the bird wasn't hooked precisely in the throat, it could rouse the household, and the farmer, his dog and his gun would give even these cautious and resourceful gypsies a bad time.

The next day we were invited for curried chicken. The gypsies are extremely clean, neat people, their pots spotless, their palm huts swept and tidy. The cooking was done by two women over a small, open fire, the chickens cut up and simmering away in a pot blackened by countless log fires, while the curry was prepared by pulverizing small red chilies and a handful of other herbs—one I identified as coriander—in a wooden bowl. Then the milk was taken from four coconuts and put in another pot, the chicken transferred, the home-made curry stirred in, the fire arrested by use of a green palm leaf, and the pot capped with a wet palm leaf. Rice was cooked in the broth of the original chicken pot.

We ate the chunks of spicy chicken over a mound of excellent rice on a palm leaf. The gypsies watched carefully, grinning as it became increasingly evident that their visitors liked vagabond food.

Three days had passed before we had the opportunity to go chicken-fishing with the gypsies and eat that meal. It all started the day we discovered their camp and had to wait two hours for the men to return from the hunt.

They came like victorious warriors, the younger men running ahead with the barking dogs. The tall chief came next with the elders, then the ordinary members of the clan—only a dozen of them, but with the noise and confusion they looked like an advancing barbarian army. Their torsos were bare, gleaming with sweat. Some of the men wore bright red skirts, others white, some flowered in vivid colors. Prancing before them was Japah, the chief's son, a handsome fifteen-year-old in a purple turban, his chest and face shining as though they had been dipped in oil.

The chief was more than six feet, his black uncombed hair swinging wild as a mane as he came over to see what we wanted. His name was Ariaih Moony Ramaswamy. At first he was as arrogant as a bandit chieftain, but soon became friendly.

After entering camp they took the results of the hunt out of a large cloth bag. A half-dozen large monitor lizards popped out spitting like dragons. Two men quickly tied the creatures' tails around their necks so they wouldn't run away. Then they broke off their front claws so they couldn't climb trees. We called it a cruel but practical method of storage. The dogs do the catching, digging the lizards out of anthills. These ugly scaled reptiles are the gypsies' chief diet. The meat is white and as tender as chicken. They eat the best parts; the rest goes to the dogs and the snakes.

Denzil talked with them in Singhalese but claimed that they had their own language—Telugu, a mixture of Tamil and Hindi—which they reverted to when they didn't want you to know what they were saying.

"We believe these are the original gypsy chaps," Denzil said. "Came over from India so long ago that no one knows when. These are snake people."

Sure enough, in half a minute a short bearded fellow got out his flute, sat by a snake basket in the classic pose, started his high weird music, and the painted head of a cobra came out of the basket. The man with the flute was Humamah; he had blue tattoos of birds, tigers, monkeys, lions and snakes on his body. With pearl earrings, a white cloth around his head, curly hair spilling over it, he had a way with the flute, the sound going through the grove like a live thing. The flute was a small brown turnip-shaped gourd, *thiha labba,* tapering at one end into a mouthpiece.

Now another gypsy, Sinaiya, handsome, with a toothbrush mustache, a silver cross hanging from his neck on a chain, came over to sit by the flute player before three reed snake baskets. Three cobras slowly began to dance up, the painted design on the back of their heads looking like frightening clowns' faces. So long as Humamah played his flute the snakes swayed before him, keeping time with his music. There are arguments about these Eastern snake charmers, some critics claiming that all snakes are deaf, so the music can have nothing to do with the seeming hypnotic enchantment. They believe it is the movement of the charmer's body as he sways in time with his own music which causes the snakes to dance. I couldn't tell. But the cobras continued to sway even while Humamah sat still. When the music stopped, the snakes fell back into their baskets, dropping as if dead, the spell broken. Quickly Sinaiya capped on the basket covers —the show was over. Japah, smiling and using his abundant charm, came over with a small reed basket. Denzil dropped a coin in it and we did the same.

The men were now at ease, sitting and talking, some shaving, others skinning lizards. I noticed the white weal of a scar running across the chief's back like the livid mark of a whiplash, and asked Denzil what he thought it was. The forthright Denzil asked him. The chief smiled and told us that when he had been ill several years before with a high fever and much pain, he had had one of his men burn his back to release whatever evil was within him. Then he changed the subject and asked how we liked the *polanga,* the snakes. When we said fine, he smiled and shook his head, making his hair bounce. He told Den-

The gypsies, Sinaiya and Humamah, performed the unusual feat of luring three cobras from their baskets.

zil that his men were the best snake charmers on the island of Ceylon, that they had a pact with all the cobras they captured, releasing them always within five years, often even a year, giving them their liberty to enjoy their twenty-year life span.

Then he got a half-dozen of the children, and they made a little circle, slapping their arms sharply against their bodies in loud splats of sound as they danced. They went on so long that we thought they would split their ribs and we asked Denzil to tell them thanks. They smiled at us, bowed slightly and went back to their mothers who were all beginning to start cooking fires beside the palm huts. The chief came over then, hunkering down beside us, and asked us to stay for a meal of lizard.

Denzil advised us to stay if we wanted to see more of them; otherwise their feelings would be hurt. We had grave doubts about lizard until it came curried and steaming out of the chief's family's black pot, served by his wife, thirty-year-old Sinmana, a lovely woman with a warm smile and skin like brown satin. The lizard was tasty, its flavor reminding me a little of wild turkey. We talked, Denzil translating. We were a long way from the tourist trail.

We discovered that there were a number of gypsy bands on the island, each governed by its own chief who is supreme arbiter in all disputes, marriage broker and priest. The clan under him is a direct reflection of the power and wisdom of his rule. He governs by unwritten law, which Denzil claimed was better observed than the laws of Ceylon. Never does a gypsy end up in court. If there is a major issue or crime, the victim or the accused can make an appeal to the old chief who is the head of all the gypsies on Ceylon. There is a gathering in Anuradhapura at the same time each year for this purpose.

Ariaih told of one extreme punishment, given only when the accused is convicted of a serious offense. A shallow pit is dug, the accused put in. Thorn branches are placed on top of him and driven in by the feet of several gypsies who trample them down. But that rarely happened, he said. He punished mostly by making the accused buy toddy for the tribe. He was a cheery man whose clan reflected his good nature. To amuse us while we were talking, he had one of his men shinny up a tall coconut tree. The climber tied rope from ankle to ankle, which acted as a belt along the trunk of the tree, helping him to ascend. It was a skillful maneuver. The man went up the tree as fast as a monkey; the rope between the ankles moved him steadily as a cable to the top. Once aloft, he thudded three coconuts dangerously close to us. The chief took a curved knife from his waist and deftly split the coconuts in half, giving us each a section. We drank the cool milk, then picked out the white meat, eating as we talked.

He told us that his gypsies made a good living with snake-charming and helping people get rid of cobras on their lands, smiling as he said this. I tried to get an invitation to go along on a snake hunt but he would have none of it, claiming that it was much too dangerous.

He said that gypsies have intimate knowledge of snakes, that they sell stones that have the magic power of sucking out snake venom, and stems of a plant named *nagatharana,* which when held before the cobra, frighten him so that he becomes a coward and flees. His clan also know where to get a root, *suthaclavara mulle,* which the mongoose chews to destroy any poison in his body after he has had a fight with a cobra.

Several times a year his gypsies go after sambur, an elklike animal, tracking it with dogs and using spears as weapons. The chief said proudly that he and his people were considered an asset to any area, for not only did their donkeys rid the coconuts of beetles, but also they and their dogs found and destroyed most of the rats in the region, feeding them to their snakes.

Their meager possessions include knives, spears, axes, cooking pots, donkeys, dogs, and the snakes which are their most prized possession. "We are a happy people," he told Denzil proudly. "We ask no charity. We make no trouble, we dance and sing every night, and we have warm huts and good food. Who can want more?"

Those refreshing days with the gypsies took us away from a civilization that is becoming the same everywhere. Their practicality and common sense are good guidelines for anyone. The chief's wife told Denzil that the dowry a bride offers her husband consists of three pots, a mortar and pestle, a rattan basket with a performing cobra, a flute to charm the snake, a spear, and a trained mongrel dog—a prize food-getter. No nonsense. Each item is aimed at setting up and maintaining their transient household. Our brides could learn.

We were there the day they moved. Ariaih and his son Japah had their talipot palm hut dismantled and folded upon the backs of two donkeys in exactly ten minutes. Another donkey carried household belongings, blankets, palm mats and pots, and a bright-eyed infant. There was something sad about the exodus. It was a strangely quiet operation.

Ariaih was in a somber mood as we said good-bye. His hair wasn't bouncing. He seemed to have acquired more dignity.

"This is our curse," he told Denzil. "We cannot stay in a place longer than one week. This curse was laid upon us for our sin of ill-treating the snakes. If we stay, this ground will breed worms."

We watched them move off, each man leading a donkey, the dogs running easily beside them, the women holding their children by the hand. They waved as they left the palm grove. But not a head turned as the proud little procession went down the dirt road, spirals of dust rising behind them in flags of farewell.

The gypsy chief, Ariaih Moony Ramaswamy, dismantled his palm leaf hut and prepared to pack it on his burro.

The Ceylon sun was setting, giving off rays like thrown spears around the old woman who sat beside a pile of water-soaked coconut husks. Beating these with a rock, she was breaking them into fiber to be plaited into rope. Four feet from her was a belt of lush green grass. As I moved closer, raising one foot to step on the grass, she stared coldly. Denzil suddenly shouted, "Stop! Don't move!" Without another word, he picked up a rock and heaved it at the green grass. It plopped and gurgled as it sank in deep water.

"Another foot and you would have been in slimy water fourteen feet deep," he said. He went on to tell me that the "grass" was a water plant introduced into Ceylon during World War II as a means to destroy Japanese flyers. From the air the green plant looked like a level landing strip. The Japs would come in for a landing, and plop— the plane and man would disappear.

"A good idea then," Denzil said, "but now it has become a pest in Ceylon, growing all over the island, wherever there is water."

The old woman knew what the grass was hiding but she just sat there staring impassively. Maybe seeing a stranger vanish into the slime was her idea of amusement. "Fooled you, you old monster," I said. She smiled, showing two teeth and a lot of ancient gum.

We were on another excursion that had started a couple of days after we watched the gypsies break camp. Denzil, as usual, led into it in his tantalizing way.

"I've found some shells for your shotguns, sir," he said.

"Yes?"

"I've been thinking that while you are here, perhaps you would like to do our rice-growers a favor, and perhaps have some good wing-shooting besides."

"Sounds good. What does it involve?"

"Well, it's a sort of waterfowl, a bird of peacock blue—"

"Peacock blue? Is it a game bird?"

"Yes, sir! This chap is a game bird all right and we want them shot too, sir. They do much damage to rice-paddy cultivation, eating not only the newly sown and ripening grain but also the tender stalks of the growing paddy."

"But just what is it?"

"Well, sort of a duck chap. In Singhalese it is also called a *vil-kukula,* but most of us use the Tamil word for it, *kitta.* Its length is about seventeen inches and it is purplish-blue. It has a bright red beak and red legs; the feet are rather webbed, but it doesn't have the spoon bill of the duck. And those chaps are delicious. *Kitta,* and a little rice with a spot of arrack, and I'd say you have the best meal in Ceylon."

But the trouble was finding the blue bird. After I had almost met the wet death, we went on to a tank where Denzil was sure there were *kitta*. Here we met four teen-agers, the De Silva family, who took me out in a boat that looked like a sleeping crocodile. The water was shallow and muddy and I fell out twice before I realized that balance was all that kept one aboard. But I kept my gun dry and finally, with some pushing and pulling, we got the boat into water deep enough to navigate.

About the only words in English that the boys knew seemed to be "shoot," and "don't shoot," and they sometimes got these mixed up. Twice I brought down coots, smaller than any species I had ever gunned. The boys were pretty glum about them.

I kept saying *kitta,* and they kept shaking their heads. Finally I saw the brown eyes of the smallest De Silva brighten. He pointed and said, "Shoot!" It looked like a brace of cinnamon teal on the water

"The De Silva family . . . took me out in a boat that looked like a sleeping crocodile."

about one hundred yards ahead. I couldn't shoot at that distance even if I wanted to and I asked the De Silvas to move closer. We got in about thirty yards and sure enough three birds took off with that telltale teal zing. I got lucky and dropped two. As I was shaking hands with one of the boys, there was a flurry in reeds twenty yards from us, and something went through the air that looked like a blue-bird that had never stopped growing. I fought to get my hand loose from the admiring grip of the strongest of the De Silvas. He grinned broadly and said, *"Kitta!"* I will not record what I said.

That was all we saw of the vaunted *kitta* that day. Somehow we got the boat to shore and I gave the De Silva brood six ducks and two coot. They weren't the best boatmen or the most skilled duck guides I have ever met, but they were the most enthusiastic.

As I left they kept asking, *"Kitta? Kitta?"* and laughing. I never did find out what the joke was. The *kitta* had become no laughing matter. We spent the next three days touring as many tanks and rice paddies as we were permitted to enter. Nearly every paddy owner welcomed us when Denzil explained that we were after *kitta*. "Ver' ver' good," they said. "Kill the *kitta*. *Kitta* is the enemy of rice plants, those chaps the enemy of people of Ceylon."

The only difficulty was that they seemed to be a hidden enemy, or one that had gone underground. Denzil explained that actually they were all around us, but they were clever. "You see, sir, these chaps hear us coming and they sneak into thick paddy or reed growth and hide until we pass by. Unless we step right on them I don't think they will get into the air." At this point I was beginning to think that maybe I was the butt of some local joke.

The next step was to consult with a friend of Denzil—Sanchez, a car mechanic in a Colombo garage. "This chap is a real hunter, sir," said Denzil. "He knows about bird-shooting. I should have thought of him before—"

Sanchez did know all about bird-shooting. "The *kitta*," he said, "is not such a fast flyer. He is wary, hard to get into the air. But once he's up, he isn't as difficult to hit as a snipe or a teal." He went on to tell Denzil about paddy fields and a tank two hours from Colombo. "The paddy fields will be in water," he said, "and the noise you will make will drive the *kitta* out into the tank. Go prepared to do some wading." He told us of two boys living near the tank who knew the habits and the location of the *kitta*. We seemed to be making head-way.

Driving from village to village, we finally found the boys, enthusiastic *kitta*-hunters, Spmanader and Daniloo. We drove to the paddies, enormous ones. The rice had been harvested and, as Denzil's friend had said, were full of water.

We rolled up our trousers and got into the mud, the two boys ahead of us in loincloths, moving fast. They gabbled something back to Denzil. He translated. "They say to hunt the *kitta,* you must be quick. They already saw five. They are running through the paddies heading for the tank."

What followed would have made an interesting film sequence. We pulled our feet out of the muck of the paddies as fast as we could, splashing muddy water as high as our eyebrows. Then I saw the *kittas.* They were running through that mud as if it was a racetrack. They were too far away, but I saw that the paddy did run almost into the tank, and the birds would have to take to the air or swim the pond.

Nine of them took off, the sun striking blue fire from their beautiful plumage. They were such an inspiring sight that I just stood and stared. By the time I was through admiring them, they were out of range but down on the ground again, not far from the pond. The two boys just stood and looked at me. Denzil chuckled. "Pretty chaps, aren't they, sir?"

"The most vivid blue I've seen," I said. "If they weren't such destroyers of rice paddies, it would seem a shame to gun them—"

"Just consider that they're rogue birds, sir," Denzil said slyly.

Now something else happened to prevent me from getting a closeup of a *kitta.* Moving carefully, we got within twenty yards of the birds before they took to the air like a Broadway production. I dropped two just across the pond in a clump of tall reeds. One of the boys searched for them, hidden from our view as he looked. In ten minutes he came back, shaking his head. He said something rapidly to Denzil; translation brought out that a pair of giant lizards were in the underbrush, had the birds that we shot and were eating them. "Vicious chaps, they are," Denzil said. "Big as a dog and can cut a man badly with their tails. There is a large fine, perhaps imprisonment, if you kill one. They eat the worms that attack the rice plants in the paddy. Our government protects them zealously."

Finally we worked out a plan. The boys would go into the bushes with large sticks and drive the lizards into the open, preferably into the tank, out of our way should we drop any more *kittas* in their lair. They did it, but it took some eloquent urging from Denzil.

The lizards came tearing out of the undergrowth like a nightmare.

They were as large as a half-grown alligator and scaly, shooting out long tongues and whipping tails like swords. They were small dragons. I was glad that I wasn't the one annoying them. They went into the water, swam the pond and disappeared.

We waited silently for an hour and then the *kitta* flights began. They exploded from the paddies in frequent small bursts of color. Wading waist-deep, Mary Lou and I managed to bag a half-dozen.

I examined the *kittas* closely. They looked something like coots that had got glory.

I said, "Denzil, would you like—"

I never saw him move so fast. In milliseconds he had three *kitta* in each hand, saying, "Thank you, sir. My wife likes these chaps better than fresh beef."

So we never got a chance to see what this mysterious *kitta* was like between knife and fork, and it was doubtful if we could be talked into hunting this brainy bluebird again. It would take two days to recover from this bout. Denzil's suggestion before we left, to visit the gem mines and maybe do a little skin-diving or underwater-fishing, sounded relaxing.

"Don't you think that Denzil is a little too zealous?" Mary Lou said as we reached the hotel that night. "He's got something going every minute."

"He's only trying to show us that there is more here than meets the tourist's eye."

"I know," she said, "but sometimes this being the traveler is a little tiring. That *kitta* expedition has me thinking with favor on things like tour buses and a gentle day by the sea."

We broke into the fishing in easy stages, first going out of Hikkaduwa in a glass-bottomed boat, peering at the vast beds of pink and white coral, watching the fish—some like lighted gems in a jeweler's showcase, others large and dangerous-looking. The latter moved through the coral alleys like prowling wolves. "Grouper," said Denzil. "Harmless, good to spear, good to eat." The man who owned the boat had a knot of hair at the nape of his neck and his head speared with a jeweled, circular crown comb. Denzil told us this is supposed to be a mark of high caste, attesting that the wearer's head has never carried a burden.

After the boat trip we went scuba-fishing—the simple way, using goggles, swim fins and the snorkel. We each had a small spear gun, which was fired by compressed air and was as easy to operate as an ordinary rifle. We swam along the surface, occasionally submerging our faces and looking for fish.

The second day we tried going deeper and did rather well. Mary Lou speared two mackerel of fair size, and I got a Jack—probably an amberjack—a creature of rainbow hue that had a lot of life in it.

Toward mid-afternoon, we were coming back to shore, which was less than one hundred yards off, when I saw a huge shadow. Experienced scuba men, the cautious ones who are still around to talk about it, have told me that the time to get out of the water is that moment when you see something larger than you. This is the yardstick the big fish use before attacking. If they're bigger than you are, it is possible that they will attack—especially sharks and barracuda. But this shadow vanished as quickly as it came. I didn't see it again as we swam shoreward. Three days in those crystal waters of the Indian Ocean off Hikkaduwa brought no other scares. It was the most relaxing time we had had in many months.

A wise friend once told me that the best investment in life is memories. I believe him. Those hours in a blue sea full of sun, off a beautiful tropical island, have supplied me with memories that come back often, bringing a peace and tranquillity of mind hard to come by in this hectic time. Today when I sit in a traffic jam I often click on this memory and the ulcerous period disappears.

You may remember the old story in *The Arabian Nights' Entertainments* in which the adventurer writes: "The island of Sarandeeb is under the equinoctial line; its night being always twelve hours, and its day also twelve hours. Its length is eighty leagues; and its breadth, thirty; and it extendeth largely between a lofty mountain and a deep valley. This mountain is seen from a distance of three days, and it containeth varieties of jacinths, and different kinds of minerals and trees of all sorts, of spices, and its surface is covered with emery wherewith jewels are cut into shape; in its rivers also are diamonds, and pearls are in its valleys." The ancient traveler then went on to tell about the gifts of precious stones and "a cup of ruby a span high" that he delivered to the Caliph Harun-al-Rashid in Arabia. He was writing about Ceylon; of Ratnapura, the "City of Gems," in particular.

Ratnapura lies fifty-six miles from Colombo in a hollow surrounded by hills. The world's largest sapphire, 466 carats after being cut and polished, was found there. We found it a place to stir the imagination with its busy goldsmiths' shops, the gem dealers arguing in the streets, the hypnotic open stalls where Moorish gem cutters sat on the floor carefully moving their polishing wheels to get the right facet here, the correct bevel there—working with such concentration that you could stand and stare for an hour and the craftsman would never lift his head. Most of the "gemming" for sapphires, rubies, cat's-eyes and other stones is carried on in the low-lying wet land where the illam, or gem-bearing gravel, is found at depths from four to fifteen feet. We watched one operation where pits were dug, then surrounded with long flat stakes to prevent the sides from caving in. The man we were watching wore only a breechcloth, his brown body shining like a polished statue. He worked much as our Western pros-

We saw a man "gemming" with a heavy reed basket which retained only the precious gravel.

pectors did in the old days, panning the streams for gold. His "pan" was a heavy reed basket designed to let everything but gem gravel sift through.

Another method was used in the rivers, where the gravel was dragged up by hand with seventeen-foot wooden hoes, then washed in cone-shaped baskets; the principle being that the stones sink to the bottom. I mucked around in the stuff and came up with a small cat's-eye that I had cleaned and polished. Remember the old poet's line, "And all the world a ruby for your finger ring"? Well, today I wear the world of Ceylon in a ring. Whenever the sun or a bright light hits the smoky cat's-eye, memories of that fabled island stir and the dreams come alive again.

Two miles from Ratnapura is a temple worth driving out of your way to see. It is Sama Dewale, a shrine housing the golden bow and arrow of the God Buddha. After an hour in the temple, we drove down from the hills and through the ricelands, following the sea back toward Colombo. Denzil slowed to fifteen miles an hour and we crept along, caught in the peace of this old land. The sun, blazing like ignited oil on the Indian Ocean, suddenly highlighted some odd figures.

We stopped and sat watching a half-dozen men on stilts standing in quiet offshore water like giant predatory birds. They fished for hours strapped to those tall stilts, their poles protruding like bird tongues darting for insects.

"Now, sir," Denzil said, as he started the car, "I think before you leave the island you should act just a wee bit like a tourist chap. You must see our fortress in the sky, Sigiriya Rock." He touched the brakes to make his point. "You haven't done any planned sightseeing yet," he said accusingly. "This rock is living history, sir! Those chaps had quite a time back in the old days."

I don't recall if I mentioned that Denzil was a man of colorful, even poetic expression, which was especially evident just after we had stopped at one of those little palm-thatched go-downs and he had had a quick glass of milky toddy, a sour and potent drink distilled from the flower of the coconut palm.

"I mention going to Sigiriya," he said, "because we are already halfway there. It is a village situated 103 miles from Colombo, famous for its massive rock built into a fortress by a king."

He went on talking like a combination travel-folder writer, native historian and representative of the tourist department. It seems that in the fifth century King Dhatusena was ruler over Ceylon. He had two sons: Kasyapa, by a wife of inferior birth, and Maggallana, born of a wife of noble birth. He also had a daughter who was married to the commander-in-chief of his army.

One morning Dhatusena's daughter complained to him that the commander-in-chief had whipped her savagely. Weals on her body proved her statement. In a fit of fury Dhatusena had her husband's mother burned to death.

Powerless to avenge his mother's death by a physical attack, the commander-in-chief did the next best thing. He used the king's low-born son Kasyapa as a convenient instrument.

What wiles he used, history does not reveal, but it is evident that they were effective: Kasyapa not only turned against his father, but had him buried alive. Then he seized the throne and converted the Rock of Sigiriya into a fortress. His brother Maggallana fled to India.

Eighteen years later Maggallana returned with an army and met Kasyapa's forces on the plains at the foot of the rock. When the battle had turned decisively against him, Kasyapa committed suicide.

It was with great skill that Kasyapa built that fortress-palace. A storage tank, cisterns, sentry boxes and living quarters occupied four acres on the rock's summit. Every inch of space was used. Elaborate precautions had been taken against damage in any form. A carefully planned drainage system captured water from the heaviest downpour of rain, ran it over the edge of the summit to a cistern below, and from there by easy stages to the plains.

After about an hour of this storytelling, Denzil stopped the car before what looked like a flat-topped mountain. It was a geological freak rising six hundred feet straight up out of the landscape.

"Sigiriya!" said Denzil, making a sweeping gesture with his right hand. "A monument of which even Pharaoh could have been proud."

Following limestone steps we came to a four-foot gallery flanked by a parapet wall twisting around the rock. An overhanging crag shielded the wall from sun and rain. This, according to Denzil, is called the Mirror Wall, on which are inscribed the famous Sigiriya graffiti, writings going back to the sixth century. The graffiti consist of 650 verses, their characters varying from one-eighth of an inch to three-fourths of an inch.

Denzil was talking in a reverent whisper now, which somehow fitted this ancient place. "No one knew what the writings were until three years ago when our Commissioner of Archaeology, Dr. Paranavitarne, after years of study discovered that they belonged to verse-making contests in which wit played a large part." He pointed to one cabalistic white line. "This reads 'Hail, O friend, the damsels indeed are at present deformed in certain parts. In certain places their color is faded. Are there none whose hearts were attached to them in those days?' "

We went higher, taking a newly built spiral stairway to come close to a rock pocket forty feet above the gallery. This was covered with vivid frescoes of twenty-one big-busted maidens in various forms of undress. We stood watching the light play on these nearly nude ladies of long ago and listened to Denzil as he told us more about this rock. On the summit was a tank, still full of clear water, and a perfectly planned garden.

As we went down the twisting stairway Denzil said, "A clever chap, King Kasyapa. He had everything here."

"Not so clever," said Mary Lou. "Why did he leave a protected place like this to go out on the plains to die? They never could have reached him here."

Denzil looked at her and said, "Madam, you have a point. I never thought of it just that way." He was silent all the way back to Colombo.

We arrived at Reclamation Street in Colombo at 5:30, toddy time. The dock workers and laborers and Tamil women in their soiled saris were gathered at the dozens of toddy taverns that line this waterfront area, many of them sitting on the curbs drinking the milky stuff from coconut shells. Others clustered in groups, tilting their evening cocktails from bottles. It was a noisy session as they stood eating and drinking, laughing and singing. The sour odor of fermented toddy rose from the street. The lights started coming on in the little taverns, giving a festive air.

As we neared Mount Lavinia we asked Denzil if he would come and get us in the morning and drive us to the airport for the next leg of our journey. Tomorrow we would leave for Thailand.

He walked to the lobby with us, then suddenly said, "Our King Kasyapa was sort of a dumb chap at that, wasn't he?" Then he said good-bye and stood in the lobby until we had gone. When we got to our room he was in the street looking up. He gave us a lonely wave.

The crows had come into the room again. We shooed them out and stood on the balcony and watched the moon shine on the Indian Ocean. Waves were washing white on shore; the turtle rocks crouched in the sugar sand. The palm trees were still gracefully nodding, and a woman was walking along the beach, the wind lifting her red sari.

CHAPTER THREE

THAILAND AND CAMBODIA

One of the advantages of air travel is a dramatic arrival. As we flew over Bangkok, the sun glittered on red-tiled roofs and the spires of hundreds of Buddhist temples gave us the impression that it was being guarded by thousands of raised spears. The bus ride from Don Muang airport to Bangkok is eighteen miles but worth every second of the jolting journey. Roadwork was being done by slender women who looked as if they had just stepped out of the pages of the resort issue of *Vogue*. They wore long wrap-around colored skirts of red, orange and flaming pink, and straw lampshade hats over scarfs tied under their chins. Men in wet fields walked behind plodding black water buffaloes trailing ancient wooden plows, probably planting a ricefield. Often as we watched, a bare-chested peasant sank up to his knees in the ooze. Then the buffalo turned a patient head and stared back at him until forward motion began. In narrow canals running along both sides of the road, men in *praus*—slender, pointed boats loaded with vegetables and fruits—stopped and waved wooden paddles at our bus, while the bus driver kept up a monotonous running commentary in a strange high English.

"Thailand is situated in Southeast Asia between Burma on the west and Laos and Cambodia on the east. We have land area of 198,247 square miles and a population estimated at 23,219,287, made up of ninety percent Thai, 3.4 percent Chinese, 3.4 percent Indian and Malayan, others 3.2 percent. Beautiful Thai people come from Yangtze River valley in China in thirteenth century." He paused for breath, waited for two water buffaloes and five men in shorts to saunter across the road, then cranked up the high voice again.

"Bangkok with two million peoples is largest city in Southeast Asia. There are over three hundred temples in Bangkok; though we only nine hundred miles from equator, our temperature is moderate and best month' are November through Februar' when temperature ranging from sixty-two to eight'-four. May through September are the rainy month' with the temperature going as ninety-five." He ended on what could roughly be described as a high note as he brought the bus to a stop before the Erawan Hotel. "This is our first and last stop," he said proudly. "We hope you enjoy joyous, gracious Thailand."

After a blank no at the Erawan, we began the weary trudge to other, overcrowded hotels—the Oriental, King, Plaza, Princess and six others—finally ending up in a dim, dank, airless fleabag where we shared a bath with two others. The unmade bed was still warm from former occupancy. On a shelf in the bathroom was a dirty comb full of shiny black hairs, a shaving brush with vestiges of soap and an open package of Gillettes. If one had the time and the inclination, it could be interesting to ruminate upon what sort of traveler had just left this hot, humid room. We were out in ten minutes, in a cab to SAS where I sat with the manager—sorry that I hadn't sent him a cable days ago—while he called for a room fit for human habitation. This was to be a brief stop. We were actually on our way to the Philippines, but felt that Thailand would be exciting. Or so we thought.

Getting to SAS was itself an adventure. We stopped a cab with a young driver wearing a short-billed uniform cap who sat indolently behind the wheel, cigarette dangling from his mouth. He said, "Where-youwannago?" I told him the SAS offices, and he took off with a jerk. The ride was a little over a mile. Before he stopped he said over his shoulder, "Eighty baht!" Boning up on exchange on the plane before we landed, I knew that twenty baht is about a dollar and I refused to pay it, enunciating slowly, "This is too much for this short ride! But I will be generous. I will pay you forty baht. This is still twenty baht too much."

He leaped from his seat as we got out of the Austin, waving his arms and screeching, "Liar, cheat! American robber!" until a crowd gathered, all evidently on the side of the cab driver. I took Mary Lou by the arm and hustled her into the SAS offices. There a beautiful young lady behind the ticket counter—who I later discovered was a Thai princess—upon hearing my story and seeing the cab driver beating at the door, advised me to pay what he asked.

"You made the mistake of not settling the price before you got into his cab," she said sweetly.

"How could I know? I've been in your country exactly two hours." She kept shaking her head negatively, a fixed smile on a face that was rapidly losing its beauty. While the cab driver shouted and rattled the door, I asked for the manager. The calm Norwegian who came agreed with me. I gave him the forty baht and he gave it to the princess and said, "Send him away!" She did it in bad grace, scowling as she went to the door.

From that time on we had a running battle with cab drivers. They rule the city, taking visitors for as much as they can. The efficient-looking police in khakis, white helmets and Sam Browne belts, and others, like the uncoöperative little ticket-selling princess, ignore the situation, or are in league with the cabby gangsters. This can take much of the pleasure from a visit. But I was determined that it wouldn't place Bangkok in a bad light and I got as tough as the drivers, settling on a reasonable fee or not getting into the cab. Often I let hotel doormen take care of the haggle, but then they extracted so much for doing this that the whole thing turned out to be a losing battle. It became common practice to bargain with six drivers in order to get a cab to take us on a three-mile trip.

The SAS manager finally did get us a decent hotel, the Ratanako-sin, which cost nineteen dollars a day and was a distance from just about everything. It was an enormous pile of tan granite blocks, the façade sooty and all in all, a cold, uninspired place. But the room was air-conditioned and after about a day of licking our wounds at the "Rat," as it is called in Bangkok, we were ready for the city.

We are dedicated cat-fanciers, so from the moment we entered Siam we started looking for Siamese cats. In two days we hadn't seen one. I suddenly remembered talking with a traveler who had said that they were kept inside, in homes, in temples, or on the boats in the Floating Market. So we made our way to the Floating Market.

The manager of SAS had suggested Harry's Tours on New Road near the Princess Hotel. In ten minutes we were in the hands of a smiling young guide. "I am Sobham Sotara," he said, "but to you please call me Joe. You American. All Americans like call me Joe. This is nice name. I like you call me Joe." Within minutes he was telling us that he was studying photography at the Technical Institute in Bangkok. He wanted to become a great artist with the camera and come to the United States and give us the benefit of his art. He kept studying Mary Lou's cameras, the Tele-Rolleiflex, the Nikons, F and SP. He asked us more questions than we asked him. But questions weren't really needed. All that was necessary was to sit in the boat and watch this ancient spectacular in full color.

We started off in Harry's Tours craft, a fifteen-foot inboard motor-boat moored behind the Oriental Hotel, and chugged up the Chao Phraya River, "The Mother of Waters," on our way to one of the many branching canals. Our boatman cut through the traffic of floating houses, barges, paddle boats, sampans, steam launches, *praus,* sometimes skillfully, sometimes with idiot abandon. When Joe could get his eyes off our cameras he said, "Two Floating Market. We for Klong Bang Luang."

As we came in sight of a huddle of gleaming tin and tile-roofed buildings we moved off the river into a broad canal, the water flowing brown and heavy as syrup. "This it," said Joe, ever the perfect guide. Now there were only sampans, some partially covered with bamboo

The Floating Market was an Oriental hubbub of color and confusion where East met West.

matting, and the *praus*. The latter were loaded with food of every kind, and the boats were paddled by two women in lampshade straw hats, or by men in khaki shorts. One that attracted my attention was a floating butcher shop. The man was paddling with one hand, arranging a pig's head to the best advantage with the other.

One sampan, with two women who could make forty dollars an hour as models in Manhattan, had a load of onions, dried fish, roasted ducks and baskets of tiny red peppers. In another a woman leaned across to a *prau* and traded a duck for a basket of garlic and eggplant. One *prau* was loaded with dirty-white duck eggs; another was alive with white chickens; while still another had a half-dozen very dead-looking suckling pigs. Everywhere the trading and bartering was going on with much smiling and waving of thin, elegant hands. The buyers were mostly housewives afloat looking for bargains. In one flower-banked craft was a slim woman and three little boys, their hair in topknots. Joe pointed at the boys. "Topknots are for lucky," he said. "Kids wear until twelve year old."

Thai children were everywhere, the most beautiful youngsters I have seen, with their luminous brown almond eyes, their perfectly shaped skulls and honey-brown skin. When they saw foreigners they shouted, *"Lai! Lai!"* which Joe said meant *"Welcome! Welcome!"*

The youngsters kept diving from the boats and swimming to the unique houses on stilts along the shore, sometimes delivering a purchase, holding it high out of the water with one hand while sidestroking with the other; some just jumped in, splashed around, submerged, then popped to the surface spouting water, as graceful as dolphins. This sounds like fun, a colorful and pleasant sight among the market craft on this old canal where bartering had been going on just this way for hundreds of years. It was and it wasn't, for floating on the turgid water were dead things, a goose, decomposed chickens, unsalable fish, debris of all kinds. From one canalside home a young girl dunked breakfast dishes in the water, an old woman sank a full basket of rice—cleaning it, she thought.

As two dead dogs floated by, bloated and almost hairless, Joe said, "This year we send thirty thousand dogs to Hong Kong. Chinese he eat dogs. Thai don't eat." Then I remembered something I had read about Thailand. Two years ago five thousand Thais had died of cholera along this ribbon of dirty water; over twenty thousand had been struck with the disease in a country the size of Texas.

But we weren't here to watch diseased dogs floating in the Klong Bang Luang. We wanted to find the country's seal points—Siamese cats. Mary Lou had asked Joe. She should have known better. Now every time he saw a cat Joe shouted, "There cat!" startling us and the occupants of the boat where the animal lived; twice men held their paddles motionless, staring at Joe in surprise. Mary Lou attempted to explain that we were looking for the real Siamese cat so well known throughout the world—the seal point with blue eyes.

"Oh, *oh!*" said Joe sagely. "These cat on boat Si Sawat. You call for Dok Lao."

Mary Lou nodded in bewilderment. "Where can we find Dok Lao?"

"I not know," said Joe. "I hating cats."

It was dusk when we returned after traveling more canals and taking lunch at a curious waterside teahouse. We sat by the Klong and talked for hours, Mary Lou and Joe exchanging photographic doubletalk. As we moored behind the Oriental Hotel, little lights began to blink on in the gently bobbing boats. Savory smells from cooking fires wafted from the canals. The trill of a woman's nightsong rose above the creak of boats, the splash of paddles, and the faint roar of taxis on New Road. Joe suggested that we go to Sampeng Lane. "World's narrowest street," he said, walking ahead and leading the way.

Sampeng Lane was an alley, not much wider than a man's body. I recommend it for anyone who wants to get the color of a country—fast. Smells were raw; the crowd Chinese, Malays, Indians; much of the riffraff of the Far East washed in here, all selling anything from paste jewelry to overripe fruit and fish. A blind man standing against the ruin of a building poked at us with a bamboo stick, probably smelling that we were foreigners. One bearded old fellow in a filthy turban, a tattered Bengali shirt and little else, held a long-dead fish so close to me I could see that its scales were stiff with age. A man in a faded pink robe trotted after us singing "A Foggy Day in London Town" in a weird, high voice, obviously not understanding a word of the song. One dark character in a burnooselike hood kept trying to place an enormous white cockatoo on Mary Lou's shoulder.

Bangkok is a temple town. Guidebooks say the city has three hundred of the spired beauties. Four hundred would be more accurate. Cat-lovers in the United States have long been convinced that the Siamese are temple cats, that they are sacred in Siam, that every temple has one. This isn't exactly factual, and the temples aren't really temples. They are Buddhist monasteries located in compounds called *wats,* where there are several other buildings. The largest is the

Bote, the place of prayers, and is usually the most beautiful and imposing in the group. The entire area is a religious sanctuary and every animal in it is supposed to be sacred, which means that life cannot be taken. If there is a Siamese cat in this compound, it is protected like every other creature there. White, the symbol of purity for the Siamese, is worn at all rites and ceremonies. Because Siamese kittens are born white they are given especially respectful treatment while in this stage. Such is the extent of "sacredness" of Siamese felines. I am sorry if I have upset the thinking of the cat set, but these are the facts given to me by a Buddhist monk.

We started searching the *wats* for cats. This could have gone on for weeks if I hadn't talked with the monk. Future travelers who want to look over the best of these religious edifices can profit by our trudge. Probably the most beautiful temple is the Wat Benchamabopit, built entirely of elegant Carrara marble; the most extensive is Wat Po, which has a reclining Buddha forty-nine meters in length. The structure is twelve meters high, built of brick, covered with cement, then gilded; the Wat Indra Viharn is probably the most active of all the temples. It has a huge yellow Buddha standing thirty-two meters, and is highly venerated by Bangkok residents. The Emerald Buddha, Phra Kaeo, stands thirty-one inches high on a thirty-four-meter golden throne in the Wat Phra Kaeo, where we talked with the monk.

These shaven-headed monks abhor the killing of living creatures, theft, adultery, untruthfulness, drunkenness. They observe absolute chastity, live exclusively from alms, do not take food after midday, turn from worldly distractions, are against perfumes and finery of any kind, and will not traffic in gold or silver.

Our man was slim, the first Buddhist monk I ever saw who didn't appear overweight. The people feed them so well that even with the one meal a day that they beg with their rice bowls, they all seem to thrive. This one stood before the Wat Phra Kaeo on the grounds of the royal palace, his saffron robes flaming in a shaft of sunlight. He was smiling as I approached.

"Your temples are beautiful," I said, trying to move him to speech.

He looked at me, still smiling.

"We've been looking for your famous cat, the one with the blue eyes and the dark face. The temple cat, the one that is sacred."

"Every living thing is sacred," he said. "I have just talked with one of your countrymen who told me that he is a jeweler and that our Emerald Buddha is not emerald, after all, but jasper. Very interesting. He has a sharp eye. Fortunately we have known this for centuries. But I did not tell the good man. He was being helpful." His smile returned.

He went on to tell us that the cats used to be seen around the temples often, but not so much in recent years. "I see few of the dark-faced ones these days, mostly the silver with the orange eye, the one we call Si Sawat, or Khorat, believing that it comes from our northern province by that name. It is our belief that most of the others, the dark-faced ones with the blue eyes, the Nopakow, are in America."

Returning to the Ratanakosin, I mentioned our search to the hotel desk clerk, a dapper old man who spoke seven languages. He laughed. "Why didn't you ask me? You could have saved yourself time. But it was good for you. You've seen more of Bangkok than you would have, had you put yourselves in the hands of an organized tour." He went to his desk, returning with a slip of paper. "Here is your man."

The name was Chompoo Arthachinda; the address, 7 Boon Siri Road. "A famous lawyer," the clerk said. "A nice chap who has many cats." We went to his office after telephoning for an appointment. "Not law," I said. "Cats."

"My favorite subject," he replied. "Do come along."

His office was up two flights in an enormous old building less than a half-mile from our hotel. One large room was filled to capacity with desks, girls at typewriters, and men hunched over ledgers or standing at steel filing cabinets. Mr. Arthachinda was a successful lawyer. He was dressed in a white linen suit and had that honey-brown skin peculiar to the Siamese, brown eyes that sparkled, and a smile that put you at ease immediately.

"We are told that you have the world's largest cat house," I said, regretting the corny wordplay immediately.

He stopped smiling, looked at me intently for a second, then laughed. "Maybe not the world's. But surely Bangkok's."

After twenty minutes of getting acquainted we went down to his car and he drove us to his home. As he drove he told us his feelings about his cats. "I have several hundred," he said, "several color phases that I am developing. The seal point is native to Siam, but I believe that the blue point was bred in your country. As a matter of fact, you Americans have taken most of our good specimens and I am devoting myself to bringing them back to Siam. It was not unusual for you to look for days and not discover a seal point. In the old days the good specimens that were found around our temples were often put into the hands of dependable villagers who would breed them and return a kitten to the temple or let the monks distribute them. Then you cat-lovers and dealers descended and before we knew it, all of our beautiful cats were gone. I shouldn't say all. But in truth I am only interested in breeding wonderful specimens and seeing them about our country the way they used to be."

We entered a winding drive that took us up to a house that looked Spanish with its brilliant tiled roof and cream stucco. At eye level to the right of the residence was a toy house on a post. Mr. Arthachinda excused himself and bowed respectfully before it.

He returned and explained that many of the homes in Bangkok had the miniature monastic temples called Phra Phum, which means lord of the land and is the shrine or the guardian spirit of the house. "The first thing we do when our land is cleared and our house built is find a suitable place for Phra Phum. Only certain persons versed in the art can tell us where to build it and it can be erected only on certain astrologically calculated days or months. The shrine must face either north or south, preferably north. A mound of earth is raised, the shrine erected in its center. Great care must be taken that no shadow from the residence falls on it. Otherwise the Phra Phum will not come and stay in the shrine. This is so because man and spirit are of different worlds and cannot logically live in the same place." He pointed to some candles, a bouquet of flowers and some fruit before the tiny temple with its three-tiered sweeping roofs. "We make daily offerings."

We followed him along a path to an enclosure, and went in behind him as he carefully opened and closed the gate. Here, under wire, were more cats than I have ever seen in one place in my life. They had so many colors and combinations of colors that one run of them looked like a bed of iris. Three men were moving among the cats, feeding and watering them; the runs were spotless, the wire of a strong and expensive variety. Mr. Arthachinda asked us to remove our shoes if we wanted to go inside to see the cats more closely. "Diseases are carried on our feet," he explained.

I immediately fell for a solid chocolate that stood looking up at me. Mary Lou was so busy with her cameras that she seemed to have six hands.

Mr. Arthachinda proudly pointed out the different types while we walked. As he talked I suddenly realized that I knew absolutely nothing about these animals that had been in my life for so long. There were seal points, blue points, solid chocolates, chocolate points—and

The cat farm in Bangkok—"They had so many colors and combinations of colors that one run of them looked like a bed of iris."

"Mr. Arthachinda proudly pointed out the different types while we walked."

the silvery Khorat. "This may be the cat of the future," he said. "I call it Siamese blue and am trying to breed in the bright blue eye of the nine gem seal point."

We walked into other wired areas, each with its well-built cat house at the rear. Here were cats in colors seen nowhere else in the world; startling lavender points, red points, lilac points, black points. Points simply mean that the cat is a solid shade with the distinguishing color on the tip of its tail, part way up the feet and legs, on the face, ears and tail. There were cats so beautiful and unusual that we just stood and stared.

I still was fascinated by that solid chocolate and asked if I could purchase one. He shook his head gently, saying, "I do not think I want to let my cats out of Siam; especially I don't want them in the hands of Americans. You people are so enthusiastic that you immediately set about 'improving' a breed or designing a new version." No, none was for sale, at least right now. He had spent a fortune on this hobby, a patriotic endeavor if I ever saw one.

Later at the Sukasom Restaurant, one of the few where you can get genuine Thai food, not the fancied-up Chinese version, I did manage to give him a check for a chocolate and extract a promise that it would be flown to me when I returned to the States.

The Sukasom, in the Thai Niyom Building, Pharn Fah, opposite the Charlem Thai Theater, is seldom discovered by tourists and travelers and is presided over by a motherly woman who comes and sits at your table while you order, advising you on what she believes you should have. The lights went out while we talked. She calmly lighted fat yellow candles and sat explaining that the basis of Thai food is rice, that a complete meal starts with soup, an assortment of vegetables, usually very hot with peppers, and fish or meat curries to be eaten with the rice. Then comes fruit or sweets made from a combination of rice, milk, sugar and coconut.

Eating in a pool of candlelight, we started with *kaeng chued,* a vegetable soup floating little pieces of white fish; then *kao pad,* fried rice; with this she brought a bottle of dark brown liquid, "fish sauce," she said. It was powerful, one drop converting a plate of ordinary rice into one of the tastiest dishes Mary Lou and I have encountered. Next we had *kaeng ped kai,* a marvelous bitey chicken curry which we ate with rice; then *mee krop,* crisp noodles served with *preaw wan nua,* sweet and sour beef. It was one of the best meals we had anywhere in the Far East.

Mr. Arthachinda had suggested that we talk with Witt Sivasariyanon, Deputy Director General of the National Tourist Organization. We approached him without much enthusiasm, our experience having taught us that the people of tourist departments had mentalities that coincided with their positions. They were exactly what they said they were: tourist representatives, offering the common sight, the traveled trail, the beaten path; the paid prophets of the easy-to-reach, much-seen delights.

Mr. Sivasariyanon followed pattern. A quick little man with beady eyes, he reminded me of a starling in the way he hopped from his desk to a table holding countless pamphlets and brochures extolling the wonders that were Thailand. After a hard sell on the temples, he turned toward the Floating Markets and the building housing a snake pit, suggested Bang Poo and Bangsaen, both seaside resorts. "Where there are beautiful beaches and dancing," the Deputy Director said proudly, as if every American should be instantly enthralled by the combination. Out of the two-hour conversation came two thoughts. The train trip to Chiang Mai, second largest city in Thailand, seemed worthwhile, for at its termination were the teak forests and the trained working elephants; also, slipping out of the Deputy Director's routine speech, was the advice: "You must see Lopburi, our most ancient city. It is a little like Angkor, that fabulous lost city of the jungle."

"The lost city of the jungle" set us to doing a little research on Angkor. It was in Cambodia, an hour away by air. Apparently a fantastic ruin, it was described in the book we read as "a haunting mystery, one of the wonders of the world . . ."

The director of tourism didn't tell us that the trip to Chiang Mai would take fifteen hours, passing through some of the most spectacular country in the world. If you like girls, this train ride is a must. At every village were beautiful women, often on bicycles, in *cai-ao*—loose trousers and long, colorful, slashed tunics. Many walked the roads in *chanai,* a revealing chemise, and *pasin,* a bright piece of material tucked around the waist like a bath towel. When the train, an old Scottish job, burst through the Khun Tarn tunnel, the highest point on the rail sector between Lampang and Chiang Mai, it was suddenly another world. Gone were the canals and flat land, replaced with lush green forests and hills and long stretches of jungle. This was the north, the teak country. Here is found the most important export of Thailand, 243 million bhats' worth being brought in yearly by the elephants and the men who wield the axes.

Chiang Mai, again attesting to the religious fervor of the Thais, was full of gaudy temples. Flaming rose gardens were everywhere, with many deep-red giants.

We found our elephants at a teak plantation on the outskirts of Chiang Mai. Mahouts were dressed in Western khaki shirts and trousers and leather-billed caps. Two elephants, men up, rolled huge teak logs toward a pile; heads down, they butted the logs across the ground. Two others dragged logs, the chain harness trailing behind tied onto the teak. The last two, without mahouts, were arranging and piling logs as neatly as a child does his Tinker Toys. They worked slowly but methodically. There was no harsh treatment and little use of the *ankus,* the hooked steel rod.

The overseer, Mr. Seng, in crisp khakis, was delighted with our admiration. Taller than the Thais, he didn't have their Chinese look; his skin was darker and he had a heavy gold ring in his left ear. He spoke a good, ringing English. I think he was either a Malay or an Indian—from his knowledge of elephants, probably an Indian. These people had been training them to be friends of man in war and peace for thousands of years.

And then we got the lucky break that comes once in a lifetime; again a testament to the traveler who goes off the beaten track.

"You like elephants?" he said.

I told him that we had hunted with them in India, and had grown so fond of them that I was beginning to build up a violent dislike for men who thought it was sport to hunt and kill them. He beamed and said, "We go to catch wild ones for training tomorrow. Would you and the madam like to come? It will be of three days duration, this trip. If we have trouble and do not find our elephants, I will bring you back to Chiang Mai so you can catch your train back to Bangkok."

We were ready at six the next morning when Mr. Seng picked us up in a rather ancient truck. With three of us in front, we drove most of that day, rapidly running out of civilization and anything that passed as a defined road. Moving deeply into the jungle, I noted the same trees; the sal, peepul, and thick bamboo were here as in India. But the undergrowth seemed heavier, the treetops closer, the light dimmer.

Just as I thought we had made a bad bargain, with the truck coughing and laboring, the road vanishing as undergrowth erased it before our eyes, I saw the elephants. Twenty stood a hundred yards to our right, their ears moving like great fans, tails flicking in little splats of sound as they slapped their backsides. This was dense jungle, the light giving the impression that we were underwater. Tents were pitched. Thirty men stood around a fire. Seng drove near the elephants, turned off the motor, and we joined the fireside group. Little brass teapots stood in the ashes rimming the fire and we soon had steaming tin cups in our hands.

Seng introduced us to the men, telling them that we were lovers of the elephant, and those who spoke English greeted us, the others nodded respectfully. They were short and dark—all Thais, I believe. We were shown our tent, told dinner would be ready in a half-hour and that we would move off after the elephants at five the next morning. A wild herd had been located and they were hoping to isolate some of the younger ones for capture. The meal was curried leg of jungle fowl, rice and tea. Then we went to our tent, listened to the jungle sounds and that familiar soft nickering of the elephants that had put us to sleep in India at a time that now seemed years ago.

There was no problem about awakening. The mahouts were shouting at their charges, there was bustle about the fire and the clanging of pots and pans. We had tea and a piece of hard bread in the tent and were dressed and ready before Mr. Seng came and softly said, "We are about to go."

We rode on a big female elephant with Seng in a *houdah* that easily took the three of us. With the mahout on the neck, we went single file, our elephant bringing up the rear. The ride was a familiar one, a swaying motion, almost that of the roll you get in a boat in certain kinds of water.

There were three sections of elephants; the fighters, beaters and captors, with fifteen animals used in teams. The leading elephants, the fighters, carried one man; the others two; with the man who was going to lasso the wild animal riding the captor. He bore a long stick with a rope of plaited buffalo hide on the end—the free end which is coiled on the elephant's back.

"The idea," said Seng, "is to move in on the wild one, drop a noose around his hind leg and then tie him to a tree."

He told us that a small herd had been located by the trackers and that we were slowly approaching from downwind, trying to reach them despite their remarkable sense of smell. We came out of a screen of bamboo that ran for a quarter of a mile. Four hundred yards to our right in a partially cleared glade seven elephants stood eating the leaves from some second-growth saplings, ears fanning, tails swatting. We had skillfully approached from the rear. They didn't know we were there. We sat and watched.

Flanking them, our beater elephant, a vital young animal full of zip, started running for a young elephant that was separated from the wild herd by twenty yards. At the noise the others wheeled, stood staring at us for a moment, then whirled with trunks raised, and rushed into jungle cover. The youngster, escape cut off, was chased in a circle by the crafty beater whose purpose was to tire out the wild one and prevent him from joining the others. Confused by this older and stronger animal that seemed to want to play and yet not play, the youngster finally stopped his rushing about and stood, evidently exhausted. It took about a half-hour to wear him down. Instantly the captor elephant moved in with a Thai on his neck, holding the rope on the stick. Skillfully, in a movement like a hockey player streaking the puck into the net, he hooked the noose under the foot of the elephant, deftly working it up around his leg. The rope-coil on the back of the captor played out, and the beater elephant came back, reversing his former operation. This time he tried to chase the wild one into the jungle. The captor followed. Once inside the jungle, the man with the rope jumped off and tied it securely to a tree. Brought up short, the wild one slammed to a halt. Turning fiercely on the man with the rope he charged, trunk raised, his little red eyes wild.

Now the fighter, an enormous animal, came rushing in and placed himself before the frightened but angry youngster, pushing him back with the sheer bulk of his body. The man on the ground escaped, running back to the captor elephant who stood waiting for him. Standing by to rough up the wild one if he showed any more signs of aggression, the fighter now moved in, butting him with his big shoulder. It seemed to do the trick. The wild one now stood calmly and stopped tugging against the rope. The rest of the trained elephants moved in, and the young captive was taken away, encircled by his captors. It was a skillful but sad drama. I didn't care for the sight of the small elephant with head down in dejection. His wild freedom was gone. The carefree days were over.

"He will be well-treated," Seng said. "A mahout will be assigned to him. They will live together in the compound for months while the training is completed."

"When will he be put to work?"

"In three months' time we can use him on teak logs. It is our most important industry. We must have elephants. In one year the wild will go completely. He will be dependable and happy with the others who work with him."

Civilization. Progress. Sometimes they seem unimportant.

When we got back to Bangkok I discovered that we could get a plane early Sunday morning that would take us to Siemreap, Cambodia, in ninety minutes. Within three hours after leaving Thailand we could be walking through the lost city in the jungles.

In less than that time the fabled jungle city rose before us, hanging there like a cloud mass. Instantly it dwarfed the publicized ruins of Rome and Athens. Angkor Wat, called by archaeologists the largest place of worship in the world, is one of the greatest structures attempted by man since the Tower of Babel. Hidden by vegetation, it was discovered in 1861 by Henry Mouhot, a French naturalist hunting rare insects in the Cambodian jungles. Today it is an acknowledged wonder of the world.

We entered it by a quarter-mile causeway, the area surrounded by a two-hundred-yard moat. It is poetic and magnificent beyond ordinary description. The temple in the center moves up in three flights almost three hundred feet from floor level. Five central stone towers rise within a rectangle of pillared galleries that could easily enclose two Canterbury Cathedrals. Two hundred startling faces of dancers, kings, slaves, snakes, and characters from Hindu mythology are cut in bas-relief. Believed to have been built during the first part of the twelfth century by a race called the Khmers, the Wat is a shrine to the Hindu god Vishnu, constructed to represent the legendary Mount Meru, mythical abode of the gods. Stones, all weighing more than a ton, were brought from a quarry twenty-five miles away by boat, then moved to the temple area on rollers powered by elephants. No expert has yet determined how the huge stones were lifted into the high places. The Khmers, who vanished as mysteriously as they came, were a remarkable breed of men. Using two hundred thousand battle elephants and huge armies, they brought entire nations into slavery to quarry the rock for these temples and buildings.

The marvel here was so strong that not one of the dozen persons wandering through the ruins spoke. You could hear the rustle of a Buddhist monk's robes as he went by, bald head high, looking at the decorations on a temple. Everything from Vishnu blessing his followers to seminude celestial dancing girls came alive in stone. We stood listening for the music that had prompted the postures of the dancers.

Angkor Thom, the "great city," is said by historians to have been the largest in the world, with more than a million people. Its creator and king, Jayavarman VII, a twelfth-century egoist who believed that he was a living Buddha, lost his head when it came to erecting temples. He built them everywhere, filling them with treasures of jade, emeralds and rubies, even topping them with solid gold. His personal place of worship, Bayon, had chapels facing every direction and fifty-four towers, each with the remarkable sculpture of three or four gigantic faces, all in the likeness of the king.

The Khmer society was supposed to have been the most luxurious ever known, even above the Romans. Maybe it was the soft life that did them in. Anyway, in 1431 the Siamese, formerly slaves of the Khmers, marched to Angkor and took the capital. The Khmers, always superior warriors, managed to rally and drive the Siamese out. But one year later when the Siamese rebuilt their army and reappeared, they found the city deserted, the Khmers gone. Where they went, what happened to them, how and why they disappeared remains one of the great historic mysteries. Some historians lay it to a plague, a "Black Death"—but there were no bodies. Others say the slaves revolted, killed their masters and fled the place of bondage. But again, no bodies.

We returned to our plane, dazed by that strange city eaten up by the jungle and discovered by a bug-hunting scientist. Shortly after strapping on her seat belt, Mary Lou checked the map given her by a svelte Thai stewardess. Minutes following our take-off for Bangkok a vast sea fell beneath us to our left, molten in the approaching twilight. The window framed it like a painting. "The China Sea!" Mary Lou said, touching the map, then the window. Across it lay the Philippines. We would be there within hours.

CHAPTER FOUR

THE PHILIPPINES
AND HONG KONG

Our great ship is coming down through a fog of cloud, so solid that it looks like the wall of a glacier. Suddenly there is a tear in the cloud cover to my left, as if someone had hacked a hole in canvas with a knife, and the steely glitter of the Bay of Manila appears.

We have arrived. The flying miracle is over and the pilot and co-pilot look like ordinary men once more as they come to earth down the ramp. I stand still, put our bags down, and wait for a confusion of emotions to subside.

It is always that way. The drama of arriving is almost as great as the exhilaration that comes from suddenly finding yourself in a new place. It is mid-morning by the time we unpack our bags and check our position in the Bay View Hotel, a place that lives up to its billing. There is an excellent view of the bay, with island rock-heads poking out of the harbor murk—Corregidor, and to its right Cavite and Langley Point, the United States Naval Base. I didn't fight in the Pacific, having spent most of my war in the European and Near Eastern theaters, but standing here now, looking at these famous places, is like opening a history book to a painful chapter, and scenes come of half-starved men imprisoned on these islands.

Mary Lou's voice brought me back. "He was right," she said. "See, that *does* look like a woman lying with her back in the water, her face to the sky—"

It was the low chain of mountains behind Cavite in this bright morning sunlight looking like a reclining woman with long-flowing hair.

"Just as he told us," Mary Lou said. "The Lady of Manila Bay, the Sun God's Wife. I remember his saying back in New Delhi that the skies over the bay are the domain of the Sun God and Goddess—"

It is possible that we came to the Philippines because of the charm of a man we met in New Delhi. He happened to be the Philippine

Ambassador, a short, bouncy diplomat who said, shortly after we met him, "Don't spend all your money in one place! Drop in on the Philippine Islands. We have more to offer the real traveler than anyone." Among the lures he dangled were hunting the francolin partridge, boating a swift river, walking through a tropical rain forest, and wing-shooting the mango groves where there were so many bush quail that "you had to beat them off."

My contact here, arranged by the Ambassador, was Jesús B. Alvarez, Jr., senior biologist with the Philippine Parks and Wildlife Service. I placed a call for him and watched life moving below us while I waited. On the grassy island of the boulevard several old men in straw hats and shiny leather sandals were sitting in the morning sun with their precious fighting cocks in their arms; the sun shooting sparks from the roosters' iridescent necks. One lank old fellow got up in a limber movement and walked his warrior rooster, the bird tugging at his cord, strutting arrogantly. Boys were lined on the seawall dunking fishing lines in the bay; cars hummed by; a woman stood by a gaily painted cart full of the green-gold gleam of mandarin oranges, apparently singing. A tourist in a red shirt and white pants stood taking pictures of the boys.

In the harbor a half-dozen old freighters from as many faraway places, cargoes unloaded, floated high. Then the phone clacked at us, bringing me from the window that was beginning to have the appeal of a cinema screen. Mr. Alvarez had a soft voice that asked questions: did we bring shotguns and shells and would we be ready to hunt francolin the next day? Not a time waster. He also said that he would send over some information on the islands by messenger so we could read up a little on the Philippines while we waited. He would arrive at six the next morning.

While we waited for the messenger to leave this special information at the hotel desk, we walked around the park that was opposite the hotel beside the American Embassy, working up an appetite for lunch, which we had in the Swiss Inn close to the hotel. The place was full of Americans drinking beer and eating gigantic pork hocks smothered in sauerkraut. They looked and talked like construction people.

We had excellent cold San Miguel beer and a spicy tripe dish that had been slow-cooked in tomato. The waiter told us that the beer was brewed by a German family who had migrated to the Philippines, had become millionaires and famous "because of the nicest taste of San Miguel."

Back at the hotel, I went through Jesús Alvarez's facts on his islands. They were short and hard. I was glad I followed habit and hadn't involved myself in a complicated book on the Islands. This was information I could retain. The earliest known inhabitants were three dwarf aboriginal races, which presumably crossed over from the Asiatic mainland by way of land-bridges then in existence. Later, Indonesians, Malays of Hindu-Mongolian mixture and, finally, the Chinese came to the Islands. The early Filipinos were literate, using a phonetic alphabet, prosperous in agriculture and skilled with textiles and metals.

The Philippines derived their name from the Spanish Filipinas, the name given the Islands by Miguel López de Legaspi in honor of King Philip II of Spain. In 1898, as an action in the war against Spain, Commodore George Dewey destroyed the Spanish fleet in Manila Bay. The Treaty of Paris of December 10, 1898, ceded the Philippines to the United States.

The Japanese took over in 1941, entering Manila on January 2, 1942, and capturing Bataan on April 9, 1942. General Douglas MacArthur announced the complete liberation of the Islands on July 4, 1945. On July 4, 1946, the Philippines took their place among the independent nations of the world when the Republic of the Philippines was born.

The Philippine Archipelago, composed of 7,107 islands of volcanic origin, lies approximately a thousand miles off the southeast of Asia, just above the equator, extending 1,152 statute miles north to south between Formosa on the north and Borneo on the south. It is about the size of Italy, a bit bigger than the British Isles and somewhat smaller than Japan proper. The archipelago is divided into three island groups: Luzon, Visayas and Mindanao. The land is generally mountainous, although it has fertile coastal plains, rolling uplands and rich valleys.

The climate, though the Islands are entirely within the tropic zone, is merely mildly tropical. In the highlands, the air is cool and bracing. There are two seasons: dry—March through June; wet—July through October. The remaining months are cool. Mean average annual temperature is 80.3° F.

There are three official languages: English; Tagalog, the national language; and Spanish, used socially.

The bay water was gleaming like newly minted nickel as we waited on the sidewalk outside the Bay View for the senior biologist. We didn't wait long. An old black car, of a year when size was uppermost in the designers' minds, lumbered to the curb. The man who got out was slender and looked like Tyrone Power with a heavy suntan. He was young, under thirty, and after introductions told us that he had been in the United States and would like to go back. He grinned. "Nice place to visit, but I'll take our islands for living."

"Have you heard of the francolin?" he asked, as we drove out of the city. We were already calling him Jess, as all his American friends did.

"Yes," I said. "A partridge, isn't it?"

"The natural range of the francolin in all its fifty forms is Europe, Africa and Asia," he said in his best biologist's voice. "But again we thank America. In 1916 a major from your country established them here, brought them from Hong Kong. They are thriving—so much so that we are paying you back in a way."

"You mean by taking us shooting?"

He laughed. "That too, I guess. But no, I mean that one of our part-time field men, Adriano Navarro, is trapping one hundred pairs of francolin for shipment to Hawaii."

We were on our way to Muntinlupa, Rizal, a huge estate of mango groves, forests and open meadows. This was a spot to which the francolins had naturally gravitated, the area where Navarro was trapping them for shipment to our fiftieth state. In ten minutes we were free of the city, traffic lessened, and the world changed rapidly.

Rice paddies were everywhere; some with nothing but muddy water; others standing hip-high in green; others where rice was being harvested. In little open shops in the villages we sped through, men were working over crude ovens, puffing rice, blowing it up like that grain we use as a breakfast cereal.

We entered the area on a long, winding dirt road and stopped when we saw a slender brown man waiting for us beside a stilted bamboo-mat hut. He shook hands and said, "Good morning." This was Adriano Navarro.

We started off with Adriano carrying a mongrel pup in his arms, a brindle fox terrier-type that bore the brave name of Tigre. After we crossed the road and got into the trees, great mangoes with shiny green leaves, Adriano put the dog down and said sharply, *"La! La!"* The little fellow took off in a rush, heading for a stand of hip-high, heavily bladed grass. Cogon, Jess called it.

"Don't yank any of it with your hands," he said. "The blades are sharp and give a nasty cut."

The dog was silent but you could see the grass swaying as he moved. Adriano, burlap bag over his shoulder, machete sheathed and hanging behind him, followed the dog swiftly, motioning Mary Lou and me with a sweep of his hand to follow. Just before we got to him, there was a sound like a window smashing and up went a covey of bush quail. I raised my gun, but Adriano said, "No! *Pugong Americano!*"

Jess explained: "Adriano doesn't want you to shoot quail today. Just the *Pugong Americano,* which is what our people call the francolin, in honor of the American who brought them here. It means American quail. Of course they aren't quail at all, but here in the Islands everything big and good is American. So it follows that American quail have to be as large as partridge."

"We saw a slender brown man waiting for us beside a stilted bamboo-mat hut. . . . This was Adriano Navarro."

The next time the birds went up I was so close to Tigre that I almost stepped on him. My bird was a hen, fast and swervy. I got her on the second shot as she swung back, crossing at an extreme right angle.

Adriano shook his head and smiled. Jess said, "Excellent, now we have Adriano with us. He likes a good shot."

"I hope he likes a lucky one, too," I said.

It was mid-morning now, getting hot, and there was a sweet smell from the big mango trees. Suddenly we were joined by a slender man in a big straw sombrero, Caimiro Navarro, Adriano's brother.

As we walked through the ocean of cogon that was getting higher and heavier, I lost sight of the dog and consequently missed the turned-head-and-tongue signal. The bird towered forty yards away, flipping like a clay target in the wind, and I shot twice, missing. But Mary Lou didn't. She made a right crossing shot that caused Jess to stop and the Navarro boys to remove their straw hats in a sweeping gesture of respect.

We started off again seeking the big pools of shade flung by the mangoes, and came finally into an open field. The grass was shorter now and we had the privilege of watching the little brindle mongrel work. He seemed to have no sense of direction and he ran with his nose to the ground in a manner that would have disgusted any Southern quail hunter, but it was a sight to behold. Suddenly he would slam to a stop, turn his head, flip out his tongue, and there would always be a francolin. In this great stretch of field I missed twice, but connected with three shots. Mary Lou also got two in quick overhead action.

When we got back to the two-room palm and bamboo hut on stilts, I shook hands with Adriano and pressed several pesos in the grip. He quickly took his hand away, put the money back in my hand and made a movement with the edge of his hand, bladelike, across his throat. I asked Jess to tell him that we had taken his time, used his talented dog in the hot sun, and it was only right that he be paid for his time, just as he was paid to collect the francolin to ship to Hawaii. Jess did, but again the knife-across-the-throat gesture.

"He says he will take no money," Jess told us. "He says anyone can take money. But a good deed is what makes a man."

This was a new experience for me—people not taking money, especially when they had earned it. Jess shrugged. "He is a proud man. I wouldn't press it or he will be insulted."

Now Adriano's wife, a cheery, overweight woman with snapping brown eyes, appeared on the porch of the house with three children ranging in age from four to ten, tense little antelopes who smiled and ran if you approached. She spoke rapidly to Jess in Tagalog, smiling and looking at us.

"You will also insult Adriano and his wife if you do not stop and eat with them," Jess said.

So we ate—on gigantic banana leaves, while sitting on the ground before Adriano's hut, with spectators—carabao. These black fierce-looking beasts with a big spread of horn stopped within five feet, sniffing, to be shooed off by Mrs. Navarro.

We had seen her killing a white chicken when we arrived. Now the fowl was evidently in a black pot which she brought, sending out an aromatic spiral of steam. "This is *guinataan*," Jess explained. "Few of your countrymen will ever get the chance to taste it. It is a true Filipino dish with fish, chicken, vegetables and pork cooked in co-conut milk. Garlic and vinegar, eggplant, *ampalaya* (fruit) and *sitao* is probably added—"

I've never tasted anything like it: pungent, creamy, the meats firm yet tender. I tried, as I usually do, to get the recipe, but it got so involved that we decided to enjoy it and not delve into the hows and whys.

After we had finished the feast, Adriano, his wife and shy children, and his brother Caimiro, shook hands with us. We told our hosts how much we had enjoyed it and the day itself. They stood solemn and proud, waving as we drove back toward Manila. I had managed to leave the francolin we had shot without being observed by Adriano and was thinking now as we wound through city traffic of the magic Mrs. Navarro would call up in cooking those birds.

Just before he left us, Jess said, "There will be a taxi driver waiting for you in the morning, name of Alfredo Zamora. He will take you to Barrio Kalawaan to see one of our largest industries, the raising of duck eggs. I don't think many travelers have seen it—"

They probably hadn't. If you asked them whether they would like to see duck eggs, it is fairly certain that most people would pass in favor of a boat ride on the bay or a shopping trip for the native sea-shell souvenirs. They would be missing one of the most interesting sights of the Islands, and one of the world's most astonishing foods.

Alfredo Zamora, a broad, dark man with the blood of the old Spanish legions of Miguel López de Legaspi coursing through his veins, arrived in a big black American sedan gleaming with the hours of loving care he had given it.

"Are you Mr. and Mrs. Scott for the ducks?" he said, approaching us where we waited before the Bay View.

We said we were and he laughed. "I've never taken any visitors out to Pasig, Rizal, where most of our ducks are. I once mentioned it to an elderly Englishman and his wife and they looked at me like I was crazy." He laughed again.

As we drove he told us that raising duck eggs was one of the largest industries in the Islands. "Not ducks. Eggs. Of course you must have ducks to get duck eggs." A logical man, Alfredo Zamora, and a cheery one. He explained that the reason for the eggs was a dish called *balut,* which was simply a boiled egg. "But taken at the right stage," he said, eyes twinkling. "We must see that you get one with a cold bottle of San Miguel."

The dark, fast-flowing Pasig River moves from Manila many miles inland in a long, twisting loop. Forty miles out we hit one of the loops at Pasig, Rizal, and the village of Barrio Kalawaan, which is not accessible by hard roads but only by native boat or *banca,* a narrow, pointed craft, sometimes propelled by motor but usually by paddle. We left the car near the Pasig Bridge, and walked down a flight of steps to the shore where Alfredo got a boat for us. There were three in the dark water, two with motors, one without. We got into a motored craft and started down the river, with the boatman saying, "You like see duck. We got duck. Many duck."

On both sides of the river, large pens wired right to the water were full of ducks, thousands of ducks—Alfredo said there were seventy-five thousand here—of a breed I didn't recognize; some brown and white, others with solid black heads flecked with white, some all white.

"From China they come long many time ago," our boatman said. Boys in T-shirts and baggy pants, and broad old women in brown dresses and aprons were busily feeding the ducks some kind of whitish mash from large circular baskets. There was an incessant quacking as if ten thousand children's toys had been stuck on a high note in the winding, and there was the ripe smell of barnyard. Occasionally there would be a woman sitting well back from the shore, a huge basket of duck eggs gleaming greenly in display beside her. We managed to convince the boatman that we wanted to stop and walk through a duck area, a place of soft ground and ducks so tame that they came running for a handout. Often, as we cruised this village of duck breeders, a woman would come running to the bank holding aloft a basket of eggs. Three times duckyard owners offered gifts of eggs; one old woman tried to press a loudly quacking black duckling on Mary Lou. We moved up and down the river for over an hour looking at duckyards which are said to be the largest collection in the world.

Alfredo was waiting for us when the boat made a doubtful docking, working through the suck of mud, the old motor wheezing with effort. "That white stuff they are feeding the ducks is ground sea shells from Laguna de Bay," he said. "Eggs, the best ones, are bought by men for eight centavos and taken to the *balut* makers of Pateros, Rizal, who sell them for twenty centavos. The best ones are fourteen days old. These are boiled and sold hot. *'Balut sa puti,'* we call them."

When we reached the top of the stairway and got to the highway, he said, "I have found a place where you can get a *balut* and a beer."

On this delicacy, Mary Lou passed. The eggs were sold from a cart, not unlike some of the hot-dog rigs you see on the streets of New York, from a heated aluminum container. Alfredo went to a nearby *sari sari,* a store where you can buy anything from a skinned lamb's head to a pineapple shirt, and got two cold bottles of San Miguel. Following his example I cracked and shelled the egg, salted it from a shaker offered me by the *balut* peddler, and took half in a fast bite as Alfredo did, washing it down with San Miguel.

"It's very good," I said, looking down at the other half of the egg in my hand. Nestled in the white was half a duckling; a little featherless soft-billed head stared back. I had just eaten half an embryo.

Quickly Alfredo said, "This is our national dish, full of vitamins and food value. Delicious! Don't you think?"

I didn't want to think. But I had to admit the astonishing fact that it was good, the whole effect not unlike Austrian boiled squab.

"Aren't you going to finish it?" Mary Lou said sweetly. "It looks to me like an interesting and clever dish. Egg, soup and bird all in a bite—" When I finished, she stood staring at me as if I had just jumped off Pasig Bridge, which I was tempted to throw her from.

Alfredo beamed proudly all the way back to Manila, thinking he had just made a *balut* convert. "You are a good sport, what we call a *balutero,*" he said, adding that he would pick us up again in three days and drive us to the Pagsanjan River. "Suggested by our tourist and travel office as something very unusual," he said. "It will be a thrill!"

The *balutero* skipped dinner that night.

The following day we went out to shoot quail after meeting our

The astounding national dish of the Philippines was balut, *boiled duck eggs with a surprise inside. The eggs shown here were ready to be sold before boiling.*

guide, Santos, a grinning little capuchin who spoke a wonderful English without paying much attention to tense and gender. We were getting ready to go afield when it started to rain, a fierce, sweeping downpour that made it impossible even to see quail. I went back the next day for the shoot but Mary Lou and Jess decided to spend the time searching for camera types. Her shotgun was acting up, but I took it along anyway as a spare. I had quite an adventure.

. . .

The sun shone on the horns of the carabao and I was watching the play of light as it moved up into the angled scimitar of bone, when the animal made a sound like someone breaking a barrel with a sledge and started for me. Now I had been carefully told that the carabao, even though an extremely close descendant of the wild buffalo, had been completely domesticated and was as nice an animal as they had in the East. But apparently this one didn't know. He obviously was in a nasty mood and coming for me when I decided that a mango tree had virtues besides bearing fruit. I was up in the tree as the big black animal's rush carried him five feet beyond. He stood and looked at me for a moment, his stupid eyes rolling.

Then humiliation. Two beautiful little girls riding a water buffalo came over to my wild animal. One, probably fourteen, slid off the carabao they both had been riding, ran over, got on the killer. Then the two of them rode off in sidesaddle posture on the ugly beasts, waving as they went.

It was early morning but hot and the high cogon was dry now, beginning to wave in a slight ground breeze. This was the Madrigal Estate in Alabang, said to hold the best quail in the islands. Here we saw the lushest mango orchard in existence—one hundred acres of the valuable trees, some in fruit, some not. These trees were so perfect, so symmetrical, that they looked as if they had been pruned into that plump shape. A faint perfumed odor came from the orchard; the sunlight was casting sculpture in shadow on the ground as it fell through the leaves.

Where was Santos? Suddenly he came over the hill with three men and two small dogs, a white-and-brown and a brindle mongrel. As he got closer and I waited for introductions that never came, I said, "Am I right about the carabao? Didn't you say they were harmless?"

"Harmless, yes. Yes, harmless?" he said.

I told him of the episode of the black bull.

"But oh, I forget," he said. "You stranger, yes? Not dressed like Filipino farmer. You not wear a straw sombrero like mine. You wear little hat with band of colors, and she does not know you, and she afraid and she then run at you to see if perhaps you like him. If you like him like Filipino you will show this by shouting loud, by being fierce. Our carabao not dangerous! Did you see the quail while you wait?"

I had seen no quail, even from the vantage point of the limb high in the mango. The two dogs went ahead, moving slowly, holding up

The dangerous carabaos were placidly ridden away by two young girls while the author, disbelieving, watched from the safety of a tree.

the single-file line of men that followed. And then I forgot the carabao completely. The birds went out of the cogon ahead of us so fast that it seemed they were being hurled from some type of spring machine invisible in the grass. They were smaller than our bobwhite, and I missed with both barrels of the Browning 20 over-under. Every man in line wheeled and looked at me with disgust. I handed the Browning, empty, to the nearest man and took the Winchester 12 from Santos.

"They are small quail, Santos," I said, "and there are too many helpers. I should be first in line, then you, then the others."

Santos agreed and we switched positions. We walked about a mile, passing through many mangoes, when I felt the fire burn my bare arm. There were three big red ants intent on taking the arm off. I killed them, but as I stood under the tree doing this, the ants got replacements from above. Looking up, I saw a nest, a cluster-nest, high in the mango, saw ants moving on the mess, and stepped out of the way.

Santos stood watching me. "Terrible!" he said. "Ibok! Hantik! Our wild red ants. They live in the tree and bite the very hard."

"The very, very hard!" I said. My arm was welted. These Ibok make a mosquito bite seem like a massage.

This was quail-hunting the hard way: the charging buffalo, the ants that bit like a blade, and now it was obvious that the dogs had come along to help the quail. They trotted just far enough ahead to slow our progress, and when the quail flew out of the grass without any help from them, they leaped into the air as if they were after a bouncing rubber ball, barking and having the time of their lives.

If I had fired at the second covey of quail that went up I would have bagged both dogs. On the next two coveys the dogs did their hurly-burly in the air, completely blocking my shots. Twenty-five birds were up off the ground, hitting the air as one, making a sound like applause. Despite the dogs, I got a double. They were about half the size of a full-grown bobwhite. Santos called them turnix, but they looked like bush quail, the tiny African or Indian bird that flies faster than any game bird that I know and is so smart that you have trouble getting enough of them to fill a plate for a meal. Even a bobwhite is small, less than the size of the clay birds that the skeet boys make such a big fuss about. Without feathers the bush quail would be the size of a half dollar. It is slightly larger in the air with the wings churning and the feathers fuzzed out, but as far as quail-hunting is concerned, I would say it was similar to shooting at a puff of smoke.

Now I patiently asked Santos if he could send the dogs and their master back, pointing out that we would never get any quail if these hazards were with us all morning. Santos, I knew, was looking forward to some quail and rice for supper, to go with the dozen bottles of cold San Miguel I had brought. He coöperated with alacrity. Dogs and master dirty-looked me but submitted to Santos' authority and went back toward the bamboo huts.

I'm not saying that the quail had things their own way for the next couple of hours, but let's agree that the Philippine sun in April is not ideal for wing-shooting. And there are the *tivegs*. They are sparse trees that dangle strings of green balls that look like limes, and when the quail take off in shattering squadrons they head for the *tivegs,* with the result that you bag many of the little green limelike balls but few quail.

Santos was an asset. He made himself my official gunbearer, giving me the distinction of being probably the only quail-shooter who ever used one. But I must say it is a handy thing.

Take a covey that broke into two segments, flying in different directions. I luckily put two birds down with the Browning, then took the Winchester .12 pump that Santos ran over to me and went after the other flying wedge of birds that had gone to earth thirty yards away. When they went again I got two on the rise. Santos was beside himself. "Wait I tell you husband what the shoot you are," he said. "She will be ver', ver' happy—"

Once I was so eager that I fell flat on my face as I made a clumsy little two-step after a single that had scooted out of formation too soon. Then, again, it didn't help when the master of the two dogs that loved to defend quail came back with a friend and watched dourly from a distance.

Then the birds got sparser and slower and it was evident that it was getting too hot even for them. They were too smart to take off from the cooling grass into the sun and so we sat and ate a mango and counted our take. Eighteen. Enough for Santos and his brood and for my "husband," Mary Lou.

The mango trees were a blessing. Not only did they offer pools of deep shade, but we unparched ourselves often when we saw a ripe mango hanging luscious and yellow. This makes quail-shooting in this area a sport that should catch on.

I'll admit that my favorite adventure is one that puts my feet under the table at its ending. As for my traveling companion who had spent the day riding in a breezy Buick, she was smug about getting her quail without the run in the sun.

"Wonderful!" she said, watching one fall apart under her knife. "Do it again tomorrow!"

"Can't," I said, "even if my legs agreed. Tomorrow we shoot the rapids of the Pagsanjan River."

Can you remember getting excited in geography class looking at the bright maps and aching to visit the thousands of places named on the colored patches? Remember how it was always the extremes that you longed to see—the largest city, the longest valley, the highest mountain, the swiftest river, the coldest country, the hottest desert, the deepest jungle? In this regard I never grew up and was fortunate enough to marry a girl who also has that youthful spirit and the urge to move.

Alfredo had shined up his car again and drove through the

morning traffic as if he were at the helm of a yacht, regarding the cars around him as bumbling little craft that shouldn't be in these waters. He told us that the drive would be more than one hundred kilometers, that we would probably have lunch by the river, then take to the boats. "One passenger to a boat," he said. "They go by balance. Fast. You will like this thrill, I think." Everything to Alfredo was a thrill— the way his car ran, his cigar pulled, his wife sang, his city grew, his dinner digested. So we didn't know what to expect.

Luzon is blessed with good roads, but even with this narrow yet good roadbed it took us almost four hours to get to the river with the hazards of driven herds of carabao invaded by tick birds, slow wagon traffic carrying everything from mounds of green-gold oranges to rice and stacks of bananas, and old trucks humped with purple eggplant. At one point we waited ten minutes while two boys guided to the roadside about fifty piglets, all pink and white and squealing. These were the raw material on the hoof for the national dish of *lechon,* roast baby pork stuffed with papaya.

Our destination was an ancient three-story restaurant beside the river, a somber gray building with the faded name Pagsanjan Falls over its doorway. The restaurant was on the lower floor overlooking the river that sprinted and foamed outside. Boatmen in khaki sat at tables eating rice and fish. Little brown bottles of the pungent *bagoong,* a concentrated sauce of shrimp and fish, were on every table, often the mark of a good place. Andy, the head boatman, gray, slender, not young, came to our table and told Alfredo that if we wanted to go he would assign the men. "Martin Coro for the camera lady," he said. "And Fred Mendoza. After you eat good food we go."

This place could be one of the best in the Islands for native dishes. The background was simple: bare, well-scrubbed plank tables, clean napkins, stainless steel and heavy china plates. With Alfredo translating and adding his own recommendations, we finally ordered *lumpia* and more of the foamy local beer. Paper-thin pancakes covered with soy sauce arrived. I opened one. It was stuffed with coconut pith, pieces of shrimp and pork, and assorted vegetables that I couldn't identify. A light and delicious dish. Alfredo had *diningding,* leafy vegetables with dried fish, insisting that we taste it. Excellent. Tea, and then the river. Andy introduced us to the boatmen, Coro and Mendoza, little men with the fine, trained-down look of jockeys.

When we saw the boats riding in an easy swell I could understand why they were small men. They had to be. The *bankeros,* primitive canoes hollowed from logs, were gaily painted in red, pink and purple stripes. They measured twenty feet long and three feet wide. Andy, who came to see us off, explained that they were kept afloat by balance, cautioning us to sit upright without side-to-side movement. He said that the boatmen must have seven years' experience before they are allowed to take out paying passengers. Coro, in my wife's boat, was about forty-five years old and had been on the river half his life; Mendoza had been on the Pagsanjan for ten years and the others for the same length of time.

We sat in the bow, paddles were dipped and we started toward the rapids—fourteen of them, according to Andy. Alfredo sat this one out. "Water," he said, "is for taking the bath. I have already taken my bath. This is not the thrill for me." I wasn't certain that it was for me either, but we were rolling now, caught in the fast sweep of the river.

Now we were passing through a gorge, a huge, theatrical stone curtain towering several hundred feet, that looked as though it had been cut from solid rock. Farther on, the shoreline rose, furred with trees; some of them were hung with beards of air-spun moss. The jungle walked down to meet us. In places the Pagsanjan was deep and green; in many places shallow and pebbly. When we hit these thin areas the boatmen were quick, leaping out and pulling the boats through. Then they made a cat-hop back into the sterns, the four-foot paddles with the broad blades spun as if electrically powered, and we were in deep water again.

Have you ever had the dream of falling, the somnambulant horror of dropping, dropping through space, and then thankfully awakened just before you hit the earth and broke your head, and lay there shaken by the experience? Shooting the rapids of the Pagsanjan was something like that. Mary Lou was ahead; Coro, apparently the dean, had eagerly paddled out first, and now after shooting through three small rapids, watching their boat half vanish in the spray, we came to a big rapid. I could tell it was a big one by the tensing of the man behind me, feel it in this delicate craft that telegraphed every movement, hear its current brawling and raving ahead of me. Then, quickly, we left the security of the smooth-flowing river and were lost. Lost and blind. The fine spray threw a curtain around me, blanking out the day, the river, encapsulating me in fear, in that old dream of hurtling through space. The boat wobbled, I felt water on my head, coming down my neck, and I was still falling. Then a bump and frantic motion from the man behind me, and the mist lifted. I was in a long, smooth glide on unbroken water. I turned and looked behind while the rapids churned as white as milk and as violent as sin. I looked down into deep green water and was thankful that the boatman had spent ten years on the river and had kept me from going down there to join my ancestors on the bottom of the strange, sunken land.

Mary Lou's boat was gliding ahead of me; suddenly it stopped, halted by a clever churning of a paddle, and she pointed. On the bank of the river was a small black wild boar, head down, drinking; to his right about twenty yards were two silvery-brown rhesus monkeys staring at us. Farther on, a rock wall came up and lush green foliage ran down its side in precarious symmetry. Giant begonias threw their color as the banks flattened again, and huge green ferns stood like pruned hedges waving in the offshore breeze.

Now the sun was bright on the water. There was no sound except the dip of the paddle and the crushing noise of another rapid ahead. Kingfishers darted by, smalt-blue in the sunlight. Then this peace was suddenly shattered. We fell again. We fell eight more times. I began to have firm confidence and respect for my boatman and his sturdy craft. We stopped by a burst of water coming off a cliff, a fragment of rainbow caught in its mist. *"Magdapio,"* said Mendoza.

After what seemed to be a long time we came to the end of our journey at Pagsanjan Falls. Here water roared from three-hundred-foot walls, a sight that I sat and watched in respectful reflection as my boat floated heavily in the churning buttermilk-white water. A heavy rope had been fastened to the cliffside by some idiot and floated nearby, in case anybody lost his mind and wanted to pick up the line to pull himself through the raining blows of the falls into the dubious sanctity of the cave behind.

Mendoza pointed to the rope. "For lovers," he said. "They pull boat through waterfall into underneath where they are alone." They could be alone for a long time.

Such was our passage on the Pagsanjan, the river that falls.

After resting for two days, we were ready to meet Alfredo, who was turning out to be as helpful as Denzil in Ceylon. He was eager to take us to a *pintakasi,* a special cockfight. We had seen the stately old men all over the city holding their fine-feathered birds in their arms, walking them on thin rawhide leashes, standing in doorways loudly discussing the merits of the rugged roosters. We even had seats beside one old fellow in a cinema who sat hugging his bird. It was after dinner when Alfredo arrived and drove us to the northern suburbs

We shot the rapids of the Pagsanjan, the "river that falls."

and La Loma, which he said was the best arena in the islands.

"There are others but here you get the real thrill, the feel of the earth and our people—"

We stopped in a dark, musty-smelling section where dancers were practicing native steps that they would exhibit at a fiesta. "We won't stop long," he said. "Just a look. They don't like people to watch while they are practicing, but one is my wife's cousin."

We were in an alley, lighted by wick-fed lamps held by two girls in bare feet and long native skin-tight dresses. They were doing ballet-like movement. Rotating the flickering lights from hand to hand, the girls glided to a squeaky Oriental tune played by three young men who were blowing reed instruments. "That is the *pandango sa ilaw*," Alfredo said proudly.

The girls soon stood by the musicians, their lights casting shadows into the street as two bare-chested young men appeared. In stiff, styl-ized motions, holding bamboo poles ankle-high, these men gyrated in what Alfredo called the *singkil*. We left with the shrill instruments pouring sound into the dark street while the young men, light mas-saging their chests, seriously engaged in some of the most intricate dance steps I have seen.

La Loma arena was a barn of a place with earthen flooring, the cock ring a matted circular section boarded low enough so you could lean on the barrier and see into the fighting pit. It was full of smoke and the sound of men in enthusiastic conversation. Now shouting rose as two men came in carrying the fighter birds, one flecked with white, the other red; stillness followed for a moment as the birds were placed in the ring. These gamecocks looked exactly like the East Indian red junglefowl (*Gallus gallus*), from which all domestic fowl are believed to be descended.

The centuries fell away as the hubbub rose and we were in Rome in the time of Columella, the first-century agricultural writer, who was forced to claim in public denunciation that his people spent their entire patrimony at the ring pit betting on the brave birds with the iron spurs, or *tela*.

The betting here began with the *kristos*, the professionals, so called for their habit of extending both arms, Christlike, to emphasize their bids. The words "*Sa Pulti*" (for the White) and "*Sa Pula*" (for the Red) were being screamed. As I looked around I could see men winking at one another, making slight nods, lifting a finger at the *kristos*—indications that they were betting, as binding here as a writ-ten contract. One old fellow in a gay yellow and red blanket-shawl and a deep-brimmed straw sombrero made a ticlike movement with his left eye that rippled his entire cheek into a long quiver. Beside him stood a trim dandy in a gray silk suit.

Alfredo, his broad face streaked with sweat, his smile fixed, raised a clenched fist for his bet, and whispered, "Take the red bird! He is a fierce one, that fellow, and he has been in training near my neighbor-hood. It is said that he can tumble any cock in the Islands—"

Trying to be nonchalant, I fumbled with the knot of my tie, evidently a betting gesture, for a *kristo* quickly raised his arms at me, and the bet was made. For what amount would be discovered at the climax of this fight. I began shouting *"Sa Pula!"* for the red fighter, along with Alfredo, while my wife stood entranced with the collection of Filipinos. One portly fellow dressed in faultless white linen was hopping up and down in excitement, a motion like the cha-cha.

The birds, placed breast to breast, were backing away, feinting with their beaks. Suddenly the red one, kicking, sprang atop the one flecked with white. There was much commotion, men screaming, both birds kicking, the terrible steel talons flashing in the doubtful light. Now they were apart, feinting again. The white one, in a curiously ungraceful motion, batted the red cock with the full force of its left foot, sending him sprawling. Hackles up, he flashed to his feet and, wings partially outstretched, rushed his opponent. This fight had more action than most boxing matches. There was a curious silence. The man beside me, black cigar in mouth, unconsciously drooled, the spittle streaking down his chin.

The white-flecked cock gracefully sidestepped the rush of the red; whirling, he lanced out with his talons. The red, until this moment fiercer and stronger, was caught off balance. He fell, blood streaming down his breast. He lay there, feebly kicking while the audience speculated aloud what he would do. He did nothing.

Finally, with the white bird standing aloof, the two owners entered the ring. Placing the birds breast to breast, they stood back waiting while the crowd clucked in encouragement. The white one raised his hackles but the red one rested, all fight gone. The owner of the white rooster, placing it on his wrist, bowed grandly to the crowd and its rousing cheers. The owner of the red cock took his bird and slunk from the ring.

While waiting for the next bout, Alfredo explained the fine points of this ancient sport. He apologized for the red losing. "Overtrained. Did you see how thin he is? I told his owner that he was working him too hard!" Ah, the seasoned sports in Madison Square Garden could alibi their losses no better than Alfredo. I had apparently lost five pesos, about two dollars, which is the normal bet. If you want to raise it, you signal the amount with the fingers.

Alfredo said that the brave cocks are challenged at an age of one to two years, and he explained the artistic requirements of the techniques. Only the skillful can do the "heeling," or proper fastening of the spurs, and "cutting out," trimming the wings so they have the right slope and cutting the tail by one third its natural length, shortening rump and hackle feathers. The comb is cut very close to remove it as a target for the opponent's spurs. The arena birds are fitted with either "short heels," steel spurs an inch long, or "long heels" of two and a half inches. Their training is much like that given boxers. From ten days to two weeks before the fight, the cock goes on a rigid diet and is given intensive exercise and sparring practice. It is against the rules to touch a bird after he has been placed in the cockpit unless it becomes necessary to untangle his spurs, which sometimes become caught in the matting.

Cockfighting is illegal in most parts of the world. Popular in ancient India, Persia and China, this unusual sport was introduced into Greece during the time of Themistocles. It is said that while advancing with his army against the Persians, Themistocles observed two wild cocks fighting fiercely. Halting his troops, who were rapidly losing their vigor against the strong enemy, he rallied them by pointing out the courage of the battling roosters. In honor of the victory that followed, cockfights were held annually in Athens, at first in a patriotic spirit but later just for the love of the sport.

"And then the Romans borrowed it from the Greeks," Alfredo said. "We take to it in the Philippines because we love brave things."

As we drove back to our hotel, he said, "You will be happy to learn that in the first international *pintakasi* between us and Cuba last May at Santa Ana Turf Club, we won with the score of six to three!"

A day after our cockfighting experience we were back with Jess and on our way to Makiling National Park. Following Route One, we drove south for forty miles while Jess explained that he thought one of the great free adventures left in our world was a walk through a tropical rain forest.

"I don't think there is another experience like it," he said. "It is like moving through the stage set of a dream."

The officer in charge, Ceferino Datuin, a short, cheery fellow in his early thirties, was enthusiastic about our visit, telling us that forestry experts from the United States had helped establish this national park, that all the birds and animals here were under the protection of the government. "Sometimes," he said, grinning, "a deer or some other succulent animal is relieved of this protection. But only momentarily. Mainly this is a place of peace and quiet."

We stopped at a forestry go-down and bought cans of wieners, bread and salted eggs, picked up a couple of forestry boys and started our walk. Our destination was a hut a number of miles into the rain forest in the vicinity of a hot spring.

Jess and Ceferino stepped out after the two boys, moving in long, easy strides, with Mary Lou and me bringing up the rear. In less than an hour we were in our first rain forest. As we walked, a vast wall of trees rose before us, a splendor of growth that reached eighty feet toward a sky that we now couldn't see. One incredible fern stood fifty feet high and was so bushy that its width could cover the body of an automobile. As we moved deeper into the forest, the whole effect became theatrical; there was no noise, not even the sound of a bird, and damp heat rose around us as if we were standing in a gigantic greenhouse. Because little sunlight filtered through the closely growing trees and plants that struggled to raise their heads high enough to get light, there was virtually no undergrowth. Ceferino talked about rain forests as we walked through the opaque light toward the forestry hut.

Genuine rain forests cover one-tenth of the earth's surface, a tropical area where it doesn't rain constantly as the name seems to imply, but where rain comes in quantity, dumped by cloudbursts. The treetops, so high that the wind doesn't whip them, retain evaporation, and Ceferino said that even at night the great trees trap the sun's heat to such an extent that humidity is a twenty-four-hour thing. This is tenuous, heavy, all-enveloping, a mist of heat unlike anything I have encountered. The deep jungles of India, even in the heat of May, are cool in comparison to these rain forests of the Philippines. I understand that there are rain forests in Puerto Rico, the Virgin Islands, Africa and South America, even one on the Olympic Peninsula, in the State of Washington.

There is also a ghostly process of "trying to fall down" going on constantly. As all living things must, trees and bushes die. But here they are crowded so closely together in their determined scramble to get their share of the sun that when they die they just slump, resting against one another, falling inch by inch.

Ceferino pointed out one old dead giant, a *dao*—something like our redwood—leaning as if exhausted between two sturdy *pili* trees, a mahogany type. "That one has been trying to fall down for two years," he said.

The colors were dazzling, coming from hundreds of different kinds of flora—burning yellows and startling scarlets, fading off into old rose and violet. From the proliferating green wall of climbing bamboo standing fortlike to our left, the greenish-white arm of a white *lauan* tree stuck through, seeming to beckon. A shaft of sunlight had sneaked through the prison of treetops, illuminating the gesture.

Ahead of us, blocking our path like soldiers guarding the entrance of a castle, stood a line of *agohos,* exotic trees not unlike the tamarack. Ceferino pointed out the trees and their names, but there were so many different kinds that the poetry of their names became confusing and I only remember a few. The background became even denser, and now, after two hours of walking, I felt dwarfed, shrunken, like a captive Lilliputian.

Then, coming through the great shadows cast by the soldier trees, the *agohos,* we could see the forestry hut, a bleak gray unpainted shack lost in the terror of the trees, its grass roof spotted with the rare sun that dribbled off the heads of the forest giants like raindrops.

The yard that had been scrabbled out of the forest was bare, with scrawny chickens that looked like poor fourth cousins of the shiny fighting cocks we had seen. Three nondescript dogs with blunt muzzles rose to their haunches and gave half-hearted growls. Two young men came to the open door of the hut. Five men of varying ages and sizes were sitting at a bare table in the center of the room which held a banana leaf and a mound of rice. Using their hands, they skillfully scooped rice off the leaf into their mouths without dropping a grain. Jess and Ceferino talked with them for a while; then the four of us sat at a spindly table, its bamboo legs trembling as we unloaded our lunch—wieners, hard bread and salted eggs. The eggs—the Filipinos do the damnedest things with eggs—had been dyed purple, soaked in brine for two weeks, then heavily salted. The yolks were dark orange and smelled strong. Mary Lou ate one without comment and quickly followed it with a hot dog and a gulp of water. Jess and Ceferino calmly ate eleven salted eggs and polished off the rest of the bread and two cans of wieners. If their leg muscles were as strong as their stomachs, those two could walk the forty miles back to Manila without taking a deep breath.

After lunch we went out and walked through more of the monster trees looking for a boiling spring. We saw the breath of the boil before we did the spring, the steam rising in constant spirals and eddies. It was a large area, perhaps one hundred feet wide by two hundred deep, a caldron on the earth's crust. Mud bubbled and shivered, sending out little groaning sounds as if it were alive, imprisoned and trying to escape.

"It is a true volcano," Jess said. "Sometimes it erupts and throws mud as high as six feet."

We stood and watched the strange spring making its strangled sounds and then Jess suggested that we go back to the hut, have a drink, and start back before it got dark. "I don't like to walk in the rain forest after dark," he said.

Ceferino laughed. "Nothing to worry about, Jess, I am here. I know the way."

"I know," Jess said somberly, "but there is something about those big trees at night that gives me the creeps."

I knew what he meant. I don't think I would have liked to walk three hours through the living damp of the rain forest as night came down, and dodge the dead trees that couldn't lie down, and listen for sounds that never came.

As we came back to the hut and Jess passed tepid soft drinks to everyone, the forestry workers again were grouped at the big table. One seemed to be telling a story. The others were rapt.

"He tells the story of how the Filipino people came upon earth," Jess said. "I think you should know it." He translated, telling how his people were created in a fight between the sea, the sky and a giant bluebird.

We were anxious to take advantage of the light that remained, and pressed on. As we moved swiftly, the light fell through the umbrella growth overhead, like that half-world glow you get underwater. The old giant *dao* was still leaning drunkenly between the two sturdy *pilis,* patiently waiting to fall down dead.

You get to the Eighth Wonder of the World by driving to Baguio, the summer capital, a beautiful city five thousand feet above sea level on a pineclad plateau 130 miles from Manila. A permanent springtime city, it has a climate that makes you feel that hot summer is acomin' in but never quite makes it. The ride is akin to shooting the rapids of the Pagsanjan River in reverse—a harrowing trip up a steep mountain on a ribbon of a road with more curves than a hungry boa constrictor.

North of Baguio one suddenly becomes aware that the hills drowsing in the butter-colored sunlight are not covered with some kind of thick mountain grass, but are, in reality, hundreds of cogon-thatched Ifugao native huts. Alfredo stops the car and says, "Here we are, at the center of one of the most extensive areas of rice terraces in the world."

The Banaue terraces rise in tiers to an altitude of five thousand feet, four times the height of the Empire State Building, stairways to the sky in an incredible tautology of design. They were dug out of the mountains by Malays four thousand years ago—so expertly that they are still in use.

Alfredo informed us that the fields are eight times as long as the Great Wall of China, are twelve thousand miles long, and if laid terrace to terrace, would reach halfway around the world. Entire mountain ranges have been reshaped in an art lost forever. A mist lifted as we stood in silence staring at the masterpieces of patience, ingenuity and backbreaking labor, and it curled around the carved-up mountains like smoke, giving the whole thing a dreamlike effect.

Finally moving away from the spectacle, we had lunch a few miles away at the Beyer Inn at Banaue, a dish of rice and shrimp chased down with *baya,* a light rice wine. (We ordered everything with rice or made from rice out of sheer respect.) Then came the ride back to Manila down the roller-coaster mountain. There is more to the Philippines for the person who is seeking adventure than is recorded here. It is a group of islands where little pockets of old cultures have somehow escaped modern erosion; the Zambales, Mindoro with its pygmies, the tree people of the central islands, and, in Mindanao, the Moslem settlements of Moros still living in the fourteenth century.

As we coasted down the road, to take our minds off the curves, Alfredo told us of an old custom of the Bagobos of Mindanao. It seems they used to sacrifice human victims annually for the benefit of their crops. In December, when the constellation Orion appeared at seven o'clock in the evening, the people realized that it was time to clear their fields for plowing and to sacrifice a slave. This was done to present to powerful spirits a payment for the good year the natives had enjoyed, and to secure the spirits' coöperation for the year ahead. The slave was led to a tree where he was tied, back to tree, arms upraised. He was killed with a spear thrust through his body at the level of his armpits. The body was then cut off at the waist. The upper part dangled, while the lower lay in blood on the ground. Finally both parts were brought together in a shallow trench beside the tree. Just before this a line of people waited to cut off a piece of flesh or a lock of hair and take it to the grave of a member of their family, whose body they believed was being eaten by a ghoul. The fresh piece of corpse would attract the ghoul and he would then leave the person in the grave alone.

Alfredo was successful in taking our attention from the road. I didn't notice a curve all the way down. I'd have to wait until I got to a good library to check Sir James Frazer's *The Golden Bough* and discover if Alfredo was an inspired storyteller or if all this was based on fact. I had an idea that it was. He knew his country well.

It was dusk as we stood staring out of our hotel window at the Bay of Manila, watching the marine traffic coming from the far places, the street lights bursting on Dewey Boulevard in little blossoms of flame. We wanted to spend more time here but couldn't. We had a long way to go: Hong Kong, Japan—where we expected a message that might take us to the North Pole in a boat four times the length of this room. Half of the excitement of this searching for the extraordinary is in the seeking. Tomorrow we would leave for Hong Kong.

One of the lessons learned the hard way by much travel is seldom to stop at the famous so-called "deluxe international hotels," the best in the city but full to the roof with the type of tourists who give you the immediate feeling that you have never left home. When deplaning at Kai Tak Airport in Kowloon, we didn't check in at the island's most popular hotel, the Peninsula, as nearly every other passenger on the plane did, but made our way to the small Grand on Carnarvon Road in the middle of the Oriental hubbub. There was no huge lobby here filled with mink and small talk, nor was there anything about the place that reminded one of home or Hilton.

I can't comment on the rest of the hotels, but the service at the Grand was swift, superb and startling. Laundry was hardly off your back when it was returned still warm from the iron and crisply clean; several old men performed a ritual of efficiency and skill at room service, providing a five-course meal—hot! Everything in Hong Kong is done in a smooth, ingratiating manner that is far from servile. With this, plus its captivating climate and Oriental outlook, kept in reasonably ordered focus by the British, Hong Kong makes much of the accessible Far East seem almost dingy in comparison.

Selling everything from antique ivory chess sets to sixty-foot sloops with teak decks, Hong Kong is noted for extremely low prices in its marts. You can buy a Swiss watch cheaper than you can in Switzerland and a Japanese camera for less than in Japan. With the U. S. dollar valued at just under six Hong Kong dollars, and with the place at times resembling a gigantic discount house, it has become the mecca of international shoppers. Even under such conditions, Hong Kong's personality is so strong, its civilization so unique, that you don't notice the tourists. Your own kind are somehow made invisible by many things: by the coolies in crow-black trousers and shirts, running easily between the traces of rickshaws; by a wizened old man sitting on a curb carving a camphor wood chest, the perfume of the camphor rising to the nostrils from twenty feet; by an old woman with an exquisite face, tottering under her headload of lacquered ducks; by quick, handsome boys rushing about the streets delivering steaming pots of tea to everyone from a shop clerk to an impatient banker.

A slender man in peasant black, with the bright-eyed, lean face of a learned ascetic, was talking to two English tourists, an elderly man and his wife, who had stopped and were staring in amazement at what was spread on the little tripod stand. "*Toad* skins?" they repeated as they were held hypnotically by his sales chatter in good English. "Yes," he was saying, "in 2300 B.C. our warriors used these to stanch the flow of blood. They worked so excellently that today modern science has discovered something in the glands of toads called epinephrine that is antiseptic and used by surgeons to stop bleeding and stimulate the heart—"

Over all rose the din of constant bargaining and the singsong voices of street peddlers melding into a strange insectlike hum rising above all other sounds. And let's not forget the slim girls in their high-necked dresses that fit like a second skin. If Hong Kong lingers in the mind longer than most strange cities, it is because of the girls. It is said that the Tang Dynasty brought poetry in China to its highest level. I'll go along with this if they have dedicated several odes to their women who walk the city streets like living poetry. Otherwise, the Tang people go down in my book as promoting inferior verse.

Perhaps this next thought can be construed as a lack of patriotism or even one of treason, but I offer it merely as an observation. If Red China really wants to conquer the world and enslave it under its particular brand of communism, I see the whole matter as a relatively simple one. All they have to do is gather up these elegant honey-brown sloe-eyed creatures in their *cheongsams,* the form-fitting dresses slit to the thigh, which show intriguing portions of flesh as they gracefully sway along the streets in quick little two-steps as sensuous as the promise of an assignation. I figure that these bronze beauties, in slit-skirted regiments, could take the world without firing a shot.

Although everything in Hong Kong, from a walk down a street to a ferry ride, can be considered a genuine adventure, we were slightly slowed down when we stopped in Ruby's, a famous restaurant in Kowloon, and watched how the West had apparently conquered the East. We were the only foreigners there; the other diners were Chinese, mostly vivacious youngsters. We were also the only ones ordering Chinese food. The Orientals ordered rich French-type pastries wheeled in on a cart, iced tea, orange drinks. One slim young girl had a mushy pile of spaghetti and a bilious-looking green drink, while her companion had coffee with a big gob of ice cream. A woman and her daughter were drowning golden American waffles in maple syrup; another sedate couple sat eating steak and fried potatoes.

Although I consider the Chinese close to being the world's best cooks, I wasn't too impressed with the native food, except for *hokien mee,* a noodle and prawn soup floating crunchy vegetables, and *satay,* skewered pork rolled in pungent sauce and grilled, and some superb seafood. Even though all the varieties that you get only in China were represented—Peking, Shanghai, Szechuen, Foochow, Swatow—and everywhere, of course, the familiar Cantonese, the heavy-oil cooking odor of which is one of the standard smells of Hong Kong.

We spent an entire evening trying to get a Peking duck, that crisp-skinned creature with the moist, delicate flesh, cooked in a manner that only the old Peking experts know. It was a discouraging search with everything from Suzie Wong salads to Kobe steaks being offered. We did find one place that specialized, but it was so smoky, dirty and noisy that it took both breath and appetite away. It is certain that exquisite native food exists in Hong Kong, that old hands there could guide me to some places where all wishes in the matter could be fulfilled. But I must report that my own search was unproductive.

The great advantage is the extremely low price of *all* food. In one restaurant I had a plate heaped with Iranian caviar. It cost $1.50. In New York it would have cost twenty dollars. Hong Kong is not to be disparaged; it is an amazing city that rejects a precise descriptive tag.

Its history is testament to the fact that the impossible is always possible here. After the Opium War (when England was profitably trafficking in the drug to the displeasure of China, who tried to retaliate on the false notion that if the Chinese withheld their rhubarb exports to England the people would die of constipation) the defeated Chinese had to permit free trade at five ports, and hand over a twenty-one-million-dollar indemnity plus "a properly located island from which Her Majesty's subjects in China may be alike protected and controlled . . ."

For reasons then unknown, Sir Henry Pottinger selected Hong Kong (Fragrant Harbor), a rocky, waterless place that caused much laughter in England—"Hong Kong" replacing certain dirty words. But the warehouses that soon went up became jammed with opium and one hundred ships delivered the happy stuff to the Chinese along the four thousand miles of mainland coast, laying the foundation for much British wealth and affluence. Officially outlawed in 1845, opium was replaced with ordinary merchandise and Hong Kong became a free port, taking in the Kowloon Peninsula in 1860 and the New Territories on a ninety-nine-year lease in 1898. World War II left the place a shambles, financially and physically. When Japan occupied the island, she cunningly withdrew all other currency, replacing it with worthless duress notes. After it was all over, England, in a bold, much criticized stroke, redeemed every bad note at face value, spending thirty million but solidly restoring Hong Kong's prestige.

With the advent of the Korean War, the United Nations slapped an embargo on the export of strategic commodities to the mainland of China from Hong Kong. Without trade with China, the island could have become a ghost community again, but the Chinese themselves saved it. More than three million Chinese moved in, bringing their money and their talent with them, converting Hong Kong from an island that produced nothing to a fantastic place that produces and sells everything. Hong Kong is full of success stories of every nationality. Linden Johnson, a Kansan who was with our air force in the Far East, is a colorful example. He didn't act like a ball of fire to me, with his lazy, soft-spoken drawl. There was nothing in his personality or physical make-up to set him apart. But he obviously had plenty of something. As the poet said, the brain has many forms of camouflage. He arrived in Hong Kong broke, borrowed some small capital from a Chinese friend and started a dress business, Dynasty. Now his clothing is sold throughout the world, and Johnson is among the most affluent in Hong Kong, a place of spectacularly successful men.

Hearing that there was a floating restaurant with wells of live fish to be selected and cooked, right from the water, we decided to take a look. To make the experience worthwhile, we gave it some trappings. We rented a Chinese junk, the *Sea Dragon,* and went to the Typhoon Shelter to look at this floating city on the way to our fish dinner.

The *Sea Dragon* was an orange and green forty-foot teakwood three-masted sailing junk. Eighteen tons, she was equipped with a marine diesel engine and manned by a crew of three, two of whom spoke English. It was identical with the craft, so I am told, in which Richard Halliburton sailed away, never to be seen again. I can recommend as an unmatched experience taking this junk around the Fragrant Harbor, running close to the dark green barges of Red China flying the yellow stars, virtually rubbing noses with craft from

Zanzibar, Istanbul, Oslo, Abidjan, Miri—flags seldom seen in any other port. The junks and sampans with faded red, yellow, orange, white and black sails billowing in an offshore breeze, drift like brilliant fall leaves on the quiet water outlined against the rise of Victoria Heights.

And then, suddenly, dramatically, one is in the Typhoon Shelter within the largest, most fantastic floating city in the world, the place of the Tam Ka people, who are born, live and die on these ragged old junks and barely buoyant sampans. They lie there humped with old canvas like a mass of water beetles. They have come here from all of China and there are so many boats and people that no one knows the population. As you stare in amazement you see several girls beckoning you to their sampans. These are houses of prostitution. Close by, in other sampans, two men are being shaved; in another an old woman is stirring a pot over a raised charcoal fire. Next to this one floats a school in session. Four boats away from the chanting schoolchildren are several market craft full of everything from fresh vegetables to huge cooked pigs that look as if they have been sprayed with orange paint. Now coming toward you is a junk with musicians and dancers, actually a Chinese opera in full swing. Small boys swim to the *Sea Dragon* for contributions and when they go back, the dancers stop and bow and the musicians smile. The Oriental tune comes across the water in a weird wail, perfect background music for this bizarre setting of impossibly bunched boats.

Now you are reminded that it is only a little distance to the fishing village of Aberdeen, and the boat where you will get your fish dinner. Aberdeen is another floating city, much smaller, full of fishing boats and many sampans paddled by women. They are the taxis to the Sea Palace. We left the *Dragon* to try a sampan, climbed down into it and sat on cushions as we got under way. It was a wobbling sensation akin to riding an English bicycle on a wet street. We were paddled toward the Sea Palace by our skinny but powerful Chinese woman dressed in coolie black and a dishpan straw hat. It came at us suddenly, alive and monsterlike, the red and blue painted hull and dragon face towering. But the evening mists suddenly swept away and we saw it for what it really was: an ancient double-decked ferry, a fat old lady of the river, retired but now called back to duty with face painted and full of cheer at a new assignment. We were helped aboard by many hands, went to the well in the ferry beside the open kitchen with its dozen cooks, gleaming pans and open fire, both gas and charcoal, and took the net we were handed. After groping in the water for a likely-looking fish, we netted lively red ones that looked like snappers, but were a new species for us—*garoupa*. Then we went back to a table laid with white cloth and waited, feasting on a heaped plate of hot broiled and boiled shrimp, which were small, sweet and delicious. When the *garoupa* came to us in a bowl of lobster and fresh tomato sauce, we ate the flaky-white sweet fish until there were only small pools of sauce streaking the bowl.

At the next dinner we had, I avenged myself on an enemy that had

This was Typhoon Shelter—"the largest, most fascinating floating city in the world."

scared me half to death in India. It was a special affair given by a Cantonese friend, a cheery little man who watched us closely as we ate. One dish was delicious, seemingly a mixture of chicken, pork, some kind of seafood, and bamboo shoots. It came to the table steaming, with side dishes of snowy rice.

"How do you like?" our Chinese host asked after my wife and I had polished off the first serving and nodded to the servant that we would like another.

"Delicious!" Mary Lou said.

"I am happy," our host said. "It is a dish that is very good for you. Banded krait is especially fine this time of the year. When I eat it I can feel its wonderful warmth go traveling down my throat and spread throughout my system. It is very healthful."

"What did you say it was?" my wife asked. "I thought it was a mixture of chicken and pork and—"

"Abalone. And snake. Banded krait," the Chinese said.

There was a long silence, broken finally by me. "When I was hunting tiger in India in 1958, a boy on a beat just three feet from me was bitten by a krait. The thing almost got me too before we killed it. I didn't sleep much in the jungle for a week after that. Kraits kept coming out of the walls. They are deadly, faster and more poisonous than a cobra."

"Well, you've gotten even now," Mary Lou said. "You've eaten your old enemy."

"Cobras," our Chinese friend repeated. "We like them, too. There are three million of us Cantonese here in Hong Kong. We eat more than a million snakes every year. All kinds. A special delicacy is snake liver that we simmer with onions and soy. I also like snake soup. Good medicine, too. Last year I had a dreadful cold. My wife cured it with krait bile mixed with rice wine." He was lost in reflection for a while. Then suddenly he said, "Will you be here next week?"

I shook my head.

"A pity," he said. "Seeing that you like snake so well, I thought you might come to a special dinner we are having at a friend's home. It is our greatest combination. In your language it is known as dragon, tiger and phoenix."

"What is it?" said Mary Lou weakly.

He smiled brightly. "Snake, cat and chicken, cooked together. A heavenly treat. I am most sorry that you won't be here."

"I am too," I said, "but our plans are made. Thanks so much

though. It sounds like a dish we should try."

"Yes," said my wife, "we are sorry to miss it."

Our Cantonese host smiled. "It is rare that we get Westerners who appreciate our special foods. I would have been proud to show you off."

The rest of the night of the krait was a bad one—a sleepless one, a night of indigestion. Probably all a matter of mind not rising over matter.

The next day we saw a couple of shops with revoltingly realistic snake art in the windows and stood fascinated watching a big black cobra being prepared for the pot. The butcher put his right foot on the snake's tail. His left hand pulled the cobra straight out. Then, with a sharp knife in his right hand, he ran a rapid line straight along the snake's body, ending by cutting a ring around the neck. Then in one quick motion, he stripped the skin from the cobra. The butcher, who proved to be the owner, told us that on a good day he sold over two thousand snakes.

The krait experience made us cautious. When you get friendly with the Chinese in Hong Kong, they go all out to win your friendship with special treats. During the next few days we politely declined dinner invitations which featured braised thigh of chow dog, fifty-year-old compost-bedded seabird eggs and a broiled cobra luncheon.

But esoteric dining isn't Hong Kong's star attraction—or distraction. Reading my notes now, I take these brief jottings from them as places to see and things to do, activity that won't exactly mark you as full of derring-do, but even the ordinary is extraordinary in Hong Kong.

Take the surprisingly spotless and timely Star Ferry from Kowloon —where your plane landed, and where your hotel most probably is— and enjoy the spectacular display of Chinese femininity aboard as you cross sun-struck water to the real city, Victoria, on twenty-nine square-mile Hong Kong island. You pass weathered junks waving torn sails, so old and salted by the sea that they move like solid silver ships out of an Oriental canvas, and sampans that make progress clumsily, their paddles protruding like the legs of a sea mammal splashing across the harbor. The Tiger Balm pagoda rises in tiers from the far shore, pagan in its posture, gleaming now in a sunlight as palpable as dripping butter.

Wander in Wanchai, supposedly the world of Suzie Wong, with startling neon-dripping night clubs and the all-pervading smells of the East: tea, noodles frying in heavy peanut oil, rice cakes simmering in soy sauce, cooking vegetables sending forth a strange steaming aroma, roast ducks hanging, so heavily oil-lacquered that they swing on their strings before the markets like pieces of huge costume jewelry. Old women trot by in their colored cotton shirts and flapping trousers, carrying everything from protesting chickens to bland babies strapped to their backs. Just stand still in Wanchai and let your eyes and ears and nose discover sights, smells and sounds that they will never find again.

Take the funicular railway that moves like a Chinese dragon switching its tail to the eighteen-hundred-foot Victoria Peak, and the heights where the old British merchant *taipans* once lived; but among the places pointed out now is "where William Holden, your actor, had a house." From the summit look down on the great harbor—one of the three most beautiful in the world, sharing honors with Rio de Janeiro, and Sydney, Australia—still crowded with history, with ships arriving from strange places, with a glittering Oriental splendor that makes even the Bay of Naples seem ordinary. Far off you can see the Portuguese island of Macao flying its plumes of city smoke, the soiled banners of civilization.

Try Cat Street, the thieves' market, where there are so many Chinese "antiques" that it takes hours to determine what to buy, and the wise usually leave buying nothing, although American tourists alone drop twenty-nine million dollars yearly in Hong Kong. But watch the barter, the sly sales pitches, the bewildered, the beckoned and the beckoning. It is more dramatic and amusing than most theaters, and admission is free—if you can use your will power and good judgment.

Walk to the end of Shanghai Street, the place of fortunetellers— Yung Shui Tow—where dignified, bearded old men will not only sagaciously delve into the future of your love life but will tell you how to grow rich by planting a certain tree at the correct moon time, a tree that will in time grow gold pieces among its roots.

And now, after working your way through countless Chinese dinners, many of them seemingly concocted for the international trade, try Jimmy's Kitchen in Victoria, in the China Building, Theater Lane. Jimmy, rotund and cheerful, had a pioneering father who came out from England many years ago, bringing good taste to the East when he opened Jimmy's. Old hands tell me the food was superb then, as it is now. I recommend the Sydney Rock oysters *mornay*. In fact, tell Jimmy I sent you and order *anything* he suggests—that is, after you have sampled the Australian oysters that are flown in daily.

"Wander in Wanchai, supposedly the world of Suzie Wong . . . roast ducks hanging on strings before the markets like pieces of huge costume jewelry."

Take the twenty-mile drive through the New Territories moving among rice terraces so precisely planted that they look like a problem in geometry laid out in the damp soil of Kam Tin Valley. Pass the ancient walled city of Leung Yuk Tao, now double-walled with silence and isolation, until you come to Red China's border. The landscape, suddenly marred by rusty barbed wire, is guarded by the newly awakened China's soldiers with their stone faces and their dirty yellow uniforms. Beyond, in the distance, blue hills rise. Here more than 600 million people live like animals, yoked to lives and livelihoods not of their choosing. I look past the hooks of wire and the emotionless men with guns, caught in the sudden realization of the terror and the power and the confusion that wait over there. I also wonder how long civilization can go on pitting ideology against ideology, and suddenly remember the words of an old man in Accra years ago when he was asked if there was any way to cure the enmity, stop the fighting between the Gold Coast tribes. He looked at us with red-veined, rheumy old eyes and said: "Hate has no medicine."

CHAPTER FIVE

SPITSBERGEN AND SCANDINAVIA

A cable was awaiting at the Grand. The diesel ketch taking us to the North Pole would be ready in a few days. We would fly to Norway across the top of the world, nonstop from Japan to Alaska, then Copenhagen.

A jet brought us in a swallow-swift flight to Tokyo, which we didn't have time to see, for our plane to the north was to depart in a matter of hours.

Harry Backelin, an American employee of the Scandinavian Airlines System on his way to Sweden from Tokyo, was tall, blond, looking more Scandinavian than the short, dark Norwegian purser who kept our glasses filled. He told me about the flying miracle performed when the dream of this Northwest air passage over the earth's most dangerous terrain came true. We struck up conversation when I commented on the excellence of the '55 Chablis that accompanied a luncheon of chicken breast in aspic, to be followed by a tender Kobe steak and a superb Bordeaux. Our talk began out of mutual respect for wine, and appreciation of the remarkable fact that we were speeding above this untracked icy wilderness in such luxury with the velocity of a .45-caliber bullet.

In pioneering this air lane, the airline had seemingly unsolvable navigational problems: the magnetic North Pole, the polar twilight and the disappearance of direction at the Pole. In this region ordinary compasses point due south when they should read north, or go wild. SAS had to find something that would point in one direction and stay there. From this need they developed the Polar Path Gyro. The size of an orange, it works like a top; electrically powered, it remains fixed in space for twenty hours. Ordinary maps were also useless, necessitating a change of course every few minutes as the plane cut across one meridian after another. The further complicating fact that all meridians meet at the Pole where all directions become south forced SAS to develop a new method—the Polar Grid System.

The grid is simply an accurate chart of the polar regions over-printed with a series of parallel lines. All meridians are ignored except the center line running from Greenwich, England, across the North Pole and on down to the South Pacific. The direction of the line is north—grid north, remaining north even after the plane has passed the geographic North Pole and is technically going south. The chart is the key to this amazing flight.

"So we sail right over the top of the world," Backelin said, "with the flight-watch help of five special radio stations below, Andenes, Isfjord, Nord, Dundas and Point Barrow. Each has ground-wave transmitters with a range of seven hundred miles. This is the first time ground-wave stations have been used on such a large scale. We furnish them with position checks, using them as a navigational cross-check. They feed us weather and other ground data.

"It may seem smug to point out that we're doing in sixteen hours what it took Fridtjof Nansen, Robert E. Peary and Roald Amundsen a year to accomplish," Backelin continued. "Then they traversed just part of the Arctic. We hop from Tokyo to Copenhagen. It took Peary twenty-three years of preparation to reach the North Pole with dog sleds, moving from Ellesmere Island, west of Greenland. It took him thirty-six days to cross, sixteen to return." He waved his hands. "I could talk this up to you all the way to Copenhagen. It gets boring."

"Not to me, it doesn't," I said. "When did SAS make the first trip?"

"On November 19, 1952, we flew the first commercial flight over the arctic area, from Los Angeles to Copenhagen. Then on February 24, 1957, we inaugurated the world's first air service over the North Pole, linking Europe and the Far East via Alaska. Our first 'Northwest Passage' flight straight across the Arctic Ocean was in May, 1954, with a DC-6B, from Bodø in northern Norway to Fairbanks, Alaska, then on to Shemya Island and Tokyo."

We were moving smoothly without battling air currents. "I had an idea this would be a rough flight," I said.

"Our weathermen point out that the Arctic is like a desert," Backelin said. "A region of generally light winds, low humidity, infrequent or thin clouds, little rain or snow. When we do get clouds over the polar area, usually in late summer, they never move above ten thousand feet. In the tropics, clouds form at fifty thousand feet or even higher." He smiled. "I'm not a talking machine. I primed on this before flying over the Pole to Tokyo, for my own information. And, like you, I'm curious. Anyway, by flying at thirty thousand feet we avoid clouds, icing and the bumps. And at this height, air temperature above the North Pole is the same as that above Europe and North America. Actually, the lowest temperature ever recorded, 90 degrees below zero centigrade, 130 Fahrenheit, was taken at fifty-five thousand feet above Java in the East Indies, near the equator."

We came down at Fairbanks, Alaska, to refuel and to change pilots. The airfield was ringed by gray buildings as bleak and forbidding as anything I had seen during the war. It was cold and damp. Water collected in little pools that glimmered in the gray light, reflecting the hunched figures of the passengers from our flight as they sloshed dazedly through the mud. Now that we were on the ground, a sudden exhaustion overtook us; our faces flushed and our steps dragged. We were anxious to get to Copenhagen. The hour wait before reboarding the plane seemed like six.

Wonderful, wonderful Copenhagen. Short hours since Alaska, and now the lights of the gay town were twisting down there like worms. *The worms of light,* we said to ourselves as the plane circled, waiting for landing instruction. *The worms of light, they twist and they dance in a land of solid smörgåsbord, running with rivers of foaming beer.* And with thoughts beginning to blur, we realized that we were very tired; the bed at the Terminus would be welcome.

Johannes Jensen, then director of the Terminus Hotel, a trim, blue-eyed Dane with the direct, pleasing manner of the Jutlander, had become a friend. He waited for us in a room of thick red carpets and polished brass. "Welcome, Mary Lou and Jack!" His hand swept toward an elegant brocade banquette. In an instant a blond boy in uniform appeared as if from a hole in the floor, with foaming glasses of draft Tuborg. I could feel myself relaxing as it went down. Mary Lou said, "Mr. Jensen, this is what we needed!" He smiled. "I know. Now for bed—"

Beds in Copenhagen—at least in the Terminus—are not beds at all. They are clouds, captured by the canny Danes. Our room overlooked the old stone Danish tourist office flying its red and white flags. Hunting prints on the walls of our room showed woodcock and pheasant shooters doing everything wrong, but they were bright and cheerful, nevertheless. The last thing I saw before sinking into the softness of the goosedown mattress and pulling the goosedown *dyne* over me was the picture of a brown and white spaniel flushing woodcock on the wall at the foot of my bed.

The morning was gray as it often is in Copenhagen, the sky the color of putty, the red-and-white national flags flapping violently in the wind off the Kattegat. The deep voice of the tower clock at Town Hall struck the half-hour, and the city's copper towers rose in medieval green splendor as the taxi made its way to Kastrup Airport. We were to catch flight SK-302 for Bardufoss, first leg of the journey north.

The plan: get to Tromsø and pick up passage on the S.S. *Lyngen,* an old coastal steamer that was taking a group of scientists on a preconference seminar cruise to Svalbard before they attended sessions of the Nineteenth International Geographic Congress at Stockholm. Every country except Russia was supposed to be represented aboard the *Lyngen.* At Longyearbyen, an arctic coal-mining settlement, we would then board the *Havella,* a specially constructed 57-foot diesel ketch, and sail toward the North Pole.

The prop plane was rough in comparison to a jet and you suddenly realized how quickly modern man is converted to machines of the future: the jet hasn't been around long enough for any passenger to become critical of these reliable planes with propellers, but that is exactly what I found myself doing when the Metropolitan hit air currents with a pash not unlike that of a motorboat cresting a wave. As we made our descent, the runway at Bardufoss came up—a narrow strip of concrete that lay gleaming in the morning sun like a piece of adhesive tape stuck to a hairy arm, sparse grass sticking up all along the strip that was too short to accommodate the land-eating jet.

As we walked to where the bus was waiting, I stopped and talked with a pilot still in blue uniform who was showing a creel of trout to passengers. The fish glittered like jewelry, so fresh that the iridescence was still there. "This is great fishing country," he said in schoolboy eagerness, "trout everywhere. The best salmon in the world are farther north!"

"As far north as Spitsbergen?" I said.

He looked at me. "You're really going far out, aren't you? That's pioneer country! They tell me one of the great fish is there, the Spitsbergen salmon." Weeks later I discovered that his information was accurate. Standing before the bus were two hatless men, obviously Americans. One, in a loud checked gray and black sports jacket, was blond and stout; the other, in a suede coat, tall, lean and dark. As we approached, the blond man said, "You must be the Scotts." When we nodded, he said, "I'm Ben Berg from Madison, Wisconsin. This is Ed Bryant from Stoughton. We're going along on the *Havella* to have a look at polar bears."

This was the first we knew that we were going to have company, but I should have known that Odd Berg, the ship's owner, was not a man to send off a cruise without squeezing out all the profit he could. I was skeptical as I stood there in the bland Norwegian sunlight, wondering how the four of us would get along for over a month in close quarters. It can be uncomfortable and annoying to be thrown into such close contact with strangers, especially if they turn out to have personalities that aren't compatible. I shouldn't have given it a thought. Berg and Bryant were a cheery asset to the trip, and as I look back on this stirring adventure now, I know that it wouldn't have been half as pleasurable if the two from Wisconsin hadn't been aboard.

The bus drive to Tromsø took four hours through farm country where entire families were in the fields haying: women with bras showing much creamy-tan skin, tow-headed youngsters, shirts off, using pitchforks with dexterity. In one field, a man, woman and child were passing around a coffeepot. The land looked thin and rocky; the only crops hay, potatoes, and a few carrot patches. Every family had a horse, some three or four cows; most houses had a deep sod roof which seemed to be growing. Several had small trees sprouting. The roughly paved road had been patched so often that it was covered with little blister-like bumps. It was so winding and narrow that when we met another car, one had to pull to the side to let the other pass. Our bus, like buses everywhere, was a bully and we pulled over seldom.

Tromsø finally swam into view, a bleak frontier settlement of fifteen thousand, two hundred miles above the Arctic Circle on an islet between Kvaløy and the mainland. Frosts arrive in May; the autumn freeze in early October. Fish and seal oil factories and a couple of tanneries dominate, but it is also noted for making sturdy boots and once was famous for its whaling vessels. I remembered that the Germans occupied it in 1940. (Later, on an uninhabited island, we would see some weird results of that occupation.) It is a historic jumping-off point for northern explorers, and the town square has a towering, heroic statue of one of the most famous, Roald Amundsen, who lost his life when he flew from Tromsø to rescue the Italian, Umberto Nobile, who, against Amundsen's advice, attempted to reach the Pole in the dirigible *Italia*.

Norwegians are a notoriously proud and independent people, sometimes carrying these character traits to an annoying extreme. We couldn't stir a soul into helping us take our baggage to the Grand Hotel, which proved to be a place full of small rooms, the smell of boiled cabbage and fried mutton, over-age bellboys who seemed weary of the whole thing, and yet an air of excitement, which made up for its shortcomings.

We expected to board the *Lyngen* in a couple of days so we unpacked only the necessities and went to the lobby to meet Berg and Bryant and to await Odd Berg's representative, Wilhelm Bolin. He came trudging in, a slender, tired-looking man, with blond hair that was beginning to go, startling blue eyes and an odd, lilting accent. He carried a thick, old-fashioned, double-strapped briefcase as if it were full of rare documents. As far as he was concerned, it was. In it were papers telling us what the trip would cost, who the crew was, what food we would have aboard, maps of Spitsbergen—or Svalbard, as he called it—and some excellent literature, not only of the area we would sail but of the *Lyngen* itself.

Mary Lou and I had a bad supper—or didn't have—of overcooked cod and greasy half-raw fried potatoes before going to bed, where I went through the Svalbard material. It was a trying experience looking at my watch and discovering it was midnight though the sun was shining. There were no curtains on the windows so I couldn't even pretend it was night by masking the light. The Midnight Sun would take some adjustment.

When I first decided that Spitsbergen was a place I wanted to see, I was sitting in a bar in New York City with two knowledgeable Norwegian friends who delighted me with tales of the far places jets had made accessible.

"Far north in the Arctic," one of them said, "are mountainous islands; mysterious places surrounded by a gale-driven sea, cut off from the mainland by hundreds of miles. The Gulf Stream's warmth keeps the sea open. Midnight sun and south winds take over during the summer. Flowers grow on the islands. You can see more polar bears there than any place else on earth; several species of seals, blue foxes, thousands of birds. It is one of the great adventures left."

According to the information left by Bolin, my friend had it right. Lured by tales of great riches, explorers began looking for a shorter route to China. Rather than sail around Africa, they decided to short-cut along the north coast of Asia. A pair of Dutch ships under the command of the arctic explorer Willem Barents, started off on May 18, 1596. Less than a month later they were at the cold coast and killed their first polar bear on an unknown island. Without exerting much imagination, they named it Bear Island and proceeded until they were stopped by the ice packs, great stretches of jammed, jagged, moving ice that threatened to overwhelm them. Blinded by fog, menaced by moving ice, one of the ships still managed to turn and get back to Holland, but Barents pushed on, was finally encircled by pack ice, his ship seriously damaged. He died on Novaya Zemlya that winter. Shortly afterward many European countries had a hand in the rich whaling and sealing the region offered—England, Norway, France, Denmark, Russia, Holland. Dutch records show that this country alone took sixty thousand whales.

Spitsbergen has drawn many explorers hoping to reach the Pole. Andrée, a Swedish scientist, tried it in 1897 in a balloon. He died on Kvitoya. An American, Walter Wellman, attempted it in 1909, using an inadequate airship which was quickly wrecked. He was rescued by a party of Norwegians from Tromsø. Roald Amundsen made an attempt in 1925 by air and got as far as 87° 43′. The next year Richard Byrd reached it by plane; so did the redoubtable Roald Amundsen and Lincoln Ellsworth in the airship *Norge*. The record of those who have tried and failed is long; history is full of adventurous men who were attracted to this dangerous cold coast.

A barren, mountainous arctic archipelago, Spitsbergen lies in the northwesterly part of the large continental platform between the polar basin and the continent to the south and north. It consists of five large and several small islands, some of them less than four hundred nautical miles from the North Pole. Southernmost is Bjornøya; northernmost, Sjuøyane, 10 degrees from the Pole. Total land area is 24,-095 square miles, twice the size of Belgium. The largest island is Vest Spitsbergen with 15,250 square miles; Nordaustlandet with 5,800 square miles is next. Others include Hopen, Kong Karls Land and Kvitøya, Barentsøya, Edgeøya, Prins Karls Forland—most are situated between 76 and 80 degrees latitude North and 10 and 28 degrees longitude East. Since the North Pole lies at a flat 90 degrees, this gives a rough idea of the character of the territory we were trying to reach.

Mountains on even the smaller islands are impressive: many of them rising three thousand feet; Newton Toppen rears up 5,630 feet. The Gulf Stream makes the place habitable, bringing a mean annual temperature of nineteen degrees, which to my way of thinking is hardly enjoyable, but in June, July, and August, the temperature rises as high as forty-two degrees; sometimes on calm days even seventy degrees has been registered.

It was warm the next morning when Mary Lou, Berg, Bryant and I went to see the *Lyngen*. She was tied up at the dock with a crowd of locals inspecting her. According to Bolin, she was a 120-foot steamship of five hundred tons with hand-fired coal boilers, had been built in 1931, put into arctic service in 1934 and spent the months of June, July, August and September plying the waters from Tromsø to Spitsbergen, as far as the mining settlement of Kings Bay. She looked more like an old coastal freighter to me, was a bit rusty, and you could hear her metal bones creak as she moved in the slight swell. But she was big and she looked rugged.

We spent hours walking around Tromsø, seeing the town hall, the whaling museum and the taxidermist, who was proud that he had his warehouse stuffed with polar-bear skins, telling us one Norwegian "had killed six hundred bear! Great man that!" The houses were mostly unpainted frame, silvered with wind and seaspray; many window sills had flowerpots, geraniums and delphinium getting the lemon sun. The people were reserved and uncommunicative, walking the streets without a look at us, although it was obvious we were strangers.

It was also obvious that some tourists had made their way this far north on cruises from Bergen but no farther. Shops were stuffed with all kinds of junk, as well as some excellent products: hand-knit sweaters made to shed the cold, sealskin boots, jackets, gloves. In one we saw a magnificent polar-bear hide made into a rug with a hi-fi unit in its head that a lucky tourist could pick up for $500. A bargain. Without the radio it would cost three times that amount in New York.

As we got acquainted I learned from Berg that Edwin Bryant was president of a big company in Stoughton, Wisconsin. He was dedicating much of his time and income to the growing problem of carbon-dioxide exhaust from cars and industrial smoke, and had become an international expert. From Bryant I learned that Ben Berg had owned the largest and most successful sporting-goods store in Wisconsin, but had recently become quite wealthy by going to his basement—like many another ingenious American before him—and inventing a product that helped his country progress and its industry flourish. His mother had been born near Tromsø and he was delighted to come this far north, look the country over and see the people she often talked about.

Boarding the *Lyngen* at midnight was a gay affair; nearly everyone in town came to see us sail. Interesting-looking people in all manner of dress began arriving with weird luggage. I recognized a few words in six languages before we even got our luggage aboard. These were the fifty scientists who had come from Stockholm to take an expert look at the North. Scientists seem the easiest professional group to recognize. They have a certain dreamy air, a lack of reality about dress, baggage, clearing the gangway, getting aboard on time.

I stood behind a bearded young man leaning nonchalantly against the rail as the *Lyngen*'s engines coughed, the harbor herring gulls flew above us in bursts of black and white like an unfurled Japanese fan, and we backed away. "You ask me why I go on these explorations?" he said to a fleshy young American behind him. "I can't say, really. Human nature always wants what it doesn't have. If we are accustomed to things such as culture, civilization, luxury, we seek something else. Perhaps even the primitive—"

"As my father remarked," the fleshy young man said, " 'The beautiful girls are always walking on the opposite side of the street.' "

"Exactly!" said the bearded man in his precise Oxford English.

I hadn't seen everyone yet, of course, but I was rapidly coming to the conclusions that there weren't any pretty girls aboard. There was a quartet of determined-faced, big-busted German women in thick woolen stockings, skirts and heavy Swedish sweaters—their gay colors lost on the wearers. Moving in storm-trooper formation up the center line of the deck, these women and a few others, skinny, intense, standing at the shoreward rail as alert as cranes hunting for fish, watched the water roil with the movement of the ship as we left Tromsø.

The first-class cabins were so small that they made you feel you were living in a broom closet. But the situation had a double appeal: the unusual scenery and the scientists aboard. Between the sea views and human company—the geologists, botanists, ornithologists, oceanographers, ichthyologists and geomorphologists—it was clear that we would not spend much time in the cabin. It would take four days to get to Longyearbyen where we expected to board the M.S. *Havella*.

If I had known that we would soon run out of trees and not see a single one again until we came back to the vicinity of Tromsø, I would have feasted my eyes on the pines, spruces and other evergreens that lined the rocky shore. Instead I watched the people; they were as excited as school children as they stood at the rail, guidebooks of Svalbard in hand, talking about the icebergs and glaciers they hoped to see. One skinny young man with shaggy blond hair resembled an egret, as he excitedly stood on one foot, then the other. He proved to be an English ornithologist, and whenever anyone was in doubt about the variety of seabirds that followed the *Lyngen* like a long flowing banner, they merely had to ask him. He named the species instantly. A handsome, sullen young German, reporter from a Hamburg paper, wore stylish Swiss mountain sports clothes and beautiful suede shoes. He was on his way to Longyearbyen, planning to spend a year in that lonely outpost. He said that he hoped to write a book about the coal miners and their families who lived and worked there.

"A dude," said Berg. "He won't last three months in Longyearbyen if the place is as rough as I hear."

Bryant, Berg, Mary Lou and I luckily found a table in the dining room and were told by the waitress, who did little except clear the tables after we were finished, that the linen napkins at our places were ours for the trip. And she wasn't joking. Those soon-to-be-stiff napkins were unchanged for the voyage. Meals were served smörgåsbord style from a large central table. Everyone helped himself, but we soon discovered that this wasn't as cozy as it seemed; that phalanx of German women was now part of our dining group, and they were first and last at the buffet. They moved around that circular table shoulder to shoulder, making it a physical impossibility for anyone else to serve himself until they had heaped their plates with the best of everything.

When the sea started getting rough, the tables were liberally sprinkled with water to keep the plates from sliding to the floor. At this point we lost nearly everyone in the dining room. The *Lyngen* tossed and rolled like a bathtub and there were times when the waves got so fierce that we felt that our stomachs had moved to where our hearts should be. But no matter how rough it got, our German ladies never missed a meal.

One dreadful day when no more than a dozen people could even attempt to stir from their cabins, every plate in the dining room crashed to the floor with a sound that brought us rushing, thinking that we had run into an iceberg. There in the dining room were the four Germans complaining bitterly to the waitresses about the spilled food and the fact that their luncheon had been disturbed. Mary Lou and I grew pale at the sight in the room: food was splashed about everywhere; dishes and cups shattered. The sight and the smell further upset stomachs that we thought could take no more. But nausea began to subside as we got to the heaving deck and drew fresh air into our lungs.

We lost the treeline early on the second day, long before we got to the first stop, Hornsund, where a group of Polish scientists had established an observation station. Their leader, a regal old man with a full white beard, came aboard to pay his respects to the captain and meet the more important of the scientists. Before he left he invited them all to come and take a look at his station. The entire fifty accepted. Berg and Bryant managed to get into the boats with them.

We had encountered ice floes and the mountainous shoreline long ago. But Hornsund appeared to be carved out of solid ice. Now that nearly everyone had left the *Lyngen,* the little bay was quiet, the water gentle. Huge white glaucous gulls were landing in clumsy belly-flops near small floes that looked as if they had been drenched in a housewife's bluing. The mountains beyond, sleek in snow with some brown rock showing, were capped with cloud and mist. The icecap was there, too, streaked in a vivid blue that flared when the sun hit it, like a match being struck.

The only sounds were the creaking of the boat as she swayed in the natural swell, the voices of a few of the crew drinking beer with the waitresses and three Polish boys from Hornsund in the dining room. A generator hummed somewhere below and from the radio in the saloon, music started coming up softly—"Carolina Moon"—which reminded me that American music is everywhere. It brought back a night in the Indian jungles a year before when "Sleepy Time Gal" came purring at us at 3:00 A.M. from a small radio in the *dak* bungalow. This came to us from Peking, out of the Communist stronghold to us in our isolated forests of the night.

Our scientists, most of them clutching rocks, shards of shale, bird feathers, lichen or some other type of flora specimen—with Berg and Bryant, big-eyed in admiration of these dedicated men and women—returned at 2:00 in the morning, and the *Lyngen,* coughing smoke and rattling her bones, continued toward Longyearbyen.

During the cruise Mary Lou and I had talked at length with several of the experts and spent as much time as we could manage with R. Kay Gresswell, a slender, articulate Englishman, lecturer in geomorphology at the University of Liverpool and author of *The Physical Geography of Glaciers and Glaciation.* It was he who made this country come alive for us as no book or less literate guide could.

When he heard that we were going to board the *Havella* in Longyearbyen and go farther north cruising the islands of Svalbard, he said, "I envy you! We'll go as far as the most northern outpost, Kings Bay, then return to Tromsø. We've got to get back to that conference in Stockholm. But on this particular trip you're going to see some of

"Mountains beyond . . . were capped with cloud and mist. The icecap was there, too, streaked in a vivid blue that flared when the sun hit it, like a match being struck."

the most impressive country in existence."

An ice expert, he was prejudiced. He sketched a few facts about the islands of Svalbard and ice sheets, glaciers and icebergs so skillfully that they made you want to be able to sit in on some of his lectures at Liverpool. But here he was able to point at an iceberg and say, "When either a glacier or part of an ice sheet reaches the sea without melting entirely, it rides on the sea floor until there is sufficient depth of water to float it. It then continues to move northward, pushed by the ice behind it, becoming thinner and thinner as it gradually melts away. When it is only a few hundred feet thick, pieces often break off from the front edge—calving, this is called—and float away as icebergs. These calves are more massive than they appear. You can only see the one-ninth portion that is above the water level. The bergs drift with the current, often traveling hundreds of miles in the cold polar water before they eventually hit warmer currents and melt."

Once he pointed at some black-headed gulls sitting on an ice floe and was off again. "Floes are different from bergs," he said. "They are formed by the surface of the sea freezing. Of course, salt water requires a lower temperature than fresh to freeze, but it is plenty cold enough up this way to do the job." He laughed. "If you get short of drinking ice where you're going, don't chop it from floes. They're pure salt. Bergs are frozen from fresh water and make an excellent base for your martinis. Those innocent-looking little floes out there often break up into smaller pieces sometimes covering a square mile. This is pack ice. I doubt if we'll run into any hereabouts, but it is likely that you will on *Havella*. Pack ice can be dangerous. Some ships have been imprisoned in it for months at a time."

He also told us that the islands of Svalbard and the sea-bottom around them were covered with ice sheets, and that the fjords and valleys, although they were river valleys, had actually been shaped by the glaciers. Telling us that we would see conditions that are the same today as they were ten thousand years ago at the end of the Ice Age, he said that some of the islands were completely covered with ice. Kvitøya's entire surface was covered; Nordaustlandet was fifty percent ice-sheeted; and Vest Spitsbergen's central region was solid ice, some of it more than two thousand feet deep in places.

The professor explained that there were more glaciers where we were going than any place else on earth; that only the very small islands were without them. He told us that the frozen crust in Svalbard is nine-hundred feet deep. Even in warmest summer only one to three feet of surface thaws. Noticing Mary Lou's expression, he quickly added that there also were large areas free of ice and snow and we would even see flowers in some places. Broad valleys would extend for miles into the interior of Vest Spitsbergen. If we walked to the end of a valley we would see the receding tip of the glacier, which in its retreat had probably created small lakes, rivers and streams. Exploration inland sometimes became difficult because these rivers and streams constantly changed course, with rushing water everywhere. We would discover this for ourselves soon.

The night after the stop at the Polish station—no stars or moon; night came only on one's wristwatch—the seas became the roughest yet. We couldn't even lie in our bunks for fear of banging our heads. We stood and hung onto handrails, bracing ourselves against the lashing dragontail of the sea. More crockery was broken and in order to save enough to eat from on the return—not out of kindly concern for his passengers—the captain changed course several times, hoping to run out of rough weather. He finally succeeded and we all rushed to the deck for fresh air. Even the four German women, though in fairness to their unswerving determination, I must record that it was long past the dinner hour.

Nearly five days after we left Tromsø, on a memorable sea-calm July 28th, we sighted Longyearbyen, the mining center founded by an American engineer, John Longyear, who developed it, established the mining techniques, ran it from 1904 to 1916, then sold it to a Norwegian company. With its 1,200 people, plus the superintendent of mines and the governor, it was the capital of Svalbard.

Our first view of this far north settlement—a cluster of weathered houses, several large institutional-type buildings, the area bisected by muddy roads—was seen through a gray rain. Near the quay, where trucks were already lining up with coal for the *Lyngen*, were three workshops, a power station and a mess hall. The geologists were invited to the new community center for lunch. We spotted our sleek white craft floating like a swan among the ugly duckling Longyearbyen coal craft as soon as we entered the harbor. Scheduled to board the *Havella* at dinnertime, we trudged through biting rain up the muddy road toward the center, with Berg and Bryant leading the way. The young German who was to stay in Longyearbyen sailed by grandly in a jeep. Dry, and smiling now, he waved. I decided that Berg had been wrong. Here was a fellow who would get along.

At the center we were in for a surprise. It was a well-designed modern building with a restaurant, several spacious lounges, a theater, a gym, all brightly painted and filled with chattering people. Our group of scientists was gathered in a huge lounge drinking beer and eating reindeer stew with the mine officials. As we got dishes of the savory stew and foaming glasses, Ben Berg's ruddy face beamed. He said, "I don't know if I've told you the little rule I have in life. Have a little fun *every day*." Dunking a piece of coarse homemade bread in the stew and chasing it down with the cold beer, he added, "This is the fun for today!"

Tall, dark Ed Bryant laughed as Berg went at his stew. "Yep," he said, "Ben gets that little fun even if he has to twist things a bit to make it come out that way."

We were joined by the short American who had made the remark about pretty women always being on the other side of the street. He was Emmett Costello, a schoolteacher from Chicago, who spent his summers wandering the world picking up knowledge and pleasure. And he was generous about passing on both. He had explored Ireland last year, the Donegal Mountains and the fishing off the Erin Islands; the year before he had steeped himself in Pueblo Indian culture. He had a quick mind and a fascinating tongue.

"They're going to take a few of us through the coal mines," he said. "Mine Five. Why don't you come along? Walk *through* a mountain for once. Any of you ever seen a mine in operation?" None of us had.

The five of us went up the hill to the mine in a little electric trolley and entered the main gallery which extended horizontally for several miles into the mountain. All of the galleries were propped with heavy timber to keep mountain rock from collapsing and blocking the exits. We wore headlamps on light-metal helmets and moved cautiously through the gloom, deep in the heart of the mountain, in some places hunching as we went to avoid props and rock overhang.

Our miner-guide, a youngster with flaming yellow hair and a grin, took us to a stope—a mining term used to describe excavation of a certain kind; our guide had been on his belly cutting the lower part of a solid slab of coal with a long narrow electric saw. Costello discovered that one miner takes out three tons of coal a day. Surprisingly the underground air seemed quite good; we had no trouble breathing, but it was rather cold—twenty-seven degrees the year around according to Costello—and in the cross-cut we were walking, coal dust gathered, a black film that spread like paint. A miner was going before us spreading lime to bind the dust. This would prevent explosions caused by pit gas.

On the way out, our guide went to join the other miners, and Berg and I walked over to thank him. He was taking a verbal beating. After working for three years, crawling up to stopes on his belly for eight hours a day, spending the rest of the time in one of the world's loneliest places, he was finally going on a three-month vacation—to Paris! Right now he was getting ribald advice on just how he should handle the various situations he would encounter in the wicked city. Some of the suggestions smacked of a weirdness that could only come from womanless months spent locked up in the dark heart of a mountain.

It had stopped raining. The sunlight was warm and bright when we came out of the mine and stood on the protruding lip of rock, looking down at the bay. The boats were bugs; the trucks were crawling from the quay like long, joined insects. Beyond, Temple Mountain rose in layers like a fantastic Viennese torte. This time with the loquacious Costello aiding us, we got a ride back to the *Lyngen.*

The captain and crew of the *Havella* were waiting for us. The captain was short with dandelion hair, blazing blue eyes and a game leg—right out of Joseph Conrad. He limped forward, saying, "I am Haakon Godtliebsen, master of *Havella.* My English is not good. But Alf, my mate, his good." We introduced ourselves, shook hands, and the captain waved his crew forward.

"This ice pilot, big man in north. Sigurd Dal." Dal, a blocky man with huge shoulders, walked over and shook hands. Then came Alf Olsen, the mate, a slim blond boy with quiet, grayish-blue eyes and a hard, lined face browned with seaburn. Next was a bald man, probably in his late sixties. He wore glasses that shimmered in the sun, his skin looked like leather, and he laughed as he came forward. "I keep *Havella* going. I Harald Hansen, engineer. Forty years at sea." The last, short and dark, looking like an impossible combination of Hoagy Carmichael and Ned Sparks, was Aage Rutwold, steward. He bobbed his head shyly at us and stood his ground.

Each had a quiet air of confidence that communicated itself, and we felt relieved as we helped transfer baggage from the fat, dirty old queen of the coastline, the *Lyngen,* onto the trim white craft. *Havella,* the captain told us, meant Sea Duck. It did float there as gracefully as a seabird.

We were out of the harbor in a matter of minutes, watching Longyearbyen fade away. The mountain we had walked through was the last thing we saw. It loomed dark and cold, and we thought a little guiltily of the men sealed inside. Shaking this off, we went below, exploring the ship, finding a comfortable lounge amidships, two double cabins, a head with a shower; then the galley, small but clean and efficiently equipped; beyond that the crew's quarters.

The 150-horsepower diesel sawed like a leopard beneath us as we went back on deck and the captain told us about the ship we would live on for the next month.

Odd Berg had spared no expense to make her Arctic-worthy: Built in 1952, a fifty-seven-foot, forty-ton copy of the famed Norwegian rescue boats, she was constructed with double hull to take the pack ice and the accidental butting of an iceberg. In addition to her powerful diesel, she had 1,178 square feet of sail area, was equipped with an automatic steering, echo-sounder, direction finder, electric log and a radio-telephone. She cruised at nine knots and, small as she was, the *Havella* rode like the *Queen Elizabeth* in comparison to the *Lyngen* and her bathtub wallow.

It would take forty-five hours to get into polar-bear territory where Berg and Bryant could go after their trophies. Berg would also do a 16mm. movie of the bear and the cruise. Mary Lou and I were interested in the land, the birds, photographing the bears. In addition, I was hoping to gather enough material for a natural-history piece on the white animal.

Alf Olsen filled us in on himself and some of the crew while we made our way toward Kings Bay, another coal-mining community, where we would make our first stop and take on water and fuel. He assured us that our cases of whiskey and *øl* (beer) were aboard, that we had a good larder, and that we would see plenty of bears.

He had been a sealer for ten years, sailing most of the Arctic, had worked in the mines and had been with the *Havella* since she started her Arctic cruising in 1953. The captain had also been a sealer, graduated to mate in his twenties, just as Alf had, and been master of various ships for twenty years.

Watching Berg and Mary Lou with their cameras, both snapping at floes and resting gulls, he said, "You come at a good time. This is the season for 127 days of sun. You can take pictures twenty-four hours every day."

"How many dark days do you have?" Bryant asked. He was having trouble adjusting to the constant sunlight, staying awake most of the time, catnapping only occasionally.

"We never see the sun for 112 days," Alf said. "Those are the bad times. We live for this time."

Fourteen hours after we left Longyearbyen, we came up a shining spit of water, Kongsfjord, into Ny Ålesund or Kings Bay Harbor, passing, sometimes going through, flat floes that parted with a sound like breaking glass as our hull sliced them.

Skillfully spinning the *Havella* to the dock, the captain shouted. "Want you to see sight," he said. "Coming now across the *bukt* to us is a harbor seal, maybe ring, maybe saddleback. See how he comes!"

From the far side of the bay a dark object swam toward us, veering now as it saw the *Havella*, coming straight for us.

"A tame one!" Bryant said. "Get set, Mary Lou and Ben. Might be a good picture—"

Just its black head was above water. As we watched, the weird goggle eyes grew, became enormous. Now hind feet came splashing out of the water. Seals have no hind feet.

Treading water now, the animal said, "Hi, there! Any Americans aboard?"

The captain was speechless. Mary Lou had enough presence of mind to say, "Four of us. Hello!" The rest of us stared. What was a man doing in an arctic bay, so far north it isn't even on most maps, swimming in water that must have been so cold that it would freeze a human within minutes?

Swimming easily and gracefully now, he came close to us. We reached over and helped him aboard. He was tall, dripping water from a black frogman's rubber suit, and awkward in his long flippers. Taking off goggles and head portion, he revealed a handsome face, blond hair and snapping blue eyes.

Laughing, he said, "I'm Fred Baldwin from New York. Out getting a little practice." He shook the water off and we went below to the lounge, broke out the whiskey and discovered why he was imitating a seal so skillfully that he had even deceived our captain.

"Have a bunkhouse here in Kings Bay," he said, "working with a photographer from Sweden. He's after life in the north. I'm for polar bear, but I'm having trouble getting a boat."

"What do you want with *isbjørn?*" The captain finally broke his shocked silence with the animal's Norwegian name, ice bear.

"I've got go-ahead assignments from *Sports Illustrated* and the *National Geographic* magazines for picture spreads. *If* I pull it off. I want to photograph polar bears underwater. *Me,* I'll be underwater. Photographing them on top, swimming, killing seals. Anything I can find."

"Do you know polar?" the captain said. "I begin think you are mad! *Isbjørn* lives on seals. Seals black and shiny in water. As you in rubber suit. You will get eaten!"

"He is right, Mr. Baldwin," Alf Olsen said. "We thought you were a seal in the bay. And me, I've seen more seals in my life than people."

"I was practicing," he said, ignoring the warning. "Getting my wind. This suit is beautifully insulated. Don't feel the cold at all. I can do that bay in nothing flat. Next, I'll start swimming with the cameras underwater."

"Will you have a man with a gun with you?" I asked.

"Nope," he said. "The Swede will come along. With another camera. We want pictures, not carcasses."

"Could be your own carcass," Berg said. "I take pictures, too. This sounds like a damn-fool stunt. Polar bears. Underwater!"

Baldwin went on to tell us that he really wasn't crazy, but that photography had become so competitive, with so many expert and imaginative practitioners, that he decided his only sure way to success was specialization. Liking the out-of-doors, he had decided to concentrate on the unusual in that field.

"Got some lovely stuff in Lapland on tame reindeer herds. Went right into a herd and did some reindeer-eye views. Few months ago I went underwater and photographed a marlin being hooked. Bit sticky at times with that fish thrashing around down there, but it turned out fine."

"You've cut yourself some rich stuff," Bryant said. "Young fellow, there must be an easier way to make a living."

Baldwin allowed that his family felt the same way. We talked for a while about our plans, went to see his Nissen hut living quarters and meet the photographer from Sweden, drank some strong Norwegian beer with them, and went back to the *Havella* after promising to call Baldwin's agent in New York, who hadn't heard from him in months and would be wondering if he got speared by a reindeer or chewed up by a bear.

His enthusiasm, dedication, and just plain guts were admirable. He had lonely, dangerous months ahead, but I have an idea that one of these days we'll be seeing some spectacular photography from Fred Baldwin.

We stopped and watched coal being loaded at the dock on the way back to our boat. The *Brandal*, a two-masted coal-burning trawler belching black smoke, came to the dock. In less than ten minutes, seamen were pouring off; two of them approached me as I stood looking at the boat.

Reeling a bit, one bearded, burly fellow touched my arm. "Want buy good polar-bear skin? Cheap. Maybe two, three?" When I got it across that I wasn't interested, they weaved on toward the cluster of buildings of Kings Bay, moving as if they were on roller skates. Both were loaded. The harsh perfume of cheap whiskey drifted back.

The captain stood on the deck observing the whole thing. "Hard life, codfisherman," he said. "If not drink they go crazy, I think. But they give us bad name killing *isbjørn*. They kill all can to sell in Tromsø. We try stop but government won't help."

He suggested I come aboard and take a look at the *Brandal* from the vantage point of *Havella's* deck. In the stern, along with barrels of salted cod, was a barrel of bloody heads.

"*Isbjørn*," the captain said. "Bear skulls."

Berg and Bryant cursed the codfishermen but had to admit that with their low pay and grueling life at sea, it was a temptation to pick up much-needed extra money.

"But it's also a good way to wipe out a species," said Bryant. Berg just grunted, glaring at the *Brandal*.

On the way out, skirting icebergs that burst like huge blue flowers out of the green sea, we talked about *isbjørn*. Not once since we left the treeline had I heard the white animal called a polar bear.

Alf told us that the captain had seen over two thousand of the magnificent white animals since he had been sailing the Arctic. Because of language barriers, Alf did most of the talking, as usual. We were striking for the ice pack now, trying to get into territory where the bears would be hunting seals. Then we would try for the Pole.

"I think our bear is the only animal that stalks man," Alf said. "I know others do, but they are abnormal, man-eaters or something. *Isbjørn* has been known to stalk a man for forty miles."

"Why is that?" Berg said.

Alf smiled grimly. "Can't say for sure. But we think that the bear often mistakes man for seal. Then you must remember that he is king here and anything that moves he considers fair game."

I knew that many naturalists consider the polar bear the largest carnivorous animal, even surpassing the vaunted Alaskan brown bear in size, cunning and ferocity. Arctic explorers and geographers have recorded that there are more of the white bears in this area we were cruising than any place else in the world—mainly near King Charles Island.

During most of the year the bear wanders, making his trail along the edge of the ice where he catches his favorite food, seal, sometimes in open water. It is believed that the ice bear's main polar route of travel runs from King Charles Island and Spitsbergen to Greenland and back again.

The strange, solitary white animal follows light. In the spring he comes north to this land, moving southward in the fall, always staying as close to the ice belts along the coast as he can, for that is where the seals congregate. Seals subsist mainly on small fish that live under the ice. But a hungry bear will eat anything that moves, often is seen swimming toward a flock of eider ducks, just the tip of his black nose showing. Once among the ducks he can dive deeply and swiftly enough to scoop up a plunging eider. A hungry ice bear will even rise on his haunches and slap at swooping gulls. He likes his men rare, or will try old rope, discarded boxes, roots, anything that he can chew.

But his main food is seal. Where there are seals, it is certain that there are ice bears.

So we set up a prolonged seal watch, carefully scanning every bobbing piece of ice. This moving through northern waters is somewhat unnerving until you get used to it and acquire full confidence in the crew. We had confidence in these quiet men of the sea, but icebergs are treacherous things—like the evil in man, they are nine-tenths submerged. That's where the trouble lies. Judgment in skirting them must be exact; that hard underwater ice could poke through even the *Havella*'s special hull as easily as a hand going through a paper bag.

We were coming out of the Barents Sea now into the Arctic Ocean with Sigurd Dal, the ice pilot, standing near the captain at the wheel, still and alert like the figurehead on a Viking ship, his pronounced features jutting out, jaw hard, blue eyes squinted. Beside him the captain was humming a tune that sounded Oriental, his stubby, square fingers graceful on the wheel.

Haakon Godtliebsen was in love with this country. You didn't have to be especially perceptive to realize it. The captain seldom wore a hat and the sun seemed to tangle in that incredibly yellow hair making him look, as he stood at the wheel, as if he were wearing a cap of gold. He moved the *Havella* through floes and around icebergs like a Midwestern farmer at his tractor showing city folks through his vast fields of corn. Smiling proudly, he would point toward an island, saying, "Ice Island there. Never free from ice. No man walks her. She proud and free place."

And Berg would grunt good-naturedly and say, "Captain, who in the name of sense would want to walk over that ice cube? Freeze your bebobs off for sure!"

Haakon laughed. "I know, Mr. Berg. You anxious see *isbjørn*. Soon you get wish."

He was right. The moment of drama came in a V-shaped wave. I saw it first.

"Alf," I said, "what is that?"

He looked where I pointed. "*Isbjørn!*" he said sharply to the captain. "Left bow!"

We were way out in the Arctic now. Shorelines of islands weren't even visible. What would a bear be doing out in the middle of this cold, barren, chopping sea?

I asked Alf.

"Hunting," he said. "They can swim almost as well as seal."

"This far?"

He smiled. "This isn't far for *isbjørn*. Two years ago I saw a female with two half-grown cubs in open water almost two hundred miles north of Greenland. They were swimming north for the ice pack one hundred miles farther."

As we overhauled this one, we could see his giant forearms doing the scooping, the swimming. His back legs trailed like a rudder. He was an enormous animal, yellowish to ivory-white during this summer period. His nose, velvety black, was above the water; he swung his great head in a menacing gesture as we followed beside him, Mary Lou, Bryant and Berg using their cameras. We followed that bear for two hours, clocking his speed at a consistent three miles an hour.

One could get nauseatingly rhapsodic describing his emotions after seeing his first wild polar bear swimming in the arctic water, but the feeling that comes through most strongly is one of awe: wonder that the animal can swim so well; amazement at his size and evident strength. This one, bothered by us, slackened his swimming stride

Isbjørn—"We followed that bear for two hours, clocking his speed at a consistent three miles an hour."

only once when he stopped and floated, buoyant as a cork.

"Air spaces in his fur," Alf said, "oil glands in the skin, and a thick layer of fat keep him afloat. I've seen them lie like that for an hour."

We finally pulled away from the polar bear, leaving him paddling in peace, while we kept on our route toward Storøya, where the captain said there usually were polar bears. Seals congregated on pack and drift ice in the vicinity.

Running nearer the shoreline now, we spotted many ringed seals. These were the smallest of the race, probably no more than four feet in length, having a yellowish-gray skin dotted with darker spots ringed with lighter color; thus the name. They lay on pieces of ice, placidly taking the sun.

There was an especially large one about one hundred yards from us. Suddenly Alf said, "Captain, I would like to shoot that one. I have an idea, but I need seal blubber for it."

Haakon grinned. "I know idea. Good. But kill on first shot."

Alf explained that if the seal wasn't killed with the first shot on the ice, he would fall into the water, immediately sink, and be irretrievable.

He borrowed Berg's Winchester Model 70, .270. The captain stopped the *Havella*. Alf, as nerveless as a surgeon performing in an amphitheater before curious interns, squeezed off a slow, careful shot.

We couldn't see any motion indicating that the seal was hit, but it stayed there; then the lines of scarlet began running on the floe. Alf went over the side on a rope ladder, hoisted the seal on his shoulder and brought him aboard. The animal was butter-fat; its gray hair soft.

"This is an old one," Alf said. "A bear would get him soon anyway. I wouldn't have shot him though, except we need him for an experiment."

The experiment involved finding a large, thick floe where we anchored. Meanwhile, Alf had skillfully skinned the seal and stripped off hunks of snowy white fat, which he cut in chunks and placed in a pail on deck that was full of glowing coals.

We were puzzled, but Alf and the rest of the crew weren't talking. "We wait," the captain said. So we waited.

Smoke came from the pail in a curling signal fire, rising straight up, then flapping shoreward like a flag with the wind that came off the water. The smell was not unpleasant, like broiling a strong fish over charcoal.

We were in a place where vision was perfect, unimpaired from any direction. Haakon watched shoreward with binoculars; Hansen, Sigurd, Aage and Alf took stands on the *Havella* so that North, South, East and West were covered.

We could hear the seal fat sizzling, the water lapping against the boat, and that strange, coarse, lonely cry of seagulls coming from a distance. One hundred yards from the *Havella,* the world's most skillful glider, the arctic petrel, was giving a performance, his grayish-white chunky body held motionless in the sky by its tapering sailplane wings. These birds of the storm battle the elements with ease, catching and using the air currents to their benefit.

"He comes!" said the captain suddenly, pointing toward shore.

It was another big V-shape coming through the water; now we didn't have to be told what it was. As we watched the bear coming, Alf put chunks of seal blubber on the long-handled boat hooks. The bear had started as just a speck, even seen through binoculars, and as he grew larger, Alf said, "His sense of smell is amazing. He could scent that burning seal blubber for at least five miles."

He went on to tell us that trappers claim that the polar bear can smell this burning blubber for twenty miles; many of them use that fabulous scenting ability to trap the bear. They burn blubber, then tie a belled rope to a piece of blubber outside a cabin. When the white animal arrives, takes the blubber and rings the bell, the trapper puts his rifle through a small aperture in the cabin and shoots him.

"That's a hell of a sneaky way to take a bear!" Bryant said.

"The trapper probably thinks that is squaring the odds," Alf said. "The ice bear is not easy to face in the open."

He was right: our bear was pulling himself out of the water now onto the floe. He was enormous; he looked at least ten feet long and must have weighed over one thousand pounds. We had staked the anchor on the floe. Without hesitation, he ambled over to the anchor rope. Using his paws like hands, he pulled the boat closer to the floe, illustrating in one action his intelligence and his strength. There was little between us now, other than a big jump from this suddenly fearsome animal with his long snaky head, his cold dark eyes—and his silence. He hadn't uttered a sound since his arrival from the sea. He scaled up onto the ice and went to the anchor rope as if he knew exactly what to expect. It looked too pat. Alf said it wasn't—that they had done this only once before, but in another area. Done what? Feed the animal.

Now Alf gave us each a boat hook dangling seal blubber. When the first piece was offered, the big bear stood on his hind legs like a man. Now there was no guessing. He *was* ten feet tall. He hooked that blubber off the pole with one easy swipe and stood waiting for more. Standing and swiping, he ate all of our seal blubber in less than a half-hour. When it stopped coming, he went back down on all fours and paced the floe, stopping and shaking that elongated head at us. As he started to the far end, then rushed forward, then went back to the far end again, Alf dragged in the anchor. Without a word, Haakon got the *Havella* going. We left the giant white animal agitatedly pacing the ice floe while Alf explained the quick exit.

"The last time we did this, the bear didn't like the idea of the blubber stopping. He tried to jump into the ship—"

"What happened?" I asked on cue.

"We had to shoot him. No telling what would have happened if we didn't. But we don't think this is the way you want to shoot your bear. Do you, Mr. Berg? Mr. Bryant?"

They said of course it wasn't. Two days later we sighted Storøya, where the two men from Wisconsin went ashore and each got a bear. It took one day for each ice bear, and they had a rugged time walking up a long, slippery, frigid glacial tongue (or *jøkel*) to reach their animals—five hours, in fact. It wasn't easy; but now they had their trophies and we could spend the rest of the voyage observing.

One day we sneaked up to some pack ice, cut the motors and lay watching, hoping to catch a bear stalking a seal. We saw several seals the first day, but no bears. The second day we were rewarded. We had the good luck to see an impatient bear in action. Usually the polar bear is a patient master at stalking, coming for a seal on a floe in slow, easy movements, actually on his belly, until he is in the right position to pounce. If he swims to a seal, he seems to know exactly when he can leave the water. The timing is superb. Or so the crew told us.

This was a bright morning and the seals were out, a big one on a floe no more than three hundred yards from us. The *Havella* rode easily in the quiet water, and we stood watching in silence. The seal wasn't moving; the sunlight had him hypnotized with its warmth. After ten minutes of watching, the captain touched my shoulder and pointed. There, twenty yards from the sleeping seal, was a big swimming bear. His head was above the water moving like a periscope. How he accomplished his next action I don't know; strength, system, freak action. But suddenly he hurled himself out of the water at the seal. His swipe missed; the seal slid under the ice and escaped.

The polar bear got up on the floe, stood upright, picked up pieces of ice and hurled them in rage. Then he flopped down on the floe and sulked. We couldn't help it; all of us laughed. Hearing the sound, he backed off the ice and vanished into the water, going under for twenty yards. His head bobbed up, turned toward us; then he swam away.

"How did you like the way he used those paws? Like hands," Berg said.

"Men tell me," Alf said, "that the polar bear uses paws that way to kill the giant walrus, the one animal he can't fight. They say he creeps up on a sleeping walrus and smashes his head with a large piece of ice. I never saw it. But two of my friends have."

"After seeing that polar bear figure out the anchor rope, I believe anything about them," Mary Lou said.

We saw twenty-five bears on our cruise of these arctic waters. Once, watching through glasses off Svenskøya, we saw three playing. One went up an icy knoll, sat, and slid down it like a child on a playground slide. Two stood watching; when he finished, they joined the fun. It went on for twenty minutes; then they shambled off across the icy waste.

Travel, if it is to mean anything, should give the traveler revaluation. The north does.

One morning we were all standing on deck watching two ringed seals coyly follow the *Havella,* dive shyly, surface and move through our wake with marvelous skill. Their antics bore no comparison with those of seals in zoo pools. I can't explain the difference in emotion involved in seeing wild seals cavorting in their own habitat—the bays and inlets that ring this looping arctic coast—but it is all tied up with freedom and the vastness of the place.

Suddenly Mary Lou said, "Small, aren't we?"

Without another word, we all knew what she meant. Here in this silent land with its ice mountains—with so much sea and sky that they seem to meet in a sweep of infinity—race, religion, profession, wealth, all were left behind on the dock at Tromsø with the rest of the trappings of civilization. Here all that counted was that you were alive—and free. The freedom suddenly seemed to matter above all. I had never had a feeling like this before, as if I had escaped from some kind of imprisonment.

I was aware that I was free to move where, when and how I wanted, restricted only by weather and ocean and the *Havella*'s shortcomings, which were few; free to bask in this sun that was so weirdly wonderful in its constancy; free to stand and watch the sandwich tern with his yellow-tipped, sooty bill and tailored tail, as he swooped gracefully above the deck shouting his joyful *kirrik,* the land's own chord of music. This strange, sleeping land would change only when that master of movement, the glacier, stole forward; when the clang of its calving in the sea would be the only bell ringing out the ages.

Solitude is the sanctuary here, and man the intruder, with no significance or importance. But even now, away from telephones, schedules, cocktail parties, the envy and frustration that the clashing and meshing of civilization brings, I know that what I have is at best a synthetic sort of freedom—never the freedom of the wild things. Not that of the frolicking seals behind us, or of that arctic fox that stands on the near shore, stiff as a setter on point, staring at us. There is sadness in this realization. I wonder if I have ever been free, or will ever be free, of the bindings and pulls of civilization, and I have an insane desire to set about destroying all the world's alarm clocks, to still that angry buzzing that makes us all slave to its bidding.

Then, as I see my wife standing beside me with sunlight in her eyes, smiling at the graceful seals, I appreciate the moment for what it is. This is almost great wisdom: to be able to appreciate what you are doing while you are doing it. This is the true essence of travel. The riches of memory can be spent later.

The bright cold of the north tends to clear the mind or invest it with its own peculiar fog. Now, as if wiped from a slate, the seals vanished; the mood of the day changed. The temperature dropped, the wind increased, and within minutes we were in a rough, bucking sea.

Suddenly the sea seemed too full. It was overflowing; the waves increasing in height. The *Havella* now was catching the full force of the lashing water. The wind continued to grow in strength. We were in for it. The captain was making for a sheltered bay, if he could find one.

No one could stand without holding on to a rail. Even then it wasn't really standing, but lurching, falling against anything solid that happened to be near, catching each jolt as a strong wave hit the ship, almost as if one were being punched. The giant hand of the sea had us in its palm, playing with us, tossing us up and catching us as we came bouncing down hard.

One couldn't lie in the bunk unless he was strapped in. Now we couldn't even stand. So we all gathered in the pilothouse and sat, bracing ourselves with our feet and hanging on to the handrail.

We thought we were standing, until we looked at the sea and realized that we were horizontal, not vertical. Haakon said it got this way when the warm waters of the Gulf Stream hit the cold waters of the Arctic Ocean. "Makes boil," he said. There couldn't be a better description.

After he told us of the Gulf Stream I recalled some words from an old, almost forgotten book, *The Physical Geography of the Sea,* written by Matthew Maury. "There is a river in the ocean . . ." The words came back stronger with every thrust of the waves. "In the severest droughts it never fails, and in the mightiest floods it never overflows. Its banks and its bottoms are of cold water, while its current is of warm. The Gulf of Mexico is its fountain, and its mouth is in the Arctic Seas. It is the Gulf Stream. There is in the world no other such majestic flow of waters. Its current is more rapid than the Mississippi or the Amazon, and its volume more than a thousand times greater . . ."

Here we were in its mouth, with the feeling that we were about to be swallowed. But what happened in the next hour made us feel that we were riding comfortably in a luxury cabin of a ship twice the size, not being banged about in a fifty-seven-foot craft that resembled a tossing chip on this wild ocean.

Sigurd, who always kept his eyes moving ahead of the *Havella,* suddenly said something violent in Norwegian. The captain and Alf rushed over to him. He pointed. "No!" said Alf. "It is not possible! Nothing that small could live out there!"

We unbraced ourselves and stood. "What's the trouble?" said Bryant.

"We think there is a small boat out there," Alf said.

Now we all stood peering through the spray that the lash of the wind brought from the water. As we drew nearer we could see that it was indeed a small boat—so small that it was lost in the swells—but as it came up to the top of a surging wave you could see that there was a flag or a piece of cloth thrashing wildly in the wind. A distress signal.

It is testimony to Haakon's skill that he got the *Havella* close enough to throw out a lifeline without swamping the little craft. Now Alf and Hansen somehow got a ladder over, pulled the little boat close and helped two men aboard. They had tied the rope to their boat and as we towed it behind us, it looked like a child's toy bobbing on the rough sea.

The men were muffled in oiled raingear. One, with flaming red cheeks and blue eyes, was almost as broad as he was tall; the other, with a gray, unshaven face, was slim even in the bulk of storm clothing. The broad man spoke to the crew in Norwegian; the other talked with us in a twangy Texas drawl.

"Thought we'd had it, y'all," he said. "Got a radio, but can only receive, not send. Gave ourselves another hour at best. Never so glad to see people in my born days!"

"What in hell are you doing out in the Arctic Ocean in a small boat like that?" Berg asked.

"Not so small," the Texan said. "Eighteen feet."

He was a crude, profane little man, and he soon made himself completely obnoxious. First, he demanded whiskey; then hot food, then more whiskey. In less than one hour he took over our ship, dominating it completely, a Captain Bligh with a Texas accent. Or so he thought. Actually we were all just putting up with him. There wasn't much else we could do.

The crew had got the full story from the other man, a Norwegian sailor they knew from Tromsø. "Not good sorts," said Alf. "He does not have good judgment. Never had."

So the crew just sat and stared at our American visitor while he told his story. Their expressions were those of people walking through a zoo. Apparently he had come this far north in the outboard by hitchhiking, actually persuading the captains of bigger boats to tie him behind and tow him as far as they were going.

"Took a sight of smart lip service to get some of these jokers to give me a haul," he said cockily. "But when I hafta talk, mister, I can talk."

It seemed that he was a photographer by profession—obviously not of the caliber of Baldwin, whom we had met in Kings Bay—and had come north to photograph the polar bear.

"I got me a fat little old TV series by the tail," he said, "if I can get what I came after. Goin' take some doin'. Needs some good luck and some guts, but as my old granny said, I got me plenty of both."

He was almost as irritating as a dentist's drill; his voice whiny-nasal. How he ever got this far in his fantastic hitchhiking, where personality was a potent factor, was a mystery. I thought people might have given him the pull through the Arctic Ocean out of sympathy for his Norwegian companion, a comfortable, fat, cheery man, who sat smiling and puffing his pipe.

The TV series idea that the Texan had by the tail involved him lassoing a live polar bear, and pulling him through the water to shore. How he was going to do this wasn't quite clear, and he had no idea what strength, ferocity and swimming ability the white animal had. But his object was photographing the roping episode in 16mm. color, not only to depict man's courage against the wild beast and the elements, but also to show how tough rope is and illustrate what you could do with a properly tied knot.

"Now you see," he said (after telling us that he had no fear of our stealing the idea because he was sure none of *us* had enough courage to lasso a bear), "the idea is for this to be a Boy Scout TV show with all that natural built-in audience. I learned how to tie all these knots. We show how to tie the knot, see, then dissolve to me up here in the middle of the Arctic Ocean. Behind each one of these knots is an adventure. My job is to explore and get into that adventure. And photograph it, of course." His partner back in Texas, whose original idea this was, would make the contract with the Boy Scouts of America—after he came back with the lassoed polar bear in the can.

Bryant and Berg just sat there listening with their mouths open, shaking their heads in disbelief.

"Thought Baldwin was off his nut with that underwater polar bear stuff," Berg said. "But this guy!"

"How's that?" the Texan said, sharply. "Underwater polar bear stuff, you said?"

"Doesn't matter," Berg said. "Nothing matters now that you told us of this looney idea of yours. You're asking for trouble aplenty with this thing—"

"What's the matter?" he said. "Think I can't pull it off? Listen. Let me tell you, I am a genius with a lariat. I can lasso anything up to and including a rattlesnake. But never you mind *my* business! Y'all tell me about polar bears. How many you see? Here—" He took a chart out of his pocket. "Let's set right down and mark me up a polar bear chart. Now. You show me where you saw bears. When. Then you can haul me over that way and—"

And so it went for hours.

Meanwhile, the sea had calmed, and Haakon and Alf were talking with the Texan's Norwegian companion. Finally they seemed to have reached a decision and came over to us while the Texan was going into the financial aspects of his TV idea that he had by the tail. "Take fifty stations. Tag 'em three hundred dollars apiece for the film. See what I mean? And who the hell would be such a stupid son-of-a-bitch that wouldn't want to see a show with a polar bear being lassoed? A *polar bear*—"

Alf interrupted, much to his annoyance. "We're going to give you some food, tow you to the nearest bay and wish you good luck. We're off our course now. We have a schedule to make. The captain feels that he can't tow you around looking for polar bears and still be fair to his present customers."

"That bastard! Goin' dump me! You guys goin' let him? What's the harm of a few more days with you? A easy tow to the bear country?"

"It's the captain's ship," Bryant said quietly. "We can't tell him what to do."

"Do you have enough equipment and things to keep you going?" I said.

He snorted. "What you guys think I am?" he said. "An *amateur?* An old *pro* like me? Sure I got enough to keep me goin'."

So we took them to a quiet bay where they immediately went ashore and put up a tent. The Texan never said thank you once during the hours he was with us drinking our whiskey and eating our food and ordering us around. I like to think that I am a character collector, but this was one that I was glad to pass up.

I've been watching TV for his lassoing sequence, but I haven't been able to catch it yet. Often now when I see driving rain or snow coming against the windows of my snug place in Connecticut, I wonder what happened to him. One thing he had, as his granny always told him, was guts. I'm sure he landed on his feet.

It was one of those quiet days when the water had stopped boiling—waves still broke, shattering in diamond-white pieces, but there was no fury in the sea now. It swaggered and flexed its muscles and rolled around as arrogantly as a bully walking among cowering schoolboys. The sun was shining up its surface as effectively as a scrubwoman with a waxing machine as we stood watching the birds float around the *Havella*. A fat orange-beaked puffin flew within ten feet, poking his head at me, looking like a parrot out of his element. Sigurd, the ice pilot, came over, tapping out a cold pipe in his hand.

"That lake could be open this year," he said. "I not see it now for thirteen year."

"What lake?" I said.

The captain came back, running fingers through his yellow cotton hair. "You mean one at Duvefjorden?" he said. When Sigurd nodded, he laughed. "That's a lucky lake! No people been at it for many year. Chinese Wall Front glaciers, hanging cliffs of ice pushed out, made a wall around little bay and nobody get in."

"Mild winter, thin ice last year," Sigurd said. "Wind from the south and southeast last summer and autumn. Ice broke, drifted in many places. Now this good summer, too. I think we could try—"

Haakon laughed again. "Perhaps, Sigurd, they all do not want to go. After all, what is it? A lake? A lake without a name even?"

Ed Bryant came up from below. "What lake without a name?" When the captain filled him in, his dark face lighted and he roared, "Berg! Get up here! We got the chance of a lifetime!" Ben came rushing up and we quickly held a two-minute conference. Result: find the lost lake. The course was changed. We had a new destination.

Now we moved along the north coast of Nordaustlandet watching the iceblinks, luminous reflections from the ice that rimmed the horizon in silver. Gulls (herring, glaucous, great black-headed) hung almost motionless before us as if inked in on a seascape. The cold coast of the second largest island in Svalbard rose out of low-hanging fog banks in a great ice mountain.

The books tell you that this gray place lies at 80° 20′, that because of difficult ice conditions the island is not accessible at all points every year and can only be circumnavigated on favorable occasions. Lying northeast of Vest Spitsbergen, it is visited only by intrepid seal hunters in specially constructed sixty-foot ice cruisers. As we moved along its dangerous coast, Alf Olsen told us that the lake we were seeking was full of fish. "Red charr," he said. "Some call them Spitsbergen salmon. They're like a salmon on the table. Pink flesh, delicate flavor. They look like a mackerel, silver, when they come out of the sea and enter the lakes made by glaciers. After a time they become beautiful with red spots."

I remembered that SAS pilot and his creel of fish at Bardufoss. He had said I might find the best of the northern fish. "Spitsbergen salmon," he said. As I stood thinking about the strange fish, staring at this lonely, ice-ridden land, Sigurd told us a little more about the island, none of it designed to make us feel that this would be the place to rush out and buy real estate.

"Icecaps there," he said, pointing. "Inside, the Vestfonna, Austfonna, Sorfonna and Glitnefonna. They up to seven hundred meters high." He was silent a moment. "On the south and east they push into the sea with big ice wall. Very dangerous."

But we had run through several kinds of danger getting here; the

Beyond this bleak Chinese Wall Front glacier calving icebergs, was Nordaustlandet, a rarely accessible island visited sometimes by seal hunters.

rough seas, the small boat, the icebergs and thick fields of floes proved to be the least of them. A couple of hours ago the captain had left his wheel in the hands of the mate and come aft to chat with us.

"We are trying to avoid islands of Franz Josef Land," he said. We could see them rising through the wisping fog miles away.

"Russian!" he said sharply. "We not been able to land there or navigate close for many year. This fog makes bad. Their boats are ready for chase should we slip too near."

"Can you imagine what Mr. K would do if we landed by mistake?" said Mary Lou.

"Yep," said Ben Berg. "They'd say, 'What are you doing here?' We'd say, 'Hunting for a lost lake to go fishing.' And they'd have themselves four choice spies."

"They don't catch us," said the captain grimly, now back at his wheel.

Several hours later the captain told us we were out of danger. "Until we come back," he said.

Through glasses I could see fjords cutting back from the jagged shore in long knife slashes, deeply indenting the entire north coast. We were looking for one that would take us back into this seldom explored area: Duvefjorden, a key fjord which would take us inside to a small cove, Duve Bukt or Pigeon Bay, so called, the crew said, because of the many ivory gulls that inhabit it. These are plump white birds that look more like prize White King pigeons than seabirds. Sigurd felt his way as skillfully as a doctor probing for pain, slowly, carefully, checking the chart every few minutes, speaking rapidly in harsh Norwegian to the captain at the wheel. In these waters the ice pilot was supreme; his experience and judgment could mean the difference between life and death.

Next day the birds were there as we came slowly from the long tongue of fjord into the bay, the mist coming off it in gunsmoke puffs, the fog lying low as if the land was on fire, the high reaches glistening with ice. The ivory gulls swooped close; you could see the short yellow bills, the young ones with gray smudges on face and chin, shrilling, "Keer! Keer!" as we dropped anchor. It was 10:00 P.M. but the sun stood high and the water sparkled.

The crew were smiling. This was adventure even for these seasoned sailors. "We are here!" said Hansen the engineer, an old man doing a little-boy jig on the deck.

"The ice is out!" said Alf Olsen at the wheel.

Havella came into the small cove, Duve Bukt or Pigeon Bay, searching for the lost lake that lay below the mountains with their powdering of snow.

"See run from the lake," said the captain, pointing toward land. "I think we make it!"

From where we had dropped anchor in the middle of the little bay, you could see a streak ashore moving in a rush of white light, a tiny stream coming from fresh water farther inland, perhaps from our lost glacial lake.

We stood there on deck, silent now, realizing that if we made it we would be the first to visit the hidden lake in more than a decade, probably the first Americans ever to see it. The captain, as if reading our secret thoughts, said, "You will be the first from your country."

He was busy at his charts for a time then, working out that we were at 80° 23°, less than ten degrees from the North Pole. It was then I asked the question and gaiety went from our group.

"May we take a look at the fishing rods?"

"Ya," said Alf. He went below and came up with a small, ancient casting rod. The line on the reel was old and thin, and there wasn't much of it.

"This it?" said Ed Bryant in a dead voice.

Alf nodded.

And then with some waving of hands I said Odd Berg had told me not to bring my flyrods and spinning rod that I had left in Copenhagen. "He said you had plenty of fishing equipment aboard and not to burden myself!" I said.

"Mr. Berg," said the captain gently, "not aboard in some time. This is only equipment we have."

"A fisherman's dream," said Ben Berg, "and we have one lousy rod!"

"I think we can fix it," said Alf suddenly. He went below and came up with three whiskey bottles that had been emptied in the normal way; then dipped into a drawer under the wheel and came out with a big ball of nylon and three pieces of gleaming copper. "We make equipment," he said enthusiastically.

He held one of the bottles by the neck, tied the end of a ball of nylon line to it, winding the rest, about twenty yards, around the center of the body. On the other end he tied one of the pieces of copper, which turned out to be Swedish spinning lures. Before we could ask if the lash-up would work, he walked to the side of the boat and in a neat, graceful cast, still holding the bottle by the neck, sent the line out. It peeled off, not unlike a spinning reel. "Not good as a rod," he said, "but it'll get fish."

We all tried then. It could be done with practice. I almost lost the

Mate Alf Olsen made a reel from a whiskey bottle—empty, of course.

bottle overboard on the third try, and we decided to give it up for the time.

I don't know if fishermen are born sneaks or whether they just grow into it, but the next act of Bryant and Berg proved one or the other true. Inasmuch as it was dinnertime now, after 9:00 P.M., the captain suggested that we eat and try to make our way into the lake in the morning, taking a picnic lunch with us. This time-talk was deceptive here, for the constant light made our days timeless.

We all agreed, but immediately after dinner, about eleven, Bryant suggested that he, Berg and Alf go in, "Just to take a quick look at the lake." Mary Lou and I agreed. At this point, after battling our way through heavy seas to this quiet piece of water, we were tired and thought—even with the sun—we would try to get some sleep in preparation for the trek in the morning.

Bryant and Berg departed in the small boat. We retired to our cabin but lay tossing for hours. Sleep didn't come; neither did the intrepid explorers. Then Mary Lou spoke from the top bunk. "The boys pulled a fast one. I think they're 'firsters.' They wanted to be number one at the lake."

They finally did get back at six in the morning, tired, noisy, exultant—with three fish. "Good thing we went," said Bryant quickly when he saw me waiting on deck. "We didn't go to fish but just couldn't resist it. The bottles work, but you need sinkers. That place is full of fish, but I think you need something on the hook beside that hunk of copper." He played good Samaritan with consummate skill.

The fish, even though they had been out of water for some time, still had a jeweled look about them, much like a rainbow. They weren't large. "Two- or three-pounders," said Berg, "but real sassy."

They went to bed after showering us with more advice, and we started off for the lake with the captain and the engineer, Hansen, who lugged the fourteen-foot bamboo pole which usually carried the boat hook. Hansen also took some seal blubber for bait. It was clear that no one had been in this little bay for a long time. Flocks of black and white guillemots, usually a spooky bird, waited until our outboard was almost upon them before they skittered off. Bryant and Berg had said the going was rough and wet, with run-off streams from the glacier everywhere. We worked our way back, following the stream that bubbled into the bay.

Off to our far left, patches of melting snow on the slopes ran red, tinted by moisture running off red carboniferous sandstone that jutted out of high ground. Except for small streams that twisted under our

Ed Bryant, ice pilot Sigurd Dal, Ben Berg and engineer Harald Hansen were returning from their visit to the lost lake, "tired, noisy, exultant— with three fish."

feet, the land ahead of us looked like rubble from a hydrogen-bomb attack. The glacier, the top strata of the icecap, had advanced with enormous strength, digging up boulders, upending rocks, strewing stones in its path, tearing, scarring the earth as it moved. Its main force still lay beneath us, three feet under, untouched by the warm summer sun that for twenty-four hours for well over one hundred days had been bringing the top-surface earth up into something like a boil, spilling ridges and gouging depressions. The combination made this kind of walking a form of exercise I had never experienced.

Beyond the mountain that stood like a menace was the largely unexplored Fonna, land of eternal snow, imprisoned by a giant of ice astride its back in a cruel, hard ride that went on forever. The thought of being stranded back there without benefit of the boat in the bay or experienced northmen, gave me a quick, frightening insight into what some of the old explorers must have gone through.

Suddenly Hansen stopped abruptly, held up a hand in warning, then pointed. Directly ahead, perfectly camouflaged by the gray, stone-strewn background, was an animal. It turned its head slowly and I could see the antlers, still in velvet—a reindeer. We stood still; the only noise now came from Mary Lou's camera shutter. The young reindeer kept coming closer, raising its head, jutting it out suddenly in curiosity.

City people, or those unaccustomed to wilderness places, who get their view of animal life at zoos where they can walk within ten feet of a tiger in a cage, might think a reindeer walking so close is nothing to get excited about. But for us who have spent time in the wild, it is a wonderful thing. Human beings are the untouchables of the wild places. Somehow man's cruelties have been communicated throughout the animal and bird world, and those splendid, aloof, free wild things flee from us as if their lives depended upon it. Man's stupidities toward fellow man are only outdone by his treatment of the wild creatures; if he can't tame them, enslave them for his own use, then he kills them.

This innocent came within ten feet, soft brown eyes curious, the sun shining up the gray-brown velvet on its antlers, picking out white hairs in the shaggy coat. It must have been very young; the feet splayed out too big and awkward. Now pure instinct took over; the little reindeer flicked its tail and went bouncing over the barren moonscape, sailing over rocks that had been upended four feet. Obviously it had never seen a human being.

Hansen took off his hat, ran a hand over his bald head, grinning. "Ya, ya, a baby. The closest I have stood to a wild reindeer."

You wondered what the reindeer lived on in this forsaken land, and then, looking closely, you could see, between the rocks, places turning grayish-green, like copper exposed to weather: lichen. Hansen, who told us that he loved gardening above all, even though he had pathetic little time to dig in the Tromsø earth that was frosted much of the time, walked beside Mary Lou and me pointing out and naming flowers. It is one of the puzzling miracles of nature how they grew in this rock, but there they were: saxifrage, the petals standing out against the gray background like drops of blood; the delicate yellow arctic poppies; the light red licebane sprouting from the rubble as if it had been tended by a gardener; mountain avens that ran in burning white lines, somehow symmetrical and orderly in all of this wild disorder. Mary Lou plucked an aven and stuck it in her coat lapel. It lived there for three days.

With a shrill Scotch-bagpipe keening, a brown bird suddenly flushed before us, looking like a very large woodcock, long, slender bill, grouse-colored plumage. "Phalarope!" said Hansen, and I thought, incongruously, of the title *Too Late the Phalarope,* a book of man's injustices to man. A wild bird flying before me in nightmare country carved bare by a glacier made me think of civilization. But here was a land that would never have its burdens.

The streams became wider now and the snow on the slopes and ridges heavier, the run-off streams coursing suddenly swifter, deeper, forcing us to wade in water up to our hips. And then we came over a slight rise, stumbling over the rocks, and there lay the lake. It wasn't large, but it was as blue as our captain's eyes, and it was beautiful. Beautiful like a woman caught swimming in the nude. It lay silent as if caught by surprise and I could see fish rising, dimpling the water in short reaches near the shore.

None of us said anything then, and there was a quiet look almost of reverence on the tough Viking face of the captain. Hansen took off his hat and put up his hand in a salute. It is rare in this overwhelmed world that man has the opportunity to stand and enjoy true serenity.

Then the realist took over and we walked the shore searching for fish. In some places they lay so still in the clear water they looked as if they were frozen in ice; then the tail would suddenly flick and the fish would move off into the depths. Hansen strung up his gigantic pole, baited it with a piece of white seal blubber and started fishing. He caught three before I could get my bottle into action. They were spotted in reds and gold, slimmer than a salmon, bigger than a trout, and there were color variations; two of them were silver touched with red and gold, one had an orange hide spotted with deep red.

"I think that one live on bottom in deep water," said the captain. "But no one know about red charr."

Mary Lou tried the small rod and I worked at the bottle, trying to get line out without much luck. I tried not to think of what I could do with a good flyrod, or a spinning rod and a pair of waders. And I attempted to content myself with the peace of the place, shoving underneath the thought of actually catching fish. But this always came rising back, and it was difficult not to condemn Odd Berg, the "don't bring your rods" man, into a special hell reserved for those who frustrate fishermen.

In two hours Ed Bryant, Ben Berg and Alf came up over a distant rise. They had come in from the mountain on the opposite side, tired but titillated.

"Here's the answer," said Bryant. He spilled three Norwegian **kroner** into my hand. They were **heavy coins,** quarter-size with a hole in the center. "Sinkers," he explained. "Get us the distance we need."

Tied above the Swedish lures, they were just heavy enough to send the line out where the charr congregated and we started taking fish. "Money was never put to a better use," Mary Lou said as she got action on the small rod, her fish leaping and making a fuss on the top of the water. But our bottles took them too, even if we did have to handline them in gently. We took only enough to eat for the next three days, keeping them cool and fresh on ledges of mountain snow.

It wasn't all uninterrupted fishing. We put the bottles aside and explored, once finding two fuzzy birds walking wobbily about, evidently fresh from a nest. As we stood watching their staggering, clownlike efforts among the rock scrabble, suddenly an arctic tern, easily identified by its blood-red bill, came swooping in with a shrill kee—kee. Whether she had ever seen human beings before made no difference; we obviously represented danger. Her kees increased into shrieks as she darted in courageously, coming closer and closer to our faces. Waving our arms to keep her off—she attacked me, then Mary Lou, then went high and dive-bombed Ben Berg—we finally fled that part of the lake shore, and left her in the scree walking proudly beside her offspring, clucking softly as she led them back to the nest hidden in the rocky hillside.

When we wearied of the complicated sport of casting line from a whiskey bottle, we just stood and stared at the lost lake and listened to the silence. It was difficult to leave but we started back filled with emotion, a mixture of awe and sadness, knowing that we would never again see this quiet lake, knowing in our hearts that we would never again have the opportunity to walk in a place where no man had been for years.

Hansen was walking ahead with his big pole. Suddenly he stopped, motioning wildly. We caught up with him and looked where he pointed. "Ya," he said. "No one been here for many year all right. That is arctic fox. Shyest of all."

Not more than fifty yards from us, a slim, elegant grayish-blue animal with uppricked ears stood for a full five minutes before it turned and moved off in a graceful, unhurried trot. Hansen, the oldest of us, seemed to have the sharpest eye. Again he beckoned. He was standing near the bay, back off the shore in the middle of a circle of rocks. He bent over as we approached and straightened with something shiny in his hands. He rubbed it on his sleeve and it began to shine. It was a button.

Red charr in hand, the author took a last look at the lost lake, not seen by man in a dozen years.

All around him were buttons, heels of boots, rotting bills of caps—and skeletons that were obviously human, bleached and twisted by wind and water into weird ivory forms, a surrealist horror spread there for how long? Closer examination proved that there were pieces of uniforms and the rusted remains of a short-wave radio. "Nazi!" the captain said. "These were German soldiers." He counted skulls. "Nine." He turned to us, blue eyes blazing. "They were smart, those damn Nazis," he said fiercely. "This probably some kind of outpost—"

"But why out here, Captain?" Hansen said. "This way off shipping lanes. Nothing moved here."

"Who knows?" the captain spread his hands like a butcher accused of short weight. "Maybe knowing us Norwegians they thought we would try send boats from Tromsø across Arctic Ocean. You cannot say Germans had no imagination when it came to war." Haakon, of course, was right. When it came to the art of war, the Germans were masters. Drama, mystery, loneliness, frustration, horror, and, I am certain, bravery, lay here in these rocks surrounding the bleached bones in a kind of cairn to courage. Certainly few soldiers had been given a more rugged or challenging assignment: establish an outpost on this lonely, rocky, ice-covered, wind-swept island, and if you don't freeze to death or starve or get eaten by polar bears, watch for ships that may never pass.

We went back to our ship in two loads, stayed in Duve Bukt all night watching the ivory gulls fly, enjoying the best dinner our short, dark magician, Aage, had ever prepared: charr fresh from their cold, clear lake, poached in sea water, accompanied by tiny boiled potatoes and a sharp mustard sauce that only the Norwegians of the north country know how to concoct.

As we sailed away in the morning, ten reindeer came to the shore and watched us go, heads high, standing like a curious crowd seeing a big ship off in Manhattan. They stood there until we sailed out of sight.

I didn't know it then, but wild reindeer would soon give me the opportunity to do some of the most exciting wing-shooting of my life. In two more days the charr were gone and we were once again eating from cans and bearing down on the last fresh meat. Fog had become so heavy that we decided against trying actually to reach the Pole, or

Our dark magician, Aage Rutwold, was about to convert red charr into the best dinner anyone aboard the Havella *had ever eaten.*

at least the latitude designating the Pole. This was a bitter disappointment, for we were only four hundred miles from it. But the fog continued to come in waves from the north, wisp settling upon wisp, smoky threads that wove into a blanket that closed off vision as effectively as if one had suddenly gone blind.

This sudden fog is one of the great dangers of ice navigation. When enveloped in it you cannot observe the moving pack and drift ice, with the result that it may close up behind you without your knowledge, perhaps locking you in its creeping circle for weeks.

Beyond, as everywhere, lay icebergs and floes. Even Sigurd with his knowledge and his skill was helpless in that bank of wool. So Haakon changed course to try to evade the drifting fog and the danger of ramming a great berg that could sink even our double-hulled craft.

In several hours we ran out of the arctic smoke, skirting cliffs that signaled that a fjord had been sculpted by a glacier, and Sigurd said, "Soon, Bockfjorden."

As we came closer you could see just a scarf of fog draped around the bony neck of the cliff where the red stone began to show. Below that the snow ran red, then drifted into pink, colored probably from the Devonian rock.

If you're one of those who started dreaming in geography class when the teacher said of a fjord, "A long, relatively narrow arm of the sea, bordered by steep cliffs, as on the coast of Norway . . ." then you'd be as fascinated as I am by these sunstruck stretches of water that leave the sea and slide mysteriously into hidden places. Bockfjorden was an especially pretty piece of water. The sun bounced off the strange red cliffs, making reflections in the clear water that looked like Oriental palaces or Scottish castles, and in one sunny spot the upside-down cliff reflection looked a little like the Empire State Building. But one thing the books never tell about fjords is their loneliness. These bits of sea that stole in here to brood in peace give you the instant feeling of isolation. And you feel like an intruder.

The captain evidently had no such feeling. "There is supposed to be herd wild reindeer behind Bockfjorden," he said. "Maybe we stretch legs and see?"

Mary Lou and Berg and Bryant thought that was a great idea. I was standing beside Alf.

"Eider ducks in Bockfjorden," he said. I looked around to see if the Wisconsin men had heard. They hadn't. I motioned and we left the pilothouse and stood on the deck with the spray misting around us. "You like duck-hunting?" I said. His eyes shone and he smiled. He didn't have to say anything. "So do I," I said. "I know," he said. "Got a gun?" I said.

He said that he had a side-by-side Swedish shotgun. "Two triggers. Maybe little old and rusty, but it shoots." He shook his head. "Only one trouble. One box of shells."

I then said some unkind things about Odd Berg, who had nearly ruined some great fishing by telling me not to bring rods. He had also written that the duck-shooting wasn't worth the trouble of bringing along a shotgun and shells. Then I remembered Berg and Bryant going ashore after those charr on the pretense that they just wanted to take a quick look at the lost lake.

"Alf," I said, "my wife, Ben and Ed would rather use their cameras on reindeer anyway. Let's give them a break and not tell them about the eiders. It could spoil their day. Just think, Alf, what if they stayed out here with us looking for ducks and missed getting ashore to see those reindeer? It could be a real tragedy for eager photographers like those. Why not drop a word to the captain to take the boys and the rest of the crew ashore and let us watch the ship? I have some notes to write anyway."

"This is a very good idea, Mr. Scott," Alf said. "And it seems to me that you are a very generous man thinking of your friends like that."

Within an hour the reindeer seekers had gone and we were standing on deck looking at the pink snow and plotting our course. I could see bands of eider bursting from the water near the far edge of the fjord, and Alf suggested that we take the small boat and go after them.

"They smart?" I asked.

He nodded, and then gave me the verbal fact sheet. "These are common eider," he said. "The largest duck there is, twenty-three inches long. *Somateria mollissima* is their technical name—"

He saw me looking a little shocked. "Long winter nights, long watches aboard. I've been reading a bird book."

"Oh," I said. "Ducks, geese and swans?"

"No," he said. "Just ducks. I don't care about any other bird."

"They breed from the Farne Islands to Spitsbergen," he continued. "During the breeding season, past now, the male has a dark belly and a white back, the only duck that has. But now they look like the female, dark, reddish-brown, barred with black. They look heavy and clumsy, but they are fast and good divers—"

"How do they go on the table?"

"Great," he said. "Like a Christmas goose!"

I could see them a half-mile away, in the air now. "Peculiar flight. Alternate period of wing-beating and gliding."

"And they carry their heads low," he said.

"Too far away for me to see," I said.

"Let's get in the small boat and take a closer look," he said.

That proved to be more difficult than we planned. Apparently Alf's duck reading didn't include instructions on how to sneak up on eider. You just can't do it.

There were a dozen big brown birds, looking almost as large as Canada geese. We tried using our motor but soon found that they would spook off the water at one hundred yards. So then we tried our oars, and got within sixty yards before they dived, surfacing another fifty yards away.

Since Alf was the sailor, he manned the boat and I clutched the shotgun, but I am of the school of duck shooters who maintain that you can't bring a duck down unless he is close enough for you to see the skin scale on his legs.

We did get close enough to hear their cries, "Coo-roo-uh! Kor-r-r!" Close enough for me to see that the famous northern eider look like giant female mallards. Once I could have shot a big one on the water, but I didn't even lift the gun. Alf nodded, pleased, and I wondered what kind of duck hunters he had been with.

This went on for well over an hour, and for the first time in years of hunting wildfowl, I learned where the word *duck* came from. It was handed down directly from the eider. They can duck and dive with more dexterity than anything in feathers. And they looked almost as fast as canvasbacks when they took off from the water in unpredictable spurts, then rose straight up like the red-legged black duck.

"Maybe that reindeer visit wasn't such a bad idea after all, Mr. Scott," Alf said. That did it. I decided to get devious.

"I have an idea, Alf," I said, ignoring the reindeer repartee. "See that cliff?" I pointed at a red cliff rising like a rosy dream over the fjord.

He nodded.

"It might work if you'd drop me off on shore," I said. "I'll take the gun and sit up on the cliff. You use the motor, run way down the fjord and then back up. It may get the birds into the air, and if I'm at that elevation, that far over the water, there is a fair chance I may get a shot— It's worth trying anyway."

He thought about it. "Good idea. Doesn't look like we're going to get any this way." He swung his head and pointed. "See that movement. They're rafted up farther down too, and I may be able to get them up."

I looked, and although they were about the size of starlings from that distance, you could tell by the wingbeat-and-glide flight that they were eiders. There must have been at least a hundred in the flock.

He put me ashore, but I had to wade in water up to my hips. Glad that this was the time of sun, drying fast, I found a springy hunk of Iceland moss and sat. Luxury. I could see almost to the end of the fjord and the open sea. Alf in the boat looked like a tightly wound child's toy down there as he spurted toward the rafted eiders. They rose almost as one, heading for the sea, but broke back and came down the tongue of water for me. Halfway, they sat down again and Alf went after them. This time they came toward me, the whole sequence slow and unreal, like a scene in a Peter Scott wildfowl painting suddenly come alive, and I almost forgot to shoot.

The wind-rush of wings came like a shrill whistle making me alert. Four were hanging out thirty-five yards from the cliff and I threw one shot and an eider went down. Fumbling with the second trigger with which I was unfamiliar, I bungled the second. The ducks went away in a concerted rush, then flared back. I was dressed in a khaki parka and hunched against the rock and I don't think they saw me. I went through that precious box of shells like a knife through cheddar cheese and then suddenly realized what I was doing and stopped with two shells left. There were seven ducks down; only one looked as if it still had life, and I could see Alf going for that one with an oar.

It took him twenty minutes to gather the eiders and come for me. I was a little ashamed when I waded out to meet him but tried to carry it off lightly.

"Great ducks!" I said. "If I had a gun with a single trigger, I think I could have a real score. But I missed nearly every time on that second trigger."

He didn't go for it. "Any shells left?" he said.

"Shells?" I said, hoping I looked bewildered. "I don't know. I never thought to look—"

As I sat in the boat, he opened the box. "Two," he said. Then, "Oh, well, the cliff was your idea. Would you mind running the boat through the birds while I go sit on your cliff?"

"Gladly, Alf. I'm sorry about the shells. You know how it is. I was carried away. Ducks make you forget your name—"

He just smiled, that chill Norwegian smile. "When you hear two shots you can come for me, please. Two shots, because that is all I have."

So I went off feeling like a dog, a devious dog at that, and ran the boat through the eiders and saw him sitting high on the cliff looking like the figurehead on the prow of one of his ancestors' ships. The ducks flared back over the cliff again, and waiting for a while, I looked in the water near the cliff for ducks. None. Then I went ashore for Alf.

He came wading out to meet me, shotgun in one hand, a brace of eiders in the other. Evidently he had dropped them right in his lap.

He said, "I like double triggers."

He wasn't really annoyed though. He was smiling. "You're a real duck hunter. It's a disease." I told him he was a gentleman.

"We'll have a change for dinner," he said. "Aage is a good man with an eider."

Mary Lou was the most annoyed when they came from their expedition and saw the big, fat, beautiful eiders hanging from the pilot-house. She is an even more devoted duck hunter than I. I explained that it would have made the whole thing too complicated if I had generously told everyone about the ducks. Had I told her, both Berg and Bryant, knowing her skill with a camera and her interest in wild animals, would have been suspicious.

She didn't quite go along with this thesis, but at dinner that night Alf and I were congratulated. Aage plus eiders resulted in a memorable meal. Berg and Bryant thought that if we were around Bockfjorden long enough they might take a couple of shots at eiders themselves.

"I'm sorry," Alf said. "We have no more shells."

The rest of that delicious arctic duck dinner was eaten, as the cliché goes, in pregnant silence.

Our seventeen-foot outboard, called *Jolle* (little boat) by the crew, was the means of exploring ashore, cruising the shallower water of the fjords, or just taking a ride on those quiet days when the *Havella* was at anchor in a cove or bay. It was a seaworthy little craft, but with typical Norwegian frugality, Odd Berg had equipped it with the smallest motor I have ever seen, a two-horsepower, if there is such a thing. It moved through the water all right but at a pace that made you want to take up the thick, clumsy oars and hurry things along. I had often wondered what would happen if we needed an extra burst of speed in an emergency. I was to find out.

One afternoon with the *Havella* floating at anchor like a giant gull, Mary Lou, Alf and I decided that we would take *Jolle* and run along the shore several miles away where we saw a flock of seabirds congregating. From this distance we couldn't tell what the birds were, but with little to do now we wanted to find out. Mary Lou took her cameras, and Alf suggested that I carry my Browning rifle, a .375 Holland and Holland magnum.

Bryant was writing letters home and Berg was checking his cameras, titling and identifying film as he stored it. Aage was doing something dexterous with a piece of lean corned beef he had taken from brine, and the rest of the crew were draped in various positions on deck soaking up sun. As we left the *Havella,* water was moving against her in a susurrus and you could understand what the psychologists meant when they said that the sound of water is beneficially soothing. I could hardly keep my eyes open as we went over the side into *Jolle.* Alf swung her about and we headed for the birds, which were still in the sky and looking like a cloud that was shredding into independent, floating pieces.

The shore was mostly brown now in the summer sun but the water was full of floes and two big bergs that raised dangerous blue heads. Alf avoided the ice in skillful S-loops, sometimes going very close and showing us what a good man he was. The *Havella* grew smaller as we went along in our slow way, the little motor making purring sounds like an electric food blender.

As we drew close enough to identify the birds, I looked back and saw that the *Havella* had shrunk smaller than *Jolle* in the distance. The birds were gulls, of a variety that would send a devoted birdwatcher into name-calling ecstasies. Alf identified Audouin's blackheaded, Bonaparte's, Ross's, herring, the slender-billed. What they were interested in was a carcass, or what was left of an adult ringed seal. It lay on the shore twenty feet from a big flat floe.

"A bear kill," said Alf. "We should watch. He could be close. There is still a meal on it. And it is suspicious that the birds don't land. They are too cautious."

We sat, as good watchers do, projecting ourselves out there where the bear might be. We saw nothing except rock, ice farther back, and strips of grainy snow.

The gulls still didn't swoop down to the seal, and we sat watching for another ten minutes, then started off, moving through the floes in a circle that would take us back in the *Havella*'s direction. We were about one hundred yards from shore when Mary Lou pointed and said, "There's something swimming our way."

Alf stopped the motor—why he did that I will never know—and searched the water; so did I. Now the water broke into that telltale V —it was a polar bear.

No more circling and swooping in graceful S-loops now. Alf pointed *Jolle* straight for the *Havella,* a speck in the distance. I doubt if we were making three miles an hour.

The bear was doing twice that. As he got within one hundred yards, we could see that he was an enormous one, his hide yellowish from summer sun, ears back against his head, hind legs floating gracefully.

Mary Lou was taking advantage of the action, using her Nikons as the bear came on. Alf tried to get more speed out of *Jolle* but couldn't. The bear was rapidly overtaking us.

"I have seen one bear upset a sealing boat much bigger than this," Alf said. "Then he swam among the men and killed three. I don't like the look of this bear!"

Mary Lou did: the constant clicking sounds coming from her end of the boat signified that she was taking pictures with great speed. I counted the clicks once. Ten in a short space of time. That bear must have looked twice as large to her through the lens.

Haakon and Alf had told us that polar bears rarely flee from anything. When they see movement in their Arctic, they come right for it. Nothing, other than a killer whale or a walrus, is strong enough or large enough to do battle with them. It would be impossible to conjecture how we must have looked to the bear in this forsaken area where it is doubtful if he had seen human beings in a boat of this kind before. Actually *Jolle* wasn't much larger than he, but the three heads sticking above must have puzzled him, for now he stopped the forward movement. He remained stationary, paddling lazily to keep afloat, giving us time to make more headway. Not much. Then he came for us again.

"If he gets closer than fifty feet," Alf said, "shoot him. He means business, I think. And if he gets closer than that, even if we shoot him, he could dump us into the sea with him."

Mary Lou stopped photographing with these words, and I took a firm grip on the Browning. I didn't want to shoot that magnificent animal swimming so gracefully out there, lord and master of everything he surveyed. But Alf was experienced; he knew what he was talking about. I could feel the authority in his voice.

Now as the bear swam toward us I could feel fear coming, too. It came with the flushing of the face, the sudden sweat in the armpits. It came in the mind. What if I shot and missed? What if I shot and just wounded? We would then be in for a terrible time.

If you could only have the ability to turn off the mind during times of danger, so that you sat cold and calculating and calm. But few of us have this ability. Frankly I was scared. Then, using all the will I could summon, I tried to shake off some of the fear. I actually shook myself like a dog, raised the rifle and looked through the big eye of the telescopic sight. That was a mistake. The bear's head was tremendous. It must have been two feet across. And he kept coming.

"I think you shoot!" Alf said, his voice unsure.

As I got ready, trembling slightly, the bear swerved, and Mary Lou said softly, "No. Don't! I think he is going away."

So I ignored the word of an experienced northman and didn't shoot. It could be a tragic mistake.

But the bear had apparently seen enough. He backpaddled; then putting on an astonishing burst of speed, swam in a big circle around us, proving he could have run us down with ease. Then he started back for the shore and what was left of his seal.

The one amusing aspect of this drama was the gulls: when they saw the bear playing with us, they lost their caution and darted down on the seal. Now as we sat, silent and aware of what could have happened, we saw the bear come out of the water and the birds burst into the sky, flaring like a Roman candle. One didn't make it. The bear, standing upright, batted it to the ground in a single, remarkably swift gesture. We would have been as helpless as fish in a net in the water with that animal.

Alf didn't criticize me for not firing when he told me, but when we got back to the *Havella,* Haakon, using his prerogative as captain and master of our fate, was somber when Alf told him what happened —in Norwegian.

"That was silly thing!" he said. "We have many *isbjørn.* To shoot one more is not bad. Close you came to getting killed! Do not do again! Please! Listen Alf. He know what to do."

One afternoon we came into a tiny bay, or *bukt,* that led into a fjord, Mushamna, just large enough to berth the *Havella* comfortably. There the captain said we were going to see, as he called it, "One of the north's stirring sights." While we came in to the quiet, greenish-blue water, a clear, true color that swimming-pool owners try unsuccessfully to emulate with a paintbrush, the captain said, "This is where biggest birdcliff I see is." He pointed to the shore.

A cliff rose sharply, a vast wall of rock. Above it were bursts of white, rockets exploding—rockets of birds. They blasted up from the face of the cliff; then when they gained altitude just above it, they fanned out. Some then went their own way singly; others in twos and threes violently fought the updraft, then plummeted back to the cliff, disappearing into its surface.

We watched through the glasses for a while, identifying gulls, mostly common, herring and black-headed; then after two trips in the *Jolle* we were finally all standing on the shore, a strip of glacial stone sweepings perhaps forty feet wide that ran along under the gullery.

There were thousands of birds on that cliff. The combined sound coming from them was like that of a giant siren screaming out its shrill warning, the noise so sharp that it would have been impossible to live near this for long without going either mad or completely deaf. This was an impressive sight: the variety of gulls with their whites and slate-grays were splashes of living color against the rock. You could look up and see them in nests on the ledges, some feeding fuzzy yellow young, others courting, some half-grown staggering unsurely along a narrow line of stone ledge; here and there a fight, the flurry of feathers, the slashing of beaks. Take all the seagulls you have ever seen in your lifetime, place them on a cliff, then stand beneath, and you have an approximate picture of what we found just off that little islet.

Alf told us that there were also bird rocks like this inhabited exclusively by auks, which were shot for food at certain times of the year.

"During nesting time," he said, "it is forbidden to shoot near these rocks. We are also not supposed to use the ship's hooter until we are five nautical miles from the rocks."

Now as we watched, the birds suddenly went mad; their shrill keening increased. They rushed to their cliff nests and stood, beaks out, on guard. Above the cliff floated a giant bird, three times the size of an ordinary gull. He had come suddenly, without our noticing.

"Skua!" said the captain grimly.

"It's a gull," Alf said. "One that preys on smaller gulls. Takes mostly baby birds. Look! He can float like that for hours, waiting his chance—"

There wasn't a stir of wings as the great bird hovered above the cliff like a shadow.

"Like a shadow of death," Bryant said.

"Ed," Berg said, "I do declare, if this country isn't making a poet outta you. If you don't like that nasty fella, why don't you knock him off? You brought your rifle."

Bryant had a custom Weatherby .375 magnum, so new and so handsome that he usually carried it on a sling over his shoulder, rarely letting it out of his sight. He kept it cleaned and polished until it shone like a jewel, its blue barrel gleaming, its Spanish walnut stock shiny and soft as satin.

Without a word he threw it to his shoulder, peered through the telescopic sight, following the slow, easy drift of the arctic *skua*. When the shot went off it even startled us, although we stood there expecting it. It frightened the cliff gulls even more than the threat of their hovering enemy. They left the rock face in violent spurts.

The *skua?* Like a subject in a slow-motion picture, it made a sudden upsweep, folded its wings and went into a deep glide, splashing into the bay. Down, one villain.

"Lordy! *Lord dee!*" said Berg, expressing the sentiments of us all. "What a shot! You lucky muskrat! Now we'll never know if that was skill or pure rotten Bryant luck!"

Bryant gave a hero grin. "Never did like bullies."

The crew stared at him as if they had suddenly discovered a celebrity in their midst.

"A shot to celebrate!" said the captain. "Let's go to *Havella*. Harald Hansen can give music. Aage can cook; Alf and me, we can sing."

Aage cooked all right: a stew that he had been working on for some time with big tender nuggets of beef—or seal or reindeer; we never knew and didn't ask—carrots and potatoes, laced with red wine. Crisp homemade bread came out of the oven. He was not a cook, he was a chef, a man of creative ability, for he even saved large portions of the red wine to wash the stew and bread down—soft, velvety burgundy of a proper age that we didn't even know was aboard.

An artistically bent saw—an ordinary wood-cutting saw—provided the music as Hansen coaxed wailing but soft and pleasant sound from it with a violin bow. Hansen sat, his bald head cocked to the side, his old blue eyes snapping behind his glasses, humming as he made music from the gracefully arched steel blade.

And Haakon and Alf sang. What they lacked in musical harmony they more than made up for in sheer gusto. Swinging, short, colorful Norwegian words. Alf suggested that he translate some of the folk-songs so we could enter into the singing.

I wrote down some of the words and translations from that song fest many miles above the Arctic Circle. One, *"Bissam, Bissam Ban'e"* ("Sleep, Sleep, My Baby") was a favorite of Hansen's. They sang it over and over. "Sleep my baby. The kettle is on the fire full of porridge for you. Father is sifting the corn, mother blows in the pretty horn, sister is spinning gold, and your brother is hunting wild animals in the woods. If it's white, bring it home, if it's gray, let it go, but if it's brown, let it wander in the forest."

Another, *"Vassro-Fela"* ("Watercreek Fiddle Was Wooden"), was short, lively and full of beautiful chords faithfully produced by Hansen. "The watercreek fiddle was made of wood, it sank in the Losna Lake, but was found again by a bush and now it sounds night and day. *Suli, luli lei.*"

Suli, luli lei, what an end to a beautiful day. Warmed by stew and song, we slept that night in the little bight by the birdcliff. There wasn't much sound from the birds that night. Fog had moved in, again that northern gray heavy fog that screened the sun and made it bad for sailing.

Next day the fog had lifted and the birds were in that one big scream again as we moved off. A range of color was beginning to play on the ice, the rocks and the water. When sunlight meets and penetrates big ice, it seems to magnify; often even appears to be captured and held. There was a streak of this imprisoned color, blue edged with scarlet, in an iceberg. It even held there while Alf got off the *Havella* and chopped a bucket of ice for our drinks.

I can think of few things more satisfying than stirring a hunk of this sun-caught ice in a glass of whiskey, enjoying the peace and solitude of this man-free Far North while you sip that gold-brown soul-stirring result of man's genius and try to define the things the sun does with this country of ice and sea and sky.

It will be difficult for anyone who has never been this far north to realize that the color spectrum is so varied, so versatile, so fantastic. The twenty-four-hour sunlight helped, of course, but no artistic or poetic license was necessary to get rhapsodic: all you had to do was jot down or remember the colors as you saw them playing across or burning into the ice sheets, the icebergs, the floes and the great glaciers. One moment the world would be rose-violet, then diamond-blue; suddenly it would be rimmed in silver, and although the clouds always hung close to the glaciers, there was a permanent and strange brightness to this lost sky and sea.

Ice for cocktails was as close as the nearest iceberg. Alf Olsen became adept with hatchet and bucket.

I am certain that Edwin Bryant, a hard-headed businessman who saw the facts of life clearly and had a fine appreciation for the wilderness, had never progressed as far as Keats in his reading. But today as I stood beside him on deck, he commented on what his eyes were seeing.

"Look," he said, "that glacier is brushed with diamond dust. That berg to the left is pure sapphire. Now look at that rim of sky, sterling, polished bright, and shining with that chamois of cloud just above—"

Berg stared. "You old muskrat!" He slapped Bryant on the back. "Snap out of it! You'll be writin' that stuff home next!"

Bryant grinned sheepishly. "Can't help it," he said. "Never saw anything like it!"

Thus does the Arctic make a poet out of a muffler manufacturer.

• • •

This northern trek was about over. Bryant had to fly to London on business, Berg was needed in Wisconsin, and Mary Lou and I had a date in Spain—with a few unexpected stopovers.

Now we reversed, in time to meet the *Lyngen* at Longyearbyen for the run to Tromsø. It was a rough, lashing, stomach-churning voyage. Then the bully bus ride back to Bardufoss through the potato-field country with the women in their bras, the men and the children all still at work, as if held in an unchanging frieze or caught with relentless realism in an Andrew Wyeth painting. Here, in one swift scene, was the story of survival in a harsh land where only three percent of the earth is tillable.

Jogging along in the bus, I thought that travel means many things to many people, is as individual as human character. Some go to agencies asking to be safely led by the hand through the foreign fields; others like the camaraderie of tours, preferring the companionship of their own kind to the happenstance hope of meeting and knowing new people; others prepare for months in advance, reading every book and map, winnowing all the information they can, so that when they take their long-awaited trip they feel that they will be moving through familiar territory.

Though always interested in its history, I rarely read anything more about a country I am going to visit, in the belief that if I predigest this information I may dull observation and take the edge off the excitement that comes from seeing new places. Also, I wander. Although I must establish some sort of itinerary, it is seldom that I keep unswervingly to the plan. The real enjoyment often comes in breaking routine, taking a completely unconsidered direction.

This philosophy served us well at Bardufoss where we met an SAS pilot going back to Copenhagen for reassignment. He gave us a new direction—following which we would literally eat our way up the coast of Norway.

"Something different in travel out of Oslo," he said. "A big cruiser you can have all to yourself. Takes the inland route to Bergen. You've seen things the hard way out there in the Arctic. Why not do it the easy way? New view of our country; new people—"

It seemed that there was a fleet of Norway's finest motor vessels, used during the cold, dark winter months as rescue patrol—sort of a coast guard—available for rent during the summer and early fall. There were two eighty-six-foot cruisers; three yachts from sixty-seven to seventy-eight feet and eight ketches and cutters, running from fifty-four to sixty-three feet—complete with crews, fuel, food.

We decided to find out if we could get aboard one of these. The SAS pilot who had trapped our interest graciously phoned from Bardufoss to inquire. We learned that the *Ambassador Bay* was available for the inland cruise to Bergen. Price, reasonable; it was idle time for her.

A snowstorm of seagulls covered the harbor the morning we arrived to introduce ourselves to the captain and set sail. The *Ambassador Bay,* seagull gray, was indeed large, eighty-six feet, ten inches, with a twenty-three-foot beam. The captain, Kristian Arntzen, was cheerful and stocky, with graying, wavy hair. He introduced us to the five young crew members, telling us that on these easy summer cruises he used the ship as a training run for younger sailors. After several summer sessions, he took some of them with him on his winter rescue work.

The boys had the *Ambassador Bay* shipshape, the decks shining clean, the cabin neat. They were all happy, whistling and humming as the anchor was hauled and we sailed out of the harbor, the big 525-horsepower diesel motor thumping smoothly, the ship riding deep and easy. It could accommodate ten with ease in the five double cabins. The two heads had modern showers, water ran hot and cold; the lounge had smart Danish furniture and comfortable easy chairs. The travel possibilities of the *Ambassador Bay* were enormous: she could serve as a mobile luxury hotel, moving from Oslo to the coast above the Arctic Circle, sailing all of the big fjord country. One could visit Sweden and Denmark; even Germany, Holland, Belgium, France and Britain.

Now we moved past hundreds of small, chalet-type houses along the shore. Each house flew the Norwegian flag. Blond Norsks in motorboats played before us like dolphins, darting ahead of the *Ambassador Bay*. The mountains ahead were dark in mist; sailboats on the far shore moved as gracefully as seabirds getting ready to launch themselves into the sky.

Curious about the name of our ship, I asked the captain about her. "American," he said. "Built here in 1958, but a gift of the Texas Bay family."

The cruiser came from the Charles Ubrick and Josephine Bay Foundation. Their son had served as United States Ambassador to Norway from 1946 to 1950. Both parents had been born in Norway, moved to Texas and found oil on their land.

About **three hours from Oslo we made port** for a brief stop at

Be your own captain on a sea-sized yacht like the Ambassador Bay *of the Norwegian Summer Ship Rental Service.*

Sandefjord, the world's leading whaling center, home port of Norway's Antarctic whaling fleet. The captain told us that this town of seven thousand does nothing except whaling and shipping. Today it was like a town from another century sleeping in the bland sunlight, stirred only by the raucous seagulls as they drifted over the few boats in the harbor. I understand we could have eaten a whale steak at the New Park Hotel across from the monument of six bronze men in a small craft harpooning a whale, but we passed up this dubious treat, and the *Ambassador Bay* moved out of Sandefjord with a few laughing townspeople at the quay obviously making comment on how the captain handled the cruiser. Not understanding Norwegian, I missed the humor. But the captain, grinning, explained.

"Old gentleman in sailor's cap is retired whaler. He said I use too much oil getting *Ambassador Bay* out. Go too fast."

On our way again, we stood beside the captain at the helm, watching the steel prow cutting through this summer-smooth water. The captain bemoaned the fact that he became fifty years old this week. "That is the year you know life will not get better," he said.

"From this day it can only get worse."

I laughed. "You're the captain of your ship, the master of your fate. That's more than most men can say."

He shook his head. "Ya, captain of a ship that mostly sails stormy seas," he said. He rubbed his chest. "Did fool thing this winter, going from Shetlands on night patrol. Ran into bad storm. I watch through window, telling helmsman direction. Had a bottle of beer. Next I know I am thrown against the wheel. Trying to save bottle of beer, I break two ribs against wheel spokes." He laughed. "It was good bottle of beer. *Bokkøl*." This seemed to remind him of something. He looked at his watch. "Ya, is almost lunch time. Would you and Mrs. Scott join for a bottle of beer, please? Same kind that broke my ribs?"

Bokkøl was dark and strong. It was good, not exactly worth breaking a couple of ribs for, but after two bottles it brought more conversation from the captain.

"You know what you did to us?" he said.

"Who?" I said.

"Your country, the United States of America."

"No, Captain."

"You sent us a black man as an ambassador."

I wasn't aware that this had happened, but I said to myself, *I'm sure he is an intelligent, able man.*

"Ya, maybe you test us," he said. "But if so, it was good test. We Norwegians are democratic people. We like people for what they are. For what they do. This is good man, this ambassador. Everybody I see who know him say that they like him, that he is doing good job."

From this we got into philosophy. The captain had sailed the Far East and had picked up some thinking on the subject of marriage.

"In the East," he said, "they believe that is better to have many wives with little trouble than have one wife with much trouble." He cocked his head at me. "Good thinking, ya?"

. I agreed that a division of trouble in the manner he suggested might be a good idea.

"How many wives do you have, Captain?" Mary Lou said.

Ruefully he admitted that he had only one. "And three fine sons and a daughter," he said proudly. "Ya, I am not man enough to do as they do in some places in East. Not with Norwegian woman."

Two of his sons were following him to sea, he said, shaking his head. "The third," he said, "is going to university." A slightly bewildered expression crossed his face, as if it was beyond understanding how an upstanding Norwegian could do anything but follow the sea.

In addition to the captain's conversation, one of the unpublicized virtues of this summer boat rental idea was the food. It was superb, and unlike the *Havella* and the *Lyngen* it wasn't a hazard to sit at the table. Not only was the *Ambassador Bay* built for rough seas—so seaworthy she rode as though she were on a mill pond—but the route we were taking was near shore and we weren't hitting any rough water at all.

That day for lunch we had a choice of at least a dozen herring, *rakefisk*—raw trout that has fermented in some mysterious tart brew for weeks—and the famous *gravlaks,* dilly salmon—filets soaked in spices and dill, sprinkled with cognac and sherry, then sliced thinly. These were followed by those remarkably firm, sweet, tiny shrimp from the cold fjords, a squeeze of lemon over them as they were spread on buttered white hearth bread; then the entrée, *faaralaar,* smoked leg of mutton sliced thinly, surrounded by scrambled eggs topped with fresh chopped chives. I don't know if the sequence was proper, but next I had *gjetost,* the dark brown Norwegian goat cheese that looks like laundry soap but has a bitey-bland flavor difficult to describe. The Norwegians have long been underrated cuisinewise, if the fare aboard the *Ambassador Bay* is typical.

As we progressed, villages and seaside houses were spaced more widely, with little green mounds rising along shore. They gleamed whitely at the bottom with *fjelsbat,* a smooth stone something like granite, according to the captain.

"Our scientists work on that stone," said the captain. "We are economic people. Norway wastes nothing. Already I hear that *fjelsbat* holds material that gives nuclear power."

I thought this would launch him into a discussion of the hydrogen bomb and the cold war, but it didn't, and I was glad that it didn't. He stood smoking his pipe, rubbing his mending ribs, watching a fishing village come up off the port bow.

We had passed so many fishing villages now that their picturesque construction was no longer strange. The houses were all alike, with fieldstone reaching halfway to the clapboard second story; roofs of weathered shingles; four windows facing the water. The first story was evidently a combination boathouse and storage area for fishing equipment and the drying of fish. These were all within a dozen feet of each other on the shores of the tiny harbors.

In late afternoon we stopped at Bekkjardks. While the captain went on a mysterious shopping errand, we walked through this settlement. The houses were the same two-story, wood-shingled, oyster-white clapboard, cheek-by-jowl affairs, many of their windows filled with apple-cheeked women who stared at us curiously, smiling as we waved. A pleasant, quiet, homey place—but its odor! Fish, fish, fish. They were everywhere, drying on racks, hung from rope that stretched like a clothesline, stacked in barrels, being salted in open trays. All herring. Bekkjardks is one of the few herring villages in the world, a settlement that does nothing but catch, smoke, salt, dry and pack herring. Its fishermen are among the world's best, making their richest catches off Iceland. They are a rugged, blue-eyed, seaburned breed, dressed in dark jackets, faded blue dungarees, black rubber boots and billed caps.

This was a place that made you want to sit and talk. As we watched a torn hole in a net being rewoven, I wanted to ask questions about how the hole happened and about the dark, cold, dangerous days in the sea off Iceland. But this wasn't possible, so I let my imagination sail out of the tiny harbor with these modern Vikings as they headed for the cold coasts, the rough seas and the perilous weeks at sea.

The captain had completed his errand, and was boarding the *Ambassador Bay* again. He carried a long newspaper-wrapped bundle under his arm, and wore a broad grin on his rosy face. Later he summoned us for the unveiling. As he dramatically unfolded the paper crease by crease, he said, "I make this Bekkjardks stop every time I can. They have secret way of getting best damn salmon in all Norway."

They looked like the best. They were fat, gleaming silver, had clear eyes that you could look into without remorse—the certain sign of a water-fresh fish.

"For dinner," he said. "Norway way!"

As on the *Havella*, the salmon was boiled in sea water, but wrapped in muslin to keep it intact, and poached just long enough so that it came to the table firm yet flaky. A distinct art. Served with it were diced new potatoes cooked in heavy cream and dill, and a side dish of piquant mustard sauce. Next to the charr fresh out of the lost lake, this was the best fish I had eaten. As we started to push back our chairs, the captain laughed.

"No, no. This last night. We have Norwegian special dish!"

This was *faar i kaal*—mutton and cabbage stew. Breast and shoulder were cubed and arranged between layers of cabbage, heavily seasoned with freshly milled black pepper, and slowly boiled until meat and cabbage were tender. It sounds plebeian, but as a combination it came out savory and succulent.

Dessert was a Scandinavian specialty—cloudberries. So named because they are grown high in the mountains, these golden berries are the size of a giant blackcap raspberry. The flavor is sugar-tart, distinctly its own even when sprinkled with powdered and granulated sugar and topped with whipped cream. As the captain said, this was our gala night, the last on the *Ambassador Bay*. In the morning we would reach Bergen, city of the seven mountains.

The Norwegians have taken their way from the sea; rising from a barbaric nation that lived on the plunder of its sea-raiding Vikings, they have become a major merchant sea nation, a prosperous people. At last count, I believe, Norway was third among the merchant marine nations of the world. With its rocky soil, its two thousand miles of fierce coastline, its raging winters, it has built beautiful cities, done fanciful and poetic things with glass and stone, created great music. From their mountain-ranged sheep come the most magnificent sweaters in the world. They have also given steel a new dimension. Yet, regardless of what they do with ceramics, steel, silver and wool, they never forget the sea for a moment. For them, sailing is as important as baseball or Hollywood to many Americans. Their idols, even today, are the sea captains, the adventurous sea rovers like Thor Heyerdahl of *Kon Tiki* fame, who bring pride and fame to their country.

Consequently, the quays are always populated with those who come down to watch the ships come in. They are as vocal, as critical and as demanding as any crowd at Yankee Stadium—and they have much more know-how about how a ship should be handled than the average American baseball buff has of how to make a double play.

As Captain Arntzen brought the *Ambassador Bay* into Bergen under the appraising eyes of two hundred locals, he laughed. "If I don't do this right, I better not get off ship." He told of one captain who, accidentally scraping dockside with a cruiser, received such jeers and heckling that he was actually afraid to leave his ship.

We wouldn't return to Oslo with the *Ambassador Bay*. We would fly back. The ship was going to lie at anchor in Bergen awaiting the next charter and would spend a month doing the big fjords farther north. Good-byes were hearty—and liquid. Now that we were at port, the captain broke out a bottle of ancient whiskey and we toasted each other three times—fast, as seems to be the man-testing Norwegian custom—and left the ship in a warm glow of fellowship and good cheer.

People make travel. Captain Arntzen made this trip. Getting to know new people, to learn their ways and understand their character, is one of the real challenges—and pleasures—of a man on the move. As the Greek poet, Giorgios Seferis, Nobel Prize winner for literature in 1963, wrote:

> "How hard to collect
> The thousand fragments
> Of each and every man!"

But the fragments you do gather along the way can one day, piece by piece, form a whole that makes life better. I'll never forget Ben Berg's "Have a little fun *every* day." He has pulled life into focus for himself.

For a few days we had used Ben's philosophy on the *Ambassador Bay*. But there is a distinct drawback to this type of sidetrip provided by the Norwegian Summer Ship Rental service: Captain Arntzen was so entertaining and hospitable, the cruiser so well built and tremorless, that all we did was sit and talk, watch the fishing villages sail by —and eat. I put on five pounds, Mary Lou two; we wouldn't be able to look a fish in its cold eye for weeks—or so we thought without taking Bergen into consideration.

The public market in Bergen is at the quay, a few feet from the harbor. It was such a riot of color and activity that we decided to register at the Orion Hotel, a trim, clean, modern place, then go back and walk among the people at the market. Everywhere were tanks of water full of live fish. People stood watching the fish as if fascinated, but we soon saw that it wasn't fascination at all: they were coldly estimating how fat and lively they were, just before having their selections netted and weighed. Some were buying boiled shrimp in cornucopias of newspaper and eating them like peanuts, leaving trails of pink as they walked. We stayed in that happy place until dusk came in a sudden sweep of purple and the people started drifting away and the stalls began closing.

After Tromsø, Bergen with its gaily painted houses and its population of over one hundred thousand seemed like a metropolis. But it isn't. It is an ancient town hidden and scattered among its seven mountains, founded by King Olav Kyrre in 1070 A.D. Once one of Europe's great seaports, it even vied with Copenhagen, and was Norway's capital for almost a century and a half, from 1164 A.D. to 1299 A.D.

In its mountain fastness, Bergen is different from most Scandinavian towns. Shut off from the rest of Norway, its people went west
across the sea to Europe and England, creating new markets, bringing
back new ideas and products. Bergensers claim that they are different
from other Norwegians for this reason, believing that they in their
mountain civilization grew not only in wealth and sophistication but
in culture as well, while the rest of the country lagged. Beautiful
music did come from one of Bergen's sons, Edvard Grieg; Lud-
vig Holberg and Ole Bull also brought her fame. For two weeks
in May and June, Bergen honors Grieg with a festival in his home at
Troldhaugen, and the place is full of the music of his *lieder*.

The waterfront was foreshadowed by onion-domed churches and
had an Oriental look. In the harbor a little ferry launch was weaving
in and out among the cargo ships like a rabbit dodging hounds.
Wanting to see Bergen from one of the mountains, we twisted up the
funicular to Fløien in a fast, whipping movement. From the terrace of
Fløirestauranten, the town—with lights beginning to blink on—
looked like a toy village neatly assembled beneath a Christmas tree;
beyond was the North Sea, a vast gray glimmer dotted with islands.
Directly below us, motionless little boats looked as if they were
caught in ice.

Later at the Bellevue, an elegant restaurant run by the same family
since 1899, we dined in the Speisestuen, a beautifully appointed room
with old brass, glass chandeliers and damask draperies, overlooking
Bergen proper. There I had the opportunity to see a citizen demand
and get a live cod, which he poked with a forefinger and watched as it
wiggled while he gave lengthy cooking instructions. For a trip that
was just casually worked in, the cruise to Bergen on the *Ambassador
Bay* had many things working in its favor, including the inspiration of
confidence: I also tried the live cod gambit, even managing to carry
off the theatrical effect by suggesting that I have it poached in cheese-
cloth and served with melted butter. Sheer bravado—anyone telling a
Norwegian how to cook a fish! They tell me Bergen does that to you.

Waiting in an air terminal doesn't have to be boring: the talk as
travelers come and go is more immediately rewarding than reading a
book, hopefully counting your sheaf of traveler's checks over and
over, or even mentally blocking out what lies ahead in your own
uncertain world of travel. There is a new jet-born conversation that
easily takes your mind off late planes, cramped schedules and terminal tedium. Sitting in Oslo airport waiting for the Copenhagen plane,

Mary Lou and I heard four of our senior citizens trying to out-adjective one another, and I remembered the words of an old Danish writer, Steen Steensen Blicher: "Yet he who at first sight of the North Sea has too much to say, should never put himself to the trouble of going there . . ."

"Just got back from the Viking Tour," said a short, red-faced man, nodding proudly at a gaunt, crane-thin woman. "Simply great! Wasn't it, dear?"

She smiled. Overhead light made her hair look like heather in dubious Scottish sunlight. "*Fabulous* is more like the correct word," she said.

The other man and woman were biding their time. All were obviously exhausted, but valiantly kept trying to throw off tourist sparks of joy.

The other woman looked like a little cherub come to earth, all dressed up for a visit to a cold country.

She said, in a basso profundo, carefully rolling the vowels, "I'm sorry that we didn't take that three-day *Fairyland* Tour."

Her husband glared. "You know you liked the *Blitz* Tour. Look what we did in that length of time. Every minute counted!"

Viking Tour's interest was aroused. "Blitz?" he said. "Just what is that?"

Blitz Tour beamed. "Why, it's a brand-new idea—for those of us who can't seem to find the time for an *ordinary* tour. They set up a *special* flight from Oslo in the evening, arriving at Bodø, *beyond* the Arctic Circle, at midnight." He winked. "The witching hour. Then they take us around by car in this northern *outpost,* feed us a reindeer-steak dinner on the very top of Ronvik Mountain. Flight takes two hours forty minutes each way. Get back to Oslo for an early breakfast—"

"Don't forget, dear," his wife said, "the *sights* as we blitzed."

He blinked. "Of *course*. Most important. Fly over a great variety of Norway's most fascinating country. Valleys, lakes, waterfalls, rivers, fjords, mountains, glaciers. All in the Midnight Sun."

"And, dear," his wife said, "remember the *certificate*."

This time he scowled. "Yeah, yeah! Award you a 'Midnight Sun Certificate,' as they said, 'a token of your entry to the distinguished circle of seasoned world travelers.' "

The sparks were still flying as they boarded the Copenhagen plane. They didn't look exhausted as they entered: they had talked themselves out of fatigue. I envied them the ability.

On the swift flight to Copenhagen, the cloud formation below resembled a military contour map. The color was alive, like a fire in a forest, pink on top, growing red as the light went deeper into the cotton clouds. And the shiny red Danish cows in the emerald grass, seen from above, were a pastoral scene that painters have been trying to create on their canvases for years, but never have mastered. They can't quite get this feel of the earth seeming to turn, of the wind whisking the grass into moving lines like water running. As we approached Copenhagen, the meadows disappeared and a caterpillar of people in a single-line file of bicycles took their place, the line twisting and turning like the insect.

That first night back from Oslo and the Far North, a friend, Inger-Lise Christensen, met us at Kastrup and took us out on the town, where we danced straight through breakfast. Copenhagen is one of the few cities left in the world where this can be accomplished. I'm not commenting on the physical merits of this, but after long days on boats it has a certain therapeutic value. Especially when the strength has been built with much *smørrebrød*, a deceitful word that means buttered bread, and the legs limbered with *akvavit*, the white Scandinavian firewater.

Inger-Lise started us off at Oskar Davidsen's, a famous old restaurant where Peter Freuchen, the Danish explorer and adventurer used to do much of his glass-clinking. It was owned by her friend, slender, handsome Per Davidsen, and made a specialty of *smørrebrød*, offering a four-foot menu listing two hundred of the open-faced sandwiches.

Each *smørrebrød* was hailed with a *skaal,* the Danish custom that consists of holding up a glassful of aquavit, looking each other in the eye, smiling, saying *skaal,* then downing it, following with a sip of Tuborg or Carlsberg beer.

Inger-Lise explained that *skaal* is really a social ritual that holds much meaning for a Dane.

"S," she said, "is for the Danish word *sundhed,* good health; K, *kerlighed,* love; A, *alder,* long life; and L, *lykke,* luck." After another *skaal* and some eel, she said, "So, you see *skaal* means the most important things in life. And we Danes don't take it lightly."

Aquavit is made from potatoes; never have I had them more pleasantly served. I'm told that Denmark's inland sale is four million bottles a year fermented from twenty thousand tons of potatoes. Well fortified with this variety, we started off to see Copenhagen and do some dancing. "To get rid of those shipboard blues," Inger-Lise said.

She is a tall girl with dark red hair and brown eyes and a creamy complexion. She laughs often but genuinely. She handles her *skaal*ing well, speaks seven languages, English with just the slightest accent— deliberately, I think, to let you know that she is a Dane. And like all Danes, she is gay.

Every restaurant and night club we entered was crowded, mostly with Danes—all ages—all having the time of their lives, *skaal*ing, laughing, singing with the orchestra, doing crazy impromptu dances. For me, Copenhagen is a much happier and gayer city than Paris, Rome, London, or even Vienna. About 5:00 A.M. Inger-Lise and I walked off a tiny, smoky dance floor at the Flamingo, after trying to close the Ambassadeur, the Club de Paris and the Stork Club— aquavit makes you want to close places—and joined Mary Lou at our table, where she in turn had been joined by an unknown Dane and two beautiful, heavy-lidded, full-lipped blondes. One was smoking a cigar, a common feminine habit in Denmark. Our male visitor had a bottle of pink champagne in each hand. The girls sat blinking sensuously like pleased cats. One dainty thing handled her cigar like a Hoboken politician, chewing it and blowing great streamers of smoke over our heads.

When the champagne was finished, the gentleman took each girl by an elbow, stood up, bowed stiffly and left the Flamingo without a word. We followed in a few minutes, in time to have coffee and *wienerbrød* (which means Vienna bread, but is really a flaky, delicious Danish pastry) at our favorite, the Terminus Hotel. We made it to bed as the sun was coming up along the Bangaadsplads. The light flowed like a river along the street.

Inger-Lise, as bouncy as if she had slept ten hours, turned up at the Terminus at noon. "I have a nice little adventure for you," she said. "We will drive out to Snekkersten, to Kystens Perle. Pearl of the Coast, to you. There we will get some much-needed fresh air."

"What's the adventure?" I said.

"It will be more fun if I don't tell you. The drive is nice. Along the beachway."

The beachway ran in loops and curves along the Baltic, then in alternate long, straight and short staggered stretches for twenty miles through the area called Strandvejen, passing some of the most impressive residences I had seen in Denmark. Set beside them were simple week-end beach cottages—a democratic touch of build-and-let-build much in evidence everywhere in Denmark.

Kystens Perle was a red and white three-storied, slick, modern seaside hotel, complete with colored beach-umbrella tables, a fountain with a huge jumping fish, plush cocktail lounges, a super-modern bar, several dining rooms, and a tall, dark, handsome manager, Ove Miehs, who looked like a hardened-down, younger Cary Grant. He greeted us warmly, gave us a bitter, yellowish drink, of which I couldn't catch either the pronunciation or spelling, guaranteed to bring life back to those who needed it after spending a night on the town in Copenhagen. It did.

Ove Miehs could teach certain hotel managers I know in world capitals some tricks in manners, graciousness and personality. He escorted us through the hotel, the Film Bar, the Hamlet Restaurant, the Pearl Coast Room, and invited us to spend the night, the week, or the month. He finally showed us a large wicker hamper packed with a picnic lunch.

"Now for the boat," he said.

"Boat?" Mary Lou and I asked simultaneously.

"Yes!" He smiled happily. "Our own tuna boat. It is not right now for tuna, but Kystens Perle has a little adventure worked out for people who are getting perhaps a little bored with Copenhagen. We supply you with a boat, a captain and mate, a complete Danish picnic and take you cod-fishing from Denmark right across to Sweden. Guaranteed to give you sun, fun and relax you. Price: ten dollars per person. Good?"

"Great," I said, looking at Inger-Lise. "This will give us a chance to see what your tuna boats are like. We've just spent the last several weeks on a fifty-seven-foot diesel ketch off Spitzbergen, and came back just the other day from cruising the coast of Norway in an eighty-six-foot cruiser. But this is just fine. We haven't been on a *Danish* boat yet."

The thirty-foot boat was old and gray, but rode well—a three-ton tuna fisher with port marine engines, Miehs said. The captain, Frederick, was a middle-aged, gray-blond in blue coveralls, and the mate, Tobin, a youngster with his face wind- and sun-burned the color of a broiled lobster.

Snekkersten Bay was a bit choppy, but the day was warm and the sun felt good on the back and face. Miehs waved from the shore. "We'll have dinner ready when you get back!"

"We've been *eating* our way around Scandinavia," Mary Lou said. "No one seems to think of anything else!"

"It's what most people do more than anything," Inger-Lise said. "We just think we do it better."

"You win the championship," I said.

"This is the water," Inger-Lise said abruptly, soberly, "where we Danes crossed to escape the Nazis. You know Sweden was neutral. Or supposed to be neutral. We used everything from water skis to rubber tubes to get across this bay." We stood looking at the horizon line that was Sweden, thinking about the bad days. Then the captain passed out fishing gear.

I don't recommend this cod-fishing picnic as a stirring adventure, but it is relaxing, more fun than a tour, and a good way to see two

Codfishing on Snekkersten Bay with Inger-Lise Christensen meant a picnic in the grand style. . . . Fish were many if not mighty.

countries in one short trip. We fished our way across to the island
Hven in Sweden, taking over two hours in a casual, easy run, with
Tobin rebaiting and removing the hooked cod. Denmark is said to
take two hundred thousand tons of fish annually from the waters
around her islands. I don't doubt it. Snekkersten Bay was alive with
the broad, silvery fish.

On landing we took the big hamper and went into a restaurant
overlooking the little harbor. Café Solbacken was pleasant, except for
one thing: its record-player blared forth rock-and-roll all the time we
were there. Four young Swedes, two boys and two girls, stood before
it with dead expressions, snapping their fingers, bowing as if paying
obeisance to the God Buddha. I'm not certain that the juke box
hasn't become a reverent symbol of sorts to the younger generation
everywhere.

We fished all the way back, piling up a sizable catch of cod. We
took two apiece after Tobin skillfully cleaned them, and had them
boiled at Kystens Perle as *torsk,* which simply means codfish but
comes on the table as a first course with cups of thick melted butter
and a mustard sauce (not as tart as the Norwegian). Then we went
into the favorite exercise of the Danes: eating our way through a
magnificent dinner built around *bøf*—rare, tender beef.

When I sat down to put this collection of wanderings on paper, I
had intended to keep as closely as I could to travel, the people and
the places I had seen, the things I had done, some of them exciting
and different, some ordinary. But when a man keeps a journal of
travel it is impossible to still transient thoughts of the passing moment.

So it is with me today as we prepare to leave Copenhagen. It is a
place of pleasing people, where the past and present meet in harmony. Castles and elegant Renaissance buildings are set beside modern office structures, and shining black motor cars move along with
bicycle brigades. Shop windows gleam with princely old silver and
shine with rare crystal. The food markets display poetic arrangements of pork from the white Danish Landrace, the world's most
perfectly bred pig—everything from necklaces of sausages and pendant amber-skinned salamis to rosy hams in an artistic setting of
curled black eels, and the long, lean, lustrous loins in beds of diamond ice. Cheese shops dangle creamy wares with names that come
like songs, Samsø, Dambø, Maribø, in such variety and abundance
that you stand and count the sizes and shapes, mentally slicing a

square one, dipping a spoon into a round one, spreading a piece of bread with a soft one. This became one of my favorite pastimes.

We often walked Copenhagen's streets in the rain—red and white flags flapping from the buildings—while watching the Danes hurry along trying to use their will power and pass by the blue *pølser* stands —featuring the hot wiener dipped in mustard—before dinner. Many don't make it. The stands are always crowded; few with tourists.

The polar bear and the seal, the tiger and the lion, the small boy and the geese, the appealing girl with her white cat, all masterpieces in porcelain, stand in eternal beauty in the Bing & Grøndahl window.

The fishwives hunch at their cold stands, folded newspapers on their heads over the wool scarves tied under red, lightly whiskered double chins. They are bulky, patient old women who display like jewels on a tray their cod and plaice, their eels and haddock. They say some people want them to go. They are a shabby sign of the past. But most people in Copenhagen would miss them, so they stay.

It is a city that proudly presents and preserves its old-world personality despite the rising tide of tourists, the invasion of modernity such as supermarkets, rock-'n'-roll music and the roar of the jet.

I'm fond of cities and like to receive what they have to offer—their fine food, music, art, their combined luxurious gifts. Copenhagen's treasures include its great Royal Ballet; its several unusual art museums—one maintained by a brewery, thus encouraging the Danes to drink for the benefit of culture; its Tivoli, the world's most wonderful entertainment park with open-air concerts, symphonies, theaters, pantomime, jugglers, acrobats, comedies, plays, orchestras, dancing, ballet, superb restaurants representing most countries, beer halls, music halls, and thousands of interesting, excited people from everywhere. But when I have enjoyed a city's people, its conversation, its companionship, I like to leave. Even Copenhagen. For a city's life is an artificial one. Nothing really alive, except man, can grow in its stone.

Suddenly one day I awaken in my hotel room and discover that the noise of the city is unbearable, and when I walk its streets and see the cars rushing, the exhaust plumes rising, the sky growing dark with industrial haze, the people clotting the sidewalks, I want to get out to a place where I can watch a stream curl, see the sun on a meadow, a wagon on a dusty road. For no matter what varied pleasures the city offers, I am never at home in one—not for long. If the truth be known, no man is. At least he is not truly alive in that mass of steel and mortar.

I remember what Joseph Wood Krutch said when he left his job on a New York newspaper, caught up with the compelling desire to get out of the city: "Only those within whose consciousness the sun rises and sets, the leaves burgeon and wither, can be said to be aware of what living is . . ."

When I communicated this feeling to Inger-Lise Christensen, she looked at me soberly and said, "I know. I feel this way often. When I can, I get to the part of our country that is still mostly open and free. Jutland. This is our real farm country. Full of peace and quiet, moors like Scotland, trout streams. I think you should go there. Also, there are no tourists." The next day we were on our way.

One traveler said that Denmark was that part of the sea with land in it, remarking that you could tell the difference because the land was a much brighter green than the water. Its highest point is only 570 feet above sea level; and you never get far from what has given her strength: ships. Wherever you look there are fields with the riggings and masts of ships rising above them.

Most of the country's 16,576 square miles are made up of 622 small islands with only one hundred inhabited by the four and a half million Danes. The largest island is Zealand in the east, dominated by fair Copenhagen.

Jutland, considered by many to be the true, unspoiled Denmark— Hans Christian Andersen called it the "head and fountain of Denmark"—is not an island. It is a long peninsula, actually a projection of northern Europe, forming the continental portion of the kingdom of Denmark and including the German province of Schleswig-Holstein.

Our hotel in the village of Karup swam into view out of the light rain that greeted us—and rarely stopped while we were in Jutland. It was an undistinguished two-story gray stucco building that somehow gave me the feeling of coaches; horses standing, long plumes streaming from their nostrils in the cold air; coachmen in hard hats, long coats and gauntlets; a fat, red-faced innkeeper with his long, curving white pipe and a laugh that shattered glasses; a joint sizzling on a spit in an open fireplace.

As we entered the Karup Kro, a slim, elegant, blond woman greeted us.

"Mr. and Mrs. Scott? I'm Annalise Svendsen, the manager. Your room is ready."

It was a small, nicely carpeted room, with a huge, *dyne*-covered double bed, a bath, and a large window giving on a pond owned by a pair of swans and three cygnets. Two hundred yards back were three farm trout ponds close enough that we could see the fish jumping. A typed card on the door announced that this room with bath cost eighteen kroner per person for full pension (three meals a day)—less than eight dollars for two. It was obvious that the tourist wave had not washed over Karup.

It took less than three minutes to discover that Annalise Svendsen was a charming, knowledgeable woman who knew how to run a hotel and to treat guests. She had made a date with a banker in nearby Holstebro, a trout fisherman who would take us to his favorite stream.

After dinner I read a book, *From the Danish Peninsula* by Steen Steensen Blicher, the old poet of the Jutland heath whose work I knew slightly. It was a sad, but compelling and beautifully written, story about murder, for which a clergyman had been wrongly accused and beheaded. According to the foreword, it was the original plot for Mark Twain's *Tom Sawyer Detective*. Johannes Smith who wrote the foreword had other interesting things to say.

Writing about the pride of Jutlanders in their land and way of life, he told of one farmer living in a typical but remote part of the peninsula who had a visit from Copenhageners who raved about the beauty of his place. The only thing that they disliked about the farm was that it was so far away. "Far away?" said the Jute. "What from?"

Although it had the feel of a wild place, it wasn't a windswept, *Rebecca*-type moor, as we discovered next morning as we drove off to go fly-fishing for brook trout. Ahead of us as we drove, the moors stretched in gray gloom; the heather ran in purple fire with the lash of the wind. But everywhere the land was checkered with little farms; most of the houses were two-storied, whitewashed and thatch-roofed, all with several outbuildings in good repair. Polished by rain, the cattle looked like porcelain figurines; geese and chickens were in the grass; farmers stalked in knee-high black rubber boots. Most of the land holdings were small, perhaps from five to twenty acres. As the Danes say of themselves, defining the reason for national happiness: "Few have too much and fewer still too little." Half of Denmark's 205,000 farms are less than twenty-five acres. From these comes the great flow of dairy and pork products that make her the world's leading producer. One century ago this entire land we were driving through was an immense, desertlike heath. Today it holds two million acres of fertile land, one-quarter of the farming land in Denmark, all of it manmade. But in most of Jutland some moors and heather remain to add strength and beauty to the peninsula. Here, near Karup, we could be driving through the vast moor areas of Scotland. Except that here were many fast, narrow streams cutting through the countryside, brimful now in the rain and somewhat muddy for dry-fly fishing. By taking advantage of the few lulls and protected places, we managed to get seventeen decent rainbows, releasing all but a half dozen that we would ask to have prepared for dinner at the hotel.

Dusk came now in a long sweep like rain. As the poet said about Jutland dusk, "When down the shorn horizon the light falls . . ." And it was falling fast. But we had no trouble getting back to our hotel. "I have a drink waiting for you by the fire," Annalise said, calling a waitress to take our fish. "Would you like these as first course this evening?" Thus did she keep my first vision of old-world hospitality bright.

Shedding our raingear, we went straight to the lounge for the warmth of fire and the promised drink. The sign above the door, *Opholdsstue førboende Gaester,* informed us that it was reserved strictly for guests. It was a relaxed, intimate room. The fire was blazing and we were dry before the bourbon arrived. This was the way to end a day: before a crackling log in a quiet room full of memories of happy days that had gone before, waiting for fish we had taken from a small, clear stream to be poached, the smooth old bourbon warming and relaxing us while we talked about fishing tomorrow. Then a hot shower and a change of clothing. The world of travel never looked brighter.

The dining room was also pleasant with a soft red and white carpet, hanging lamps, geraniums in the windows, great white carnations in vases on the tables, which were laid with starchy white tablecloths, Jensen silver, wine goblets and huge linen napkins folded like flowers blooming from the service plates. The chairs were big leather ones with arms, designed to imprison you comfortably at the table. You could see rich grass, a flower garden and the hotel's trout pond through the window.

A buxom, cheery waitress who gave the air of just having come from the kitchen where she had personally cooked a superb meal, told us that the trout would be ready soon, but in the meantime we should order hot soup and a local dish to follow the fish.

She suggested *aegte skildpaddesuppe,* the fish, then *inbagt hamburgerryg med gemyse.* The soup proved to be genuine turtle with succulent pieces of the green creature floating in it. Our stream-fresh rain-bows were crisp and golden and fell apart at the touch, flaky yet moist. The last, complicated item, that sounded like a German tank division being ordered to counterattack, was a simple dish: ground meat formed like a shell steak, with a natural but well-seasoned flour-less gravy; the meat, a combination of pork, veal and beef, was a Jutland specialty served with hot creamed potatoes, garnished with chopped parsley.

The next day further convinced me that we had indeed found an undiscovered oasis in this churning world of elbow-to-elbow tourism.

We went to Holstebro, a larger town than Karup, to meet the banker, Gunnar Muller, who was there waiting with a gift. "From the mayor and the town for two Americans who come fishing," he said. The gifts were two beautiful pieces of white china hand-painted with the coat of arms of the town, a knight on a white steed.

Gunnar Muller turned out to be young, short, voluble, friendly, and full of enthusiasm. He had been to Detroit for two years as an exchange student studying banking, and he liked Americans, but bet-ter still he liked fishing. "We will go this afternoon," he said. "The Raasted—and we will take my assistant Paul Andersen with us—"

Andersen was tall, thirty, dark blond, and he talked trout all the way to their special stream. The Raasted was a swift-running ribbon of water fifteen yards wide. Muller and Andersen were Danish hosts to the letter. When they got a rise they would immediately call me to their place on the stream and insist that I try my fly. When I said no, they would say, "But you must. It is best to try another fly now at this time. Perhaps the fish will like your fly better than ours."

Andersen would walk beside me and point out places in the stream. "There is a good trout there," he would say. "But we will go farther and work back. Another is usually in that run, waiting for flies to drift to him. He is a fat one and a smart one."

Muller and Andersen were masters with the rod, and they sat-cast, the first time I ever saw it done. They hunkered down as if they were tying their shoelaces and suddenly the line would sail out like a bird, the fly gently light on the stream as naturally as a stone fly puffed in by the wind, and they would mend line so smoothly that it was ma-chinelike.

"The trout see you when you stand and cast," Andersen said. "This is why we do this." Beside, I think this position is about the easiest for fly casting. Don't you?"

I tried it but didn't like it. My wife did no better. We had to take our chances standing and scaring the trout. But the Danes delivered. They took scrappy ten-inch rainbows consistently, releasing all under that size, creeling just enough of the keepers for dinner that night. They couldn't understand why we weren't getting results. I could; we just weren't skillful enough to make a sitting game of casting the fly. Twice when the sun went under the clouds scudded over black and full and I had no shadow on the stream, I took good fish. Muller and Andersen offered me their entire catch but I politely refused, even though I had promised the blond Annalise Svendsen that I would bring back enough for dinner. Fish seem to taste better when you catch them yourself. The Danes agreed.

We went to Muller's apartment, a bright, modern place full of that Danish furniture that looks as if designed to prove there are 125 ways to sit and recline. Mrs. Andersen was there, too; both women were blond and charming, one slender, one not. The talk was fishing and America. How many people in our country owned two cars, did everyone have television, did we only eat canned fruit and instant foods, were baseball, Hollywood and television really the American gods, was it true that only the people in the far West walked, that the new developments that were going up were without sidewalks because they wouldn't be used? Were we really suppressing the Negroes and the poor people from Kentucky who lived in Chicago, was Frank Sinatra going to be our singing ambassador to Italy? Muller, having been there, helped some, but it was evident that they didn't place full faith in his observations. Mary Lou and I were hard pressed to answer some of the questions.

I must confess that charming and thoughtful as Annalise Svendsen was—inviting us to her elegant second-floor suite for champagne and classical music from her hi-fi, helping us plot places to see and fishing holes to try, having special fat trout lifted from the pool in her garden and served to us in that rare blue color that comes only when a live fish is immersed at the proper time and poached by an expert—she also had an annoying habit that would rub any self-respecting fisherman the wrong way.

Whenever a local caught a sea trout, somehow she got hold of it. Waiting until dinner, she would walk into the dining room and make a grand entrance with the huge gleaming blue, white and gold creature on a tray.

"Caught by a local," she would say. "Today. With one of those shaggy old flies I gave you."

Perhaps I deserved this. She had got me a fly, supposedly the champion sea-trout lure of the peninsula. It was large and shaggy, tied from the neck feathers of a red rooster. I tried it on my heavy salmon rod and had little trouble sending the shaggy thing where I wanted. But I never had a strike: the lure floated there like a bunch of chicken feathers, which it was, never tempting even a rise. Telling Annalise that the local fly must need a special fisherman or technique, I changed to a Canadian salmon fly that had done nobly by me in New Brunswick. I did manage to get several swirling rises in three days of trying, but no sea trout. The only reason I knew that this mysterious fish wasn't the object of somebody's imagination was that repeated dramatic entrance of Annalise Svendsen's.

I am told that the sea trout come in from the sea all over Europe like the salmon, from Limfjorden here in Jutland and up the Karup stream to spawn, then return to the sea. The young grow; when they have enough strength they leave the Karup, go to the sea to mature, then return to the stream of their birth as salmon do.

Salmon devotees—I am one—will not believe it, but in my opinion these Danish sea trout are more impressive fish than the Atlantic salmon—bigger of head, slimmer of body, more color, socked with silver. They also have that mysterious quality that appeals to the imagination and keeps you trying to get one on the end of your line.

On the eighth day in Karup I awoke to a driving rain as usual, but I was inured now. It was cool, the wind was fresh and the winding Karup stream was waiting. I took my four-ounce rod and flybox and went to Phillipsen's, a classic thatched-roofed farmhouse, where two sisters and their brother had a farm. A license here means that you pay the farmer whose land you enter to fish two kroner, about thirty cents; then you walk through his gate to the part of the stream that he seems to own or at least control. I walked down to the Karup behind the farmhouse, where it made a wide curve, and wondered again while I rigged my rod if I was being kidded, whether the locals had really taken sea trout on those flies or whether they used the big, heavy Danish spinning rods and worms as I had seen many using on the Karup.

At the first turn in the stream, a fisherman in a long black rubber raincoat and hat was tying on a fly. As fishermen will, I stopped and chatted, glad that he spoke English. He hadn't caught a fish all week and he had been out every day. But he was smiling and evidently glad that there was another willing to stand in the rain and let a fish make a fool of him.

"We in Denmark have a saying," he said. "If you want to be happy for an hour, take a drink. For three months, marry. But if you want to be happy forever, learn fishing." The rain ran off his billed rain hat in a long stream that somehow managed to find its way down the back of his neck. His face was wet and his rimless eyeglasses were fogged, giving him the look of a blind man.

He was interested as I opened my flybox and chose a salmon fly. Offering him one seemed to shock him for a moment, but he recovered and made a careful selection. With the polite and thoughtful manner of the true fisherman, he made certain he took a fly that I had duplicates of. I went off upstream and started the business of trying to discover what made these sea trout so hard to get along with.

On the fifth cast, a long one that I drifted to a point where the curve in the river began to straighten and get deep, the thing happened that keeps all fishermen fanatic. The strike was gentle at first, then a sharp jolt as if I had banged my rod against a tree. Line stripped off as if a man held the other end and was running; happily Wes Jordan of the Orvis Rod Company had suggested I have all that backing. The fish ran upstream, then switched suddenly, still taking line off, and went downstream bulling stronger than any salmon I had ever hooked. Then the jumps began and he broke water three times in a minute. It seemed a long time before the slack came in, the fish cleverly trying to slacken the line and take the hot weight out of his mouth.

This sea trout took fifteen minutes of stream-running to keep up with, of reeling, of holding the rod high, of watching it bend like a buggy whip until I thought it would snap. Then, suddenly, as it always happens, I beached him and he came in, molten silver, big in the water, tired now after one of the grandest battles I have ever been on the other end of. I would have released this old warrior so he could make his way back to Limfjorden and the sea but this was my first sea trout and I needed his profile on film. I wanted him in the flesh to prove that he wasn't something I had caught in my imagination.

That night as we dipped our soup spoons in the *aegte skildpadde- suppe* just before the *inbagt hamburgerryg med gemyse,* the lovely Annalise Svendsen took an enormous sea trout around, exhibiting it to her guests as was her custom. A sea trout not caught by a local.

Jutland has more to offer than fishing, low prices, fine food, moors to walk and interesting people to talk with. I suggest a tour to the

Dollerup Hills, a walk searching for the old Viking graves that are marked with ancient, upended runic tombstones; a drive to Daugbjerg Daas, the Flyndersø Hjerl Hede with its famous open-air museum, and the old farmhouses that stand today exactly as they have for hundreds of years.

We visited towns: Viborg, surrounded by lakes, the woodlands of Silkeborg; the ancient places, Ribe, Tønder, Kolding, and walked their narrow, winding cobblestone streets. All the houses are small architectural masterpieces with carvings and gingerbread and windows that stick curious bellies three feet out on the ground level. These are houses with the quality of fine old lacework. In Abenrå, the houses had spectacularly pitched, almost straight up-and-down, roofs. Retiling them would take an acrobat. All seemed to have been whitewashed that very day, and those strangely sloping roofs of tile or thatch gave them the look of those cunningly contrived places that illustrate the pages of fairy tales.

The thatch roofs interested me and I dug for detail on how they were made, getting it from a farmer, a town official, and an old man who came down from a ladder, where he had been replacing a piece

"These little houses with their blond, slanting thatch roofs sitting on the edge of the Jutland moors are the most comfortable-looking houses I have ever seen."

of red tile on a roof, to put the final touch of expertise in the conversation.

The roof thatch is made from reed or wheat straw; reed from the north side of the peninsula, where there is even more wind and rain, is preferred because it is stronger and said to be naturally weatherproofed.

For an average roof, a master Jutland thatcher uses four million reeds or wheat straws cut to exact five-foot lengths, and needs two months to shape them into a proper roof. In addition to his know-how, which is passed from father to son (and is now a disappearing craft), he uses a long, sharp knife, a wooden mallet, shears and a long, curved stick called a *leggett,* which is used to pound the reeds into exact position.

Thatch roofs came into being here from necessity. There are few trees and the thatch is much cheaper than wood or even tile, which used to be brought from Germany and some of the Danish islands. As woven in Jutland, a thatch roof of reed is supposed to last forty years; one of wheat straw, twenty. The thatchers are doubly assured of a continuing livelihood: once the roof is up, it must be maintained. Only the experts know how to reweave a weak place or patch a hole.

The old man who had climbed down from his ladder had the final say. "Well-laid Jutland thatch," he said, "will keep a house warmer in winter and cooler in summer than any roof made in a factory. I know. Lived in one fifty year."

I would like to live in one. I think these little houses with their blond, slanting thatch roofs sitting on the edge of the Jutland moors are the most comfortable-looking houses I have ever seen. Comfort *and* charm seem a combination of assets fast disappearing in modern housing.

We sampled oysters from the Limfjorden's cold waters, the sweet black little *muslinger* (mussels), and the Danish caviar from lumpfish caught near Iceland—salty and tasty but not in the same league with the real thing from the Russian or Iranian sturgeon. Then a meal of *rødspaette,* a spotted plaice fresh from the water, served with creamed potatoes, and either an "ape" of *akvavit* (a half-bottle) or a "chicken" (a small, individual bottle). Jutlanders don't bother with beer to ease the burning stuff down; that is for weaker folk from the islands.

Then the ride back to Karup across the moors, the wind running like water through the purple heather, and that fresh, clean smell of earth and rain and weed coming from the heath. But we had a date in Spain soon and our next move was back to Copenhagen and the Terminus Hotel to schedule our plane reservations, repack, make some notes, then take off for Madrid.

A letter awaited us from Walter Peters, a producer-director of American Broadcasting Company's television department and an old friend from *Yank* magazine, World War II. Pete, a craggy-featured, warm-hearted individualist, rarely does things the usual way.

"Dear Mary Lou and Scotty," the letter ran. "I got your address from SAS and hope this reaches you in time. I have a trip in mind that I'll take within a few days. I would like you to come along.

"Bought a new, big Land Rover in England, which I am going to drive to Paris. My final destination is Yugoslavia, where I am scheduled to make a documentary for ABC. Meanwhile I am on vacation and would like to drive through the Pyrenees Mountains to Spain.

"We would stop on the way at the most fantastic little country in the world: Andorra, a mountain kingdom on a peak of the Pyrenees, that I had heard about but never visited.

"From Andorra we could drive to Barcelona, then you go your way, and I will drive on to Italy and Yugoslavia . . ."

He went on to say that he had got the Land Rover so he would have no difficulty in moving across difficult Yugoslavian terrain. He would use it for his cameraman's raft of equipment, outfit it with cots and sleeping bags.

He ended: "But the important question: Will you come along? If so, wire me or meet me at ABC in Paris. I'll take it from there!"

Two minutes after finishing the letter, we sent the cable to ABC: "Delighted join you. Meet you Paris two days."

Meanwhile, I had a little intrigue at the Terminus that I still haven't been able to solve. It had all the ingredients of a spy thriller.

The Terminus, as I have said, is an intimate place, singularly free of tourists, filled with an old-world charm that makes it the perfect setting for what followed. Its charm comes from soft lighting, great red Oriental carpets, murals of busty ladies and periwigged gentlemen of another time. Gleaming marble stairs flanked by shiny brass balustrades lead to the second floor. The elevator is an old-fashioned, single-cable lift, and the bar small, dark-paneled with soft green banquettes; the bar itself, shiny dark mahogany. On a shelf behind it stand two white Chinese mandarin figurines. Music is piped into the bar from a ship three miles out in international waters.

As I took my seat at the bar this evening, Frank Sinatra was singing "Autumn in New York," which came through in a soft, sugar-slick nostalgic wave of sound that had the three men sitting there staring into their glasses.

One was enormous with red hands and face and a great lion head. He had on a blue suit and white shirt with a striped tie and a stiffly starched collar. He kept running a finger under his collar and shooting his shirtcuffs out. I think he was a farmer from Jutland. Many of them came here, because it was quiet, central and they felt at home in its Danish atmosphere.

The man next to him was thin with a gray mustache and beard. He was bald, wore gold-rimmed glasses, a gray suit that looked as if it had been fitted by a master, a dark blue shirt and a darker blue bow tie. He wasn't English, nor did I think he was Danish. He kept darting side glances at me.

Beside me sat a dark man in a grayish-green suit, white shirt and maroon tie. He was handsome, with smooth black hair combed straight back without a part, brown eyes, a straight nose, full mouth. He had a scar on his left cheek, broad enough and white enough to be the result of a saber slash. He nodded to me as I ordered my drink.

We sat there silently drinking, listening to the soft music until the alcohol had warmed us up. "Good bar." I made the first thrust at small talk.

"Best in Scandinavia," he parried.

"I keep a bottle of white crème de menthe here, makings for a stinger when I get exuberant enough to think of a stinger. They use green crème de menthe in Denmark. Horrible!"

"Worse," he said. "Poison!"

Neither of the other men made conversation, even the vapid kind we were attempting. Finally they both left. The man with the beard said good night in a high, girlish voice. My conversation with the dark man grew; after two more drinks we knew something of each other.

He was German, living in South America—he didn't say which part —was in business there. But he didn't say what the business was. After another drink, he said, "They're stupid, those South Americans! I went there after the war. By end of next year I think I will have made a million. And I make it because of their stupidity! Not my own good sense." He had that hard, cold thrust about him like the few Nazis I have met, an armor of bitterness against the rest of a world that didn't think the right way. Even with the warming influence of alcohol—and he was well into his seventh drink as we sat there—he was cold and hard. He kept tearing into the South Americans.

Hoping it would quiet him, I took out a silver pen and a notebook and started making notes of things to do the next day, the day we were scheduled to leave for Paris to meet Pete. He watched me for a while, drank two more Scotches, then took out a long, heavy silver pencil and also began writing.

After another drink, he said, "Nice pen you have there."

"A Cross," I said. "Works well, that's the best thing about it."

"Let's trade," he said suddenly. "Silver pen for silver pencil. Good luck!"

His speech was blurring now. The bartender looked at me, eyebrows up.

"I'll be getting the best of the deal," I said. "More silver in your pencil."

He laughed. "Yuh will atthat. Nevermindsilver. Letstrade."

To avoid an argument, I did. Minutes later he rose unsteadily from the bar stool, bowed stiffly to me, said, *"Auf Wiedersehen"* and left.

Now the mystery.

The next morning we went out to make plane reservations and run some errands. I returned before Mary Lou and walked up to our room on the second floor. There before it, trying key after key from a large ring, was my German friend. I remained where I was, watching. He was cold sober this morning. He couldn't open my door. He jammed the keys in his pocket, swore harshly in German, and stalked off in the opposite direction toward the elevator.

I checked at the desk; he wasn't registered at the Terminus, at least in the name he gave me. I asked the bartender. He had never seen him before.

"Nazi, I think," he said. "I saw many here during the war."

I spent two hours examining the silver pencil he traded me. It didn't have a secret compartment with a map in it; nor was the lead anything but ordinary graphite. I bit the pencil; it was silver. I dropped it; it didn't fall apart spilling microfilm. Maybe it wasn't the pencil. But this man wasn't a sneak thief. Why was he trying to get into my room?

The door was tried again late that night, cautiously—just once. Mary Lou was sleeping peacefully. I never told her about the German and the pencil. What was the point? I didn't have the answer. I still have the pencil. It keeps its secret.

CHAPTER SIX

FRANCE, ANDORRA, SPAIN AND THE CANARY ISLANDS

I am not about to take you on a guided tour of Paris and its restaurants, because the purpose of this book, as previously announced, is to recount our adventures in the search for the little-known and offbeat places of the world. But to avoid being called a barbarian if I don't visit at least one of the great restaurants, I will purr over one that was suggested to me by the knowledgeable president of New York's Carlton House, the late Gaston Lauryssen, a man who never graded more than a half-dozen restaurants as great or even worth visiting.

It was Lasserre, in an elegant villalike building, No. 17, on Avenue Franklin Roosevelt, between the Champs Élysées and the Seine. Chairs were covered in silk damask, table linen was lace trimmed, the tableware was vermeil, wine from the eighty-thousand-bottle cellar was poured into antique crystal decanters. There were more efficient, polite waiters than customers, and superb is an inadequate word for the food. *Steak Dumas, canard sauvage flambé, casserolettes filets de sole, timbales Élysées, le cygne royal.*

Our stop in the City of Light was just overnight, to meet Walter Peters and start the first leg of our journey to the mountain country of Andorra. That evening we stood on the little terrace of our room in the Crillon overlooking the Place de la Concorde, drinking icy martinis and eating tiny Danish sausages we had brought from Copenhagen, watching the traffic below. To the left, the great cathedral of Notre Dame brooded over the Seine; the Eiffel Tower rose, pointing an admonitory finger; beyond was the Arc de Triomphe and the famed Champs Élysées; the ancient grandeur of the city came up in a sudden, almost overwhelming wave of nostalgia—for the magnificent architecture that dreams had wrought into stone and steel? Or is it just Paris at night, the golden city glowing? Then the lights winking out in the American Embassy close below brought reality into focus, and Pete began talking about our journey and Andorra. As usual, he was enthusiastic. He has so much of this quality that it spills over into everything he does, including his ABC-TV documentaries.

"We'll cruise these little French villages, find the good restaurants, see the real France," he said. "We'll take our time. And, *brother,* is that Land Rover comfortable! I got the largest one they make." He hesitated dramatically. "Then Andorra. Right up the Pyrenees to the little rooftop republic. Maybe it's the world's smallest country. Only six thousand people. And they're independent too, believe me! Been independent since the thirteenth century, even though they were surrounded by Spain and France, who wanted to peck away at them."

"How do they live in the mountains?" Mary Lou asked.

"Smuggling!" Pete said gleefully. "Or so I hear. The place sounds so good I may come back and do a documentary for ABC."

He went to his briefcase and took out a book—the *Encyclopedia of World Travel—Europe*—and started to read.

" 'Situated between France and Spain, and for many years bypassed by progress of any kind, is the independent state of Andorra. Nestled among high mountains, the scenery is majestic and breathtaking. The towns of Les Escaldes, Andorra, and San Julian reflect the half-French, half-Spanish background. A proud and reserved people, the Andorrans claim descent from Charlemagne.' " He closed the book with a snap. "And that's all! Some mystery there, believe me! I think we're in for something!" These were prophetic words. We really were in for something. But first we had to drive through the real France, as Pete said. We would leave early in the morning.

Anyone who has ever driven in Paris will have sympathy for us starting out that morning. It is a scientific fact that a conscientious motorist in traffic of this sort undergoes twice the emotional pressure of an astronaut in his steel ball hurtling through space. In fairness, I tried to figure out why the French are such dangerous drivers. Behind the wheel they become creatures that curse, snarl, shout, take chances that would pale circus devil drivers and send sports car racers into retirement. In Europe all cars coming from the right have right of way. Proceeding peaceably on a straightaway, you suddenly are attacked as if by sharks that keep tearing at you until you turn and let them dart through, or pass, or whatever they seem to want to do in their spur-of-the-moment thinking.

Another suicidal driving habit the French have developed: when a driver discovers another wants to pass, he immediately accelerates. Insulted, the man behind then sticks to this car until he finds the

opportunity to pass, both meanwhile breaking all speed laws. When
he does pass, he does it in what is called a *queue de poisson,* or
"fishtail," which is a tail-flicking motion that dangerously cuts off the
other car. Then it starts all over again. Deeply chagrined, this driver
makes the mad chase to overtake the fishtailer. The French call this
dangerous and childish business élan, a pretty word for stupidity.

Anyway, Pete, pale and breathing hard, took us out of the city in
his sturdy Land Rover. I think we made it because the English had
put such steel and strength into the vehicle that it moved along the
road like a small battleship. The contest might have been just a little
too formidable, even for the French.

But not for the gendarmes. One, resplendent in blue cloak, waved
our Land Rover to a halt. Pete had neglected to use his signal light
when he passed a couple of cars. It wouldn't have mattered, I am
certain, if he had driven too fast, darted in front of cars, honked his
horn all the way out of the city, but it was not right that he wasn't
using those signal lights. "It is only fair," the gendarme said, in the
most humorous remark of our trip, "to warn that you will turn."

I took over on the outskirts. I had never driven a Land Rover
before, but owned a jeep and, according to Pete, the principle was the
same. It wasn't. The Land Rover is a much clumsier car, built for
desert and jungle cruising, for safari and *shikar.* It wasn't made to
pass through the narrow, winding streets of French villages. And its
shift is complicated. I scattered villagers before me like chickens,
until I got onto the idea that I had to make all four forward shifts,
and make them slowly until I got her in high gear and running
smoothly. Many miles and frightened Frenchmen later, I had conquered the Land Rover, had the old girl under my control. Or at least
had her gentled so that she didn't buck and quiver as I worked the
forward speeds. I considered this quite an accomplishment.

Working on the basis that experience is the prime developer of
both character and intellect, I would say that it is worthwhile to stay
at one of the many French chateaus converted into hotels. Before
leaving Paris we had made contact with the tourist department. They
were enthusiastic about one not far from Tours. That would be our
first stop.

In the interests of accurate reporting I must explain that chateaus
are a big thing, with the French tourist department publishing beautiful full-color brochures describing the lovely places where you can go
and get separated from your cash and good nature. For example, the
Loire Valley is known as the chateau country and there is a beauti-

fully illustrated folder listing 125 of its chateaus. "Fabulous Chateaux Throughout France Are Now Welcoming Guests!" it informs the reader.

It was nearly midnight when we arrived. This was a castle in the grand manner, modernized for the comfort of travelers, with winding marble staircases, statuary, and carpets running the length of the enormous entrance hall, which was hung with elegant crystal chandeliers.

The next morning we ate our breakfast on a stone terrace overlooking a small stream and neat farms set on the edge of a green meadow that looked like a lake. Pete had ordered ham and eggs; we asked for melon, croissants and tea. After forty minutes the waiter brought three orders of poached eggs with sausages and a pot of coffee. We finally got that straightened out. But later when he brought the check, we were charged for six breakfasts.

When we complained, the waiter looked blank. So we tried to explain it at the desk. The man nodded pleasantly and gave us our bill for the rooms. We had been charged for a suite, although we had had a double room; the overcharge amounted to forty percent. Pete's charge seemed all right, so he spent his time trying to get the breakfast check straightened out while I saw the manager about the room. When he realized that we had come here upon the recommendation of the tourist department, he warmed up, smiled tightly and said, "To even matters I am going to give you a twenty-five percent discount."

I told him that we didn't want a discount, that we just wanted to pay for a double room and not a suite. He spoke sharply to the clerk at the desk, put on his hat and left. But on balance I decided that my brave counterattack, whittling the forty percent overcharge down to a mere fifteen, was probably quite an accomplishment. So I gave up.

At breakfast we had decided that we would drive on to Les Eyzies where Pete had heard that there was a good hotel, also caves near by where Cro-Magnon man had probably done his first painting of pictures, recording his history, on the walls of caves.

"Be good to see how far we've progressed," Pete said, grinning. "Besides, I heard that the Hotel De Cro-Magnon is worth visiting. Friend told me not to miss the *confit d'oie,* a way they have for preserving goose in that region that makes it tasty. It's on our way. Might as well make the stop." The clerk was nice enough to call the hotel and make a reservation for eight o'clock that evening. He said that we could make it by then easily.

Mid-morning was sunny, so we decided to find a village, shop for wine and cheese and have a picnic on the way. It was shortly before noon when we came to Châtellerault, the Land Rover bringing people in a staring circle. Mary Lou and I shopped while Pete walked slowly around his Land Rover like the proud owner of a racehorse before the big race.

Our first stop was a *charcuterie,* a clean place run by a red-haired woman, pert and active as a chipping sparrow. We bought some Port Salut cheese, a stick of veal tripe sausage and a half-dozen young, boiled artichokes. In a bakery—bread just coming out of stone ovens —we bought two long sticks that smelled so good that we could barely keep from sampling them as we walked to the wine shop.

In the wine shop among kegs and bottles sat an old man with a noble head of white hair, young blue eyes, and hands so leathery and gnarled that they looked as if he were wearing gloves. He had probably been a vineyard laborer before he came to sit among his bottles. His sunny smile gave us the freedom of the place. I finally selected a bottle of red *vin ordinaire,* which can be excellent if drunk at the place of its creation. The old fellow didn't agree on our choice, pleasantly getting across that this bottle was only ten percent alcohol and that we could buy a quart containing twelve percent for the same amount—forty cents. When he discovered there were three of us, he went into the dark recesses of the rear of the shop and came out with three plastic cups which he carefully washed and dried. Smiling warmly again, he shook hands before he would take payment for the wine. He refused anything for the cups.

It was with good cheer that we drove out of Châtellerault looking for a place to picnic. This was rural France with seas of green meadows merging into one another. We found one with a brook that obligingly gurgled, guarded by a sentry line of seven great oaks. The wine had a wallop, the cheese was superb, the sausage was spicy with a garlicky personality. The bread was worth a poem.

There is a moment in travel when you cross that invisible line dividing the hackneyed from the new and refreshingly foreign. Here it could have been the stream singing over the rocks, the white clouds in a galleon sail over the oaks, or the fresh, penetrating smell of the newly turned soil in a nearby field. But as we left our picnic meadow I thought of that old man in the wine shop. He was the France you see on the travel posters, warm, smiling, offering more than he received.

After losing our way three times, darkness came, and with it an intersection of roads merging like angleworms after a night rain. We saw a woman at one turning, stopped, and Mary Lou asked the way. In fairness to Mary Lou's French, perhaps it was the Land Rover looming in mechanical military might that annoyed the woman. Anyway, it was with distaste that she eyed our blue monster, grunted and stalked off.

It was nine o'clock when, without the help of the French populace, we reached the Hotel De Cro-Magnon, a comfortable place of dark beams and half-timbers. A blond woman behind the desk seemed surprised to see us.

"We thought you weren't coming," she said.

"We have reservations," said Pete.

She shuffled papers. "For seven o'clock."

"The clerk at the chateau told us eight," said Pete.

"That makes us just an hour late," I said.

She smiled sadly. "People come every hour. We wrote the reservation for seven. That is two hours past. We have already rented your rooms."

Pete was puffing with indignation. "That's one devil of a way to treat three tired people who have driven all day to get to your hotel!" he said.

She shook her head. She was kindly. She was attractive. She was sorry. But she had no rooms.

We decided to have dinner. It was too late and we were too tired to drive on looking for a hotel. Pete thought that he would have the *confit d'oie*. We had soup and excellent broiled veal. Pete's breast of goose, apparently stored in a jar of its own fat, was hard and greasy. All the cheer had run out of him. You could almost see it go. It was the first time I had seen him unhinged. We had about determined to spend the night in the dining room when the blond woman appeared.

"I feel badly about this," she said. "But so often have we held rooms and people never came. But my husband and I have talked. We would like you to stay in our winter apartment for the night. Not as comfortable as our hotel. But it should be fine for one night—"

It was. About a half-mile from the hotel, the house was sewn on a hillside like a button on a sleeve, with a ragged cliff towering above. It had a feeling of impermanence not unlike a tent on a gravel bank. But the beds were comfortable. The next morning over a breakfast of croissants and freshly ground coffee—watching from the terrace that tremendous hanging cliff fold like a giant lip over this part of Les Eyzies, with the feeling that it would crumble and crash upon the town at any moment—Pete read choice sections from a guidebook,

"The house was sewn on a hillside like a button on a sleeve, with a ragged cliff towering above."

picking them out like a man cuts the lean away from the fat on a steak. Pete liked to read guidebooks, interpreting in his own style.

"Folks, this little corner of France has been inhabited since man crawled out of the sea on his belly. Remains of the mess he made, industries and prehistoric art, are preserved hereabouts in caves."

After another cup of coffee, he went on. "Under these Hollywood cliffs are rock shelters where our ancient litterbugs flung huts together. They left ashes from their fires, kitchen rubbish, and flint tools, mixed with eroded rock in layers like the pages of a book."

After digesting this and our breakfast we went into the hotel to thank the owners of De Cro-Magnon, pleasing people who were trying hard to do the impossible—satisfy everyone who visited their hotel. They firmly refused to let us pay for that night in their winter apartment. I can recommend the Hotel De Cro-Magnon in Les Eyzies. But come early.

The caves? We never did get to see them. There were quarter-mile-long lines of tourists waiting to walk through. So we went back to the hotel and called the Hostellerie De La Barbacane in Foix, the last village in France before the climb to Andorra.

We were on time in Foix. We had asked for a room with a bath and it had been confirmed. But we didn't get it. The man at the desk was firm about it.

"That bath in the hall is a *private* bath. Very private. Only for hotel guests."

It was a pleasant place with Spanish overtones and help. The waiters were good, the wine excellent, the food satisfactory.

A man named Samuel Johnson said that the use of travel is to regulate the imagination by reality, and instead of thinking how things may be, to see them as they really are. Ever since Pete had talked up Andorra on that terrace at the Crillon, I had been thinking that it would be a rough, mountainous country full of peasants in capes carrying great hooked staffs, perhaps faithfully followed by giant mountain dogs. The villages would be tiny perches clinging to the hills like lichen, the roads would be narrow, winding dirt tracks with great drop-offs on either side, and there would be eagles circling as we made our way up. The wind would be coming off the slippery rock of the cliffs like water, in a screaming sound that would pluck at the nerve ends.

As we went I could see that the Pyrenees were not so lofty or dramatic in abrupt and unexpected rises as the Alps, but they have a spectacular run from the Atlantic Ocean to the Mediterranean in a 270-mile chain, dividing France from Spain. This road we were driving would be impassable in winter. Although the roads are supposedly kept clear, it is still dangerous under snow conditions to cross this eight-thousand-foot pass, the highest in the Pyrenees.

Quickly the mountains rose as we drove, the land sloping so steeply that it looked as though even the sure-footed sheep were having trouble walking along the slopes.

As we pushed the Land Rover up I rapidly disciplined the imagination with reality. The shepherds didn't carry staffs or wear cloaks. Except for berets they looked like rural people everywhere. No eagles soared; we passed no villages, although some houses did hang from the mountain like lichen, with brown tobacco leaves draped from stone walls near them.

In the distance huge massifs raised lion heads and the passes began to get steeper. It was at one of these, coming up the French side, that Roland stood heroically blowing his horn for help for the beaten rear guard of Charlemagne's army.

My imagination had been right about one thing. The road, although paved, was narrow and winding, and drop-offs of several hundred feet were not protected by guard rails. If you went out of control, you just fell off the mountain. And traffic: the few little buglike European cars had now grown into a steady stream. They behaved naturally—passing on curves, honking horns, speeding. It was frightening. There was no margin for error here.

With Pete at the guidebook, we did some detouring and made our first stop at the Cirque de Gavarnie, a wall in vertical terraces of stone, shooting up fifty-six hundred feet, its semicircle two miles in diameter. Ten-thousand-foot peaks rose from the wall, snow capping some of them. These half-circled walls, or *cirques,* make the Pyrenees different from all other mountains.

But Andorra, as we would discover, is what really makes them different. Pete had now given up the idea of driving the Land Rover, saying that he was no good at the special art of mountain driving— proving it by running down a steep road in high gear. But Pete is a clever fellow. It would be easier to watch the scenery if he was not behind the wheel. Also it gave him the opportunity to indulge one of his favorite pastimes—reading from a handsome tourist folder.

As we continued climbing past the sheep on the slopes—and now an eagle was in the sky—Pete gave us his word-picture of the strange country we were about to enter.

"The Valls [valleys] of Andorra are the heart of the Pyrenees. Seven thousand citizens. Co-principality since 1278. Bishop of La Seu d'Urgell and Charlie de Gaulle of the French Republic are the joint bosses. Also sounds a little Commie. It says here that the only private property consists of buildings and farm land. Everything else is communally owned.

"The place is cut up into six parishes. Chief towns, Sant Julia de Loria, Encamp, Canillo, La Massana, Ordino and Andorra la Vella. Last is the capital of Andorra."

"Then Andorra isn't its own country," Mary Lou said. "She's ruled by President de Gaulle and, who is it in Spain?"

I had secretly read a guidebook also. "Monsignor Ramón Iglesias Navarri," I said.

Pete dropped his folder. "Why am I wasting my time translating this stuff?" he said accusingly. "You been readin' up on the place?"

"Not much," I said. "I prefer your personalized readings."

Now we were passing through the little villages of my imagination. They did indeed perch on mountaintops. Most of the houses were of gray and brownish stone; they looked grim and weather-beaten. Scattered around the villages were the *bordes,* old stone, open-fronted cattle and sheep sheds, leaving no doubt as to the main occupation of the villagers.

We came by La Costa, Canillo, Molléras, Les Bons, Encamp, picturesque little places, as you would expect. Then, without warning, we entered Les Escáldes—teeming with tourists, juke boxes blaring from cafés along the main street, modern buildings, hotels. We should have been warned; if this city was booming, what would the capital be like?

Andorra la Vella reminded me of Hong Kong. I had been there when the first refugees from Communist China streamed in. This also was an overturned anthill, people scurrying, poking their faces in shop windows. The main street was lined with shops of every description—gift shops, auto accessory shops, camera and luggage stores, liquor and wine shops—name it, Andorra la Vella had it. It was a pushing, noisy mob that greeted us as we entered the capital city of what was reputed to be a quaint little mountain country time had passed by. Something was wrong. Time had caught up with Andorra with a vengeance.

We drove slowly, looking for the Park Hotel where we had reservations—hotels were everywhere. But no Park in view. Farther along on the main street, away from most of the crowds, was a butcher shop, rabbits in fur hanging in front, the window full of dressed and undressed lambs. Before it, extending down the street for almost two blocks, was a line of men waiting to get in. They were talking, smoking and laughing, and they were all ages. This was the first time

"Scattered around the villages were the bordes, *old stone, open-fronted cattle and sheep sheds, leaving no doubt as to the main occupation of the villagers."*

in Europe that I had seen men shopping for food. They do go to the wine shops and occasionally you will see one in a bakery. But standing in a shopper's line waiting to buy food for the family is definitely a woman's job. What made these Andorrans different?

We stopped and looked. A woman at her butcher's block was busy carving a lamb. Her customer stood by in silent admiration, watching as the cleaver swooped in skillful, silvery strokes. But he wasn't looking at the cleaver.

She wasn't a woman to be admired especially for her skill. But she was undoubtedly the sexiest butcher in Europe: blond, with hair cut long, her eyes were blue, her skin satiny, her legs long and well-shaped. She had on a white jacket reaching to her knees, but it didn't disguise the fact that her bust was full and firm.

"I feel sorry for the wives," Mary Lou said. "More money is probably being spent on meat in these mountains than can be afforded."

We finally found the Park Hotel on a hill at the other end of town. It was a dreary attempt at mixing Spanish Hacienda with French Chateau, resulting in a turreted, bulging bastard. The room clerk was an officious little man in striped pants, a tight double-breasted jacket, a dirty white shirt and a black bow tie. He said he had a room for us.

"One?" I asked.

He lifted his eyebrows. "Why, yes, of course. Consider yourself lucky to get one!"

It was evident that the entire town was crawling with tourists— why, we would find out later—so Pete decided to scout out two rooms elsewhere while we looked at the reserved room.

We walked up three flights of narrow, winding stairs to the top floor, then another flight beyond to an excrescence that undoubtedly was stuck on to resemble a tower and had been pressed into service as a room. It was so small that Mary Lou and I couldn't view it at the same time; it had a shower, conveniently located over the toilet, presumably for those in a hurry to combine functions. It was stuffy, with one small, narrow window built like an aperture in an old Western fort.

The clerk was at his desk, behind which he resided like a judge listening to hardship cases. He held up his hand to stop the flow of language from a fat Spanish lady in a white silk dress, pink shoes and large pink pendant earrings that dropped like fire from ears mysteriously hidden in a great mound of blue-black hair.

"Well?" he said, turning to me.

"Not well at all," I said. "That isn't a room. It's a broom closet."

He sneered. "This lady will take it. Sorry we couldn't please."

While we waited in the Land Rover for Pete, I had visions of that Spanish lady taking a shower in the bathroom which was just about large enough for her to get into—sideways. The management would have interesting days ahead.

Pete turned up in ten minutes with reservations. He had a Jimmy Durante kind of humble but penetrating charm, and could talk most people into anything.

"The Mirador," he said. "It's a room for the night, that's all I can say for it. But this place is jumping! People here from all over Europe. It's a free port, free city, no taxes on luxury items. All duty free! From booze to bath salts. Fantastic!"

He had a shocked expression. His dream of a quaint, seldom seen, mysterious mountain country was being rudely shattered by a city getting more like Coney Island by the minute.

The Mirador looked as though it had gone up in two weeks, but the manager was pleasant and so were his room clerk and the bell-boys.

"Doing a little blasting behind our hotel," the manager said. "Making room for another hotel. We need a dozen more. They're at it now."

We could hear the windows rattle as we went up to our room. It was neat and clean, with a bath, and it looked out on a narrow, winding cobblestone street. At least if you looked out of the window you got the feel of the old Andorra that was letting the rest of the world roll by.

We made the mistake of opening the window: simultaneously the blast came, raining shale on our roof, flinging earth and rock dust into the room. The operation was going on directly behind the hotel, but we could see it. One side of a rocky hill was being dynamited by two boys. I had the thought that they were doing it without pay for the sheer joy of watching the dynamite explode.

Their technique was that of youngsters at a Fourth of July celebration putting the match to firecrackers. They lit the dynamite fuse, watched it curl and sputter to the hillside, then ran and stood two hundred feet away, covering their heads with their arms. There was no adult there; no foreman or supervisor. Apparently it was so dangerous that it was child's play. It also was too dangerous for us. The next blast placed a piece of rocky hill the size of a cantaloupe on the roof, just over our heads. It landed like a cannonball.

We took our bags to the lobby. Pete was already there with his. "I know," he said. "We're under siege. I found us another room. Only trouble is I can't get the Land Rover out of this street."

The management of the Mirador was understanding. They refused to charge for our short stay and seemed to be sorry to see us go. A bellboy volunteered to watch the Land Rover while we registered at the new hotel, the Pyrenees. This was on the main street; it was packed with people in the lobby; a line waited to get into the restaurant. It was dirty but the room had a bath. The smell of turnips cooking permeated everything.

After unpacking a few things rugged enough to take the turnip attack, the three of us went back to the problem of the Land Rover, almost got arrested (with the tri-nation police system in Andorra, getting arrested can be a complicated business) and nearly became tools for a smuggler.

In the street across from the Mirador a bare-chested boy was digging a ditch, probably trying to get at a water main—if the city had such a thing—and a girl who ran the music shop was outside leaning against the door, making eyes and watching the boy's muscles flex as he used the pick. A record player was going loudly inside with "I Can't Give You Anything but Love, Baby!"

The Land Rover looked like a beached whale in that narrow street. The problem was obvious: you could drive that broad vehicle in, but there was no room to maneuver on the dead-end street, and it was so narrow that you couldn't reverse out, especially impeded by a swarm of Fiats and Volkswagens. First job: find the cars' owners and ask them please to move long enough for us to get out. But no one standing on the street, watching Pete as he tried to get his giant away from the curb, knew who owned the cars. Licenses were from Spain, France and Germany. The owners were probably in that crush of shoppers on the main street.

Meantime, Pete and I took turns trying to get the Land Rover away from the curb. After an hour and a half, in one skillful spinning of wheels and a back-and-forth rocking movement, Pete finally managed to get it out and to the end of the street, but once there he couldn't turn around. The parked cars occupied the maneuvering space.

So he got out of the car, and the three of us after a quick conference decided to try to push the cars out of our way. We tried several, but they all had brakes on or were in gear. We were still trying when someone said, *"Bastante!"* It was a Spanish policeman; beside him were a French and an Andorran policeman.

It quickly developed that they thought we were trying to break into the cars. We finally got to the Mirador and asked the manager to intercede for us. After much argument, when the police finally understood that it was just a traffic problem, they harumphed and stalked off.

As we went back to the Land Rover, a slim, dark fellow came over and said, "I will take the responsibility of getting you out! I will find these car owners and get them to move."

Pete said, "You will?"

"Yes," the man said, "if you will do me a small favor. You are driving to Spain, yes?"

"Yes," Pete said.

"Would you take a little gift for my aunt in Barcelona?"

"Sure," Pete said.

The man excused himself and returned, staggering under a huge cardboard box.

"Shall I put it inside the car?" he asked. "The address is on the side."

"What is it?" I said.

"Yeah," said Pete. "It isn't such a little gift."

"Just some cigarettes," he said.

Now you could smell the tobacco coming from the box.

"Cigarettes!" we said.

"Yes," he said. "My aunt is a big smoker."

Knowing what the Spanish border guard would do if we were stopped while carrying a box with at least fifty cartons of cigarettes inside, we thanked the man for his offer of help but politely declined.

"We probably won't be going through Barcelona anyway," Pete said.

The man shrugged, picked up the contraband that he had almost gotten into Spain, and staggered away under its aromatic weight.

After three more hours, the car owners began to drift back and we finally unbeached the Land Rover, garaged it at the Pyrenees Hotel and walked about the town.

The people-to-people push was still on—all kinds and shapes. There were girls in skin-tight, behind-bulging slacks and ski pants; men with hairy legs in shorts, in red and green slacks and gay sports shirts; women in prints and silks tottering along on incredible spiked heels. If this had been near a seashore or an amusement park it wouldn't have been such an amazing spectacle. But here we were, tucked away in an isolated fold of the Pyrenees.

And cars: every European make you could name. Fiats, Peugeots, Volkswagens, Mercedes, Hillmans, Rovers, Renaults, Citroëns were bumper to bumper. It was the worst traffic jam I have seen. Pete's mysterious little country sounded like the Elks and the American Legion combined in an uproarious convention. The noise was unbelievable. The high and dangerous mountains, the crowded hotels, the terrible food notwithstanding, people poured in from all over Europe like an endless stream of ants heading for a sugar bowl.

In one shop I saw Johnny Walker black label and White Horse Scotch selling for two dollars a bottle; in another, Nikon cameras were selling for less than you could buy them in Tokyo. French cheeses, paté, even caviar, were bargains. Shops were full of tweeds and silks, radios and gadgets. Chanel No. 5 and other French perfumes were cheaper than in Paris. Luxury items of every description were going for less than half the price anywhere else. This was a greater bargain mart than Hong Kong. It was an international shopper's paradise. Yet the shopkeepers had a furtive air about them, like speakeasy proprietors in the old days—the Andorrans seemed unable to believe that what they were doing was legal. One old man in gray trousers, a white silk shirt and thonged leather sandals sold me two bottles of Scotch with a conspiratorial air, quickly slipping the money into his pants pocket and vanishing into a back room.

Even the hotels, such as they were, were a bargain. At the Pyrenees we paid five dollars a day for our double with bath; this included dinner. Designed and operated to force the hotel's customers into dieting, the dining room was huge, dimly lit, painted a dismal gray, with every inch of space occupied by tables. There was always an impatient line of bargain-hunting tourists waiting to get in. Most of them seemed to be wearing some raw perfume that they obviously had just picked up on bargain street, or else they had been drinking Scotch like water. The resultant odor made a brave battle with the perpetual scent of turnip. Dinner was served in four shifts, starting at six, ending at nine. One tablecloth took care of everyone for the evening. By the time we got to a table (the first and only time we went to the dining room), it was a repulsive horror. The overworked waiters, all slim as eels (had to be to move among the closely packed tables), just brought food. You didn't order. Turnips were indeed the order of the day; the chef must have loved them. There was overcooked lamb or tough, thin steak and cold, gummy mashed potatoes. And always there was someone standing and staring, waiting to take your place at the table. Waiters hurried you, dropped dishes, stuck thumbs in the soup and wiped served dishes with filthy aprons.

But in the morning when we came out of the hotel, with the sun on the blue peaks that surround Andorra la Vella, and watched belled sheep tinkle around cars with practiced ease, it was difficult to believe that all of the charm had been overwhelmed by the tourist horde. We did our best to find it and uncover more of Andorra's character.

It took less than two days to drive its 175 square miles, taking us from the largest city, Las Escáldes, to Lo Serrat, the most northern. The country's Y shape is formed by three valleys, all with several small streams that run into the regal Valira, a tributary of the Segre, itself a feeder of the Ebro in Spain. It is surrounded on all sides except the southeast by great mountain peaks, running from five thousand to ten thousand feet. No valley is below three thousand feet; the main Pyrenees crest line, always visible to the north and east, is over eight thousand feet.

This could be treacherous terrain in winter, but now grass was growing on the rocky slopes, and sheep and goats were everywhere. In some sudden flat areas cultivation showed in gardens where women in black worked with hoes and men plowed with donkeys.

In winter, when there is no natural food—Andorrans apparently store little for the cold months—the sheep are driven across the mountains to France, where the shepherd is given quarters and a bottle of wine a day by a vineyard owner. The sheep graze in the vineyard where the deal is made, growing fat by keeping the rows clear, making spring plowing easier. But their most important function is fertilizing the vineyard. It is even said that some bargain-driving Frenchmen who decided to do without the Andorran sheep for a winter had poor crops of grapes that year. So it is a sensible arrangement that has been going on for many years. We who enjoy good French wine are richer because of Andorra's sheep.

Once we stopped and watched a shepherd of sixteen assemble his flock, mostly rams with horns curving like pirate cutlasses. When he called them by name, they moved from the field, responding like dogs.

Most of Andorra's houses are constructed of stone taken from the fields, with roofs of mountain slate laid on, overlapping. The result is primitive, as if these grim gray places were actually growing out of the mountain.

If you were to sit down and dream up a region that would be the ideal stronghold for a race of smugglers, you could come up with no more perfect place than Andorra. There is no moral blemish attached to the profession, for there are no duties or taxes, and few laws. I believe that its foreign affairs are handled by France, its churches by Spain, and the courts by both France and Spain. There are Andorran police—perhaps a dozen. There are also French and Spanish police who are supposed to set the pattern of law and act as a model for Andorrans. But Spain and France seldom agree on what is to be done in the tiny country, so confusion is the result.

The language is supposed to be Catalan, but actually there aren't any true Andorran schools; most of them are French or Spanish, with the teachers trying to instill loyalty to those countries. Andorrans speak all three languages fluently; in their homes they speak Catalan.

In the winter when things get slow, even the farmers load up their donkeys with contraband and take off across the mountains, getting through places in the passes at night that the border guard doesn't patrol—usually taking tobacco in some form to France or Spain. (Since our trip I've wondered if some clever herder hasn't worked out a way to use his sheep, that he winters in France, as a flock of innocent smugglers.)

In Andorra cigarettes cost about eight cents a pack. I bought seven brands, Charlemagnes, New Havanas, Ysers, Reig Luxes, Duxes, Im-

On the road to Andorra were many sheep, the rams' horns curving like cutlasses—but were they sheep or smugglers?

perials and Golden Suns. Ten hundred metric tons of tobacco a year are produced—itself an act of magic in that rocky country. The two factories making the cigarettes claim that most of them are smoked in Andorra, which means that every man, woman and child would have to smoke about six cigarettes a second. They don't—most of it goes over the mountains on donkeys, or in false bottoms of cars without duty being paid, using the cover of night, bribery and sheer bravado to get the contraband across.

One smuggler worked up an interesting trade taking out vast quantities of cognac in a car's false bottom converted into a tank. Without tax this sells for less in Andorra than in Spain, or even in France where it is manufactured.

Things are taken out by many ingenious means, including the use of boobs (which we nearly were), watches, gold, medicines, food, silks, nylons and thousands of car parts. I also discovered one of the reasons there are so many cars, which in a way is also part of the smuggling activities.

Low duties make it the largest car-owning country in Europe, with a paper ownership of one out of nine—this includes women and children. Not all actually own cars. A racket has evolved. If a visitor or a "speculator" wants a car cheap in Andorra, he buys it in the name of a citizen made agreeable with a bribe. Then the car with Andorran plates is driven to Spain or France and sold for a huge profit, usually more than one hundred percent. Many of the young Andorran car-cowboys whipping along the streets and country roads at seventy are speculators in their own way. They can own as many cars as they want—on paper—and make enough to buy flashy new ones for themselves.

President of this startling country is Seignoir Francisco Caerat, also called First Sindic, a short, white-haired man who is usually found in his tobacco shop in his home town of Sant Julia de Loria. Whether you wish to consider France and Spain as two masters or defenders—and Andorra considers them defenders; no one is her master—the president is left with little to occupy him. There is almost no crime in Andorra. Away from the towns and the tourists, and the Andorrans involved with them, they are "leave-me-alone-and-I'll-leave-you-alone!" people, going their own ancient ways as farmers, herders, hunters—and smugglers.

Even an ordinary place like a post office can be extraordinary in Andorra. There are two, French and Spanish. If you make the mistake, as I did, of sending a cable to Spain from the French one, you pay full international rates—as if you were sending it from Paris. Down the street at the Spanish post office it would have cost me eighty percent less. They both have their own stamps—valued collectors' items which bring quite a bit of income into Andorra, used to finance its schools. Prices and hours of business vary according to each country's holidays and rules. It's all very confusing—even for Andorrans.

Should any stomach-respecting reader decide to visit this country to see its smugglers, its mountain scenery and its bargains, I'd like to report that we found a decent restaurant in Andorra la Vella. It was the Cisco de Sans, on a side street, up a cobblestone lane past a cage that then held a huge eagle, making you uncomfortably aware of the cruelty of man. Imagine taking a magnificent creature such as this from his clouds and putting him behind bars where his feathers drop off in a molt and his head hangs low in dejection.

Cisco de Sans was a place that few tourists found; it was populated by peasant types and workmen who ate at a long, communal table, and it was notable chiefly for its low prices, its pleasant mountain atmosphere, and its tasty food. Andorran food is not outstanding, being a mixture of French and Spanish and retaining few good features of either. But broiled young goat with a squeeze of lemon or a savory potato omelette, plus a *porron* of bitey red wine and instruction in its use, made it a worth-while restaurant. The *porron* is a glass bottle with a thin gooseneck spout. The Andorrans hold it more than a foot away, tilt it and let the wine emerge in a stream, landing in the mouth.

It looks simple but is not. After squirting Pete in the eye, and turning my white collar a spotty pink, I finally managed to get most of the wine in the proper place. It is an interesting way to serve wine; I suggest its introduction at any dinner party that seems to be going stuffy.

The Andorrans sat watching the *porron* play as if they were at a tennis match, following the action with their eyes, commenting in joyous Catalan when Pete got it in the eye, and Mary Lou sent a stream of wine over her shoulder, missing an approaching waiter by inches.

Pete's vacation was running out. He wanted to get to Barcelona and a garage that knew Land Rovers, for he had to have his thoroughly checked before driving to Yugoslavia. We left Andorra on a gray day, driving the twisting road down the mountain, feeling our way slowly like explorers passing through a strange pass in Tibet. As we ran out of the Pyrenees onto the plain, the landscape became bleaker, with red soil and rocks and a broad, sunlit river that ran swiftly, probably still the Valira on its way to form the Ebro.

Travelers say France is for food and landscape, and Spain is for people. I believe it of Spain. We got some understanding of this at our first stop on a long, uninhabited stretch of road, at a small road-side stand and gas station. This looked much like its American counterpart, found everywhere, except that it was painted in gay Spanish reds and greens, had some attractive gingerbread, and a tiny glassed-in patio where you could sit and take your snacks in comfort. Its owner was a handsome young Spaniard who smiled warmly and said that he had everything we could possibly need.

"Hamburgs, hota dogs," he said, beaming, "and malts milk. Everything for Americans!"

This was exuberance that couldn't be dampened, so we had taste-less hamburgers and soft drinks. He said that he got the style for his place from a photograph in an American magazine, that he had built it himself. He wanted to know how we liked it.

"Just like our places," Pete said.

"Prettier," Mary Lou said.

I nodded in approval.

He was delighted.

When he discovered that we were going to stop overnight in Barcelona, he insisted upon telephoning for reservations for us at the Ritz. Which he did, refusing to let us pay for the call. We hoped that Spain would be populated with many like him. He walked out to the road, waving good-bye until we were out of sight.

We discussed Andorra over dinner that night at the Ritz—our last meal with Pete.

"I'll never forget that you made it possible for us to visit that mysterious little mountain country," I said.

He grimaced. "The Coney Island of the Pyrenees!" he said.

"I don't know," Mary Lou said. "Andorra had something good about it. One thing for sure. There isn't another place like it."

"It's a character," Pete said. "That country's a character."

Our destination in Spain was the north, Santiago de Compostela, and the great salmon rivers, said to be an area little traveled. From our room in the Palace Hotel, a place of marble and shining brass, deep carpets, efficient ten-year-old bellboys and old women on their knees polishing and scrubbing, I called Osten Klintborn, SAS's man in Spain. We made a date to meet for lunch at Antigua Casa Sobrino de Botín, Calle de Cuchilleros, or Street of the Blades.

Someone once wrote, "To enjoy Spain completely, to love her, it is essential to allow her to dominate you before even trying to understand her." This is no problem. Spain does this the second day. My taxi, heading for Botín, passed several fountains; the sun caught the water as it shattered and shimmered in an endless rise and fall. And I thought of the effort New York City was supposed to be making to beautify the narrowing regions around its rabbit warrens and its great bird-cliff buildings. I remembered an old Arab prince grown oil-rich, who visited New York, studying how he could bring progress to his own mountain-and-desert wilderness. When he saw the towering, unlovely apartments and office buildings in Manhattan, he said, "They live like the swallows in our cliffs. But they have no freedom. They cannot fly." One visiting official had come up with a solution. "Build fountains," he said. "I have just returned from the beautiful cities of Europe, and they all have fountains." He may have something, but most of the cities he visited have other aesthetic assets—the kind that New York cannot create with a slide rule, or an architect with form-concrete, steel and glass.

The Calle de Cuchilleros is a winding stone lane where the sun paints a patina on the old buildings. This is the street where the swords of battle used to be forged and sharpened, where a few businesses still cater to the sharp edge. All the buildings are ancient; there is a feeling that the clock has stopped, one that you get often in Spain. The oldest of these crumbling brick and stone places could be Antigua Casa Sobrino de Botín at 17 Calle de Cuchilleros, in operation there as a restaurant since 1725. I remembered, as I entered the door past the window with suckling pigs arranged in an enticing pink semicircle, that this was the restaurant Ernest Hemingway had called one of the best in Spain.

Osten Klintborn was waiting. He looked as a healthy Swede should —ruddy complexion, blue eyes, short blond hair; he exuded energy. With him was a Spaniard, baldish, smiling. Alberto Poveda, SAS public relations, a newspaper man with a lively brain and a warm personality.

"We have some ideas," Klintborn said, as soon as we sat, "after we have lunch."

Poveda ordered.

The owners came, Antonio and Pepe González. Antonio was a

slender, handsome youth; Pepe obviously the junior, more reserved
and with less facility in English. The conference was intense and
voluble, but finally food began arriving. Ceramic pitchers of *tinto
Valdepenas o Aragon,* a light red local wine, had been placed on the
table. First came individual sizzling casseroles of *angulas a la Bil-
baina,* emitting a scent of garlic and olive oil, and looking like a bowl
of gray spaghetti. These were baby eels—and they were delicious.
Each casserole contained enough to populate entire states with eels.

Then with Antonio and three waiters in attendance came *cochinillo asado,* roast suckling pig, a long-time specialty of the house. It
was served in its earthenware cooking casserole. Antonio himself
carved, with a plate. The piglet was so tender that he simply inserted
the plate behind the portion he wanted to cut and pushed. With it we
had tiny roast potatoes and a green salad and much more *tinto Valdepenas.* Ending with wine-soaked *fresones,* fresh strawberries, we
talked over coffee. I was convinced, even before trying the rest of
Spain's restaurants, that the knowledgeable Mr. Hemingway was right
about Botín.

"You will go after salmon in the north first?" Klintborn asked.
"Then what do you think you will do?"

"I don't know. See the country, look at all the El Grecos I can
find."

Poveda smiled. "There is going to be a good red partridge hunt
soon. When you come back from Santiago de Compostela, I think we
can arrange this shoot. But while you are there, I want you to stay at
what we think is the best hotel in the world."

Klintborn laughed. "That takes in a lot of territory. Alberto just
came from there last week, and insists he has discovered the only
hotel worth staying at."

Madrid's Ritz and the Palace are both superb hotels. Poveda must
have really found something.

He went into glowing detail. It seems that in the year 1499, Ferdinand and Isabella built a Royal Hospital for the convenience of pilgrims coming to the Cathedral of St. James in Santiago de Compostela. A magnificent baroque building, it stood empty for years, until
1954, when the government decided to convert it into a hotel, preserving all of its old structural glory.

"And they have done it," said Poveda. "It is truly *magnifico!* Old
paintings, carvings, courtyards. And it is not expensive. I won't tell
you more. It will be more rewarding if you wait and see for yourself.
When will you go?"

"Three days," I said. "I want to see the Prado first and get the feel of Madrid."

But it wasn't three days. A completely unexpected adventure kept me from going north after salmon—one that would turn the centuries back to medieval days.

Ernest Hemingway once wrote that he found art museums helpful in his career; not only were they cheap places where he could spend useful time out of the cold and the rain, but he claimed that he often found inspiration in a good painting. He believed that a scene, a facial expression, a frozen gesture, started something working in his brain that was beneficial when he sat at a typewriter.

This doesn't seem to work with me. I get mired in admiration in the galleries of geniuses. But I wonder if during his museum days

In the kitchen of a famous Spanish restaurant . . . Jack Scott examined a dish of the house, cochinillo asado (suckling pig), *held by owner Antonio González.*

Hemingway the hunter, not the writer, was as fortunate as I was in Madrid when I walked around the great Prado museum, looking for those haunted, ascetic faces of El Greco, who remains my favorite. I had gone back to view his work in the Prado five times, until one day, before a huge painting of a medieval chase, I discovered I had sated myself. It was a vivid hunting scene of men in heavy leather costumes, with big, shaggy dogs, beautiful horses, some carrying black wild boars taken on a chase. The colors were a brilliant combination of the striking and the somber.

A man beside me was also admiring the painting. Slim and elegant, with a mustache and sleek black hair, he looked like one of El Greco's dons come alive.

"You like this?" he said.

"Very much," I said. "The artist makes it breathe."

"Lucas Cranach the Elder painted that for Carlos V centuries ago. It is the end of a *montería.*"

"*Montería?*"

"A big-game hunt in the bush. They used teams of dogs then, one with scenting ability, one fierce. It has changed little during the centuries."

Conversation developed that he was Francisco Mengotti, an avid hunter, a big landowner, and he had read some of my sporting stuff in American magazines. In fifteen minutes there was an invitation.

"Some of our nobility are forming a *montería* in a few days," he said. "A herd of wild boar are tearing up valuable vineyards, ruining our finest grapes. So they intend trying to drive them out. It will be in the old way, as always. I can arrange for you to come. If you are interested?"

I was so interested that we talked about it for another hour. Then I talked about it all evening with Mary Lou. The salmon in the north could come later. It would be fascinating to see that painting from the Prado come alive, watch the centuries roll back.

Two days later the telephone call came from Francisco Mengotti. We would leave for the *montería* at five the next morning.

Here, from my notebook, is how that day went.

"I sat on a sunny hillside beside a villager who spoke no English. (If you speak ten words of Spanish, this makes for an interesting association.) And here I was about to be transported back to the twelfth century and hunt wild boar in the manner of the ancient kings of Spain.

"The villager was Julian Garrido and he established rapport with me by proudly showing two well-thumbed, greasy photos of Virginia Mayo and Elizabeth Taylor that he stored in a worn leather billfold along with pictures of his fat wife and three small children. He looked at Elizabeth Taylor at length and said with vigor, *'Bella, no?'*

"Julian's shoes were pieces of old auto tire held on the heel and toe with leather thongs and a strip of canvas sewn in a way that kept them ingeniously together. He had scuffed leather leggings, a small, very old, faded black beret, worn black corduroy pants with jacket to match, two days' growth of very black beard, a brilliant smile—and a smell not unlike that of a goat.

"Finally he got up and went up the hill where he started tearing up small *tara* bushes and began constructing a blind. It is February, but the sun was warm as I watched two hawks floating gracefully like bits of windblown cloud, working for their mouse lunch. A flock of crows came drifting across the valley, ink blots on the piece of white sky, one of them making a noise like someone smacking his lips after a glass of good wine. Two hundred yards from Julian a magpie burst out of the brush, flew straight up, then dived, the sun shining on its odd streak of white. It was so quiet you could hear the insect hum coming from the hill miles beyond.

"Below the hill lay thousands of acres of vineyards, gnarled plants, skillfully pruned to pour strength into the grapes rather than the leaves. But the leaves that remained hung like green jewelry, the off-hill breeze stirring them into rhythmic motion. To the far left lay a great grove of olive trees. Dust spirals rose from the dirt road that twisted like a coiling rope across the countryside as a horse and wagon, miniature in the distance, slowly moved through the grove of trees and into the ancient village of Yebenes beyond.

"This was a place to sit and dream of snow in far places, of the ratrace in New York. Frenzied civilization seemed generations away. A hillside in Spain has much to recommend it.

"The blind was finished now. Julian came back and we sat on rocks behind its lacy screen and divided our lunch. It was two o'clock as we broke a huge sandwich of *pan,* a delicious peasant bread enclosing a thick slice of pearly fried pork. We washed this down with a small bottle of local Toledo white wine, so light that one has to swish it in his mouth to know that it is there. Then a *marzipon,* a small ripe sweet pear, and I got snake-lazy in the sun. We were waiting for the sound of the dogs now and the resonant call of the signal-conch shell of their masters. By pointing at my watch and with slow, deliberate hand language, I got from Julian that it would be another hour before we could expect action.

"Less than a quarter of a mile to my left I could see the portly figure of 'El Pastor Poeta,' Julian Sanchez-Prieto Redondo, a former shepherd who had become a famous poet, and a pet of the intelligentsia in Madrid. I wondered if he was still miffed because I didn't buy the heavy, ornately scrolled leather chaps that he had suggested in the shop in Yebenes this morning. He was standing outside his blind now.

"El Pastor Poeta was a short, enormously husky old man with a wine-red face, who had mastered the difficult feat of smiling and talking simultaneously. This morning he wore an olive-green felt hat, its brim heavy with silver figures of wild boar, deer and duck, and when he put on his leather hunting chaps, he looked a little like one of the Marx brothers getting into costume. But he was a devoted hunter, they told me.

"This morning, too, one of the countesses blinked her lovely brown eyes and said in elegant English, 'He will write an eloquent poem about the chase today.' Another one said, 'And there will be a boar in every line.' At the reproving look, she added quickly, 'Wild boar, I mean.'

"Now the sound of dogs came faintly like a roll of distant thunder, and Julian, my ever-conscientious guide, belching a little gust of wine, reached for my Browning .375 rifle, bolted it, checked chamber and cartridge. 'We are ready,' he said."

We had met for the hunt in Yebenes. As Mengotti said, the illustrious were there: S.A.R. (His Royal Highness) Infante D. Alfonso de Borbon, S.A.R. la Infanta Da Alicia de Borbon, Duque de Peñaranda, Marquesa de Valdueza, the handsome, knickered Austrian Ambassador and a brace of beautiful countesses, one called Mercedes who made the *montería* successful before it even got started.

After a brief visit to a cantina where we had some strong black coffee and picked up our lunch and a couple of bottles of wine, we were off, but not before El Pastor Poeta had herded me into a fascinating little leather shop that had an appealing variety of shooting equipment hanging from walls and ceiling: goatskin shell pouches with hairy, handsome belts, hand-worked leather shell belts, a beautiful soft chamois shell vest, and, of course, *zahónes,* the leather chaps, were all over the place in several different colors and textures of leather. While I was trying on a pair, the poet, through Countess Mercedes who came along as interpreter, told me all about the virtues of *zahónes.*

He said that it was well known that the American cowboy took the idea from the early Spanish in Mexico and that here it was a badge of honor to wear them on the *montería*—honor, because it is an unwritten law that the hunter must go into the brush after any wounded animal. The brush usually was tara, with thorns and flowers like a wild rose, and other tearing plants like *tomillo* and chaparro (the bush that gave chaps their name); so the *zahónes* were really most necessary, said the poet.

After sizing me up, the proprietor, a thin, alert little man with a face like an African gray parrot, announced that inasmuch as I was a friend of El Pastor Poeta—and here the poet grinned; a gentle, abashed little exercise—I could have this particular pair of *zahónes*, "which were the very best in the house," for the insignificant sum of forty dollars. I couldn't see him letting them go for such a pittance, even as a favor, and the poet then parted company, stomping off to join the rest of the group in their leather badges of honor.

Feeling completely undressed in my bird-shooter canvas-fronted pants, I walked out to join the royal party. We got into cars and the *monteros* were off, driving through magnificently medieval country to our *finca* (the large hunting area) where we stopped at a farmhouse. There the group gathered in a circle and little blue cards were passed out, designating blind positions and allotting guides. Within this *finca* was the smaller area of the vineyards which was called, for hunting purposes, the *mancha*. Actually this meant the target area within the area where we would place our party of guns.

Then it happened: the ancient painting from the Prado came alive. Dogs, men, horses and burros began arriving from both directions— dogs in packs of twenty, each with a handler. In addition to leather chaps, these colorful men, from another world and time, had goatskin jackets with long leather sleeves laced on so they could be removed.

The Austrian Ambassador, a tall, silvery-haired man in knickers, moved in to explain what was happening. "That jacket the men are wearing is called the *caleto*," he said. "It's strong as iron and the sleeves protect them not only against brush but against the teeth of dogs. Not that they need it for that. These dogs are beautifully trained and I've never seen a savage one. At least with people."

The dogs were chained together in pairs; a *podenco*, looking like an especially husky greyhound, and a *mastín*, or mastiff-type, a heavy dog. From the moment their training starts at the age of four months, these two are chained, coming to know or hate one another, like Siamese twins. They were joined thus to keep them from fighting other dogs when they gathered at the *finca,* and it also taught them to run as a team: *podenco* with the good nose; *mastín,* the fighter.

The dog trainer, or handler, was called the *podenquero.* He arrived at the hunt with twenty-five dogs; twenty for the chase, five in reserve in case some were injured. The dog pack is called *rehala,* and as we waited for assembly, I counted three hundred, some still arriving.

"That big conch shell the dog handlers are carrying," the ambassador said, "is used to reassemble the dogs. Each dog knows the shell sound of his master. It's an amazing thing. *Al Tope* they call the system when the dogs converge from left and right. Half of the animals will move many miles to our left, the other to the right, then guns will be placed in strategic positions in the center. Moving slowly, without much barking or noise, the dogs will drive the boar toward our shooting posts."

The dog team will attack a charging wild boar, and if urged by their masters, they will go into the brush after the wounded pigs. The handler shouts the leader of the pack's name when he starts to move off. All the handlers were doing it now.

"*Anda,* Machito! *Ola,* Chico!" And the enormous pack began to move to right and left, stirring the dust on the road.

The former king's brother, Infante D. Alfonso de Borbon, a jolly man who must have weighed three hundred pounds, started off on his milk-white horse, waving his hat at me as he went. The rest of us were collected by our guides and started walking or riding burros to our posts. We were told to listen for the words "*Ahí Va!*" "There goes!" When the cry went out from the *podenqueros,* it meant that you were to get ready to shoot.

It was quite a procession; 150 dogs in either direction followed by men and women on horses and burros, or walking. If I had been a wild boar, I would have gotten the hell out of the area long ago. But they tell me the Spanish wild boar, an animal with a decided mind of its own, is a devil in the brush and can run so fast that it takes a skilled shot to bring one down.

So with the panoplied party gone, the living spectacle of the medieval painting vanished in the dust hours ago, all the royal bloods in their blinds, and the *podenqueros* and the dogs out in the sun doing the work, I was ready to jump up from my rock and see what I could do about bringing down a boar, should one come my way.

The dogs didn't make much noise but there were some barks, and the sound of movement in the brush grew closer after our three-hour wait. Julian was getting nervous. He would peer through the brush of

The dogs of the montería, *chained in teams of two—one to scent, one to fight—assembled for the ancient sport of Spanish kings.*

the blind, then arise and stick his head over, sit down suddenly, then renew the process.

Suddenly our poet went crazy. The Spaniards each had two guns in their blinds, but from the sound of the gunfire that now came, El Pastor Poeta must have been lugging a half-dozen. I counted seven fast shots; then, spaced a little more slowly, three more. Julian's face was as red as the finest Rioja wine now and he was so excited that his right foot was doing a little special dance all of its own. Then he said, *"Pronto! Pronto!"* and pointed.

Running as if they were joined together with a lit fuse on the other end, came six wild boars. They must have been a family, for four were half-grown and two were big black lusty animals.

I tried sighting them but they were out a good eighty yards, with bush tangle coming between them and my rifle sight every few yards, and they were moving so fast that I didn't think I could drop one.

Besides, I didn't want to break up the family group. Julian almost went crazy when I didn't shoot, as I tried to explain that I didn't want to wound one and go into the brush after it, that I didn't like herd-shooting wild boar. Anyway this was the sport of the Spanish kings and there was plenty of royal blood around to hold the standard high.

The poet on his burro joined us on the way back to the farmhouse, waving his hands and chattering all the way. I didn't understand a word except that he hadn't bagged a boar.

A pillar of dust heralded the approach of Mary Lou. She had gone off with one of the countesses, hadn't seen the action, but was very excited.

"The dogs," she said, getting stiffly off the donkey, "are magnificent! The way they move as a team through that rough country. I have never seen anything like it!"

It developed that several wild boar had been bagged. One was being hoisted onto a jeep as we walked into *montería* headquarters.

El Pastor Poeta immediately became the center of attraction and was apparently writing a poem then and there for the benefit of his admirers. Some of his observations were translated. The six wild boar I had seen, four young ones and parents, had grown to a dozen, all giants, the smallest weighing over three hundred pounds. According to the poet's version, the whole wicked, seething mass charged straight at him, and if it hadn't been for his calm gunfire it was certain he and his guide would have been tusked to death. His guide, unsmiling, kept nodding approval.

Then the poet walked to the boar on the jeep and pronounced that it was a small one, not fit to keep company with those he had driven off.

I never got the chance to read the poem that was to appear in *Informaciónes* in Madrid in a couple of days. It must have been a beauty. As the countess said, it probably had a boar in every line.

One of Spain's main assets is its people. Unlike the French, who inextricably mix francs and friendship, the Spanish are noncommercially warm, full of the joy of living, whether they are poor, middle-class or landed aristocracy. There was no snobbishness on the *montería*. The nobility was friendly and down to earth; the peasants proud and sure.

In one of his lesser known stories, *Don Fernando,* Somerset Maugham, a devout Hispanophile, said it better than I.

"And if I am not mistaken," he wrote, "here is the secret of the greatness that is Spain. In Spain it is the men that are the poems, the pictures and the buildings. Men are its philosophies. They lived, these Spaniards of the Golden Age; they felt and did; they did not think. Life was what they sought and found, life in its variety. Passion was the seed that brought them forth and passion was the flower they bore. Their preëminence was a preëminence of character. In this I think they have been surpassed by none and equalled only by the ancient Romans. It looks as though all the energy, all the originality of this vigorous race had been disposed to one end, and one end only, the creation of man . . ." In Santiago de Compostela I was to meet a man who would prove that Mr. Maugham was not overstating the situation. This ancient city, an archiepiscopal see and university center, is in the province of Galicia, in the mountains of the northwest, with the Bay of Biscay to the north, Portugal to the south, and the Atlantic Ocean breasting the west. According to Alberto Poveda, who briefed us just before we left, it became famous early in the ninth century when the tomb of Saint James the Apostle, who brought the gospel to Spain, was found there. King Alphonso II had a church built on the site; the remains of this and the basilica later raised by Alphonso III are still evident in the Cathedral of St. James.

"It was second only to Rome in all of Christendom," Alberto said. "Hundreds of thousands made the pilgrimage to Santiago to the tomb of St. James." He looked at us soberly. "People don't seem to make pilgrimages any more." Then he brightened. "But the best salmon rivers are there, and this time of year there will be no tourists. I have made arrangements for you. You will be surprised." That turned out to be a classic understatement.

An Iberian Air Lines plane brought us from Madrid to the little Santiago airport in an hour and a half. There was a new royal blue Renault bus waiting with a uniformed driver—the words HOSTAL DE LOS REYES CATÓLICOS painted on the side. We were the only passengers. The drive was about a half-hour from the countryside, with its pines, chestnuts and stately plane trees, to the old city, its narrow streets paved with great blocks of stone worn smooth by the tread of generations.

The bus halted at an ancient sunlit square, the Plaza de España, where the famed nine hundred-year-old Cathedral of St. James rose in medieval might. The sun was shining on its Quintana door in seventeenth-century baroque. Directly opposite was the Palacio de Rajoy, the town hall; on the far corner of the square, the Colegio de San Jeronimo, the municipal school (with a magnificent romanesque entrance); and then back to the corner where our bus stopped, the elegant hotel, a palacelike building, regal and imposing even beside such a pile of architectural splendor as the basilica of St. James. Thus, the Spaniards, who are great for reading symbolism into everything, claim that this plaza in Santiago is the most significant in the world, and represents perfection, squared as it were by hospitality, religion, science and justice. It is actually the most beautiful I have seen.

As I sat in the blue bus taking in the exterior of the hotel, the exquisitely carved stone doorway with its lacy granite filigree, its recessed archway filled with stone statuary of saints and sinners, the crystal sparkle from the window fan above the entrance, and the gargoyles peering over the roof edge, children circled us rolling hoops and a woman dressed in crow black walked by, carrying a basket of vegetables on her head.

A group of four boys and three girls, dressed as if they had just come from a Yale gala, was suddenly divided by a huge woman, also in dead black, carrying a basket on her head filled with round loaves of bread, a bunch of waxy-white calla lilies, a huge fish and a pig's head that stared with sad, accusing eyes.

As I got out of the bus, a short, young man with a cap of shiny black hair and alert brown eyes aglint with humor, greeted me. He was Marcelino Arias Artola, director of the hotel.

It is considered weasling for a writer to beg off description by saying that you have to see something to believe it and appreciate it. But this time it is true. This is a hotel for the eye, for the touch. It is filled with rich and rewarding beauties of the past.

It is a place of antique angels and cherubs, of great rugs and draperies, Goyas and El Grecos on the walls, statuary and wood carvings, lacy ironwork and long stretches of old, age-smoothed stone floorings, courtyards abloom with flowers, three well-appointed, silver-gleaming restaurants, one intimate and one gregarious cocktail lounge, and a concert hall.

It is also a place that considers the amenities. Each suite has two of almost everything, including marble bathrooms. Built by Ferdinand and Isabella as a hospital and place of rest for pilgrims making the holy trek to St. James, the monarchs had decreed that any pilgrim be taken in, regardless of his means.

"It's almost the same today," said Marcelino Arias Artola. "Our most expensive suite is about half of what you pay in America." He was conservative; their suites were less than half, costing about what the average American tourist spends for a motel room. Restored by an ingenious architect, Fernando Moreno Barbera, who used a method of injecting cement into and behind ancient walls, the *hostal* was ready for Santiago's holy year in 1954. Costing 150 million pesetas, it took two thousand men nine months to bring back its original beauty.

Marcelino Arias—in Spain, to make matters more confusing, the last name of the male is his mother's name; the middle name is the one the man claims for his own—was even more enthusiastic about salmon than he was about his classic hotel.

"The salmons," he said, "go back to Roman times, and even word salmon, 'jumping fish,' is Roman." He then proceeded to teach me that rod was *cana;* reel, *carrete;* lure, *cedo;* and spinner, a word which he used with much enthusiasm, *cucharilla.*

"I suppose you are the expert fisherman," he said, "but I have learned the good word for the salmons, and I will tell you what I know of this fish, one only of which I have catched. Trouts yes, many, many; salmon, they are the smart ones, the kings of our *ríos.* Anadromous they are. They swim in the salt and the fresh waters, mostly in the ocean, yes. They come up Ulla—this is a *río,* a river— but first they come in Ría de Arosa. This is the estuary, doorway of the salmon from the sea. In spring they come in long silver streams, like one great fish, and they do not reach the place of their youths until fall.

"Meantime this is where you fishermens come in. Now, April, May and June they like the pools, the big, deep pools. And now, my guest and my friend, this is where Marcelino comes in. He has leased for the *hostal* the Rufugio del Couso, perhaps the best pools in the Ulla for you to fish for these silver ones who come up our river. But you must be strong; you must be quick, and the *cana* must be stronger than the fish. Please, may Marcelino look at your *cana?*"

I took the Orvis 8 1/8-ounce rod out of the long aluminum tube, jointed it, and placed the 9½-foot whippy bamboo in his hand.

He gave it a flick, using spinning-rod wrist action, stared at it for a while, then said slowly, "I do not wish to make the insult to my guest. This is the *cana* for the river trouts but not for the salmons. We on the Ulla use the spinning rod; the big one, the thick one; one that the bull salmons cannot break like the tree twig. Yes, you will use the Galician way? The spinning?"

Several hours later Marcelino introduced me to a slender, gentle man, M. Elegido, Doctor-Ingeniero, Jefe De La 2. Region De Pesca Continental, the foremost fisheries expert in Spain. Marcelino embarrassed him by telling me that he had just returned from the States where he had lectured and had given our experts pointers on fish hatcheries and a new circular tank system he had invented.

The doctor told of a great restoration in sixteen salmon rivers of northern Spain. Netting at the mouth and in the streams had been

This was the entrance to Hostal de los Reyes Católicos, perhaps the most beautiful hotel in the world.

prohibited; poaching was practically nonexistent due to the practice of opening certain areas in the rivers to the local fishermen and requiring registration of every salmon sold.

The doctor recommended that salmon fishermen bring along their favorite trout rod for slow days. "I believe we have more productive trout streams than any country in the world," he said. "Most years, on the River Tormes alone, there are recorded catches of ten thousand trout."

The first day, Marcelino went with us in the blue bus to the Couso, pointing out odd corn cribs on stilts, *hórreos,* some of brick, some of wood and stone, standing like strange sentinels in the sunlight, as we passed through rolling green hills over quicksilver creeks, with valley views that would have watercolor artists apoplectic. The mountains in the distance were capped in white, but wild flowers flared in the fields: bluebells, larkspur, daffodils, and whole fields of daisies lying like new-fallen snow. As we drove along this road I thought of the thousands of pilgrims that had come this way, walking, riding horses and donkeys, coming to the tomb of St. James the Apostle to pray for recovery from a dread disease, or for spiritual peace. Not too many years ago, all roads didn't lead to Rome, as the historians have it; all roads led to Santiago de Compostela and its cathedral, which contained the world's greatest masterpiece of Romanesque art, the Pórtico de la Gloria.

Marcelino was talking of his countryside. "And besides, *señor,* the sea, with some of the most beautiful beaches of white sand, places without the many people, is less than twenty miles from here. So, you can see, Galicia has everything."

We turned off the paved highway and entered a dirt road, winding for miles to the river. Then we followed the Ulla to the Couso.

"But I think the big treat for you who like the people will be the man of the river you will soon meet, Antonio Claro Chico. He is one who knows everything about the Ulla, the rocks, the insects, the rapids, the pools, the salmon."

We stopped at a green glade beside the river that was big and swollen with recent rains and walked from the bus to meet two men standing beside a modern fieldstone-and-wood building. A bull salmon was leaping eternally in stone over the doorway and I could see the dado flash of pink paint over white on inside walls. The river went by roaring like a tiger.

One man, short, chunky, with grizzled gray hair and a slightly hooked nose, came forward. He held a stiff canvas fishing fedora in his right hand, wore khaki pants, thick black rubber knee boots and a black-and-white checked cotton shirt. This was Antonio Claro Chico. He said *"Buenos días"* in a gravelly voice. The other, darkly hand-some, was wearing a black corduroy uniform, with three stripes on the sleeve. He was Andrés Lopez Martinez, chief game warden, the Guarda Mayor of the Ulla. He also said, *"Buenos días."*

Marcelino stood in the background smiling as I jointed my flyrod, and Antonio Claro Chico started to clip my reel to its base. Then the old fellow did a comic double take, started spitting short Spanish words, strode off to the building, and came out with a big spinning rod. With a determined expression, he took the flyrod from my hands, pushed the spinning rod at me and began a harangue, pointing at the river, then me, then the flyrod. Suddenly he stopped, laughed and turned to Marcelino for help.

Marcelino translated. "He says that his friends, the other river men, will laugh if they see you with the flyrod. For the sake of his dignity, would you use the spinner?"

This was a new experience. Everywhere the flyrod man is consid-ered the top of the craft, the elite, the master of the sport, and the spinning devotee the meat hunter.

"Please tell our river man that this rod has killed one twenty-five-pound salmon in New Brunswick, Canada. I'm not saying it was skillful. But if I like hard work, let's please try for a day or so." Marcelino laughed and gabbled to Antonio. The old man nodded his head and we made for the river.

It was big water, muddy, stirred by spring rains, and it ran with twists and turns, the pools quiet and deep. I worked one pool for a half-hour, slowly, carefully, doing everything in my limited repertoire to agitate a salmon into striking. There were no swirls, no water broke. I changed flies often.

This went on all the first day. Meanwhile, back at the *hostal,* the adept ministrations of the *maître d',* Rafael Melcon, in the way of tender veal and some gentle white Rioja, helped me forget defeat.

The next day brought a dark dawn and some rain, but Antonio was cheerful and enthusiastic when I arrived at the stream. He had the belief that by talking loudly he could make foreigners understand his language. It must have made an intriguing sound sequence as he tried to tell me which fly to use when the famed Jock Scott brought no results.

And then, as sometimes happens to devious fishermen, I had an idea. I had been told that fishermen could get their own price for these early-run salmon, and I was almost certain that this was the reason that the big spinning rods were used. Salmon, at this time of year, were a business, not a sporting, proposition.

About noon a white-jacketed waiter came out to the stream where I stood plotting, bearing a tray with a cold, white martini. "Lunch will be ready, *señor,* any time you are," he said. Marcelino was making defeat sweet. He had transferred his luxury operation to the stream for the day. I asked the waiter to do a bit of translating for me. "Tell Antonio," I said, "that he may have all the salmon we catch. All I want is the fun and a few pictures."

His eyes widened. "But, *señor,* these fish are worth their weight in

The guide, Antonio Claro Chico, tried to dissuade the author from using his flyrod—unsuccessfully.

gold at this time! If you catch many fish, Antonio Claro Chico will be a rich man—"

"If we catch any he deserves it."

He translated, and Antonio's blossoming smile was a sight to behold. It was a poem of pleasure, unspoken, but it said as plainly as if he had placed his hand on my shoulder and spoke in English, "*Señor,* you have the rights on one of the best stretches of salmon river in Spain, and you are giving me the opportunity to catch these great fish and make much-needed money. Poaching is a crime in my country now, but Antonio Claro Chico can now show you how much he knows about the secret ways of salmon . . ."

What he really said was *"Muchas gracias, señor."*

I said, *"De nada,"* one of the few phrases of the language I knew, which means "it is nothing."

And then, because it was noon, we went back to the beautiful little house beside the river and had a three-course luncheon with inspiration in the shape of a local white wine, *gazpacho a la Andalucía* (cold, biting soup), *langostín* (large shrimp or small lobster, take your choice), breast of herbed chicken, a special thistle-light cake, coffee strong enough to pour itself, and Spanish brandy.

Now I was ready for the salmon. So was the river man. He took a thermometer out of his pocket and tested the water in a deep pool. It read fifty-five degrees; so we walked until we found medium-depth water. There he assembled his own spinning rod, a clumsy, businesslike weapon, and put on a large, crude lure, a homemade *cucharilla* that looked as if it had agitated a lot of salmon. Again he recommended that I use the Black Doctor, watching while I had a few pool-covering casts; then we moved on to a slightly larger, shallower pool, and I was into a fish in three seconds.

It was a slashing attack. The salmon took the fly as though he had been building up a special hate for this particular Black Doctor ever since he left the sea and entered the stream. I was grateful for all the backing on this reel. He bulled and ran, this salmon, and he looked five feet long when he left the water, running silver in the air, and when he came back into the water he led me a hard chase. I ran with him; I reeled when he permitted, paid out line when he dictated; reeled it in when he said so. My rod was taking punishment, and for about fifteen minutes I was afraid that the spinning-rod boys had something. But then superior strength took over, surely not skill. After all, I weigh 160 pounds and the salmon when he came in, exhausted after the battle, weighed just under twenty pounds. Also exhausted, I sat on the bank then and watched the old master use his spinning rod. It was a study in skillful determination.

It took him another hour, but he beached a salmon slightly larger than mine, and that smile that talked came onto his face again saying, "*Señor,* thank you very much. Here is 2,400 pesetas more for my pocket. You are truly my hero!" But what he really said again was a gentle, "*Muchas gracias.*"

He said it twice more that week. We caught two more salmon, giving him a total of seventy pounds to peddle to the fish-hungry people with the pesetas.

Marcelino Arias Artola was a man with a dream: he wanted to go to America. But not in the ordinary way of most who hunger for the shores of the country that is supposed to have everything. He wanted to look at the hotels, inspect the kitchens, the bedrooms, watch the service.

"The best," he said. "The country with best of everything."

I disliked puncturing a dream, but there was no other way.

"No," I said. "There is no hotel in America that I know as good as yours. None with the treasures you have, the service, the bathrooms, the beauty and the charm of the old that you have kept."

"I feel much pride in what you say," he replied. "Today I feel much good."

He felt much good every day. For the next few days he ran us around his countryside in his small car at a speed that made us feel that we were in need of racing helmets and goggles. The Galician technique seemed to be to accelerate when one saw a pedestrian. He, in turn, would stand nonchalantly until the car was almost upon him, then make a quick, graceful jump to the side of the road.

The area was full of small villages. Marcelino just got the Volkswagen into its top speed on the outskirts of one settlement when he ran into another. He used his horn often, his brakes seldom, and his gas pedal constantly. It was a nerve-wracking business. He also talked while he drove, which increased the hazard. He told how he took care of himself, exercised often, walked, fished, liked the out-of-doors.

"There is the Arab philosophy about the health," he said. "They said that the health is figure one, love is zero, glory zero, success zero. Put the one of the health beside them and you are rich man. But without the one of the health everything is zero."

Marcelino also had inside information on the national drink—

sherry. He gave it while trying to get the Volkswagen to do sixty in second gear. "Everybody will tell you the best to the drink is Tío Pepe. Good old Uncle Joe. True, it is good. All Spanish sherry is the ver' good. But the best—and believe Marcelino for he has had time to do the fine test on sherry—is 'Fino la Ina' Botaina—*seco*. Ver' dry."

He took us through the ancient Roman town of Betanzos, the fishing village of Cambados, the old places of Abegondo, Sada, Mino, Petra, past the great oyster beds of Sabio. We stopped on Puente del Pedrido, a bridge over an estuary, to view the *viveros,* skeletal wooden frameworks that trap mussels and oysters, and from a distance look like ships sailing out to sea.

On another of his runs he took us to the Isla de la Toja, an island reached by a narrow bridge, to see a little church constructed of gleaming white clam shells. Whipping the Volkswagen around S-turnings at seventy-five miles an hour, he told us a story about the knight off to the wars who had a twinge of conscience regarding his wife's chastity belt. "If he became the killed," Marcelino said, "then what was the poor woman to do?" So he gave the key to the belt to a close friend. The knight and his fellows were only a few miles away when his friend came pounding up on horseback. "Sire," the trusted friend said, "you have given me the wrong key!"

Marcelino laughed at that one all the way to Casa Pepe, a restaurant in El Grove where you could eat seafood so fresh that you could see some of the fish still jumping on the big wooden table in the kitchen. He ordered *vieira,* which he called a scallop oyster; *cigalas,* delicious prawns; and also *merluza,* which Marcelino said was Spain's finest fish. I think it is hake. It was flaky white with a light but hot sauce of red pepper and butter. This was what Marcelino regarded as a quick lunch. He was anxious to show us what he called his secret beaches.

"The white sand," he said, "without the peoples. You won't believe."

It was an area called La Lanzada, about twenty miles from Santiago, where we came in the whirlwind Volkswagen, stopped and walked over to the cliffs that faced the Atlantic. The sun was on the water, the waves curling white on shore. The beach was spotless, thick, white sand, broad stretches bordering the sea for miles. And there wasn't a soul in sight. It was a simple matter to walk down the cliff side to the shore. There was little habitation for miles. We drove, looking for the blemish in this perfect picture. There wasn't any. A house on one of these cliffs looking toward the Atlantic would be my idea of the way to live. Land is reasonable; the area interesting; the people pleasing.

Next to Marcelino, Rafael Melcon was the most valuable person in the hotel. The first night we were there he explained the Spanish philosophy about meat.

He was a handsome, soft-spoken man, with curling, slightly graying hair, always with spotless tails and white tie. Usually when we asked for a suggestion, he would say, "Beal from the billage would be my first choice." And it was always good veal, tender, never overcooked.

"We in Spain," he said, "especially here in Galicia, are just beginning to elevate the cows for the meat. Up until now we use them for to work, for carrying, for plowing. When they become old and useless they go to the pot. So you understand, we eat other things. Lambs, goats, pigs. Now that we have elevated the cow to the table, we have the beal." Through his efforts we found that Galician food had a personality and a flavor different from any other in Spain, or in the world for that matter.

One evening he had quite a dinner arranged when we had returned from a day of trout fishing in the Río Umia with Marcelino and his friend, Jose Manuel Loureiro, "Lolo." That morning we had picked up two *secretarios* apiece. These eight-year-old boys from the nearby village of Caldas were bright, flashing youngsters who knew the position of every trout in the stream. These unusual guides we had to pick up and carry across the river.

"*Muchas truchas!*" they kept saying, running ahead and pointing into pools. We caught so many trout that I am hesitant to give the number. (We couldn't count them anyway; there were too many little-boy heads over the basket every time we tried.) It might have been the best trout fishing we had had. But I digress. The dinner.

Rafael started with small bowls of Galician soup, *caldo gallego,* lusty, with potatoes, white beans, turnip tops, spicy *chorizo* (a sausage) and salt pork. He poured a white wine, *Albarino de Fefinanes,* and brought in some of the salmon we had caught (which Marcelino had purchased from Antonio Claro Chico), *salmón a la primavera, guisado a la cazuela, con distintas clases de legumbres,* cooked and served in an earthen pot surrounded by fresh vegetables, tiny fresh peas and lemon peppers predominating. When this was gone he brought a bottle of *ribero* and thin goblets and served *conejo en su salsa,* young rabbit in its own sauce, which I suspect was strengthened with brandy and flavored with pork. With it were young *alca-chofas,* artichokes. Table cleared, he brought Spanish champagne, which is not to be compared with the French, but is excellent and inexpensive—less than two dollars a bottle.

"And now," he said, "we will bring the special Compostela dessert. *Filloas!*" Which proved to be small, hot pancakes rolled in superb honey.

When we weren't fishing or exploring the countryside with Marcelino, or completing our food education with Rafael, we spent time going through the magnificent cathedral, or just stood in the great plaza. It was the focal point of the city. A clock in the steeple of the church struck the hour, and every so often the cathedral bell tolled, sending its sad, sonorous sound throughout the old city. It was tolled by a tailor who lived rent-free in the steeple tower in exchange for his bell-ringing service.

Well-dressed children—no tight blue jeans or dirty khaki here—gathered in the square to roll hoops. When the school bell sounded, they rolled the hoops right into the building. The older girls and boys, books under their arms, stood in groups, talking and laughing. The sound of laughter was always in the plaza. Priests moved across it constantly—in long black frocks with brilliant blue sashes, some with tricornered bullfighter type hats, others with the round, flat, broad-brimmed variety. Tradesmen pushing loaded carts or bicycles halted for a rest in the plaza; women with baskets on their heads stopped before the cathedral, looked up at it, baskets tilting, and crossed themselves.

At night electric lights came on. Shaped like antique lanterns, they hung from the old stone of cathedral, school, hotel and town hall. A light rain fell often in the evening, and in its mist, with the lanterns throwing spears of light, the townspeople moving quietly by in their black clothing, the bell tolling, the plaza became another world far from the modern mainstream.

Some mornings we would go to the open market, where everything from a basket of pigeons to a bolt of silk is sold from open stalls or carts on the cobblestone streets. We saw one woman approach another, who was selling live chickens. After much discussion and expert feeling of a big rooster to see if it was fat enough, she was convinced and bought it. Then, to our horror, the woman cut the rooster's throat, the bird flopping and bleeding to death on the cobblestones as the customer counted out pesetas.

•   •   •

The day was climaxed by Jack's tying into an old warrior trout in a deep pool.

The secretarios were eight-year-old fishing guides we had to pick up and carry across the river.

Perhaps before he became famous for his inside reporting, John Gunther once wrote: "Note, for instance, the worthy *calamar*, a species of octopus, and there is at least one Madrid restaurant where you may have squid cooked in its own inky juice . . ."

If Mr. Gunther had moved farther north in his Spanish ramblings, as we did, he would not have made the mistake of calling *calamar* an octopus, which it is not. We learned the difference from a sixteen-year-old busboy working his way into the respected profession of waiter. In aspiring to the trade of taking care of tables, he had also learned English.

"*Calamar* is the squid. We eat the very small," the boy said. "*Frito*, fried. Or in its own sauce. Only the babies, never more than this size." He held up his hand. "The octopus is *pulpo* and we eat him this the large." He made a circle the size of a large serving plate. "He is the tough. He must be beaten first before we eat him."

But then, everyone in Santiago de Compostela knows El Pulpo. He sits in gristly glory on plates in the windows of every restaurant in town. In fact, in one careful census I observed that there wasn't a single restaurant that didn't have the pink monster in the window.

In fact, the array of food in the restaurants didn't inspire me in the least to rush in and order a meal. They put the raw material in the windows to tempt patrons. The only item that is cooked is the *pulpo*, usually in the central position of honor, its horrid limbs with the suckers astutely arranged so every feature of the octopus is clearly visible. And they are always good size, the smallest a foot long and more than that in width.

In one restaurant they lost all restraint. Its window had a white cheese, an exact copy of a woman's bare breast; a whole beef tongue; a *merluza*, curled with its tail in its mouth; bloody dishes of calves' brains and kidneys, a whole skinned kid. In the center, sharing the spotlight with the octopus, was something that looked like a snake with teeth, which I discovered was a lamprey. This despicable creature lives by hooking its toothed and suckered mouth on fish and sucking the blood from them. Galicia has the dubious honor of being the only place in the world where lamprey is considered a choice item of food.

Marcelino, after answering our questions about some of the objects in the restaurants, made an offer. "Let us make adventure for the food," he said. "We have many things for to eat here in Santiago that you will not get in any place else. For the example, *lamprea en su salsa* (lamprey in its own sauce). Tomorrow we go. Marcelino will

At the open market in Santiago de Compostela, women sold fine-looking chickens, then obligingly cut their throats.

be the guide. Galicia food from the sea! Yes?"

My wife was more interested than I. This is a grudging admission, for I am usually the leader in trying esoteric food, but the lamprey dampened my ardor. I was hoping Marcelino would forget about his kind offer, but he didn't. We had a note from him at breakfast: "Do not eat the too much. We will have adventure with the food from the sea tonight."

The restaurant, Casa Castano, was in the village of Puentecesures, not far from Santiago, a smoky place with plain wooden tables. The owner was a pleasant, fat young man with one eye disconcertingly crossed.

"Galician seafood you want?" he said. "Casa Castano has the ver' best! Shall we begin?"

We began with a crisp, white *rioja,* which was poured throughout the meal. Next came a whole loaf of *pan de peso,* a large round of local bread, light and fluffy with a hard crust. It was delicious and saved the day for me. Any time there was any doubt about whether I was eating the food, I chewed the bread vigorously, forestalling questions.

It seemed that we had come here because the restaurant made a specialty of lamprey—*lamprea guisada.* Marcelino insisted that we go into the kitchen where it was being prepared. It was half cut through in two-inch slashes along the entire body, then placed in a pot; olive oil was added, salt, chopped onion, a clove of garlic; then it was covered with brandy. Meanwhile, while it simmered, we ate other things from the sea—none available in any restaurant I know.

First came a steaming serving dish covered with something that looked like barnacles. *"Percebes,"* Marcelino said. "Galicia's best!"

He ate them with gusto. They were good; when you pulled them out of the shell and dipped them in butter, they had a flavor somewhat like littleneck clams.

"Delicious!" said Mary Lou. "What are *percebes?*"

"They are what you call the barnacles. The insects of the sea that stick to the bottom of the ships. Yes?"

Next came some more insects from the sea. *Necoras,* tiny spider crabs that you ate whole, shell and all. They were followed by *mejillónes en salpicón*—mussels in olive oil, vinegar, chopped hard boiled egg, parsley and pimento—served with white wine and bread.

This was followed by a huge platter of snowy white disks, the size of half-dollar pieces. The waiter squirted lemon over them, then some olive oil and salt and pepper. They were eaten cold. I was about to ask what they were when I spotted a sucker on the edge of one of the circles of white meat. This was old El Pulpo himself, the pride of Santiago. He tasted something like sea scallops on the tough side.

Marcelino explained the dish. "This is ver' famous here. *Pulpo estilo feria.* The way we serve them at the fairs. We eat them the way you eat the hot dog in the U.S.A." He beamed. "Delicious, are they not?"

Now the owner came bearing the *pièce de résistance,* the famed *lamprea guisada* in a large serving bowl. From a platter of small slices of toasted bread, four slices were arranged on our plates; then the lamprey, which had cooked long enough to fall apart into two-inch pieces, was spooned over the toasted bread.

In the interests of culinary science, adventure, this book, and because I did not want to insult my host, Marcelino, I ate the lamprey, scourge of fishermen everywhere. Surprisingly, it tasted somewhat like eel—the white meat was delicate, a bit on the oily side, but palatable.

Marcelino, thoughtful person that he is, never mentioned having a second helping. He quickly poured more wine and ordered dessert and coffee. We had another Galician specialty, an extremely good almond tart—*tarta compostela* or *tarta de almendra.* It successfully ended Marcelino's "adventure for the food" and our stay in Santiago de Compostela.

In Spain they wear dark glasses regardless of the hour. At night they stumble along in the double darkness created by the glasses, almost as if they were blind. They wear them while they dance, while they drink, while they eat dinner. I don't know whether they affect the dark lenses in the manner of the Hollywood and theatrical types in an effort to appear mysteriously glamorous, or just to mask the eyes so they can stare without being obvious.

I mention this because we nearly ran over several sunglass-blinded pedestrians on our way to Madrid from the airport, which put our driver in such a bad frame of mind that he took us to the Palace Hotel by a direct route. When we arrived, a message awaited us: Osten Klintborn would be over within the hour. We sat talking for a long time. An easy man to be with, he had been an SAS manager in several countries. Among the last was Poland, and he had been there when it was overrun by the Russians. He began telling some grisly details.

Alberto Poveda's arrival changed the subject. He had arranged the partridge shoot. "It is with Señor Mengotti," he said. "The gentleman you went on the *montería* with. He has leased much land not far from Madrid where there are many partridges. He tells us that he would be delighted if you and Mrs. Scott would join him."

Klintborn had some other ideas. "After that I think it would be exciting to see the Canary Islands. It will be difficult to get reservations, but I think I can manage it."

"Not the Balearics?" Poveda said. "Majorca, Minorca, even Ibiza?"

"Overcrowded," Klintborn said. "Besides, what are they but islands in the sun? The Canaries are dramatic. Also, I hear that on one of the islands there are people who communicate by whistling. No talking. Whistling."

"This I didn't know," Poveda said. "Mr. Klintborn, you surprise me."

"Sometimes I surprise myself." Klintborn laughed. "Four more gins and tonic!" he called to the waiter.

Poveda had something else. "Three hours from Madrid is a man who has never slept. Perhaps it would be good to talk to a man like this?"

"Never slept!" Klintborn said. "That is impossible!"

"No," Poveda said. "It is true. It has been confirmed by medical science."

Before acting on Klintborn's and Poveda's suggestions, we went to the old city of Toledo to look at more of Domingo Theotocópuli's masterpieces. El Greco, born on the Greek island of Candia, was called The Greek by the Spaniards shortly after he came to Toledo where he lived and painted for thirty-seven years. Against the advice of some who admired his genius, he lived in the house of a Jew, Samuel Ha-Levi, in the Jewish quarter. He liked the Jews, their sensitivities, their appreciation of art, their warm friendship and their eager, exciting way of life. The ancient house is an unusual museum with paintings by El Greco, Rubens, Bassano et al in every room. Another museum building is attached to the house, where, with other art, hang El Greco's thirteen paintings of Christ and the twelve apostles.

The painting I most wanted to see, "The Burial of Count Orgaz," was in the parish church of St. Tome. A somber, living thing, it is one of the most impressive works of art in existence, with Spanish nobles gathered around the dead count who is being held by a young priest and a bishop. El Greco brushed his own lean features into the painting in several places.

Toledo, only forty-three miles from Madrid, is best seen on foot, an excursion that the Spanish National Tourist Office is delighted to arrange. They provided us with a lovely guide, Luisa, who took us through the tremendous Santa María Cathedral and while so doing uttered a remark that made our day.

One of the most beautiful in the world, with five entrances, eighty-eight pillars, seventy-two vaults and 750 magnificent stained-glass windows, the gothic cathedral of Toledo was built on the ruins of a sixth-century Christian temple in 1226. It is full of impressive religious paintings by the world's foremost artists. Cardinals of Spain are buried under the stone floors inside the cathedral, with the words *Hic jacet pulvis pulvius cinis et nihil* (here lies dust, ashes and nothing) chiseled in the stone of each floor tombstone. The red hat of the cardinal, suspended by a long cord, hangs over each stone.

"When the hat falls," Luisa said, "the soul ascends to heaven."

She stood looking at the hanging hats for a moment, then said thoughtfully, "But never has a hat fallen."

After Toledo we drove to Segovia to see the gypsies who live in caves beneath a mountain overhang. These are old burial caves, and a mushroom industry now thrives there. We walked through the Alcazar, the most beautiful castle in a country that is full of them. Our guide said Walt Disney had used it in his picture *Sleeping Beauty*. We ate in Spain's most famous restaurant, Candido, again having piglet roasted over oak coals, not so good as it was in Madrid's Botín. Under the shadow of the most magnificent Roman aqueduct in existence, that runs through the center of Segovia like a fortress, we sat and drank *cinchón,* a thick, sweet, aniselike drink, and watched the peasants in their shiny black suits. In from the country for the day, they celebrated by having their shoes shined. The bootblack polished only the toes, but the farmers were hugely satisfied. Then they crowded at tiny tables and sat talking and drinking anise, occasionally casting pleased glances at their shiny toes.

We met Poveda's man who never sleeps, in the village of La Gineta one hundred miles south of Madrid. Valentín Medina Poves, a sixty-three-year-old peasant who works on the farm of Juan Cuesta Hidalgo, is a pleasant, stocky man with a wine-red face who says that he never remembers having slept. He claims to be happy about his affliction. "If I could sleep I would be just like everybody else," he says. He finds beds uncomfortable; his body aches all the next day if he tries to spend a night on a soft bed. He does lie down and rest, always on a hard surface, often the floor.

Everyone in La Gineta, including the village doctor, Tomás Hidalgo Muñoz, believes that their *maestro tesoro* is indeed a sleepless man. The doctor has tried everything in his medical repertoire. Sev-

"We walked through the Alcazar, the most beautiful castle in a country that is full of them."

A Roman aqueduct ran through the center of Segovia like a fortress.

eral men in the village once plied Valentín with six liters of strong local wine in an all-night attempt to make him drop off. It didn't work. They fell asleep themselves.

Several news-agency men in Madrid had Valentín sit in their office for forty-eight hours while they watched in relays. He didn't even yawn. He told them that he talked with animals—not with a language but with a feeling. He also said that he lost eight toenails every year and that he bathed in the river even in winter. In Madrid, Dr. Luis Tomás Casamayor tried his hand at putting Valentín to sleep with sedatives. He failed, adding, "Valentín is apparently a genuine case of total insomnia."

La Gineta's famous citizen doesn't look sixty-three. He told us that he thought he owed much of his good health to the fact that he had been drinking two bottles of local wine a day for as long as he could remember.

People in Madrid and La Gineta say Valentín believes that the day he sleeps will be the day he dies. He has a lifelong dream of touring the world as the man who never sleeps, and wishes that someone in Spain, medical scientists preferably, would place him under constant surveillance in a hospital for several months so that it would finally be proved that he speaks the truth about his sleeplessness.

No one should visit Madrid without dining at Horcher's, a restaurant in the grand manner, with mossy rugs, snowy tablecloths, fine service plates, sterling flatware. But it is Herr Horcher who makes the place. Many say that he was chef for Goering, that he was the pet of the Nazi elite and fled to Spain when he saw the handwriting on the wall. But I doubt if this rumor has any basis in fact. It is a fact that he is one of the finest restaurateurs in Europe. Horcher is a short man with piercing blue eyes, sparse hair over a finely shaped head, and a composed face with all of the expression of an ox. He is also a martinet, running his establishment like an army.

He does nothing haphazardly. If he has boiled beef as a specialty, it is wheeled in on a cart, an entire haunch covered by a dome of silver. It comes to your table directed by Horcher and attended by the waiter brigade, one wheeling, another slicing, another serving, another pouring the wine. I wouldn't go to Horcher's for a dish of the country (Botín is the place for that), but for game, meats and fowl it has few equals in Europe. The rigid German would do well just running a school for waiters. The service is superb to watch.

A man of immense aplomb, Horcher is seldom thrown off by the actions of his patrons. But one night, in my presence, he was. As is his custom, he approached a table after the first serving of larded haunch of venison had been finished, offering the customer a second helping. First the courtly bow, inquiring how he liked the dish. Then the regal summoning of the waiter who came pushing the cart. As Horcher himself was about to cut another slice of venison, the man, a thin American, said, "Sorry, Mr. Horcher, it was very good. But I can only have small portions. Never second helpings. I have only half my stomach."

Horcher who could easily handle drunks, bores, cranks, check quibblers, querulous royalty, obviously was out of his depth with a man with half a stomach. He paled, smiled weakly and fled in bewilderment.

The morning after I saw Herr Horcher run out on the poor fellow with part of a stomach, we joined the partridge shoot, and that was about the end of our stay in Spain. We had come forty miles from Madrid in an hour and a half. Now we waited in the square for Louis, the Guarda Mayor of the forty thousand acres of land we were to beat for the famous red partridge, the *perdiz*. Finally, clacking toward us down the cobblestones of the old village of Casarrubios del Monte, came a man on a horse. He sat the saddle as if growing out of the animal. This was the elite guard of the thousands of partridge. I was told that the poachers were deathly afraid to trespass on the acreage he guarded. "He will toot his brass horn and put the birdshot where it do the most good in the poacher," said the man nearest me. "He knows where is every partridge, almost by name."

Louis was barrel-shaped, swart, smiling, with a voice like a bell, his husky girth encased in brown leather, sporting a cocked-brimmed black headpiece that was almost but not quite a sombrero. He rode a fine red stallion and had a polished brass hunting horn slung over his shoulder. Today Francisco Mengotti wore a well-cut green jacket and a green felt porkpie hat with silver pins of red deer and stag. With his lean don-face and air of authority, he dominated the gathering. With him was Miguel Escobedo, a young lawyer, who was also gun editor of the Spanish sports magazine, *Caza y Pesca*.

Now Señor Mengotti was doing the talking, and the knightlike Louis came down from his horse, listening with close attention. There were to be eight other guns and thirty *ojeadores,* or beaters, usually three to one gunner. Each gunner would have a *secretario,* or shooting-butt assistant, who would reload guns and mark birds when they fell. When the rest of the guns arrived, blue cards with butt numbers would be distributed. You would use one number all day and move from butt to butt, in five drives or beats. Mengotti gave me a slip of blue paper bearing his organizational crest, a silver circle embossed with the head of a stag reading "Diana Cacerías, Madrid," and bearing eleven paragraphs in English—the rules of the partridge hunt.

The beginning of each drive is announced by three successive trumpet calls. It is forbidden to shoot before this signal is given, to leave the butt during the drive or allow any of the *secretarios* to leave it. It is forbidden to shoot game crossing between two guns. Shooting obliquely is permitted (minimum 45°), provided it does not represent any danger for the neighboring guns. The maximum distance for shooting straight ahead or behind is seventy yards, obliquely twenty-five yards.

The approach of the beaters is announced by several prolonged trumpet calls, signaling that it is only permitted to shoot behind. The end of the drive is signaled by brief trumpet calls when the guns and their *secretarios* can collect the game. This is handed over to the chief gamekeeper by the *secretarios* to enable him to establish the total bag.

Roils of dust whipped up by two cars coming down the hill into the village announced the arrival of the other gunners. When they opened the trunks of their little sedans I could see that they were jammed with boxes of shells. Introductions were made, translated when necessary, courtesy of Miguel Escobedo. Wing-shooting in Spain is a sport for the illustrious. Among the eight was a duke, a famous international lawyer, a surgeon, a landholder, and three of the best wingshots in Europe. One, I discovered later, was a Frenchman.

We climbed into the back of an open wagon pulled by a tractor and went off across the countryside traversing several narrow dirt roads that threw dust into the air as the sea throws spray. This was vineyard country—*tinto* grapes for the fine red wine—and there were many groves of silver-trunked olive trees and open meadows that flowed ahead of us in the morning breeze like water.

We were surrounded by mountains suspended in the mist of distance, the Guadarramas, the big spine that separated the old Castilian country from the new; to the left, purple now even in brilliant sun, was the camel hump of Gredos; to the right, somewhat smaller and gray, the elephant flank of La Ceballera. The air was spring-water clear and every once in a while someone would shout and point excitedly as a partridge broke across the road and vanished in the grass. As I rode I could feel civilization peel off, even as I had changed my wash-and-wear for khakis and shooting coat that morning.

A distinguished man with a gray toothbrush mustache (the lawyer) filled me in on the conservation side of the shooting.

"This is all leased land," he said. "Mengotti leases it and charges a fee to put on these partridge drives. But it's quite complicated. He needs eight men and Louis full time to patrol, keep off the poachers and control the varmints. Magpies, crows, weasels and lizards kill the partridge young and eat the eggs. All of these are shot on sight. The magpie is the worst. I use three or four cases of shells every year shooting the terrible birds. They peck out the eyes of the young, carry away the eggs, even attack the females on the nests. When you realize that this land, Término Municipal, consists of almost forty thousand acres, that it costs over a million pesetas to lease it, that Mengotti must plant food, till the soil, sometimes irrigate it, and then pay to patrol it full time, you will immediately see, dear sir, that this is much more than just a simple matter of riding out and shooting partridge."

I was impressed. The ride was getting rough now, the wagon bouncing hard every time it hit a hole in the road, throwing us against one another, forcing camaraderie. Everyone was chuckling and laughing; this was a lark; this was sport; this was the way it was done.

"The bruises of pleasure," the Frenchman said poetically and started singing a song about a girl who had five lovers and that didn't seem to be enough. My French is meager but apparently this song was one that was designed to be sung on such a trip for a wagonload of men.

Then we were there. Coming up over the buffalo hump of a rise were the men from the village, hot and sweaty in their corduroys and heavy shirts. How they got there so soon was a mystery. I asked. "Cross-country," said the lawyer. "Short cut," said Mengotti. "Legs of steel," said the duke.

We got down from our dusty wagon, checked our guns, collected our shells and waited for our host to give the word. The eight famed gunners and Señor Mengotti strapped two hairy pouches around their waists, one hanging from each hip—pouches looking like something new and alive in ladies handbags—and filled them with shells. Mengotti and Escobedo then passed out little blue cards about half the size of a playing card, assigning butts. I got seven, which is supposed to be a lucky number—at least with dice men. Then the fight started.

The forty men began pushing and shouting about who was going to be a *secretario* and who was going to be a beater. *Secretarios* were the elite; they sat behind the gunner at the butt and didn't have to walk in the sun; also they got more money because the gunners tipped, sometimes lavishly—especially if they had excellent bags—even though the instructions told them not to do so. Each man got fifty pesetas a day whether he was *secretario* or beater.

Mike Escobedo strode among them speaking sharply, and when the tumult subsided Mengotti tapped each *secretario* on the shoulder. I noted that he selected men who had stood aloof from the bickering.

Louis was still on his horse, holding his curved brass horn in his hand like a badge of office, shouting in his strangely melodious voice: *"Quitar! Viva!"* The beaters followed him; in ten minutes they were out of sight.

"They will be gone hour," Mengotti explained. "Then come back. Louis will sound trumpet and men will walk and make noise and the birds will fly. Have you shot partridge coveys?"

"Coveys?" I said, thinking of the occasional king of the game birds I had managed to bring down.

"Sí, sí," he said. "Yes. They flock."

Flocks of partridge. This was something that I would have to see. Such a sight would unnerve the best gunners of my acquaintances.

My *secretario* turned out to be the dark and serious Julián Morales, from the village. He came over, took my gun, a Browning 20 superposed, and my four boxes of shells, and said something rapidly in Spanish. Mike Escobedo laughed.

"He says your gun looks like a rifle. He has never seen one before, and he also says that you must be a very fine shot because you have only one gun, shoot a gun like a rifle at birds, and only bring four boxes of shells. Everyone else has eight."

"I wasn't told," I said. "I thought four boxes would be plenty."

We then walked single file along a footpath until we reached a region where we were in long, dead shadow beneath the meadows. They hung above us as if suspended by invisible means, and Mengotti, leading, stopped when we got to a place where there was a brushy blind placed on this almost subterranean path. He asked the man who had the number corresponding to the butt to stop. As Julián and I stopped at our butt, I could see that this was going to be different shooting; the birds would blast out above. They would be upon you before you could fire and swing. The angle of shot would be spectacular.

Although I had only the Browning, Julián insisted that he load after every shot. Mike had rehearsed me: *Cargado* meant loaded and *cargar,* to load. I practiced the pronunciations under my breath until I saw Julián looking at me oddly; then I stopped and, pointing at the gun, said, *"Cargar"* and handed it to him. He smiled and said, *"Cargado"* and gave it back. We understood each other; we were in business.

He said then, "Shoot, shoot!" Excitedly I looked; but he smiled again and shook his head, and repeated the words, pointing at the sky, then me, then the gun. I got it. He meant that he would watch for birds and tell me to shoot when the time was right. Maybe the name *secretario* isn't a misnomer after all.

He then went and found two rocks and we sat down while he opened the box of shells and filled one of his pockets. He had a soft goatskin winebag on a cord around his neck, the *bota* that all peasants, farmers and hunters use.

I had been told that there was quite an art involved in preparing the *bota* so the wine tasted as though it came from a grape and not a goat. A new *bota* is filled with a rich wine like muscatel and unused for ten days, while the animal odor passes. Then the muscatel is poured off, the skin filled with the local wine ready for service.

Julián took off the *bota* now, removed the plug, tipped his head back, opened his mouth, then, squeezing the soft bottom of the skin, squirted a long stream of *mora,* the soft white wine of Toledo, into his mouth. It looked easy and certainly sanitary.

He then handed the *bota* to me and I tried it, getting a stream of the precious white stuff on my nose and chin and just a slight swallow into my mouth. He stopped me and slowly demonstrated, obviously with pleasure. On the third try I had it, not perfectly but well enough to get more wine in my mouth than on my face.

He took the *bota* while it still had wine in it and then we sat and waited for the sound of the hunting trumpet. It seemed hours before it came. I didn't suppose that it could be heard from the distant point where the beaters had gathered, but when it came it was sweet and clear and exciting enough to reach the spine. It had an old sound to it, bringing to mind lords of the manor, Spanish nobility, English squires, and the hunt when the world was young.

After the third call sang away, dead in the wind, Julián loaded my Browning and handed it to me. *"Barras,"* he said—I had been told that meant a group or covey of birds—"shoot, shoot, pronto. No aim. Fire, fire. Birds fall, fall."

"We hope," I said. So Julián did speak a little English after all. You never can tell about the Spanish. They keep so many things to themselves. I didn't see the birds until they were overhead, alternating the wing-beat with gliding. My first two shots were wide, behind and low. They weren't coming in coveys. They were coming in twos and threes; I fired fifteen times and downed three birds. No, I was wrong. Now they were coming in coveys. More than coveys, they were arriving in waves.

I could hear the beaters shouting, still seeming far off, and I was trying to shoot partridge the way you do ducks. Never flock-shoot, I was taught; always select your bird. There were so many it wasn't a simple matter. Now there were several long trumpet calls, well spaced; this meant the beaters were getting close and you could only shoot behind. So when the birds zoomed over with that flap-flap, glide-glide routine that would throw any confirmed grouse shooter completely off, I swung around and shot as they went away from me. And did better.

Finally Louis loomed into view on his red stallion, and the beaters came walking behind. Julián collected the birds, doing some shoving with the *secretario* of the shooter nearest me over one bird that I was certain he had bagged. I had shot two boxes of shells; there were eleven birds. I looked at them glumly as Julián came back. *"Bueno, bueno!"* he said.

We all started along the path again; we had walked for about a half-hour when we met Mengotti and then he placed us in shooting butts again. This time we were behind cleverly constructed blinds facing the meadows, living bushes plaited into a perfect screen. When the partridge wave came this time I had the opportunity for lead, swing and follow-through and was rewarded after the trumpet's long calls by a proud smile from Julián.

There was a short conference then, and it was decided that we would lunch. We ate in a grove of olive trees. Our lunch was tortillas, an omelet stuffed with potatoes and ham, and slices of peasant bread fried in olive oil topped with pork tenderloin. Shortly after we sat down, a grim farmer came into the grove with an archaic wooden plow and a mule and did his best to bury us in topsoil. Mike started a reprimand but Mengotti stopped him with the slight regal raising of his left hand.

We got into the tractor wagon again, rode for another hour and had two more beats, then walked for another forty minutes to new territory and had the fifth and final beat. Three times I had heard the gunner next to me shouting, "Cu Cu Cu!" until I finally realized that it meant that a partridge was going from his butt toward mine and to watch out. Then I started the cooing and was promptly rewarded with a gallant wave of a hat after the neighboring gunner got the bird that sailed out of my territory into his.

Once my neighbor (the lawyer) and I shot at the same bird; both immediately conceding it to the other. Julián ran out and got it and showed me that it had been downed with shot from the left; I was shooting from the right. He ran it over to the other butt, and I got a loud *"Gracias"* and a sweep of the hat.

It is the most sporting shooting I have encountered. The partridge are in full flight with the danger of the beaters behind them; they are high, they have a curving, erratic flight, and when they see you in the blind from their vantage point they change direction, making unbelievable right and left banks, often swooping like hawks into wind current and swiftly going high.

My *secretario* looked happy after the last beat and he had quite a sling of painted red feathers over his shoulders, birds leg-tied with cord into sort of a giant, deep coral necklace. As we started walking back we were joined by two of the rural police, the Guardia Civil, Spain's oldest police service, with their flowing cloaks and black cocked patent-leather hats. All birds had to be counted by them and reported to their district chief.

We met in a group then, gunners, *secretarios,* beaters, Louis on his horse, three more Guardia Civil, and the score was totaled. Somehow —because I had a fast and skillful *secretario* who retrieved some birds that weren't legally mine—I stood third in the list of nine shooters with a bag of fifty-eight. Mengotti gave me a fat brace on a beautiful leather carrier that looped around the birds' legs. I would take them to Antonio Fernández at Botín and have in a small *paella.* The rest of the birds were distributed to the guards, the beaters, the *secretarios,* the villagers, the gunners who could use them. Not one was wasted.

Then, following Francisco Mengotti's lead, I got on the back of a shiny-eyed burro and rode along the path past the vineyards and the olive trees to the tractor wagon three miles away. Dusk was beginning to fall.

In dead of winter, the only place in Europe where you can be truly warm, and get the sun for a certain number of hours every day, is the

Canary Islands. The Islands are a Spanish archipelago in the Atlantic Ocean sixty miles west of the African coast, with a total land area of 2,894 square miles. In the winter, a warming southwest wind, the *Levante,* blows from Africa. The Romans heard of the Canaries from Juba, King of Mauretania. His report of an expedition there in 40 B.C. came into the possession of Pliny who gave them the name Canaria because of the number of large, wild dogs that were supposed to roam the Islands. (The only dogs today are those the tourists bring and a few local nondescripts.) Plutarch and Ptolemy called them the Fortunate Islands.

So do I—especially Tenerife, and its small seaport, Puerto de la Cruz, not yet overwhelmed by tourists. Although the shoreline directly before our hotel, the Las Vegas, was rough and rocky, with the sea smashing against it, one hundred yards to the right was a long stretch of black sand where the sea coöperated by meeting it with foaming white. All the beaches on the north of the island are black, ground by the sea from black volcanic lava. On the south are longer, wider, better beaches of the conventional color, which I am told comes from calcareous tufa and volcanic ash carried seaward by the wind. These beaches, El Medano and Los Cristianos, are the equal of any in Europe.

Puerto has a public park surrounded by drooping palms where it is the fashion to sit and watch the people parade while you drink a glass of excellent Spanish brandy that costs under ten cents. You can get pretty well potted for a dollar and it is not an uncommon sight to see a pair of brandy-fumed tourists sitting asleep on a bench under a palm tree, the man usually snoring.

There are quite a number of pretty women in Puerto de la Cruz, most of them French and Belgian, who have come across from the confused Congo where white is the wrong color these days. They run gift shops, work behind hotel desks, are waitresses. One elegant little thing owns Puerto's best restaurant, Petite Paris, a small, clean place with tables in a garden full of flowering bougainvillaea. The Belgian blonde takes the orders, makes the drinks and scoots the waitresses around so that your food arrives hot and your drinks cold. Specialties —both excellent—are slices of tender roast veal covered with fresh peas, and coq au vin. Both the red wine and the chicken are above average.

Our day in the Islas Canarias always began with roosters crowing and goats nickering from behind the houses that lined the street across the little square from the Las Vegas. Far from annoying at six

The little fishing port of Puerto de la Cruz lay peacefully in the constant sun of the Canary Islands, despite the tidal wave of tourists that threatened the world.

o'clock, they were pleasant, rural sounds that somehow made you feel a part of the island. And then when you looked out at the sunlight beginning to move across the square, a small dog appeared there every morning. It was his place, he owned it. He would prance stiff-leggedly around, then sit and yip a couple of times at the squadron of white fantail pigeons that came to get the sun on the roof of the little house nearest the square.

The Indians were out at this time cranking up the awnings over the Ceylon and Kashmir bazaars. Soon the tourists would come to buy leather goods, the gold-painted steel from Toledo, the brass and the ivory from the East. Both bazaars had signs claiming that the proprietors could handle customers in Spanish, German and English.

Then the girls would appear in bikinis for the morning dip before breakfast. The Canary Islands are not warm enough in winter to take to the sea just after the sun comes up. Even mid-morning is rushing things a bit. But these girls were young and blooming and it was the thing to do, so they did it and came shivering back to the hotel, towel-draped and goose-pimply.

When the red flag was hoisted at seaside, signifying that the Atlantic was too rough and dangerous for swimming, the girls got into their bikinis and other briefs and promenaded the beach. But the parade didn't last long and when the sun gets warm they lizarded to the beaches and buried themselves in sand or just spread out and looked at the sea. Peace once more would come to Puerto.

For us Puerto was a relaxing place where we could spend a morning walking the beach, and look out across the sunburned water at the mists of Africa, blue and irregular in a sawed line on the horizon. Tenerife is one of the few sunny islands left where the voyager can afford to spend a long time, a dramatic place dominated by one of the most impressive mountains I have seen—Teide with its cap of snow.

The island was named for the peak: *tener* meaning white snow, and *ife*, high mountains. The twelve-thousand-foot mountain peak can be seen for hundreds of miles and is the highest in Spain. Puffs of smoke come from it occasionally, for it is a live volcanic cone. We hired a car—for little more than a taxi ride in Manhattan—to drive as close as we could get to Mount Teide, planning to climb the rest of the way on foot while passing through one of the most beautiful valleys in the world—Orotava. The valley alone is worth the trip to the Canary Islands, thick with blue jacaranda, flowering bougainvillaea, palms, rosebay, tamarind, and great green banana plantations that flow to the sea.

As you get closer to Teide, the landscape change is abrupt and violent—lava that has stopped flowing, melting, then freezing into strange, surrealistic shapes, some black, some red, some yellow, all twisted and terrible in weirdness of design and giant size. There are volcanic stones that stand like monsters, a monolithic, nightmarish moonscape that you drive through with apprehension for the first stop at a government inn, or *parador*—a spotless place where you take lunch and a drink to put you in an easier frame of mind to watch what happens when a volcano erupts.

But snow-capped Teide puffs harmlessly in the background and her twelve thousand feet are easy to ascend—by car much of the way, then by foot. We discovered in our climbing that a single bird sings on Teide and a single flower clings to its stone. The bird, which resembles a ghost-gray starling, is the *Fringilla tedea,* the "bird of Teide"; the flower is *Viola cheiranthifolia,* "violet of Teide," light blue, growing in clusters. It is said to be the exact color of Teide in the evening as dusk starts to gather in the high places.

You feel the altitude, a dizziness, but the sight below makes you forget it: you can see them all, the green serried banana terraces of Tenerife, Gran Canaria, La Palma, La Gomera, Hierro, Fuerteventura and Lanzarote, with the tiny islets looking like specks of boats sailing away into the distance—Isla de Lobos, Alegranza, Graciosa, Montana Clara, Roque del Este and Roque del Oeste.

A wind comes now, chill and forboding, fluffing snow off the peak, a signal to go down from the high place.

After we had enjoyed much of Tenerife, I decided that I would try to find Osten Klintborn's people who talked with a whistle. I asked the hotel manager.

He grinned and said, "You mean those German boys on the beach?"

Finally, after asking everyone I could find who had spent any time on the island, I went to the little office of the Direccíon General Del Turismo and found two young English girls holding down the front office.

The older one, a redhead, was smoothing out on the desktop a travel poster of a black bull facing a toreador, the man's cat-grace accentuated by the tight pants. She said, "Yes?"

"I've been told that on one of the Canary Islands there are people who talk by whistling. I'd appreciate finding out the name of the island and how to get there."

She smiled weakly, then looked at the other, a trim blonde. "I haven't the faintest, really! Have you now, Madge?"

Madge just stared. "He's kidding us, Flo. It's a Yank-type joke."

After I convinced them I wasn't joking, the smiles went and they became businesslike. They summoned the manager, all smiles and disbelief.

"Hotels, yes, night clubs, fishing even, walks to the top of Teide," he said. "But people who whistle? I just have never been asked. Of course, I could wire our people in Madrid—"

The redhead said, "Perhaps Madge and I could scan some books?" The manager nodded. "Scan, girls. I am as interested as this guest." He asked me to come back in an hour. He would also scan.

They turned out to be excellent scanners, especially the blonde, Madge. She was abeam when I arrived. "I've found it, sir!" she said. "I'll wager no one has ever asked before, except maybe some silly scientists or something. Are you a scientist?"

"Silly, maybe, but not a scientist. Just curious."

"So am I!" Madge said. "Let me know what it's like when you get back, please. I'd like to go see—hear, I mean. People who talk by whistling! Quaint. *Real* quaint."

She had everything written on a sheet of paper. The name of the island: La Gomera. There was no airport there. Transportation would be by boat. It would take at least five hours, depending upon weather and sea. She even made the reservation. We left in two days.

There wasn't much except blue-green water and gulls until we got to La Gomera, a volcanic rock jutting out of the sea, a gray, dismal rock that got green as we came close, and developed a furry hide— trees on the slopes. Through the good graces of the manager of the Direccíon General Del Turismo, and the captain of the ship, we soon had a guide who spoke English. We started walking and learning immediately.

The population of La Gomera is thirty thousand Spanish-speaking people; it is made up of tiny villages and four small towns, with San Sebastián the capital. A single road joins the towns like a beaded necklace flung across the peaks and rocks. Paths, narrow and winding, link the rest of civilization in this precipitous place that is shaped like a tent, most of its land sloping from a 4,500-foot mountain peak to the sea. It is like living on a mountain landslide that has just stopped moving.

In La Gomera, two points five hundred yards apart as the crow flies would take over an hour to walk. With a lack of electricity and telephones, and the hazard of the terrain, communication has always been a problem. But, as Klintborn said, the Gomeros have solved the problem—with a whistle. They actually send messages, talk, tell jokes, forecast the weather, gossip, even make love with their whistled language.

The technique is called *silbo* (*whistle* in Spanish) and is actually a language, not a trilled Morse code or a signal that the hearer must define. I was told that a *silbador* (whistle-talker) can talk easily for a mile, that many make themselves heard for three miles, and that several Gomeros speak by *silbo* for five miles. I believe it: La Gomera's rocks and gorges act as a sounding board, carrying any sound surprising distances.

A Gomero told me that he believed their whistle-language goes back a long way—to the Guanches, an aboriginal race that lived in the Canaries in the fifteenth century. It has disappeared from the rest of the Canary Islands, but is still popular in La Gomera because transportation and communication has not improved here as it has in the other islands.

Antonio, the Gomero who acted as our guide, told us that Gomeros were very important people during the Spanish Civil War.

"They used us as front-line communicators," he said. "Our *silbo* was the best way to pass on secret military messages. Right in front of the enemy. Everything went well until the other side got some *silbadors* who could understand our 'talk.' " He grinned. "Then we had to go back to just being soldiers."

We listened to a comely Gomero woman talking to a man a mile away. His answers were faint, but apparently she had no trouble. As usual, she had the last word. A long, shrill blast, using the second finger of each hand in her mouth. The finger didn't distort or affect the whistle-talk; the tongue formed the words or articulation, as it does in any language.

You would assume that the *silbo* would be difficult to master, but the Gomeros say that if you speak Spanish, their whistle language is easy to master. Gomero children know their own names in *silbo* before they are a year old, and are speaking it fluently by the time they are ten.

A language student who has spent considerable time in La Gomera explained how *silbo* functions. Saying that in speech we use the larynx to generate the voice tone, varying it in duration, pitch and volume, modifying it with the tongue, lips, lower jaw, teeth and palate, he described how we make our consonants, vowels and semivowels. But the whistle is a simple sound, actually activated by two-thirds of the tongue. The lips and forepart of the tongue are inactive, with the back portion moving to vary the pitch, volume and length of sound.

In *silbo,* the key is variation of pitch, while ordinary speech depends upon complicated waves of sound and harmonics. The Gomero dialect is simple, with few unusual vowels and consonant sounds and nothing much in rhythm, intonation or stress.

Some of the *silbadors* I watched used their cupped hands as an amplifier, some stuck one or two fingers in their mouths, but hands, fingers and lips were motionless as they "talked." What they did was stick the tip of their tongue against the teeth, whistle and simultaneously articulate words as if they were actually speaking. A good *silbador* can whistle just about everything he can speak in the Spanish language.

As in ordinary language, each Gomero can be identified by his *silbo* speech. They never use it at close quarters, but I heard two women talking at a distance of three city blocks in the town of San Sebastián. My grinning guide said that they were gossiping about another neighbor.

"She must be away," he said, "or they couldn't *silbo* for the whole town to hear."

I can recommend a visit to La Gomera for the unusual experience of standing and listening while the Gomeros talk to one another across the miles of their rough, barren island. If you listen carefully you can even detect the names in the windsound—"Julio," "Maria" —and come to know the difference between man and woman *silbo* sounds that racket across the rocks.

We even eavesdropped on a pair of lovers sweet-talking by *silbo*. We couldn't understand a word, but Antonio did. He grinned, then shook his head.

"They should be careful, those two," he said. "Children can be listening!"

He cupped his hands and blew a loud blast that sounded like a train arriving twenty minutes late at Grand Central Terminal. The love-talk stopped immediately.

"That's the trouble with *silbo*," he said. "It is talk that travels. We have few secrets on La Gomera."

After our whistle-stop island we went to Las Palmas on Grand Canary to await the Madrid plane. We were due in Austria to explore the castles, climb the mountains and plan a chamois hunt. The short flight brought us back to the Palace in time for dinner—which in Spain means ten o'clock. Klintborn and Poveda had booked us on a flight that would put us in Vienna late the day of departure.

CHAPTER SEVEN

AUSTRIA AND SCOTLAND

A friend of mine has a travel theory, basing a person's importance upon the amount of fruit awaiting him in his hotel room. A much-traveled fellow, he finds that four oranges and an apple signify that you are an above average guest, two apples and six oranges that your visit is highly respected by the house, and a four-apple, four-orange, vase-of-flowers man is definitely a very important person.

If there is anything to this, our arrival at the Hotel Bristol in Vienna was an auspicious one: a vase and a bowl of flowers, along with a large basket of mixed fruit, awaited us in our room. I counted the oranges and apples, six of each. Possibly the management had made a mistake? But no, cards attested that the vase of flowers was a welcome from the Austrian State Tourist Department; the fruit and the bowl of flowers from the Hotel Bristol.

Unfortunately we weren't to enjoy this exceptional hotel's hospitality for long—at least until we returned—for the next day we were to leave by train for Schloss Rabenstein at Frohnleiten. We had been invited to spend some time in this famous old Austrian castle, and to be guests at an evening of chamber music, a *Serenade* attended by Austrian royalty and a few of their friends. It was an old-world touch that we were anxious to experience—neighbors getting together to enjoy talk and fine music. Coming from a television society of silent starers, it promised to be a pleasant and rare evening.

The trick in Austrian train travel (or anywhere) is to get hold of a husky and agile *traeger,* or porter, who can carry your bags, fight his way through the milling crowd and find your seat. We found our man, a blocky fellow who moved like a bulldozer, locating our seat shortly before the engine snorted, belched a stream of smoke and clanged out of Vienna's South Station. The train was the famous Wien-Venezia Express, not as well known as Europe's Blue Train or the Orient Express, but respected for its hospitality, its speed and its gaiety. It was full of happy young Italians on the way home and some not so gay Austrians heading for their home towns and villages along the line. On our ride, lasting more than three hours, we passed through lovely, misted vineyard country to Bruck an der Mur where we found a car from Schloss Rabenstein awaiting us.

The castle hulked up out of the night atop a cliff like a monster cat ready to spring. We couldn't see much of it in the darkness of night. We went up a steep, winding road to its gates where the owners, Sigurt and Ruth Reininghaus, waited. Both were middle-aged and aristocratic in manner as only a well-born Austrian can be. I couldn't help contrasting their warm greeting with our arrival at the chateau in France. Over coffee, with an October wind gusting outside, Sigurt Reininghaus told us that his castle is one of the oldest in Styria.

The earliest record of its existence dates from 1189, when in the nearby monastery of Rein, a knight of Rabenstein signed a marriage contract as a witness. History states that they were a mighty family; free of all duties and taxes, they held the post of honor as cupbearers of the Duke of Styria who was in residence at the Burg in Graz. When the Rabenstein family died out in the fifteenth century, Rabenstein Castle and its land became the possession of Emperor Frederic III and his son and successor, Maximilian the Great, who discovered that the castle had been built on the ruins of an old Roman fortress.

In the eighteenth century Rabenstein became private property; the owner, Count Dietrichstein, was a tutor of Napoleon's son, the Duke of Reichstatt of Vienna. But he had little interest in Rabenstein and sold it to the emperor's governor of Schloss Laxenburg, Louis von Montoyer.

On a sunny spring day in 1887, two young gentlemen on horseback rode along the road past the castle. Looking up at Rabenstein, they saw a cherry tree in full bloom on the hanging terrace. To one of the men, Fritz Reininghaus, it looked like a dream of success and splendor. He wanted to buy it immediately. An old man cutting grass by the roadside told him it was for sale; Montoyer had accompanied the Emperor Maximilian to Mexico and never returned to the castle.

So Rabenstein Castle became the Reininghaus family seat. The roofs were repaired, plumbing installed. After World War II, the great-grandson, Sigurt Reininghaus, who had held the castle at risk of his life against the Nazis, then the Russians, finally managed to get electricity into the famous old place.

I recommend as an experience worth having, a stay in a castle that still breathes history. You can almost hear the knights clanking by in their armor. That first night we were shown to a bedroom larger than most houses being built in America today. The bed itself was a carved, canopied monster straight out of medieval times. Upheld by fine amber wood, the right front pillar was Adam, the left Eve; cherub heads peeked out all along the wooden canopied edge. On the wall before the bed hung a huge painting of Lorelei brooding over her lute, with a sunset sea in the background. A bowl of wild daisies in a green-and-white stone bowl sat on a desk as large as a billiard table.

As we climbed into bed we could hear the sound of a river. It had become a starlit night, so I went to the window. The moon shone on the water below and the whole valley stretched away in the distance, its houses marked by firefly lights. It was so still that you could hear the water going over the rocks in the river bed.

In the morning we found that Rabenstein Castle hangs like an eagle's nest from a cliff, looking down on an ancient Roman road that winds along the Mur River for two miles into the village of Frohnleiten. From the rock on which the castle is built, to the south, small garden terraces reach the lower level. The courtyard was full of shade trees and a fountain with its never-ending curl of water. Wherever you looked from the high castle you saw the vast plain alive with October color.

The second night the Reininghauses hung the "dream tablet" in our room, a framed slate that guests used to chalk their dreams on when they awoke in the morning. In the old days, we were told, it was great sport at breakfast to listen to the guests read from their dream tablets over coffee. But we weren't able to add to the breakfast-table entertainment. Our great bed was so soft, the music of the River Mur so lulling, that we slept the sleep of the innocent, neither of us having a dream all the time we were in that ancient old pile on the mountain.

In the few days we were there we walked the countryside, seeing the old village of Adriach, the famous caves at Lurgotte, the high village of Schockel where you can stand and see Hungary and Yugoslavia in the distance. We walked to the ancient monastery at Stift Rein that has been converted into a wine tavern where you can sit and drink the local wines for so little that it is embarrassing.

For those seeking something "different" in their travels, a place like Rabenstein, well away from the tourist stream, could be the answer; a comfortable and relaxing way to soak up the pleasures of the past—and present. It is also inexpensive, less than ten dollars a day for a beautiful room, the price including breakfast and dinner. (On this subject, Germany and Austria have impressive lists of castles that offer all kinds of diversions—hunting, fishing, boating, swimming, skin-diving, mountain climbing. Less than half the price of the French chateaux, a stay at an Austrian or German castle is one of the real travel bargains in Europe.)

I wasn't able to observe what kind of wine Herr Reininghaus poured, for gentleman that he was, he always held the label in the proper manner toward him, but he did tell us what went into one delicious dish—*Schinkenfleckerl:* homemade noodles broken and cooked with ham, eggs and cheese. When I asked a question he called his cook, Reginia. A jolly woman dressed in a peasant dirndl, she didn't speak English but it was obvious that she was delighted when we asked about food. She made an outstanding *Powidltascherl,* pastry with potato flour, yolk of egg and semolina; stuffed it with prunes, topped with cinnamon and brown sugar. It came from her oven brown and crisp and was a wonderful way to begin or end a day.

Sigurt Reininghaus proved to be an interesting conversationalist. He was an architect with a profound interest in everything. Once, curious about the types of wood that grew in Austria and Europe, he had little boxes made from every specimen of tree, and then hand-polished them himself to study the differences in luster, grain and appearance. He showed us the boxes. They were all over the castle. A determined man.

His wife told us that he needed all of that determination during and after World War II. The Nazis, the Russians, even the English wanted Schloss Rabenstein as their headquarters. They used many ruses and approaches trying to get it, banging on the doors at all hours, demanding an inspection at three in the morning, claiming their right as conquerors to sample Rabenstein's food and wine.

"But I had a secret weapon," Herr Reininghaus said. "When things got really bad I showed them proof that I was a Swiss citizen. I told them that if they invaded my property, which was in fact a little piece of Switzerland, they would be violating Swiss neutrality and I would see to it that this became an international incident. I am sure this saved both me and the castle from destruction. Especially from the Russians. Usually anything they couldn't take over or use they destroyed."

He said that the Russian soldiers were so ignorant that they didn't know that wrist watches should be wound. They took watches from everyone, wearing as many as a dozen on both wrists and arms. When these stopped running they took them off and threw them away. He told of one Russian soldier who saw a small boy riding a bicycle with no hands. When the Russian tried it he fell. He thought that the boy was withholding from him some mysterious mechanical function of the bicycle, so he beat him.

The climax of our stay at Rabenstein was the evening of music, the *Serenade* held in the Knight's Hall. When the neighbors began arriving and were introduced, it sounded like the roll call of Austrian royalty: The Prinzessin Theresia Maria von and zu Liechtenstein-Oetingen; Prinzessin von und zu Liechtenstein-Thurn und Taxis, Grafin (Countess) Ilona Hoyos-Seilern-Aspang and friend Elisabeth de Noblet; Grafin Mariella Spiegelfeld-Goes; Grafin Lily von Herberstein; Alix Baronin von Conrad-Eybesfeld-Lembruck, and commoners Franz Gras Spiegelfel, Rudolf von Duckelmann-Thun—and us.

We walked into the Knight's Hall, a room that I doubt has changed in centuries. Fourteen suits of polished armor stood among swords, spears, maces and other ancient cutting weapons. The orchestra, composed of two boys and two girls in their teens and wholesomely handsome, sat on a raised dais at the far end. Hanging in the center of the room, a huge silver candelabra with eighteen tall white candles swayed in the October breeze coming off the hills through an open window. The candles threw licks of light on the polished armor and the great shields with their clusters of protective points. Looking ghostly, skeletal, an armored horse's mask hung to the right of the orchestra, four feet from the face of the pretty blond cellist. A painting of the famous Queen Maria Theresa hung to the left. Giant stone urns stood in each far corner, and hanging from a closed window was the coat of arms of Rabenstein—a single black raven cut from glass, wings outstretched, rampant on a yellow background.

Two violins playing first and second parts, a viola and a violoncello were the instruments. The sound was sweet and haunting in this ancient room high on a cliff. First came Joseph Haydn's *Serenadenquartett* (Op. 3, No. 5), which the youngsters handled like old pros. Then an intermission when we crowded around them, congratulating and talking and drinking coffee and eating flaky pastries. Next followed Franz Schubert's *Quartett in Es-Dur* (Op. 125, No. 1).

When this music from another age ended, you could hear the Mur River sighing past in the night. Television, rock-'n'-roll, twist and slop were a long way from us tonight. If modernity has caught you up in its rasp and its roar and its senseless sounds, try stealing away to Rabenstein and another century for a few days.

We were back in Vienna the following day. From our room in the Bristol—one of the best hotels in Europe—we looked out at the man on the horse in his eternal gallop atop the State Opera House. The black humped roof was slick with rain. (We would be inside that night attending Bohemian composer Smetana's *The Bartered Bride,* an opera in three acts that had a confused lover running around in a bearskin, a marriage broker, and several farmers and their sons and daughter singing their heads off.)

Now the streets below were glistening. The old women wearing caps and bright yellow canvas jackets, with *Kurier* written across the back, sold newspapers while weaving in and out of the lines of people moving in a slow, window-inspecting parade along Kärntnerstrasse, the famed shopping avenue.

Vienna is a baroque city. All her palaces and beautiful old buildings were created by famous architects of that period; the entire city is a sort of museum in which you can wander for days exploring narrow cobblestone streets and discovering new scenes. Covering an area of fifty-four square miles, with a circumference of eighty-seven miles, it has a population of 1,700,000. Yet, despite an urbanized air, it is one of the few cities in Europe that has managed to preserve its country scenery. The Vienna Woods and vineyards surround the city. With an area of 11,110 built-up acres, 28,440 acres of tilled fields, 8,-340 acres of meadows, 18,285 acres of gardens, 1,640 acres of vineyards, and 18,680 acres of woodlands, the result is one of the most scenic large cities in the world. Vienna has an official "green belt" policy that keeps its streets lined with lovely shade trees; everywhere you turn are quiet, peaceful gardens—there are 15 million square yards of public parks in the city.

I have heard Vienna colorfully described by many who love her. An old friend who was born there still uses the lines of a song when she thinks of Vienna: *"Wien, Wien, nur Du allein, wirst stets die Stadt meiner Träume sein!"* Vienna, Vienna, you alone are the city of my dreams!

Vienna is friendlier than Paris; its people are gay, well-dressed; the blood of German, Hungarian, Czechoslovakian, Yugoslav, Bulgarian and Italian runs in the veins of many an Austrian who believes that Vienna is the true capital of the world. The mixture is a race of creative, music-loving, food-respecting, warm-hearted people. No one visits Vienna and leaves untouched. Its people, its wine, its women or its song get to you.

In the winter, an average of 130 balls and two thousand *redoutes* (dances) are listed in the newspapers. During the dark months the entire city is caught in the swirl of the waltz and the music of Strauss, Lehar, Schubert, Haydn, Mozart and Beethoven. More great composers lived and worked in Vienna than any other city, many writing of her charms. Music is everywhere; if it isn't being played in your restaurant or hotel, it is being honored in the form of monuments, statues or plaques.

We saw another side of the Viennese the day after we arrived. It was All Soul's Day, and the city was in an all-out rush to respect its dead.

Trucks wheeled by banked with flowers; cars with passengers hanging wreaths out of the windows; streetcars with people on the back, clinging to the sides with their giant bouquets. The streetcars moved through the streets like great floral floats in a parade, which in fact it was, a parade honoring the dead of Vienna. We drove by a cemetery where flowers laid beside the graves stretched out in acres of color like one vast garden, an impressive testimony to the respect held for the dearly departed. Of course, this being Vienna, food stands were set up at various strategic points around the cemetery where the Viennese stopped, coming and going, to have a wiener, a cup of coffee or a glass of Gösser beer, one of the finest brews in the world.

Home of *Wiener Schnitzel, Apfelstrudel* and *Sachertorte*—that famous chocolate cake with a jealously guarded secret, over which a court battle was fought—Vienna's food is as classic as its music. The food, the coffeehouses and the wine, drunk in a suburb of Vienna, were taken by us in that order.

They say that the spirit of Vienna known as *Gemütlichkeit* is an untranslatable compound of coziness. I disagree. It is clearly translated into the *Gabelfrühstück,* or second breakfast, when the entire city stops for its *Guglhupf,* cake and coffee with whipped cream; and again during the afternoon pause, *Jause,* when all sorts of things are eaten, like a hot frankfurter and a piece of warm homemade bread dipped into a mixture of grated horseradish and mustard made in the house, chased down with a small glass of white wine, or again, one of the many varieties of coffee and cake, or perhaps a bowl of *Gulaschsuppe,* a thin Hungarian goulash.

Gemütlichkeit could be translated into an unexpected stop we took one night on our way to Krems. As we neared Fels village we saw a house standing alone along the road, its lights sending a warm yellow glow through the dark.

"That gives a nice feeling," I said to our driver. Without a word he pulled up to the house, went to the door and knocked. A pleasant, plumpish blond woman came to the door. The conversation was German with many "ya's" with the result that we went into the house, then to a cellar where a man was taking wine from great barrels. This was the family of Wagner, Maria, Anton and daughter Adele, who showed us what Austrian hospitality is. A vintner in the process of vatting and revatting wine, Anton invited us to sample what he had: *Most,* the fresh grape wine that when properly aged would be bottled as Riesling; then a glass of *muskat ottomel,* a smooth white wine, and finally, to send us on the road, a full water glass of *Sturm,* a five-day-old wine that was so powerful it made itself felt all the way to the heels.

Our driver didn't know the Wagners, but was sure, Austrians being what they are, that they wouldn't mind if strangers, foreigners, *die Fremden,* stopped, said hello and sampled their wine. I wonder in how many countries this would be possible?

Vienna has five thousand restaurants. You would have to live there for at least a year to be able to sample the best of them. But with the help of Professor Walter Minarz, Secretary General of the tourist department, we were able to concentrate on the best. Also, we have a friend who was born there. A talented artist and writer, she goes back every year.

"Go to both the Hotels Bristol and Sacher," she said. "And be sure you visit the restaurants Griechen Beisel, Goldene Lamm, and Cobenzl where you can dine and get the whole view of Vienna. And go to Demel on Kohlmarkt at noon. Take your lunch there. Cold. You will never forget it." We did that the first day. She was right.

As you enter Demel's, the front room is sectioned with dark marble and wooden shelves full of pastry of every size and shape; the remainder of the rooms are Biedermeier, banked with elegant mirrors; the floors are tile; the tables small, square and marble, the chairs wooden, straight and uncomfortable. The waitresses are all at least middle-aged, wearing black dresses, stockings, high-buttoned shoes; they have all been at Demel's for years and they grump around as if they owned the place and couldn't care less about whether you liked their slow service and indifference. The front room, where people sit as if they were living there, is full of cakes and pastries of every description: *Kastanienschaumbaisers,* stuffed with chestnut meringue and whipped cream; warm plum dumplings, *Zwetschkenknödl.*

In the front room also is the cold buffet, with dishes of everything from crisp, cold squab to tiny brown roast chickens *Butterteighendl,* actually pastry shells stuffed with chicken paté. There is an astonishing array of bite-size sandwiches, asparagus, crayfish, caviar, brioches with surprises within: ham, chicken, goose, duckling, foie gras, wafers of venison, slivers of game of all kinds.

Sacher's, a delightful red velvet-and-gilt holdover from the good old days and supposed to be in competition with Demel's (a ridiculous assumption), specializes in its famous *Sachertorte,* a many-layered—and rather dry—chocolate cake; *mornay,* fish baked with truffles, cheese and mushrooms and served in a pastry shell; and veal *Florentine,* fillets cooked with cream and spinach—which is better in Italy—and boiled beef, a Viennese stand-by, which its devotees claim is the best in the world. It isn't. Horcher's in Madrid is better, and so is the Hotel Bristol's, which is served with a creation of the house, applesauce mixed with fresh horseradish, *Apfelkrem.*

The good professor took us to the restaurant Zur Linde in the Rotenturmstrasse, a five-hundred-year-old landmark and the oldest inn in Austria. In this place of dark beams, oaken tables, immaculate linen and service, we tried some specialties. We started with a soup of fish roe, *Fischbeuschel,* and I followed with *Ochsenmaulsalad,* which turned out to be boiled cow's mouth served with vinegar and onions; Mary Lou had *Kalbsstelze,* a calf's shin, while the professor had *Hoppelpoppel,* a fluffy omelet with crisp chips of bacon and peas. We had asked to sample the typical and perhaps esoteric Viennese specialties—the less unusual, game, steaks, roast beef, fried, boiled and roast chicken (none better in the world) are available in most restaurants of quality. We had roast pheasant with the professor at what he called his neighborhood place, the Weissen Schwan—the White Swan—that was the best I have ever had, and I have eaten a lot of pheasants.

At Csardasfürstin the Hungarians are represented, complete with gypsy orchestra. *Badacsonier,* a Hungarian wine that makes you sit up and take notice, and *Cevapcici,* mutton meat balls broiled over wood embers on a skewer and served with diced raw onions and pickle, is another specialty. Visiting Am Franziskanerplatz and Troishussaren we tried the national dish, *Schnitzel,* in four versions: *Wiener,* breaded; *rahm,* with cream; *natur,* sautéed in butter; *paprika,* with heavy cream and paprika.

Sampling the *Wiener Küche,* the varied menus contributed by the nationalities that make up Austria, is an adventure not to be missed, but one that can occupy considerable time. I doubt if there is another city that has such a variety of good restaurants to offer the traveler. It is also typical of Vienna that coffee should contribute to the beauty of the city, for nowhere else is there more variety served and quaffed in such elegance and comfort as in the *Wiener Kaffeehaus.*

These coffee houses were the places we drank *Kapuziner* and talked, after walking Vienna's cobblestones, or after returning time after time to the Spanish Riding School to watch the famous Lipizzaner stallions perform in an elegant, chandeliered arena where Beethoven once conducted. There we sat in the galleries, looking down upon the adult white horses and the young dappled grays as they went through their amazingly intricate routines; watching the erect young riders doff their hats toward the end of the hall where the Hapsburgs formerly sat in their royal box. Everything from horses to hecatombs are discussed over coffee in Vienna.

I am told that there are thirty different ways of serving coffee and that it is rude to sit down and just order coffee. You must name your favorite. The Viennese consider coffee houses their *Stammcafé,* or clubs. The houses are usually well-appointed with paneled walls and rugs, having an air of serenity. The Viennese sit there all morning or afternoon, reading, writing, sometimes talking or playing cards, often drinking only one small twenty-cent cup of coffee. This is the etiquette of the coffee house; it is expected. We saw teen-agers studying their lessons in one coffee house, not even drinking coffee, just cold water that was obligingly brought by the waiter. It is an old, quiet way of life, still respected.

But there is nothing quiet about another way of life in the Austrian capital. Eight hundred years old and perhaps the most beloved custom of the Viennese, it is called *Heuriger,* which means "new wine." It originated when the small vintner would make a few barrels of wine every year and sell it when it was weeks, or sometimes just days, old. He would fasten a green branch of pine or fir over his doorway to signify that he was ready to sell his wine to friends and neighbors. This is called *Ausgesteckt.* He would sell only his own wine, and his customers brought their own bread and sausage. Often the farmer would make music with an accordion or zither and the *Heurige* would become a merry or a sad affair, depending upon how well they could hold the wine.

Today this custom has developed into the *Nobel Heuriger* and a big business wherever the *Heuriger* houses are actual restaurants with orchestras, remain open all year, and serve wines from all of Austria. In Grinzing we went to Poldi Kurtz at 15 Cobenzlgasse, a charming old place with exposed dark beams and plank tables. There we saw the clear white wine being served in glass pitchers, in huge glass steins, in mugs, some of it being dispensed from a carafe suspended from a wrought iron frame on the tables.

At a *Heuriger,* the new wine comes in such large glasses and goes down so easily that you wonder what all the fuss is about. Then when you've had your third glass and the waiter raises his eyebrows and brings you a platter of fried chicken, some rye bread and a dish of giant radishes, you realize that your words are slurring as you thank him. After another *Viertel* (half-pint) you suddenly find it hard to focus; chicken never tasted better, you raise your voice in song. They tell me that it has become a Viennese fad now to try to visit as many *Heurige* in one night as you can. We found one plenty.

Many of us remember Graham Greene's famous novel *The Third Man,* with the villain (played by Orson Welles in the movie) selling fake penicillin in the confused postwar atmosphere of Vienna. The intrigue of that story does live in Vienna and Austria, and you can almost hear the zither theme of the movie as you walk the city's twisting old streets or travel to the outcountry. We went to Burgenland (the land of castles), and visited Rust, a few miles from Hungary, to see an entire street of storks sitting on chimneys. Then we sat ourselves down in a huge barn of a restaurant, the Sifkovitz, whose walls were hung with sheaves of wheat and ears of corn. From the terrace of the restaurant we could see the watchtowers, the barbed wire and the guards armed with Tommy guns patrolling Hungary.

Vienna is only fifty miles from this armed border, and despite their gaiety, the Viennese are acutely aware of the iron curtain that has clanged down so uncomfortably close. While we were there, the car of a young Czech who had escaped his country and was studying medicine in Vienna was found abandoned near the border. There was blood and other signs of violent struggle. Vienna police searched his apartment and found evidence that the "student" had been working as a double agent. The week we were there the papers were also full of the disappearance of two Italian scientists who had made an important new breakthrough in physics. Apparently they vanished while making the trip from Trieste to Vienna.

Despite such intrigue, the Austrians are learning to get along with the Communist East, to live as a line from one of their operettas, *Die Fledermaus,* suggests: "Happy is he who forgets what cannot be changed any more."

.   .   .

A few miles from the ancient city of Salzburg, Schloss Fuschl—or to be more accurate, Jagdschloss Fuschl, which means hunting castle —lies beside a lake, rising several hundred feet to overlook the village of Fuschl. The conspicuous feature is an old tower where the archbishops used to store salt; the entire castle is covered with beige stucco crawling with red ivy. The ancient doorways are pored stone hung with copper doors. To the left, facing the castle, is the hunting lodge, a place with low, sweeping overhang roof, exposed timbers and whitewash.

If Schloss Rabenstein was an experience in the splendor of the past, Schloss Fuschl was an adventure in the luxury of today as well. *Luster Weiberls,* chandeliers of curved stag antlers with a hand-carved wooden nude lady surrounded by candles, hung from the ceilings of several rooms; modern and period furniture were cunningly scattered; walls that weren't natural old stone were painted oyster white; new fireplaces of warm brown marble had replaced the old; antlers of giant royal stags hung on the walls in several places; the circle bar was faced with thick brown cowhide; stone pillars ran to the ceiling in the bar room; leather sofas, and chairs faced in bright satin, velvet and linen, were placed in a well-spaced circle before the fireplace; a fine polished Biedermeier writing table flanked the other side of the room, centered with a fat, yellow, thigh-thick candle in a tall brass holder. Gold-framed oil paintings of elegant gentlemen of the past hung everywhere.

This was formerly the hunting castle of the Archbishops of Salzburg, who ruled the province for centuries until it became part of the Austro-Hungarian Empire after Napoleon. It is considered one of the most beautiful castles in Austria, located in the lovely lake district, Salzkammergut, and built on a small peninsula that extends into Lake Fuschl. The owners, Mr. and Mrs. Carl Adolph Vogel from Munich (Vogel's father is reputed to be the salt king of Europe), have spared no expense in modernizing the castle. There is a wine chamber, a grill that excels in à la carte or the special demands of diners, an international bar, a dining hall with muraled walls, and a hunting salon. In this room intimate candlelight dinners are held during the Salzburg music festival of symphonies, chamber music, Mozart operas and folk music, held in August, when it is difficult to find space for anything intimate. There is an open fireplace in the Great Hall, and best of all, a terrace with its view of the lake and Zwoelferhorn Mountain, a green giant in the misty background.

Herr Vogel has been lucky in many ways. His wife, a former Ger-

Carl Adolph Vogel stood at the entrance of his hunting castle, Jagd-schloss Fuschl, a few miles from Salzburg.

man actress, is lovely, and just having her around the place is a joy to the guests. Adolph Vogel, a blond, ruddy, blue-eyed man with much vigor, exuded well-being and good nature. He wears beautifully cut flannel trousers and handsome embroidered *Steireranzug* and *Tiroler Jacke,* short loden jackets with stagbone buttons that are customarily worn with *Lederhosen,* the famous leather shorts. He changes the jackets several times a day; the variety of shades of green that his tailor has discovered is amazing. Besides a dressy, peacock air, the pair of Vogels give a warm, relaxed feeling to the place. In addition, Herr Vogel is a hunter, which makes owning a hunting castle a thing that comes naturally to such a vital person.

Shortly after we arrived he told us a little about his Schloss, which he bought in 1958. Going back to anno Domini 476, he recited the history of the old place with pride. Then, suddenly, it got more current and more interesting.

"Then in 1940," he said, "the Nazi Foreign Minister, Joachim von Ribbentrop, became master of Schloss Fuschl. He always was a man who knew and liked luxury, even from his champagne-salesman days. He fell in love with this place and used it for state functions, bringing Mussolini and Ciano, also the Spanish and the Japanese to talk about the Anti-Comintern Pact. Then he built the bunker. All the Nazi elite built bunkers, but von Ribbentrop had one of the best ones constructed here. My architect from Munich is here this week end; perhaps you'd like him to show you through the bunker a little later. He has made it his business to know much of Fuschl. He can also tell you about the gold."

"Gold?"

"Yes, there is a treasure here somewhere. But let Schweiger tell you of that. I'd like to talk a little about your hunting day after tomorrow. The *Gemse*—"

He went on to say that he had leased three thousand mountain acres where his guests could hunt, but that although many expert hunters had been coming from Vienna and Munich, so far the *Gemse* had outwitted every one of them—including him.

"I have been out on the mountains a dozen times within the last week," he said, "but those little devils with the horns have been too good for me. I'd like one taken to break this bad luck we are having."

"But we don't really want to shoot one," Mary Lou said. "We're more interested in how it is done. The climbing. Watching the mountain goats."

He smiled. "They aren't goats. They are antelope. Perhaps the most agile in the world. And don't worry about shooting one. Most people just get worn out climbing mountains after them; some have been killed going after our *Gemse*." Then he made an appeal. "But please, if you get the opportunity, take just one *Gemse* for us here at the Schloss. It will break this spell of bad luck. Besides, it is a high honor in Austria to wear the brush of a *Gemse* on your hat."

"Is that the little shaving-brush kind of thing?" my wife asked.

"Yes. The tourists do buy them and wear them. But most Austrians worth the name only wear that on their *Ausseer Hut* if they have been successful in bagging a *Gemse*. It is not an easy sport. You can be proud to say that you have climbed the mountains after one of our antelope. Even if you do not get one. But I hope you will. It will be good for us here at the Schloss."

What could we do after this involved appeal? We promised Carl Adolph Vogel that if we got the chance we would take one *Gemse.* Just one.

He laughed at that. "You will find that getting 'just one,' as you say, is more of a task than can be imagined."

The plan next morning was to walk around Lake Fuschl, a ten-mile hike, just to limber up our legs for the mountain climb the following day, then go through the bunker built by von Ribbentrop.

Our room was not as large as the one at Rabenstein but more up-to-date, with bath and shower, and a calming view of the lake. It was room No. 5, for those who may be interested; the price, including meals, under fifteen dollars for two. The food was what they call "international," which means if it is good that it can include anything from a fine French soufflé to an American-style porterhouse. Here everything was superb. The first night we finished with a discovery: *Mondseer* cheese, a creamier Austrian version of Bel Paese.

During the walk around the lake we stopped to watch a woman working in a garden behind her farm, a patch of land near a strip of woodland. Fifty feet from her were two deer, ears up, tails switching, alertly watching us, strangers walking along the lake. They ignored the woman with the hoe so close to them.

The Munich architect, Professor Schweiger, was waiting for us at the castle. He looked like a professor, with shaggy head of fine gray hair, piercing gray eyes behind steel-rim glasses, tweed jacket, baggy knickers and a knobby walking stick.

"I find this bunker very interesting," he said as we walked away from the Schloss. "Herr Vogel claims that I am using my knowledge as an architect to try to find the gold in bunker." His eyes twinkled. "I doubt that it is there. The people from the village have gone over it like ants."

"Mr. Vogel mentioned the gold," I said. "Is there really gold hidden here?"

Before we got to the bunker, a quarter of a mile from the Schloss, he told us the story. It seemed that the Nazi elite, when they saw the end was coming, hid their fortunes—mostly stolen, including art treasures, rare stamps, gold bars—in this Austrian *Alpenfestung,* where they were preparing to make a last stand. Boxes of treasure sunken in Lake Toplitz were found in late 1960, mostly fake bank notes but so perfectly counterfeited that even the experts had difficulty spotting them. Ernst Kaltenbrunner, Himmler's Gestapo chief, confessed before he was executed at Nürnberg that his personal "operational" fund of over four million dollars in gold and various international currencies was hidden in this region of the Alps.

"Students of the Nazis know that one of the most avid 'collectors' of all was Joachim von Ribbentrop," the professor said. "He took everything he could lay his hands on, paintings, church chalices, gold in any form, fillings from teeth, anything. Servants who were here when he took over the Schloss claim that he brought great treasures with him. It is a fact that the ten million dollars in gold and jewels that Ribbentrop was known to have is still undiscovered. This was his home. He built the perfect bunker here and prepared to dig in, escape the bombings and somehow make off with his stolen fortune. As you know, he didn't make it."

The professor was silent now, slashing his walking stick at blades of grass. "Von Ribbentrop's former valet lives in Fuschl, just a few miles from here. Both of his hands and feet have been broken. He is an old man now. They say that he never talks. A bodyguard of von Ribbentrop, an SS trooper, lives near Salzburg in affluence. He doesn't work. He talks much about how he was hypnotized, how he is a good German now. He drives expensive cars, has a big house, travels a great deal."

Just before we entered the cave-mouth of the bunker, he said, "There is no doubt that ten million dollars is hidden here somewhere. Maybe in the castle, in the lake, the mountains, here?"

The bunker was dank and cavernous. Shortly after the Nazis' defeat, the people from Fuschl removed all the brick facing that had masked the natural rock from which the bunker had been carved. Three hundred Germans worked over a year, spending ten million marks, to burrow this armored hole in the hill. It runs five hundred yards straight back into the hillside, flanging four hundred yards to the right and one hundred to the left. There are thirty rooms in the underground fortress, some with bath.

It once was an elegant hole in the ground. Now it is a damp gray burrow, with water dripping and chalky lime deposits gleaming wetly on the floor. The professor moved slowly ahead of us with a flashlight as we walked to the end of the bunker, then explored its channels. There was a musty smell, and a huge gray rat scurried ahead of us as we made our way out. It was a relief to stand in the sunshine again.

"Fearful, isn't it?" said the professor. "I think most people are

actually afraid of the area. Perhaps that is why there isn't more treas-
ure-hunting in the place. I admire the construction. It is a beautiful
job of excavation."

Back at the castle we learned that we were to leave for the *Gemse*
hunt before dawn the next morning. Herr Vogel's rifles were in our
room. The head waiter asked us if we wanted an early dinner, a
gentle hint that we accepted.

It was dark when we left in the morning and climbed into a blunt-
nosed German vehicle that the D.K.S. Auto Union has copied from
our jeep.

"I have driven many guests to meet the *Jäger* this year," the driver
said, "but no one has returned with a *Gemse*. It is bad luck for the
Schloss. It's supposed to be a hunting castle."

Dawn was beginning to make brushstrokes of color as we pulled
up to a little house at the end of a long valley. Two men and a
dachshund were standing beside it. The driver made the introductions.

"Mr. and Mrs. Scott, these are the hunters, the *Jäger*. This is the
senior guide, Herr Leonhard Radauer—" A short, slender man removed his hat to nod and reveal gray hair. He had a lean, tan face
and sparkling blue eyes. "And the junior guide, Herr Herman
Oberascher." He was a husky youth; he ducked his head and smiled.

Then the driver said, "I will leave you now and will be here at
dusk to drive you again to the castle. Good luck!" And the D.K.S.
went back along the valley road.

As we stood watching, I made conversation. "Do you use dogs
hunting the *Gemse?*"

The older guide laughed. "No, this is Rusty, my friend. He goes
everywhere with me."

"Ya," said the younger man without enthusiasm.

We went into the hut and Herr Radauer took a bottle from the
shelf and poured us each a drink of *Slivowitz,* a fiery white brandy
brewed from prunes.

"Just one," he said. "We call it *Zielwasser* and say that one before
the hunt will improve the aim."

It certainly improved the metabolism. I hadn't felt much like
climbing mountains, but now I stepped along with vigor as we started
up the valley that ran like a chalk line in the early morning light
through huge green meadows that flowed away on either side.

I have mentioned earlier that my wife is a better rifle shot than I. It
has something to do with patience and reflexes. But I wasn't aware

"The professor moved slowly ahead of us with a flashlight as we walked to the end of the bunker. . . . It was a relief to stand in the sunlight again."

that it was an asset that showed. Yet, somehow, both *Jäger* seemed to know her ability right from the start. So this *Gemse* hunt turned out to be her day. It developed that I just went along for the walk. All up.

It seemed like a full day later as we stood in the Hintersee, where the *Gemse* were supposed to be, looking down at the lower hills; blue was upon them, a deep color that seemed to separate and float. A tap on the shoulder from Leonhard Radauer broke poetic reflections and

brought us back to the reality of climbing still higher. The mountain
still to be climbed rose in a cold stone head, crew-cut with spruce,
pine and hemlock. We continued up the narrow, twisting trail. After
the straight-up hours the *Jäger* weren't even breathing hard.

"Practice, just practice," said my wife, who is built somewhat like
an antelope herself. "I told you we should have spent a month moun-
tain-climbing before we tried this one." I was amazed that she could
talk. I needed all of my breath just to keep moving. "This is their
Madison Avenue," she went on. "Don't let on that this bothers you
the least bit."

That ranks as the most humorous remark I have heard in a lifetime
of sporting endeavors. My legs were numb and the noise that I
thought was the strenuous nose-breathing of Rusty, the wire-haired
dachshund who straggled along behind us, was, amazingly, my own
labored breath.

I thought longingly—and perhaps with a touch of sadness—of the
plush quarters we had left before dawn at the Schloss Fuschl. Occasionally I loosened a few pebbles on the path and they rolled, making
a sharp sound like dice in a cup. The Austrians turned and stared
sternly. When my wife turned to deliver her stern stare, I had just
about had it.

The trail we were following was less than twelve inches wide and
its constriction and steep pitch made it almost impossible to navigate
noiselessly. But in the interest of accurate reporting I must point out
that the others, including my breathful wife, seemed to have little
trouble avoiding the dislodgement of pebbles.

The alpine rose bushes, *legfohren,* were in green flame around every turning; the gentians a dazzling blue in the sun, so thick in places
that they looked as if they were sewn into a thick carpet. Even at this
height, the sound of cattlebells tinkled, and the dark roads ran like
veins in the long, narrow arm of the green valley far below. Delightful? No doubt about it. Esthetically the whole business would be hard
to beat if we weren't making that direct upward push.

The mountain was getting sparser and rockier, and even the three
ahead of me were using their alpenstocks more and moving slower.
As they came to a halt above me and looked back, waiting for me to
catch up, I said to Radauer, "Don't tell me *you're* going to call a
halt?"

He smiled. "This is one of the best spots for glassing the *Gemse*."

While he used the glasses, I asked a few questions about the animal we were hunting. "They told us back at the Schloss," I said, as

soon as I got my breath back and my heart stopped pounding, "that you knew everything about the *Gemse* and would tell us about the animal as soon as you had the chance. Could this be the chance?"

"Ya," Radauer said. "I've lived around the *Gemse* all my life. It's a goatlike antelope, distinguished from the others by short black horns rising straight up from the forehead, then coming backwards and downwards like hook. They are strong with long legs and a short black tail, and they stand two feet at the withers."

He went on with a little prodding from me to say that the *Gemse* has close hair, with a thick, woolly undertur. During the cold months the color is chestnut brown, paler on face and underparts, and there is a well-marked brown streak extending from below the eye almost to the corner of the mouth. The coat gets lighter in the summer, growing almost beige. The ears are erect and sharply pointed. Fair horns are seven inches, although some go beyond ten inches. Bucks weigh from fifty to seventy pounds. The hoofs, which seem to have a suctionlike quality, enabling the *Gemse* to make amazing leaps and land on small rocks and ledges without slipping, have edges which extend beyond the bottom of the toes. This enables them to hold to slight irregularities and makes it possible for the *Gemse* to stand on a

We glassed the Alps for the elusive Gemse, *the mountain antelope that has become a status symbol in Austria.*

base the size of a half-dollar.

Gregarious animals, they are often found in herds of fifteen to twenty. They begin feeding at dawn, eating the leaves of all the evergreens, lichens and most of the mountain herbage; toward midday rest until evening, then feed again. Breeding is in the fall with the they seek the shelter of rocks and any shade they can find, where they young, usually twins, born in May or June, after a gestation period of twenty-eight weeks. They are born with a woolly reddish coat and almost at birth are able to follow their dams anywhere. Horns show in three months; they attain adult size in three years, and it is believed that the life span is from twenty to twenty-five years.

"You have to see their sure-footedness to believe," said the old *Jäger*, "and they are wary, see like a mountain hawk. Sense of smell sight and hearing are among the best of all animals—"

Herman Oberascher interrupted with some heavy German that brought a smile from Radauer.

"He's right," he said. "I forgot to tell you that many of us call them the 'Monkey of the Mountain' because of their agility. And Herman says to tell you that they have the eyes of a cat, the horns of a demon and the heart of a lion."

He then stopped his glassing, which he had been doing during most of the conversation. He held out the binoculars to me. "There are two young ones," he said. "They are grazing just under that peak."

I looked and couldn't see a thing; then my wife looked—nothing. Radauer took his alpenstock and with a strong thrust sank it into the ground; then he did an impossible thing. Balancing his binoculars delicately on the staff, he looked through them, firmed them gently with a forefinger, looked through them again, then beckoned to us. He had them zeroed in perfectly. Two *Gemse* were cropping at some low evergreens hundreds of yards away, so perfectly camouflaged into their background that only the keenest Alps man could have picked them up.

"They're too far and they are too young," Radauer said. "We will climb still higher to the—"

"Still higher?" I said. "Listen, if we go any higher we are going to have an oxygen problem!"

"Really, Jack," said my wife. "Stop joking. This is serious business."

"That's what I'm telling you," I mumbled.

But the *Jäger* had a treat in store designed to revive the footsore and the heartsick, and I was just about both when we *really* reached the top. There was no place to go now except across and down. Although it was late October we had come so high that snow still remained near the rocks. Pale leaves were beginning to fall from the dark birches and suddenly as we followed the hunters, there appeared, almost miraculously, a snug cabin. Inside were four beds with straw mattresses and an antique iron stove, where Herman immediately started making some tea.

Radauer carefully extracted a bottle from his rucksack. *"Gebirgsenzian,"* he said. "From the gentian flower, a mountain drink to make you relax. A toast, then some tea, a rest, and we will start out for the *Gemse* as they begin moving for their night feeding."

We followed his example as he drank in one neat, swift gulp. "Just wait until we get the *Gemse,"* he said. "If we have luck, we will toast success with *Obst Branntwein,* made from the finest apples. It is worth waiting for."

This drink was pure fire, burning from the moment it entered your mouth until it reached the bottom of your belly. We could feel the tension go, and after some of Herman's hot tea we spread out on the rough straw mattresses that felt like the fluffiest goosedown.

It seemed mere minutes later that we were up, Herman urging us to go, in his heavy English. "We have much to go before the sun lowers," he said.

The alcoholic flame of the *Gebirgsenzian* still helped and I felt almost alive again. My wife was already outside the cabin raring to go. She and Radauer were looking at the valley below, talking like old classmates at a reunion. I was ignored.

I walked over beside them and looked at the valley. You could almost see the earth turn. The cattle were sun-spotted, brown-and-white cut-out toys, severe and still in the green meadows; the white chalets sat serenely, miniatures in a painting. A horse and cart raised feathers of dust on the thread of road; a hawk hung in the sky, suspended like a metal object.

Herman had moved fifty yards away to a high point. I saw him waving at us. We went over and, using his glasses, looked where he was pointing. The evening hour had brought out the *Gemse*. Their movements were short and graceful, and their brown faces, strangely like monkeys, peered from side to side trying to pick up motion that would mean danger.

"There, ah, there is a good one!" said Herman. Ignoring me, he gave his glasses to my wife and she picked out the good one. Finally I got the glasses and saw the largest *Gemse*.

"It will be hands and knees," Radauer said. "He is over one thousand yards away. We cannot walk upright on this path. He will see us, sound the alarm, and all this will be for nothing."

We had to go about four hundred yards along a narrow, stony path —a dangerous path, for it wound along the edge of the mountaintop, and when one looked over, the drop was a sheer two thousand feet. At first we resorted to a crouch, something like a duck waddle; then lower still, finally the hands and knees, just as Radauer said.

At last, when I could feel the stones beginning to stick to my hands, the old *Jäger* said, "Carefully now. Here are two small spruce. We get to them, then raise up slowly. Sit down and don't move!"

We did just that. Through the tree screen I could see the *Gemse* just under four hundred yards away. Radauer didn't even look at me. He nodded at my wife and whispered. "You are cool and relaxed. You take the shot please."

She shook her head and nodded toward me. Radauer frowned, and I said quickly, "Ladies first." What else could I say?

He smiled and my wife doubtfully put the Mauser to her shoulder. The sun threw reflection sparks off the scope. The old *Jäger* put his forefinger to his lips for silence.

I hoped that the spruce screen was hiding the sun gleam of the scope face from the *Gemse*. She took her time and just as I thought she was ready to squeeze off a shot, she shifted position and we started the tense wait all over again.

Finally the sharp crack of the rifle came and I could hear her exhale, relieving tension in a sigh. The largest of the *Gemse* straightened, ran backward a few paces.

The old *Jäger* said sharply, *"Nicht gut!"*

Herman said, *"Nein, nein! Sehr gut!"*

And then the *Gemse* crumpled and fell, going off the cliff face in a long fall like someone jumping out of a window. Herman glassed it all the way down and, without a word, took off down the path.

We watched as he made his graceful way to the base of the cliff. It seemed like an hour before he got back to us. His face was red, but he was smiling.

He poked a finger in Radauer's ribs just over the heart and said again, *"Sehr gut!"*

He had arranged the *Gemse* so that it was almost all in his rucksack. The black horns stuck over his shoulder. It looked as though Pan were riding his back. Careful examination proved that my wife's shot was just to the right of the shoulder, the perfect shot.

Radauer said, "Please, I am sorry! I didn't think you had made that kind of a shot!"

He went over to the spruce, cut off two sprigs, put one in the mouth of the *Gemse,* the other in her hat. Both men bowed deeply, took off their hats and said, *"Waidmannsheil!"* Radauer then took three little brown ceramic cups from his rucksack, and a bottle. He poured the cups full, then he and Herman and my wife toasted, and the word *"Waidmannsheil"* was shouted all over the place.

This was *Obst Branntwein,* the apple nectar that was drunk as a victory toast. I had my mouth all set, but the three of them just stood there and finished the bottle. It was obvious that they thought I had had absolutely nothing to do with the bagging of the *Gemse.*

I started up the path, with them following and chatting. When we got back to the little cabin, my wife caught up with me and said, "Now I can really wear a brush in my hat."

"Why not something a little more apropos, like the horns?" I said.

She ignored what I thought was a clever and cutting remark with "Do you know that the brush isn't taken from the beard of the old *bartgams* the way everyone thinks? It comes from the stiff hairs along the spine. Radauer is over there getting the hair for the brush now." And so he was. He had the *Gemse* hung, and he was carefully taking out the long stiff hairs that would end up bunched in a silver ring on my wife's hat. I would never hear the end of this hunt.

The climb down wasn't bad except that it worked the muscles the other way, giving the legs the feeling that they had been pummeled. We stopped about a third of the way down to watch four *Gemse* moving along the rock face of a cliff. Rusty, as usual, confiscated the one soft grassy spot, but this time I pushed him aside so we could sit and watch the acrobatics. And that is exactly what they were. When one of the mountain antelopes finished cropping the sparse grass that grew between the rocks, he would make a sudden straight-up leap, just bunching his muscles for the effort, and land twelve feet up on a rock. His suction-cup feet enabled him to balance there like a tightrope walker using a balance pole; then he would do the impossible and walk along the slippery wall of the sheer cliff until he found a few blades of grass. Meanwhile the others were hopping, looking from this distance like unique spring-wound children's toys popping into the air. It was a remarkable sight. I never would have believed such agility was possible unless I had seen it.

Back at Schloss Fuschl, we got a hero's welcome. Or rather my wife did. The champagne flowed, with everyone toasting and congrat-

ulating her for breaking the jinx on the hunting castle for the season.
There were some American guests there, a lawyer and his wife from
Washington and a couple from Pinehurst, North Carolina, who were
bewildered by the whole thing. When we left to have dinner with the
Vogels, the bartender was doing his best to explain what a *Gemse*
was and why everyone was so elated. It was a losing game and I
didn't envy the barkeep.

I had difficulty getting out of bed the next morning. I had a good
case of "Alp legs," muscles that had become banjo-string-tight overnight. But not my wife. She bounded out as limber as a lariat. It was
a good thing one of us was completely ambulatory. We had to drive
to the airport and catch a plane to Scotland in the afternoon. By dusk
we would be in the country where the Scott clan had originated. The
next day we would drive to the Highlands and engage in a "rough
shoot" for the famed grouse of the moors.

We spent that night at the North British Hotel in Glasgow, a
square, sooty pile facing the town park. Scottish hotels are overpriced
and underbathed; the best meal they serve is breakfast with crisp
Danish bacon, a good banger (excellent sausage), grilled tomato and
strong tea. The North British was no exception. Just outside our
window a rookery of starlings had clattered in for the night on the
telephone poles and wires. As far as you could see, the wires appeared to be furred.

In the morning the sun was slanting on the park across from us, its
light falling on three bronze statues, two horsemen and a head-high
man in the center of a bed of roses. Early people were about, sleep-
walking up the streets; spewing exhaust, a bus went by with a sign on
its side: "Drinka Pinta Milka Day." We were at Cameron and
Campbell on Bothwell Street early, and for a surprisingly reasonable
fee, signed up a little Ford Popular that purred out of Glasgow before
the crowds were stirring. We passed the railroad station, where a
train stood making dragon noises, and reached the outskirts of Glasgow just as the traffic began thickening.

Since I was driving I couldn't take notes, so my wife obligingly
jotted down her observations, beginning after we had stopped at Loch
Lomond Castle Hotel for lunch. This is a famous restaurant in a
small castle overlooking the Loch, distinguished for its scenery, its
hot soup served cold, and its waiters who wore tails and white ties
which were so much in need of cleaning they looked as though they
could walk by themselves. We played it safe and had lamb stew with

dumplings, uninspired but faintly warm. During the next few days we were to find that warmth was the thing we needed most in Scotland and got the least of.

Now, my wife's notes:

"Scottish Highlands. Steep, rocky mountain cliffs. Sheep all the way up. Many little streams running straight down over the rocks. A cottage here and there; well whitewashed.

"Many black-faced sheep in road stopping traffic. Not many trees, some pines, but mostly just grassy with some heather. Fog on mountains as we went.

"Saw only one shepherd; old man in long coat with a collie and perhaps fifty sheep. Some sheep in road; he and dog got them back into meadow.

"More trees now near Glencoe, still mostly evergreens. Pines and spruces. Took ferry at Ballachalish, a small boat that took only four cars. It cost four shillings per car.

"Much slate in area; saw ironmongers' factories. Sheep here have different pastel colors painted on them: spots of green, blue, red, on back, head or neck. Wonder what they mean.

"Now we travel beside the National Pine Forests that start near the road and flow up over the hills, a river of tree fur.

"Beside the road are fire warnings, red fire markers and brooms like witches' props, presumably to beat out accidental fires.

"As we go, the mountains get steeper; there are many lakes. In one, there was a gaggle of wild swans sailing away from us like a flotilla. The lakes look like the Norway fjords (much smaller), and tides seem to be running in them.

"Rhododendron fifteen feet high along both sides of the road near Fort William, and we seem to be getting into the real sheep country. Now some cattle too, mostly Black Angus; dogs and men herding the cattle and the sheep; great flocks; few lambs, mostly blocky sheep that look as if they need shearing. Now sheep keep getting in the road. We stop many times to go around them, or wait for them to go around us. Amusing road signs: 'Stray animals!'

"Lovely flower gardens in front of the cottages of the farmers, the same planting-pattern all along—first the flowers, then a row of vegetables. Scottish frugality. No waste space. Odd signs along road. 'Lay-By ½ mile ahead'; 'Two-Carriage Way'; 'Grit For Roads'; 'Double Bend'; 'A 82, Loch Ness'—this must be where the famous monster is supposed to live!"

Then she got tired. That was the end of her notes.

Soon we stopped for the night at The Clansman at Brackla, a modern hotel on a high point across the road from Loch Ness. It was a fortunate stop.

The place was new, owned by Mr. and Mrs. William Stordy. She was a fine strapping woman who took care of the hotel; her husband was the chef—and a surprisingly good one. His grandfather had been Lord Mayor of London, he told us, and he had become accustomed to good food early in life, couldn't find it as he grew older, so became a chef.

As I ate his beef-and-kidney pie that night I thought of what the late Ted Patrick, the much-traveled editor of *Holiday* magazine, had said. "Food is a determinant in the enjoyment of any place or any carrier. Food can make or mar any holiday. Food can play a potent part in making life dull or exciting . . ." Truer words were never set down. Mr. Patrick's remarks point up why our stay at The Clansman was so pleasant. Mr. Stordy also was most convincing about his famous resident across the road, the Loch Ness monster, showing us news clippings and even a copy of *Life* magazine that gave credence to the legend of a weird creature living in the little lake across from our hotel.

After leaving Brackla we entered the gray city of Inverness. If, as architects claim, some buildings are sermons in stone, then those of Inverness are grim sermons indeed, their lines straight, severe and somber. We stopped at a biscuit shop on the narrow main street that ran through the center of town, to pick up a tin of the famous oatcakes. Two old women, gray, terrier-like and quick-moving, were in command. When I told them I wanted a tin of oatcakes, one gave me a sharp, sparrow look.

"Scotsman?"

"People were."

"Name?" said the other.

"Scott."

They snorted. "Sheep rustlers, border Scots! Glad they spurited ye off to the Yew Knighted States!" said one.

The other looked at me narrowly. "Ah, but this un has the look of a Heeland mon. Good gray eyes, now. Sunshiny hair. Y'know, a few Scotts settled in tha Heelands."

The other snapped her eyes and gave me the oatcakes. " 'Tis true as y'say. The mon moght be awright itthat!"

I smiled weakly, paid and left, with them calling after me: "Cum back, laddie! Weel talk sum more!"

We came to the village of Bonar Bridge in the Northern Highlands at noon and stopped at the Bonar Bridge Hotel for lunch and direction to Braelangwell Lodge. The sky was gray with rain clouds dripping. There were few hours during our stay here that it didn't rain. The hotel dining room was overlorded by a motherly-looking woman with a bustling manner who seated us facing a small sign: "Please! No Smoking!" The tables were covered with white linen. The place gave the feeling that we were eating in a friend's home, a feeling that was heightened when, without ordering, we were brought fresh, kitchen-made vegetable soup, then a fine steak pie and, finally, apple crumble and coffee.

Our map-reading had been accurate enough: we were only five miles from the lodge. As fine a cast of characters was there as any inspired Hollywood director has ever assembled.

Braelangwell Lodge by Argay, Ross-Shire, was a huge white-washed place with many chimneys sticking up over a sloping roof, and pointed dormers and dozens of diamond-paned windows; ivy was thick between the windows near the entrance and a privet hedge needing a trim squared a courtyard.

Mr. and Mrs. Hunter, the managers, met us and introduced us to a dark, fat, cheery man, a South American ambassador relaxing from his mission in Paris with a lovely thing of svelte form, dark eyes, shining blue-black hair, a complexion like the back of a baby's hand, a devastating smile, and a relaxed, go-to-bed manner.

"They are also here to hunt grouse," said Mr. Hunter.

"Just me," said the South American. "Maria—that wasn't her name—is my companion."

Maria's smile had electricity in it.

After we had tea in the courtyard—the sun had made a weak appearance—the other three guests arrived. They were English: two, probably in their late twenties, from Birmingham; the other from Cheshire. Conan Doyle did a masterful job in portraying Sherlock Holmes' Dr. Watson, big, full of bumbling good nature, tweedy, pipe-smoking, with a nervous but blustery laugh. There actually is a national English type with this cut of character. This big fellow from Cheshire was one, younger than Dr. Watson, a little more sure of himself with a warm, friendly smile.

The others were brothers. One had tight, almost negroid crinkly hair, except that it was so blond that it startled; the other was dark and handsome with an easy manner. His left arm hadn't developed properly; it was half the length of the right and from the end of it

This was Braelangwell Lodge near Argay, Ross-Shire, where the great ones of the world have hunted game.

extended a malformed baby hand.

"No luck today," he said brightly. The blond shook his head sullenly and Dr. Watson laughed. All three had been stalking the stag.

"But we saw them," said Dr. Watson. "My stalk was a bit on the sloppy side. Better show tomorrow."

It seemed that the two guides or gillies were off on an inspection of the grouse moors to see which were ripe for the shooting, so the Ambassador and Mary Lou and I would have to wait a day at least before we could take the rough shoot.

Our room was small but comfortable with a bath and a window that looked out on the Carron River which was supposed to be one of the good salmon streams of Scotland. It was a broad stream that ran strong in the rain and it looked like a tough one to whip with a flyrod.

The first night at dinner we sat beside the Ambassador and his companion. He shook his head sadly. "My wife doesn't like to hunt," he said. "You are fortunate that yours does. So I must bring another companion." This wasn't especially amusing when he said it. It was the sort of humor that had to develop.

His companion didn't hunt either. Her main function at the lodge seemed to be changing costumes. She did this three times daily; smartly and seductively.

That first morning we walked out to the Carron to see if we could spot one of the famous salmon. Fifty yards from the river, as though planned on schedule by the lodge, we saw silver fly into the air: a giant salmon that twisted in the morning sun, as long as my arm—an old bull fish leaping in sheer good spirits. There are few sights as stirring. When we told the Ambassador and his companion about it, they rushed to the river to see if they could catch the fish in another leap.

That night, when the three stag hunters returned from stalking, a psychological drama unfolded. It had been a long, hard day for them. Stag hunting in Scotland is a sport that is observed in its purest etiquette. You never just see a stag and try to shoot it: you observe one at a distance through binoculars, then you maneuver to take advantage of the wind and the terrain. Then you stalk, crawl on hands and knees if necessary, selecting an animal with a good "head," a good rack of antlers—the prize is the "royal," antlers with twelve large, well-developed points. If an animal is taken without a decent stalk, wherein the stalker does everything but dig a tunnel to get within proper shooting range, then it isn't considered a proper go. The stalker is precise about range for he doesn't want to cripple or wound a stag. It must be a clean take.

When the three returned this night, tired, muddy, but exultant— except for the blond—they toasted the taking of a royal, routing us all out to join them in the occasion. The dark boy with the bad arm had taken the prize stag after an all-day stalk. He was in fine spirits, but his brother was not. After drinking silently for some time, the crinkly-headed blond suddenly said, rubbing his left arm, "I had a go today at a royal, too. But this arm has gone bad on me. It is numb, paralyzed, has been all day. I couldn't hold my rifle straight. I missed a dead easy shot. I think something has gone wrong with my arm!"

He drank his Scotch in a gulp, said good night and went out of the bar leaving silence behind. There is something for the psychiatrists to ponder. Boy with bad arm gets stag; boy who doesn't get stag gets bad arm.

The next day while we waited for the return of our gillie we learned that the lodge and nearby castle with three hundred thousand acres had been owned by that fabulous Scotsman, Ross, who had invented the Ross rifle and many other things. His American wife had used this royal roost as a place of entertainment after her husband died. Mamie Eisenhower's smiling picture was on the wall, framed with a letter from Ike, telling how much he had enjoyed his stay and the shoot.

I don't know how sincere that letter of Ike's was. The place was as cold as a cattle barn. There was an impressive fireplace in nearly every room, but the rich man's grouse season was over, and we quickly discovered that this was the leftover period. There was little wood, a weak fire in the bar. I doubt if there is anything as uncomfortable as a huge pile of Scottish stone in the heart of the Highlands when the wind blows, the rains fall and the temperature drops. But the Scots never were people to place much emphasis on heat. It was something that you either had or didn't have. Besides, we were here for the rough shoot, and a walk over the moors was supposed to warm the blood.

At our buffet dinner of cold sliced everything, the young Dr. Watson was in good spirits. He also had bagged an especially fine stag after an all-day stalk—not a royal with twelve points, but a magnificent head. He was relaxed and, unlike most Englishmen, ready to talk to a stranger.

"After grouse are you?" he said over a peaty-tasting Scotch at the bar.

"On what you call a rough shoot," I said.

"It'll be that all right," he said. "Familiar with the way we shoot grouse, are you?"

"Not exactly."

"Well, the best time of course is the middle of August. August 12 is the opening day. The new-hatch grouse then are fully feathered, full of flight. Way we usually do it is to have a pair of gunners in a blind. One takes the left bird, one takes the right. All incomers. Men and dogs drive them to the blinds. The birds are high and moving by the time they get over the blinds. But it's comfy. You don't have to walk. Have a nip of tea or something with you and just bang away—"

"And the rough thing?"

"Well, that is indeed another cucumber."

I must interrupt here to give a bit of advice. Never try to hurry an Englishman when he is making a point, especially a sporting Englishman who loves to be specific. He took exactly one hour and forty-five minutes to let us know what we were in for. It seems that whoever dubbed the maneuver we were about to engage in knew what he was talking about. A rough shoot is rough.

First, after many thousands of shotshells have been hurled at them from the expensive and comfortable blinds, the grouse become alerted to man and his smoking weapon. They become hawk-wild, fly high, flush at the drop of an eyelid, usually out sixty yards, and they have picked up a gambit called "hitting the heather." This means that they run in the thick heather when they hear you approach and don't get into the air at all unless they run out of heather; or if they do, they have by this time learned to judge the range of a shotgun so accurately that you must either be an exceptional shot, and run forward when you shoot to get that extra ten yards of range in, or you've got to be in such excellent physical condition that you keep after them until they run out of heather.

It also seems that the gillie and his dogs just come along for the walk to sort of point the way. The dog is kept at heel; he doesn't find and flush the bird. "But, chap, you really need that dog," young Dr. Watson said, "because if you are fortunate enough to knock a grouse down, it's damn near impossible to find it in that blasted heather, even with a dog." Finishing with that far from encouraging note, he said, "Used to rough-shoot grouse myself. Gave it up. Went into this stag thing. Found crawling four miles on my belly up a mountain a bit easier than walking those god-awful moors after those blinking birds!"

It was raining the next morning when we got out of bed stone-cold to meet the gillie and his dog. He looked stone-cold when I saw him. Over strong tea laced with honey, we made plans. His name was Edward Campbell, a slender man with freckles, blue in his eyes, and a smile that made little creases. His Highland burr was so thick I had to listen carefully to get all that he said.

"We'll go Edderton District," he said as I finished tea and was beginning to warm up. "The rain'll sure as all make it hard goin', but if the grouse birds can stand it, sure we big strong men can, too." He examined my Browning superposed 20 with a cold eye. "Prefer those side-by-side ones," he said.

The dogs were Labrador retrievers, Teal the bitch, and her son, Caper. They were on the small side, sleek, well-fed and alert, and they didn't climb all over us on the ride to the moor. When Campbell gave them a command they obeyed instantly.

As we came down the high road through the gray gloom and the wind-shifting rain, there was the gleam of big water ahead. "The Kyle of Sutherland," Campbell said. "Where t'rivers of the Heelands meet."

We left the asphalt and entered a dirt road that curved like a thrown lariat. Five miles found us at the edge of an enormous gloomy moor. We loaded up and started, gun muzzles down to keep out the rain, and Campbell said, "I'll caution ye, lass and laddie. Don't wait for yon perfect shot. When they move, mon, fire. And fire fast. On a bit of a wet day like this, they may prefer to run in t'heather, not rise and get sopped. Would ye blame them, naow?"

This was a typical Wuthering Heights moor, flat as the palm of my hand, hung with mist like a giant stretching of gauze. Caper and Teal were at heel on either side of Campbell, and we hadn't walked one hundred yards when I saw my first Scottish grouse. It went up, blurred at seventy yards away, making a fat, chuckling sound throatier than the cackle of a pheasant.

"Too far," I said.

"I know," he said. "These are fine smart birds they are."

Now it may sound inane to say that there was something strange, and at the same time romantic, about walking through the rain across this moor in the Northwest Highlands of Scotland. But the heath ran ahead of us like purple flame. Where it was sparse, there was tall grass, golden even on this dark day, and patches of odd red moss that gleamed like the stained glass of a church window. The rain combed the heather, brushed the grass, and there was an odd bluish cast to the light that gave the man beside me, and the whole landscape, the soft, shaded effect you get looking through Polaroid sunglasses.

Grouse started coming out of heather that was thinning, but they were still too far away. The boys in the blinds had done their job well. These birds wanted no part of man.

And then the *whin:* hip-high, prickly bushes that reach out and nail you. I had one grouse within range and was "whined" out of it. I stepped right into a monster with thorns like butcher blades. Then I stepped back, jabbed my leg in eight places, and made a lucky but painful shot as a grouse came out of cover chuckling as if at a huge joke and broke in a right cross before me.

Teal, with a single wave from Campbell, was out and back with it in an instant. I hefted my first moor grouse. It was bigger than our ruffed grouse, its heavy feathers shot through with reds and rich blacks and browns.

To Campbell's huge satisfaction, Mary Lou kicked up the only unwary grouse left in Scotland and downed him with a fast, graceful shot.

"Hoot!" said the gillie. But the single word came out as the nicest kind of compliment from this taciturn Scot.

It took four hours to walk across that desolate area, hearing birds get up and chuckle and blur out of sight. Then, soaked through, cold, miserable, we ended our first day of the rough shoot. Back in the car there was a bottle of Scotch to bring life again—the reason for its invention ably demonstrated.

As we started out the next morning, as usual in cold rain, Campbell said that the radio at Argay predicted gale winds today, and then he said something odd. "The winds, if they be true gale, may bring us a bit o' luck—that is, if you can stand a bucking breeze that would be trying to blow your brains aboot out." I wondered how the gale force winds could help us hunt grouse that already flew too high and too strongly.

Although this was again a moor in the Edderton District, it looked like something from another land. The heather was there burning bright in the lash of the wind, and although this moor started off flat enough, it soon climbed abruptly into sharp, steep mountains, fell again to the tableland of stereotyped moor, then humped up again. Campbell had been thoughtful. He had given us the ordinary moor the first day to test our legs and stamina, but now we were facing the

The gillie (guide), dog and gunner rested before beating another rough patch for the educated grouse of heath and heather.

really rough part of this rough shoot.

The radio at Argay had been right. The winds hurled across the moor like a physical force, lashing like a bullwhip. And Campbell was carrying it too far. He walked uphill, against the wind. If we had walked with the wind, toward the flat side of the moor, it wouldn't have been too bad. But this stubborn Scot had to do it the hard way, and I was wondering what he was trying to prove. That Americans could or couldn't take it?

I was getting ready to ask him to turn about-face and go the other way, when his actions began making sense and our trip to Scotland and its moors became worth-while. Psychology. Campbell was using psychology.

Shooting the birds from blinds had made them so scary that they would never fly in the direction of a man under any condition. So, now, with a flick of his hand, Campbell sent Teal and Caper out into the thick heather ahead, the powerful wind raising the hair on their bodies straight up into fuzz. And the grouse started flying—flying away from us *against* the wind. This brought them within range, the strength of the wind held them back within gunshot, and we started getting grouse.

I have never seen such perfect dog work. Everything was hand signals or a clucking with the tongue. Every bird was brought to hand quickly. I shot and pushed against the gale uphill until I was so wind-beaten that I had to call a halt.

Even though we were exhausted, each with a necklace of grouse around our necks, the walk out wasn't bad with the nudging wind behind and the direction down. Before we left the humpbacked moor, I made a lucky long shot on a grouse that got up and swung with the wind, going away from us. He must have been doing sixty. As he took the grouse from Teal, Campbell said, "Sure enough, mon, that daft bird flew right into your shot." The Scots don't throw flattery around.

That ended the rough shoot. We stopped at the village of Tain on the way back to the lodge and bought some tweed in Hugh Mackenzie's shop—thistle cloth, I think it is called. Magnificent. We had enough cut from the bolt to make a jacket for me and a skirt for my wife at a price that wouldn't buy a dinner in New York. Scotland has surprises.

We were to leave in the morning, so after dinner we decided to take a walk. It was a clear night in the Highlands, for a change. The stars were making light streaks, running like moonsap. Walking along the banks of the Carron River, listening to its night music in the stillness of this high place, we suddenly came upon a blot of shadow ahead of us: a man. No, the single shadow was a man and a woman, entwined. Separating were the South American Ambassador and his hunting companion.

The cheery fellow smiled as we made excuses. "We were looking for that salmon," he said. "They say it is a romantic thing to see one leaping in the moonlight."

Never have to fish around for the right word, these diplomats.

CHAPTER EIGHT

TURKEY AND GREECE

After Scotland we made our way to a place called Antalya, the Turkish Riviera, said to be one of the last of the traveler's discoveries. A place of sun, white sandy beaches, mountains that keep out the cold wind of winter—and, most important, few visitors. We reached it in a short flight from Istanbul. From the air you can see the peninsula lying along the southern Mediterranean shores of Turkey. Shaped like a crescent with most of the bend near the sea, it is separated from the mainland by the Taurus Mountains. The bays, the smooth beaches, curve in long, unspoiled stretches.

The advantage of coming by plane, rather than making the twelve-hour drive by car over bad roads, is the view you get of the serenity beneath. There are few houses, and only one city of any consequence, Antalya, which is more village than town. Nine-thousand-foot mountains act as a natural shield permitting bathing during the months when it is impossible in much of the Mediterranean area. Hotels are comfortable and inexpensive. One drawback: rooms with bath are hard to come by; planning in advance is necessary. You can spend ten days in Antalya, meals included, for as little as ten dollars a day, with the bonus of weather that remains springlike.

The hotels worth staying at are the Teras Oteli, Divan (our choice), Oteli and Park. As for restaurants, one eats only in hotels. The food isn't outstanding in Antalya: mostly *dolmasi,* peppers and other vegetables stuffed with rice and ground lamb and cooked in tomato; or the *kebaps,* lean pieces of lamb cooked on a spit served with onions and tomato. The fresh fish is excellent.

One of the most prominent monuments of Antalya, surviving from classical times, is the marble portal rising between two turrets in the eastern portion of the town wall. It was erected on the occasion of a visit by Roman Emperor Hadrian in 130 A.D. The famed Grooved Minaret, visible from any point in the city, consists of a huge square of stone and a cylindrical upper portion of bricks. It was constructed in the thirteenth century under the reign of Alaeddin Keykubat, the Seljuk king. The basilica, in the same grounds, was a Byzantine church, now an interesting archeological museum.

The Perge ruins, twelve miles east of Antalya, mark the place where St. Paul preached his first sermon. The heart of the city was the acropolis, rising on a 160-foot platform of great width. First built on this acropolis, the city gradually developed toward the flat on the south and was encircled with a wall during the Hellenistic period. The most remarkable monuments are the theater, which had a capacity of fifteen thousand, and the stadium which could seat twenty-seven thousand spectators.

Termessus, twenty miles west of Antalya on the peak of a mountain, is famous as the only town Alexander the Great of Macedonia was unable to conquer and had to bypass. It is known for its labyrinth, its agora (market) and statues. Finike is a village amid orange groves and cotton fields, with a twenty-mile sand beach—a good place to spend the day and picnic. The tomb of St. Nicholas and a church named for this bishop, known as Santa Claus, are in Myra, a village one mile from Demre. Motorboats carry passengers between Demre and Finike.

A journalist friend had suggested that we introduce ourselves to Nuyam Yigit, a Turk who used to help him with translation and local news coverage. We met him after we returned from Antalya, and sat with him over sweet Turkish coffee while he summed up his city.

"Istanbul is the crossroads of the world," he said proudly. "As you know from history, it was called Constantinople in the old days. We are also a place for refugees. They come daily from the iron curtain countries, from Eastern Europe." He paused, then with a sly look said, "There is much intrigue here. People chasing people." He went on, sounding as if he were reading from the *National Geographic*.

Known to the ancients as the "Hub of the Universe," Istanbul straddles Asia and Europe. The one and a half million residents of Turkey's largest city live and work on both sides of the Bosphorus, the body of water dividing east and west. Businessmen think little of commuting from their suburban homes in Asia to offices in Europe.

The historic and commercial heart of Istanbul beats on the European shore. Two-thousand-year-old cobblestone streets twist past spice-scented shops, minarets of five hundred mosques raise graceful spires toward the sky. The city that gave the world the table fork and the tulip is the oldest continuously occupied large metropolis.

Along the two-thousand-year-old cobblestone street we could see the graceful spires of five hundred mosques against the sky.

Istanbul residents have had the benefit of a gigantic shopping center for over five hundred years. The sprawling covered bazaar has three thousand shops selling everything from two-hundred-year-old gem-encrusted pistols to hand-beaten brass samovars. Its one hundred streets are bisected by fountains, restaurants and sidewalk coffee shops.

"So you see," said Nuyam Yigit, "your supermarkets are not new after all. They are ideas born in our bazaar."

We went to this bazaar, the largest in the world. What our Turkish adviser didn't tell us was that the one hundred streets lay like a jigsaw puzzle across the acres of shops, which hug each other so closely that in many places it seems that the streets are all one gigantic, many-doored shop. Merchants do a thriving business in an area the size of

"Merchants do a thriving business in an area the size of your clothes closet . . ."

your clothes closet; they stand in the doorway as you pass, saying softly, "Please to come in and look at my bargains. Just to *look,* please. Not necessary to *buy.* All bargains!"

In that word lies the key to shopping in Istanbul. It is not only necessary that you bargain, for every item is overpriced—often by fifty percent—but it is expected. Bargaining is the breath of life to the merchants in the Turkish bazaar. Using my wife's acquisition of an antique Turkish pistol as an example in action, I'll list a few pointers in the ancient art.

Our man and his son were in a tiny shop deep in the Istanbul bazaar; the son aggressive and hard-sell, the old man aloofly persuasive. First came admiration from outside the shop, which brought the son like a shark after a baby porpoise.

"Which? Which? Please?" he said. "That sword! It is a rare one! Cheap. A bargain!"

Slowly—never get overly enthusiastic—my wife said she liked the pistol. Now the father came, bowed and invited us in while the son took the pistol from the window. Gently the old man said, "You have an excellent eye and good judgment. That is the best piece in the window. It is over one hundred years old."

Step two. Before asking the price my wife praised the pistol. This has two advantages: it clearly shows that you are a respectful person, which all merchants appreciate; and it may give the impression that you are a fool.

"How much is the beautiful piece?" she then asked.

He smiled, spreading his hands. "Only fifty dollars. A reasonable price for such a rare old piece."

"A great bargain!" shouted the son, who had now gone to the back of the shop. He obviously was still in the apprentice stage. He lured the customers in, then the old man used his tentacles to wrap up the sale.

My wife examined the pistol carefully. "Not an unfair price for such a pistol," she said.

Never begin bargaining by insulting the merchant. Even if the price seems much too high, go along with it. The closing in comes later.

Now the old man started using Eastern courtesy, clapping his hands until his son came running. "Get us coffee!"

In seconds the son returned with a fezzed bazaar boy who carried a tiny copper pot and four white cups on a brass tray that hung from three brass supports; he was swinging it as a priest does a smoking censer. We drank in silence. The old man made quite a thing out of paying for the coffee.

"Shall I have the pistol delivered to your hotel?" he asked in a swift maneuver that often works: you have accepted his hospitality; you couldn't possibly be the type of person who would now try to whittle down a fair price.

The next approach requires some ingenuity, giving the reason why you can't afford to spend the declared price on the object.

"I'd like it," she said. "Very much! If I only had the money!"

"Madam?"

"We have just returned from Antalya, one of the loveliest places in the world. We were only going to stay a week, but I persuaded my husband to stay another ten days. We are on a budget. Then, too, we had to take the only room available at the Istanbul Hilton, which is twice as much as we were prepared to pay. And our plane people have also betrayed us. We had booked a tourist flight. Now they tell us that all they have is first class. Our money is going too fast! In ways we didn't expect."

Meanwhile, she had the pistol in her hand, turning it this way and that, admiring it as the light struck it from different angles.

The old merchant, giving me a quick look of contempt for spending money in such silly ways, said, "I'd like you to have it. I know you admire it so much." He hesitated. "Thirty dollars."

A cry arose from the son. "No, no, Father! Impossible!"

The man raised a regal hand. "Enough. We please a fine lady. We make a friend for Turkey."

Now my wife was using the last of her bargaining knowledge. "This is very kind. But you misunderstand me. I would happily pay your asking price. It is very fair." She sighed. "If only I had the money. If *only* I could afford it."

The merchant looked at her closely. "I have made up my mind! I want you to have it. Twenty dollars."

This seesawed back and forth, with my wife getting sadder by the moment until the price was down to twelve dollars. There it stayed, and there she bought it, accompanied by protesting screams and moans from the son.

Although she followed all steps of the technique skillfully, Mary Lou did violate one of the basic tenets of successful bargaining: she didn't evaluate the merchandise. She did not know the actual worth of the pistol. That is usually the stumbling block. Often merchants will blatantly ask a hundred dollars for an object worth ten, expecting to be bargained down but knowing that even if they get haggled to one-third of the asking price they will still make at least one hundred percent pure profit. So I am not suggesting that in bargaining you ever are assured of complete success.

If you haven't had enough mosques and old buildings after Antalya, I can recommend Istanbul's Blue Mosque; it is hailed as a masterpiece of Turkish architecture, the only one of its kind with six exquisite minarets. Like the Taj Mahal, it rises in unbelievable beauty, marking a place where an architect dreamed in stone.

The Ottoman palaces with marble rooms where the sultans used to store their harems are also worth the effort: the Old Seraglio, the Palace of Beylerbeyi and of Dolmabahce.

The Bosphorus, a seven-mile scythe slashing Europe from Asia, is the focal point of Istanbul. During the day the sun polishes it. Plumes of smoke rise from a pair of passing ferry boats—from Uskudar. We visited this old town—an excursion into yesterday—just across the water in Asia Minor.

Much is done the ancient way in Istanbul—by back. The city is full of slim old men with leather saddles on their backs, humped over and carrying everything from a desk to a barrel of wine. Every afternoon people line the bridge that spans the Golden Horn, waiting as the men in boats below fry fish over braziers. At the signal of a lifted fish, they walk the steps that lead to the water and buy a piece wrapped in newspaper. Food can be a fascinating pastime in this old city.

Of the twenty-five recommended restaurants in Istanbul, the best are Abdullah, Ariz, Borsa Lokantasi, Ekrem Yegen, Facyo, Liman Lokantasi and Misir Carsisi, with Abdullah the most popular. There are eight restaurants on the European shore of the Bosphorus; and only two that Europeans recommend on the Asiatic side, Deniz Klubu and the Riviera. For my taste, fresh fish from the Bosphorus was the best dish, fried, sautéed, boiled, broiled, baked, on the spit. Few meals begin until *raki* is drunk, the popular apéritif distilled from Anatolian grapes, lightly flavored with anise. *Midye dolmasi* is a dish not easily forgotten: plump mussels stuffed with spiced rice, followed by *kilic sis,* swordfish broiled on a spit and flavored with bay leaf. Tiny squashes stuffed with chopped meat and baked, *kabak dolmasi,* and slices of squash fried in olive oil and smothered with yogurt, *kabak kizartmasi,* are dishes I never tired of.

In Asia, at Deniz Klubu beside the Bosphorus, we had an Eastern meal of *iskembe corbasi,* a soup of chopped tripe in an egg sauce; *kadm budu* (lady's thigh), highly spiced lamb meatballs served with *ic pilav,* rice pilaf with raisins and pine nuts, followed by a lady's navel, *kadm gobegl* which is a dessert of pumpkin and sugar topped with crushed walnuts. Twice the meal was interrupted by a boy who came in from the garden with an earthen jug and poured *ayran,* the national drink of yogurt thinned with water.

After we had eaten our way around Istanbul, the "Hunters and Shooters Association" wanted to arrange a wild boar hunt on the Asiatic side. We were told that outside of Russia, Turkey had the best boar-hunting in the world. But we were unable to accept. We had firm dates in Greece that included arriving there by Easter.

Our plane departed from Istanbul at noon. Now, packing our bags, we watched fog draw a curtain across the Bosphorus. It never lifted until nine o'clock, and hidden boats howled like hounds as they tried to avoid collision.

As the fog lifted, the water began to show in patches, and minarets poked gold points through the melting mist. Through our open window drifted the call of the *muezzin* summoning his people to prayer, clear as a spring birdsong.

First came the march of Greek soldiers in silver helmets. They were followed by bearded priests and acolytes in vivid purple, yellow and white robes; then the dignitaries in heavy gold brocade, carrying the sacred sunburst icons and flaming torches. Preceded by a priest bearing a banner embroidered with the body of Christ, four men walked with measured tread, carrying a bier; behind came thousands with lighted candles. As far as one could see, both sides of Venizelos Avenue were lined with people holding lit candles. At 9:00 P.M. on Good Friday Athens was paying honor to Christ's death upon the cross; in a ceremony called Epitaphios (the Epitaph), a stately procession marked by muffled drumbeats moved from the Metropolis (cathedral) to Constitution Square.

Now we heard quiet, measured music from a marching band; the chants of the priests rising and falling as the worshipers moved by. From every point in the city Roman candles flared into the sky. But there was no shouting or laughter, no evidence of joy. The bee hum of the crowd's murmur rose from the streets to where we stood on the roof of the King's Palace Hotel. The burning arcs of the Roman candles died as they fell. Beyond the city, the cliff of the Acropolis threw a white gleam and over it shone the floodlit Parthenon. From our vantage point we could see the flicker of candles in the city like a swarm of fireflies come to earth.

If you go to Greece and can plan your arrival time, try to make it for Good Friday. No country has as impressive a ceremony as this march from cathedral to square. The same procession is performed simultaneously all over Greece, but this one we watched in Athens has no equal in size, solemnity or color. The Greeks make much more of Easter than Christmas. From a rooftop at night, the view of all Athens standing with a lighted candle is one you don't forget.

The next morning looked like the day of the lamb. Boys passed, tenderly carrying lamb carcasses in their arms; men had them slung over their shoulders; women brought them home wrapped in paper with the head or the feet dangling. Easter Sunday every Greek family —even the poor who save for it all year—have a whole lamb spit-roasted.

Little flocks of lambs were being driven through many of the streets, the enterprising shepherds taking the Easter feast to the doorways of the apartment houses so customers could select their own. We came across one convergence of streets that had been turned into a market place; flocks of lambs bleated; shepherds leaned on their staffs; people kneeled and felt the lambs. Bargaining was loud and emotional.

This enthusiasm is characteristic of the Greeks. They are never apathetic about anything, even poverty. Many think them the friendliest people in Europe. Their country is among the best bargains for the European traveler. This is the land that gave the West its culture and much of its language; its monuments mark a time and place all of us know.

There is so much to see that Greece can be confusing; it is one of the few countries where I heartily recommend a tour, for the Greeks do not rush or herd you about. They are too proud of their land for this. We found the Viking "Do As You Like" agency excellent. For less than fifty dollars one can take a trip to Sounion and the marble temple of Poseidon; spend two days traveling to Arachova, Daphni and Eleusis, five days moving from Athens to Delphi and the Peloponnesus.

Athens itself took us two careful weeks; the entire city is a vast monument. The Acropolis is the focal point with the monuments of Propylaea, Brauroneion, the Temple of Athena Nike, the Parthenon, the Altar of Zeus, the Erechtheum; the mountain peaks of Parnes, Pentelicon and Hymettus.

The ancient city lies below the Acropolis: the Roman Market, the Tower of the Winds, Hadrian's Arch, Temple of Olympian Zeus, the

Theater of Dionysos. Dorothy Thompson, the American journalist, once suggested to two guides, Maria Alexandrakis and Clio Mant-zoufa, that they write a book for the traveler who likes to wander by himself. The result is the excellent *Athens from the Acropolis.* Written in a simple style, it takes you by the hand and guides you through the complicated maze of monuments.

Don't rush Athens. It is a city where you take your time. I like what Pericles said: "I would have you day by day fix your eyes on the greatness of Athens, until you become filled with love of her . . ." This is easy. But if you work up the will to pull yourself away from Athens and drive about the country you will find it one of the most interesting in the world—bordered on the north by Albania, Yugoslavia and Bulgaria; on the east by Turkey and the Aegean Sea; on the south by the Sea of Crete; the west by the Ionian Sea. The mainland is the southern end of the Balkan Peninsula rising like a roof, sheltering its islands in the Aegean. Eight million Greeks live in an area about the size of New York State, four-fifths of which is mountainous. Its coastline stretches for a rocky twenty-five hundred miles.

Part of the present Greece I like is the old section of Athens, known as the Plaka. The streets there are filled with gay *tavernas,* a source of good food and the throbbing music of the guitarlike *bou-zouki.* These are friendly places where you go into the kitchen and select your meal from the pots simmering on the stove.

The harbor of Tourkolimano in Piraeus is ringed with exceptional seafood restaurants where you can sit by the water, watch the boats putter, the fishermen arrive, the cats asleep in the drying coils of nets. At Zephyros we selected our fish from a refrigerated rack in the kitchen, went back when summoned to watch it being cooked, then sat by the harbor and ate clams the size of my hand before the hake arrived swimming in butter and lemon. With this fish you drink an unusual white wine that varnishes the tongue and, like Scotch, takes some getting used to. It is *retsina,* flavored with resin from Attican pines to imitate the flavor of the wine of Homer's time that matured in pine barrels.

Someone—I think it was Winston Churchill—said you haven't seen the wonders of Greece until you have sat at the marathon table of Athanasios Vassilenas. We found the restaurant in Piraeus, a dusty, sun-shattered old building across from a wood lathe shop. Shavings had been swept into the street, the pleasant odor of raw wood mingling with the fish and old-water smell of the waterfront.

The ancient beauty of Athens is not limited to buildings alone. Here, in the old section known as the Plaka, we admired a lady in a doorway.

Beyond the brilliant yellow nets drying in the sun was the harbor of Tourkolimano in Piraeus with its outstanding seafood restaurants.

The first impression is of a grocery store ready to go out of business. Dusty shelves hold cans of tomatoes, bottles of *retsina* and Metaxas brandy; the depressing dun walls are decorated with faded autographed photos of Fredric March and Tyrone Power. Tables are varnished dark brown, chairs are wicker-bottomed, the floor bare and unpainted. A ball of light hangs from the center ceiling, a dusty globe haloed with flies. A sink stands in the rear, a marble slab that looks as if taken from a morgue.

We made our way to a table followed by the stare of a round-shouldered, gray-haired man, obviously the owner. As we sat, a boy appeared, placing a blue tablecloth on the table, then covering it with large folds of wax paper. There was no menu; no word was spoken. The food started arriving immediately.

A waiter came bearing a quart pitcher of *retsina* and a platter of *kidonia,* tiny clams buried in pimento. Then followed a salad of black fish-roe paste, brown bread, ripe olives, salted anchovies, wafers of swordfish in olive oil, three cheeses mashed and stirred into a tart spread, a pâté of headcheese, and carrots in gelatine. We finished with shrimps and tiny squid in mustard sauce—piquant, appetite-enlivening. Next we had octopus, its curls encircled by *dolmadakias,* grape leaves rolled and stuffed with spiced rice. This was followed by a platter of golden *marides*—sweet fried minnows that we ate whole.

The pitcher of wine was refilled—not a word was spoken by owner or waiter—and the specialty of the port was served: lobster balls dipped in batter and sautéed in white sheep butter. Two dozen vanished, to be replaced with crawfish, which slowed us down because of the need for careful picking of the white meat from the cracked shell.

Then a ten-minute lull while we sat toasting our discovery. This could be a psychological maneuver designed to make one ponder what would come next, to build the joy of anticipation.

We guessed lamb next, but it was a platter of tiny sausages that deepened the appetite, an accomplishment that I thought impossible. Then came the lamb: in a flaky pastry, wrapped like a cigar around the lean chopped meat. We were still eating this when the next course arrived: circles of shelled lobster, two intact pieces of claw meat in olive oil and vinegar.

We were the only customers, the center of the owner's attention. He watched every move. Now two old women in black came in carrying ceramic pitchers. Athanasios Vassilenas filled them with *retsina* from a jug he kept behind the counter, the sharp pine odor of the poured wine filling the room. As if on cue, a waiter also filled ours.

He was new, replacing the other two who obviously were resting after their endless trek from the kitchen to our table. This one was friendly, smiling broadly as he reappeared bearing a whole red fish. Broiled with butter and bay leaf, it was the tastiest I have had between knife and fork. It didn't seem physically possible that we could eat that entire fish. But we did, spurred by the stare of the owner.

Next came a soup of fish, egg and lemon, piping hot; after which, breast of squab and a bowl of chicken cooked in tomato. Then a salad, hearts of lettuce, onion, olive and aniseed. We ate this last, clearing the palate.

We sat back, folding our napkins. This had to be the last course. But no, the waiter grinned his way out of the kitchen with another whole fish—a *sinagrida,* said to be the finest of the Aegean, tasting much like a lake trout. We couldn't quite manage the entire thing.

The young waiter hesitated before he took it away. "Finish?" he said. He was back instantly with *taramasalata,* red fish-roe mashed, mixed with olive oil, onion, bread, salt, pepper and lemon whipped into a creamy paste. I didn't think I could handle it, but I did, on black bread; a new taste treat.

Incredibly, still another dish was brought: large clams known as "drunk developers" in Greece because their salty flavor calls for another drink. Here it called for a new pitcher of *retsina.*

We had been eating steadily from 1:30 until 4:00 without a break, except for that ten-minute period between courses. Now the table was cleared, the end of our feast finally marked with sweet Cretan oranges. We had eaten sixteen different dishes, most of them new to us, and yet, mainly because the portions were not enormous, the seafood rarely filling, we weren't stuffed.

The shock of the check was a sobering one, nullifying the half-gallon of *retsina.* Less than two dollars a person, including tip! After that session in Piraeus, every other restaurant experience in Athens was anticlimactic.

But let me also recommend sitting at a sidewalk café on Constitution Square at dusk, drinking Greek coffee, that isn't coffee of the country at all, but a contribution of its ancient enemy, Turkey. Often at that hour you can watch Athens turn pink as the sun goes down, then a startling stark-white just before darkness. No country I know has the light of Greece—clear, golden, it becomes white-hard as the day brightens. Our flight in had been like coming from darkness into light, even though we had come by way of Turkey, a land that sparkles in the sun.

I had taken my clue to a supposedly tourist-free Greek isle from Tommy, who had worked for the Ritz Hotel in Manhattan since he came from his country sixty years ago, and was now at the Carlton House on upper Madison Avenue. Like all transplanted Greeks, he kept pace with what was going on at home through letters, Greek magazines and newspapers. This dignified old man told me: "The island is Lesbos, a large and a beautiful one. But there are no ruins there; no fancy hotels. My cousin who works at a travel agency in Athens tells me that never do the tourists ask to go there."

Today an island in the sun without tourists is like an aquarium without fish. I'd like to find one. It is not that I dislike people. But I'd rather see three sheep in a meadow than three hundred. That way you see both the sheep *and* the meadow. Besides, how can you savor a place and a time if you have to stand in line to do so?

Testing Tommy's timeliness, I went to the Athens tourist office, riding an open elevator that did not stop—you jump off at your destination—to the fourth floor. There I was met by a Greek built like a TV wrestler. When I made my mission clear, he saw to it that I met the assistant director.

Then my test question. "Is there such a thing as an undiscovered Grecian isle?"

The assistant director smiled sadly. "No, I'm afraid not. Our sun, you know, the beautiful water, and all the glory that was and is—"

His secretary, a plump girl with ripe olive eyes, stopped typing. "Sir," she said to the assistant director.

He frowned. "Yes?"

"Lesbos hasn't been discovered. By the tourists, I mean."

Now he thought, rubbing his chin. He was a whip-slender young man who moved sharply, accentuating his words with slashing motions of his right hand. "Yes! Yes! You may be right!"

In a few seconds he had his man on the phone. "Takis," he said, "you are from Lesbos, yes? My secretary tells me that your island is undiscovered by tourists." He talked on for five minutes. Then he came back to me. "That was Takis Lalelis from Lesbos. Better still, he is the director of the Aeolian Travel Agency. He wants that you should come and see him."

Takis Lalelis was handsome with wavy gray hair. He sent out for coffee saying, "Where did you hear of my island?" When I told him he smiled, nodding, "We could use more like Tommy. What he says is true. The tourists do not come to Lesbos."

"Why?"

He smiled. "You are a traveler, so you should understand. What do tourists want? Sun? Sand? But also luxury, shopping centers, hotels, every room with a bath. Night clubs. Entertainment. Ruins. We have none of these. Hotels that have rooms with bath. Yes, but few. Beautiful white sand and good climate. But the other islands have famous names. Rhodes. Crete. Corfu. Hydra. If it hadn't been for your friend in America you would never have heard of it."

He suggested that we fly to Lesbos and return by boat. His brother-in-law, Lefteris Katsanis, would meet us, take us to a hotel and guide us to any place we wanted. "One thing," he said in parting. "Most of us from our island do not like to be called Lesbians. We Greeks have given too many words to the world. If you refer to us, just say we are from Lesbos. Other than that, no taboos or peculiarities."

Alerted to our arrival, Lefteris Katsanis met us at the airport as our DC-3 taxied to the end of the short Lesbos runway. He was slim, with burning brown eyes.

"Welcome to our island and our capital, Mytilene," he said. "We offer peace and quiet, pride and prejudice, the sea and sun, good people and bad roads." He smiled. "I had to say that. This is the island of poetry, Sappho's island."

The Lesbion Hotel, dirty cream, narrow, four-storied, was on the quay facing the sea. Moving from shore were fifteen craft that looked like weathered rowboats with sails, the ancient caïques, linked to a larger boat pulling them seaward.

"Fishermen," Lefteris Katsanis said. "The big caïque has a diesel engine. They might make it to the fishing grounds with sails but it would take much longer. The boat with the motor waits out there for them, brings them back and gets paid with fish from each boat."

Wagons rushed by the quay, the drivers standing like Roman charioteers shouting at their gaily beribboned donkeys, holding the reins with one hand, waving with the other. The sun was scouring the sides of the whitewashed old buildings, and a babble came from beyond the hotel.

"The agora," Katsanis said. "The market place. Let's leave your bags at the hotel and take a look. This is the time."

When we arrived at the market, he pointed out two old men at the entrance playing with beads. "A Turkish habit our people have adopted," he said. "The beads, called *cnbologion,* are made of ivory, bone or glass and come in many colors. They say that counting them is soothing, helpful to meditation."

I suppose this market hadn't changed in hundreds of years: stalls held live fish and octopus in tubs; clothing of every description was spread on the street; old women stood beside baskets of okra, tomatoes, purple eggplant and artichokes; loaves of bread were piled on sheets of newspaper; a purple-faced man stood between two barrels of wine, a bottle of red wine in one hand, white in the other. Oriental belly-dancer music poured from a radio in an open-fronted barbershop where a bald man sat in the chair. Three feet from the barber a dozen skinny chickens in crates were clucking fretfully; a butcher's stall had skinned lamb and goat carcasses hanging. A woman stood beside them with a rolled newspaper waging a losing battle with a swarm of flies. Another woman stood at a table that held a tub of crumbly white cheese. *"Feta,"* Katsanis said, "made from sheep's milk. We are famous for it."

As we walked back to the hotel, Katsanis said, "I wish you would call me Lefty. Everyone here does and it will get us off to a good start."

He also told us about Akis Dimitrakas, the owner of the Lesbion Hotel. He had spent years in the Sudan working in hotels, running a market, selling clothing. He had come from a poor village in Lesbos, but when he returned from Africa he bought one of the largest houses in Mytilene, a peaked, towered monstrosity overlooking the bay, and he built the hotel which he managed.

He looked like the movie character-actor Akim Tamiroff and had a pleasant but commanding personality. Sending a room clerk back with an imperious gesture, he escorted us to our room. It was small with a tiny bathroom, but clean, and the view of the quay and the harbor promised to be worth the price.

"Two dollars and eighty cents a day," Akis Dimitrakas said. "Is it a fair price? Meals three dollars perhaps?" He smiled and spread his hands. "Drinks, I am sorry, will be extra." Then he invited us for an *ouzo,* Greece's national drink.

It came in large glasses, a thick, colorless, oily-looking liquid. Following example, we poured water into the *ouzo* until it became milky. We were toasted: "The island welcomes you." The *ouzo* had licorice flavor and you could feel it burn its way down.

The view from our window was as interesting as it promised. The fishing boats made their sausage link every morning, and the sound of the motored caïque laboring to pull them to sea became our alarm clock. In the afternoon when they returned **and unloaded the** fish, the punk, punk of the motor hauling the fleet in was the signal for cocktails; the sun was about to pink out.

The first morning when we looked out at the quay, an old woman in black was riding a donkey side-saddle, holding a protesting turkey under her arm. Farther along a man was beating an octopus to death, flailing it on the stone of the quayside. Later I was told that this was routine. After the octopus is caught it is beaten to tenderize it, then

"The first morning when we looked out at the quay, an old woman in black was riding a burro side-saddle, holding a protesting turkey under her arm."

hung in the sun to dry. We saw the creatures hanging from trees, from docks, from donkeys and from the lintels of restaurant doorways.

The second day Lefty took a hotel dinner menu and wrote on it the English translation of each dish. There were eighteen never-changing items. It looked interesting, but whenever we went into the kitchen to see what was cooking, as was the custom, we found one piece of lamb. Usually a roast leg, it went into most of the dishes that were listed separately on the menu. The camel never arrived from the Sudan; the roast veal was always just coming from the butcher.

The treat was *astrakos,* lobster, and fish fresh from the boats. Meals were usually less than three dollars a day for both of us, and the bar had excellent English gin which we drank with fresh lime or orange juice. When the days were hot we had a salad of *feta* cheese, tomatoes, capers, hearts of lettuce, freshly pressed olive oil and wine vinegar.

We were met the second day by Lefty and a cab driver, Stratis Anastasellis, the local celebrity. He was handsome with a straight nose and hair flecked with gray. He smiled often but sadly. He was a poet.

"Very talented," Lefty said. "He has written a book and can write a poem about anything in a minute. He is a friend of your movie director, Elia Kazan, who comes to Lesbos when he wants peace and quiet. He and Stratis spend much time together. We think he is coming next month."

Before we drove to the Gulf of Yera, five miles from Mytilene, we went to see the statue of Sappho that an American woman sculptor had created and given to Lesbos.

"It is an historic fact," Lefty repeated, "that Lesbos is the island of Sappho, our greatest poet. It is established also that she had her school of love here. As you'll find, we have many poets on the island. But none of us are very happy about this thing that has been raised to Sappho, though our mayor took it with dignity and graciousness, in the spirit it was presented." The statue stood on a landscaped hill overlooking the Bay of Mytilene, a shapeless lump of clay that looked like a schoolchild's ode to a bullfrog. The cab driver shook his head sadly when he saw it.

"The nice lady's name was Forbes," said Lefty. "Stratis has written a long poem about his sadness with the statue. 'The Orbs of Forbes' he calls it. It is very beautiful and full of irony. But I haven't had the time to translate it into English yet."

We went to the four villages of Yera—Skopelos, Papados, Mesa-gaos, Paleokipos—and the port of Yera, Perama—dreaming in the sun, unchanged since the days of Homer. The buildings were all of gray stone, the roofs of tile. The Gulf of Yera was a cup of water as blue as the sky it reflected.

As we drove to another village Lefty wanted us to see, he told us that Lesbos had 15 million olive trees and produced thirty-five thousand tons of olive oil a year. "We have the best oil in Greece," he said. "But the last two years have been bad ones for us. Crops were thin, presses poor."

We stopped at an old inn, its closed door covered with a painting of men and women dancing in faded red and blue. "Theophilos Had-zimichail painted that," Lefty said. "He is now acknowledged as one of Greece's greatest artists. His work is everywhere in Lesbos. He once painted an entire outside mural on a restaurant for a plate of beans."

On Lesbos, in the village of Ayassos, we walked this picturesque street and saw a woman wearing the old vrakis *costume.*

The poet of Petra could create a poem to order in a matter of seconds.

On the way back we stopped at a restaurant in Petra. As we pulled up at the tiny *taverna* by the road, an old man rode by on a white horse.

"Mitsos Kanitjos," Lefty said, "the poet of Petra. I will ask him to create a poem for Mrs. Scott."

The old man came over and got off his horse. While Lefty talked with him, he smiled and his fine brown eyes lit up. He bowed at Mary Lou, then spoke softly for about a minute, climbed back on his horse and rode away, turning to wave as he went up the road.

"He's nearly as good as Stratis," Lefty said. "Here is his poem to your wife:

> "From your eyes I get drunk,
> Why drink more wine?
> From the wine that people get life,
> You are giving me to drink!"

One day when Lefty met us he was carrying a large wicker picnic hamper. "A day in the sun" was all he would say as he drove us to another part of the island. On the way we met a woman carrying a bag of sea shells. It clanked as if full of coins when she got into our car for a ride of several miles to a place by the sea where she said there was a variety of shells. Lefty said she made interesting things from them, bowls, dishes, jewelry. She had a lovely madonna face, until she smiled. She was toothless. Thanking us for the ride, she told Lefty that she was coming to Mytilene with a gift for us in return for the ride.

Lefty's surprise was a twenty-mile stretch of white sand by the Aegean. The sea was as clear as an aquarium. You could see the bottom dropping away as the blue-green water graduated in depth. There wasn't another person in sight as we walked five miles in the fine white sand before we sat down and had lunch.

There were several unoccupied cottages in the vicinity. Such is the advantage of Lesbos with its vast beaches that one can always find a private stretch where nothing promenades but an occasional crab; the only intruders are the gulls who sometimes glide in to cadge scraps from lunch. This area was Lefty's favorite. Vatera, he called it. We were to visit it several times before we left the island, one of the most beautiful, uncluttered places I have seen.

Next morning Lefty borrowed the mayor's jeep station wagon that had been presented by a group of retired American-Greek businessmen now living on the island, and we headed for Sigri to see a petrified forest. There weren't any seats in back so we rode on canvas camp stools. It was somewhat like sitting on chairs on the deck of a ship that rolled and pitched in a rough sea.

A few miles from Mytilene we left smooth road, hitting lumpy stretches that bounced us off our stools like dice flung in a box. We stopped occasionally and pulled over so the herds of sheep and goats could pass. As we sat talking we could hear the bright, clear sound of music; the sheep were belled and as they moved, now quickly, then to a slow, shagging stride, the broken tinkle rose in the air like a song— a sound I can still hear nostalgically when I think of Greece. With it dust spurted from the road behind the sheep; on one side stretched the taut-silk sea, on the other, the stony mountains rose in layers like lava.

In two hours we were climbing those mountains as we completed half the journey—mountains that were all rock and stunted vegetation, everything burned dry by the furnace flame of the sun. The dust rose from the road in long spirals and hung in the air behind us like smoke. The road was getting narrower and rockier and we were pushing now. Clattering to the top of a bony hill, we stopped and looked down. Several miles below, as if running to meet the sea that lay molten in the sun beyond, was a cluster of buildings.

"Sigri," said Lefty.

"Forty miles," I said. "It took four hours."

As we came down the hill, a group walked out to meet us. Sigri, isolated at the end of a caricature of a road, was a village that drew few guests. The president, Essiah Valoglou, hatless, with gray hair, a noble head, delicate features and the broken eyes of an old man, shook my hand and clapped Lefty on the shoulder.

He told us of his town as we walked to the coffeehouse. Sigri had two hundred houses, one school, two cheese dairies, four policemen and 650 people. They raised potatoes, some cotton, figs, wheat and fava beans, and had a flock of over two thousand sheep. Most of the young men were fishermen, selling their catches in Mytilene. "We have two fat *barbooy* for you," he said. "We tried to catch a great lobster but failed."

I noticed upright hunks of weathered, grooved stone standing about the old village. "Petrified?" I asked the president.

He smiled. "Yes, our one attraction. We have the largest petrified forest in the world in Sigri."

"And our skin-diving is the best anywhere," said the large young man who opened the door of his coffeehouse for us. This was George Psaras. He had gone to Australia to make his fortune, but like most Greeks he became homesick and returned to run Sigri's coffeehouse. It was a bare room with a dozen tables and chairs. Behind the bar hung a pigeon-holed wooden rack. Here, each man of Sigri kept his own deck of cards. On the wall was a cracked, dark painting of a woman. She lay in bed, bare feet sticking out of the blanket. Golden hair spilled onto the pillow and she held a book. There was something sedately lascivious about her—Sigri's idea of a pinup.

After lunch the president of Sigri came with us in the jeep to the petrified forest, the largest yet discovered. The forest had been found many years ago and two geologists, a German and a Frenchman, had written about it; but not until 1955 was its value realized, when a Greek-American amateur geologist, Manolaloponba, saw the trees, encouraged more excavation and began writing about Sigri's treasure.

The forest was awesome; some of the stone trees were twenty-five feet in diameter. The vast area of trees buried by volcanic action, then accidentally uncovered by man, looked as if an army of sculptors had been at work with hammers and chisels. Some of the trees, struck down in their youth, were graceful and slender, others were heavy and massive in maturity.

"A botanist from Frankfurt said that they are of the sequoia family and at least twenty million years old," said Sigri's president. "Everyone who has seen our frozen forest has been impressed. But not many come."

"Those who do are heroes," Lefty said. "Only a brave man can travel the road to Sigri."

Essiah Valoglou sighed. "I know. I am trying to convince our nomarch, George Lygeraki, that the improvement of the road would aid all Lesbos. Besides this, as you know, we need light. We have no electricity."

The trip back to Mytilene loosened our spines, but it was worth it. Sigri by the sea is one of the few places left standing still in time. They want tourists there, but as I remember the villagers happily fishing, working the soil, tending their flocks, playing cards in the coffeehouse, I wonder if once the tourists come, things will ever be the same.

The next day we found a medieval fishing village that is launching a well-thought-out plan to attract tourists. If it succeeds, Sigri will also benefit—assuming any kind of tourism is actually beneficial to the place visited. It was Methymna, most of which hung like a gull's nest on a hill overlooking the harbor. The cream and white sides of the houses gleamed in the sun like the inside of an oyster shell. The hill, crowned by a fretted Venetian castle, was a page ripped from a calendar illustrating the more picturesque places of the world.

Before we had a chance to see much of the village we were met by Michael Goutos, a Greek sociologist, a square-cut man with a red face, thinning gray hair, horn-rimmed glasses and that expression that Greeks get when they want to talk—a fixed, hypnotic stare. He had plans for bringing visitors to Lesbos with a maneuver he called "social tourism." We stood talking, or rather listening, with Mr. Goutos carrying the conversation. As he talked it was difficult to tell whether he was reciting or quoting.

"If the experiment succeeds in Methymna," he concluded, "it will be extended to other villages in Lesbos—Petra and Sigri. This means it will embrace the most beautiful and picturesque area in this district of Lesbos. We will have guest rooms in the village, where men and women, weary of the worldly life and seeking true relaxation away from radios, TV, the stock market, the mess in the world, may stay in comfort."

The articulate Mr. Goutos later went on to say that the village had plenty of room to absorb one hundred visitors without disturbing its placid life. Rooms would be fifty cents a night; two dollars a day if all meals were included. A language professor had moved in to help visitors, and soon they hoped to establish an international summer academy with small classes in drawing, painting and graphic techniques. Individual instruction would be given in English, Dutch, German and French.

The project would be kept small; neither Mr. Goutos nor the villagers want Methymna overwhelmed. Lesbos, the third largest island in Greece, is large enough to absorb without a ripple ten times the one hundred stipulated. The only visitors we had seen were those dumped ashore for an hour by a tour vessel, and two German students planning to walk the island. A woman novelist from England was staying in Methymna. She and a young Austrian chemist who makes annual visits to the island's leather factory were the only other foreigners we met.

While we were there a new motel, the Dolphin, was being constructed, a comfortable, sprawling place overlooking the Aegean with its own three-mile talcum sand beach. Its prices for room and meals will be under ten dollars a day. Less than two miles from the stage-set village of Methymna, the Dolphin could be one of the best bargains ever offered.

After indoctrination by Mr. Goutos, we stopped at a roadside dairy and bought a basket of *mizithra,* a sheep's milk cheese that looks much like our cottage cheese. We went to the top of the village, driving along a three-block street canopied with purple wisteria. It had stopped raining an hour ago and the wisteria, *paschalia* in Greek because it blooms at Easter time, perfumed the air.

The *kaffenion* was full of men who had come in to get out of the rain and stayed to play cards, drinking coffee and *ouzo,* or fingering their beads. Fishermen, farmers and a few young men sat whispering in a far corner. In one chair a yellow cat was stretched out, a black kitten draped over her. Leftover rain dripped from the roof and rolled down the mountain.

We bought a plate of *kalamarakia* (fried squid chips) and pistachios and honey, and sat eating the cheese topped with the honey. After the cheese and coffee, we had some *ouzo* and the squid. We were only a few hundred feet from the Venetian castle atop the hill and the view of the sea was magnificent.

The islands looked like dolphins leaping in the sun at this distance. The caïques, their sails spanking in the breeze, were coming into port like a pirate flotilla about to take the town. This gave Lefty a thought. "The mayor owns several caïques. We should sail one and find out about them." We met the mayor ten minutes later. Andrea Kyriakou was a blocky man with an air of authority and Apollo features, who immediately insisted that we come to the quay, board a caïque and have a sail.

This we did, in a diesel-powered one with sails stowed, chugging out of the tiny harbor past the incoming fishing boats that we had seen from the top of the hill. It was a pleasant, easy run; as we returned near dusk I knew what Odysseus meant by his "wine-dark sea." Shadows were building in the harbor as we came in, the water changing from blue to *chianti*.

Mr. Kyriakou's caïque, on which we sailed, is enormous and comfortable. He tells me that he can tour twenty-one islands in twenty days; the boat will accommodate twenty people, has baths and a dining room, and rides as smoothly as a 150-foot yacht. The cost for chartering the caïque for the twenty-one-island criuse is two thousand dollars, which includes everything—food, wine, shore excursions— even beaten octopus and roast lamb heads.

Our next trip, with Stratis Anastasellis smiling sadly at the wheel and Lefty beside him, was to the village of Saint Friday for the Festival of the Bull.

"A strange one," Lefty said. "I don't know whether anyone other than Greeks have it, but it is held once a year and something you should see."

The church at Saint Friday is carved from the side of a cliff; people were streaming from it as we arrived, gathering where a bull was tied head down to a tree and a priest in black robes stood beside a man with a long knife.

We joined the silent crowd that encircled the priest. He blessed the head of the bull. The big black animal stood there, its red eyes rolling, as the man with the knife in one incredibly skillful motion almost severed the head from the body. Blood spurted like water from a hose.

Instantly, while the bull twitched on the ground where he had fallen with a thump, the people rushed in, sticking their fingers in the blood and making crosses on their foreheads. They were silent but dedicated, scrabbling on the ground to get as much of the blood as they could. One old woman, her hands dripping, rushed to three frightened children. She quickly marked red crosses on their foreheads.

"Ayia Paraskevi we call it," Lefty explained. "It means 'preparing the food' and is a sacrificial ritual that we believe came from Asia. The blood of the bull is holy after it is blessed. It is also supposed to cure the sick. They will now boil the meat with wheat and everyone in the village will have a dishful."

It was evening before the meal was ready. The meat was stringy and strong, the wheat mushy; but the people ate it with gusto. As we left they were sitting on the ground happy and chattering, looking like some strange tribe with the blood crosses dried now into vivid scars.

We were to leave the following day. Akis Dimitrakas had ordered tickets for our voyage to Athens, which had arrived that morning. We had paid ten dollars for first-class tickets for the twenty-hour journey, but he had not yet given them to us.

"He won't do that until the last moment," Lefty said. "He tells me he is still hoping that you won't go."

This morning we walked two miles from Mytilene to an ancient theater discovered in 1958. It was a large amphitheater with grass growing between marble seats still in excellent condition. I am told that not over a dozen travelers have seen it.

"It was built three hundred years before Christ," Lefty said, "at the time of Alexander the Great. Pompeius claims that the Romans saw this theater of Sappho and Alekeos and copied it. It is one relic no other island can approach."

The acoustics of the old theater were still so good that you could hear goats three hundred yards away grazing on top of the hill. The sound as they pulled the grass was as sharp as if they had been a few feet from us. On the way back we climbed to the little mountain village of Saint Sunday overlooking Mytilene. Across from it in Turkey was Kars Dag, the Mountain of the Deer. It rose in a misty blue lump.

"Homer didn't like Kars Dag," Lefty said as we stood looking across the water at Turkey. "'Dag is unfair to Lesbos,' he wrote. 'Because of its height it takes most of the rain from our island.'" Lefty smiled. "He was a little mixed up in his knowledge of the elements, but his heart was in the right place."

The next day the *S.S. Karaiskakis* was on time. Akis Dimitrakas
gave us our tickets as we left his hotel. He gripped my hand in farewell, then my wife's, saying, "It is tragic that you go. You make our
lives bright here." He hesitated. "Besides, who else do I have to drink
gin with?"

The quay was filling as the big ship came in, her horn grunting in a
sound like a charging bull. *Vapori,* the Greek word for steamship, is
aptly descriptive. The old ferry was sending smoke from her stack in
vaporous banners over the quay where half of Mytilene stood waving
and shouting.

Women in the black bloomered costumes called *vrakis,* and teen-
agers in shorts and T-shirts, all traveling third-class, carried lobsters
and fish under their arms. One old woman had a squawking hen
under one arm; a loaf of bread under the other. Another toted a red-
necked tom turkey almost as large as she. Most youngsters carried
live chickens and baskets of fruit, gifts to their cousins in Athens.

As we walked to the ship with Lefty, we saw the woman who
worked with sea shells waiting beside the cab driver-poet, Stratis Anastasellis. He had a wooden wine flask, polished until it gleamed like
metal; she held a fragile vase of tiny pink and gold shells. She smiled
and shook my hand, then my wife's, and gave her the vase; Stratis
wrote a poem for us as the boat blasted its horn, and he presented the
wine flask. Lefty translated over the shouts of the people and the
grunting of the ship:

> "You came out of the sun to our shore,
>   You return by sea, perhaps to come no more.
>   We are saddened,
>   For you have gladdened.
>   Please come back to Lesbos,
>   The island where friendship grows."

Lefty, the shell woman and the poet stood on the quay waving
until the *Karaiskakis* had whaled her way several miles from shore.
The red roofs of Mytilene clung to the last of the sun; the quay was
emptying. A mile from us the spiny back of an ocean monster
humped as it swam toward shore—the linked boats of the fishermen
of Lesbos returning from the sea.

ABOUT THE AUTHOR

JACK DENTON SCOTT has circled the globe twenty times in his endless quest for adventure and off-track scenes. He has climbed the Alps, explored the Indian Ocean, lived with jungle aborigines, sailed a ketch in the North Pole region and hunted a variety of big game, including tigers in India and polar bears in the Arctic.

Author of nine books, he also has published more than fifteen hundred magazine articles, many in the *Reader's Digest*. For two years he produced a popular column feature for the New York Herald Tribune Syndicate under the title "Adventure Unlimited."

Jack's ever-expanding hobbies center about people, nature and animals, and epicurean cooking, though he deplores the term gourmet; participant sports ranging from spectacular shooting and fishing to a quiet game of croquet; and, of course, exciting modes of travel.

Wherever he goes, his wife Mary Lou and her cameras are close at hand. So deftly has she perfected the skills he taught her—fly-fishing, big-game hunting and wing-shooting—that Jack claims the student now surpasses her mentor, in practically all areas but writing and cooking.

The Scotts plan their long treks from a hilltop in Connecticut which commands a three-hundred-mile view of surrounding mountain ranges. They have two handsome cats, a seal point and a golden Siamese named Shan who follows Jack everywhere and thinks she is a Saint Bernard.